Cosmopolitan Power in International Relations

How can nations optimize their power in the modern world system? Realist theory has underscored the importance of hard power as the ultimate path to national strength. In this vision, nations require the muscle and strategies to compel compliance and achieve their full power potential. However, changes in world politics have increasingly encouraged national leaders to complement traditional power resources with more enlightened strategies oriented around the use of soft power. The resources to compel compliance must be increasingly integrated with the resources to cultivate compliance. Only through this integration of hard and soft power can nations achieve their greatest strength in modern world politics, and this realization carries important implications for competing paradigms of international relations. The idea of power optimization can be delivered only through the integration of the three leading paradigms of international relations – realism, neoliberalism, and constructivism. Such an integration is manifest in a cosmopolitan theory of power.

Giulio M. Gallarotti is Professor of Government and Tutor in the College of Social Studies at Wesleyan University. He has also been a Visiting Professor at the University of Rome. He is the author of *The Anatomy of an International Monetary Regime: The Classical Gold Standard 1880–1914* (1995) and *The Power Curse: Influence and Illusion in World Politics* (2010). He has also published numerous articles in leading journals across a number of disciplines: economics, politics, law, history, and business.

Cosmopolitan Power in International Relations

A Synthesis of Realism, Neoliberalism, and Constructivism

GIULIO M. GALLAROTTI
Wesleyan University, Middletown, Connecticut

CAMBRIDGE
UNIVERSITY PRESS

CAMBRIDGE
UNIVERSITY PRESS

32 Avenue of the Americas, New York NY 10013-2473, USA

Cambridge University Press is part of the University of Cambridge.

It furthers the University's mission by disseminating knowledge in the pursuit of education, learning and research at the highest international levels of excellence.

www.cambridge.org
Information on this title: www.cambridge.org/9780521138123

First published 2010, 2011
Second Edition 2012
Reprinted 2013

A catalogue record for this publication is available from the British Library

Library of Congress Cataloguing in Publication data

Gallarotti, Giulio M.
Cosmopolitan power in international relations : a synthesis of realism, neoliberalism, and constructivism / Giulio M. Gallarotti.
p. cm.
Includes bibliographical references and index.
ISBN 978-0-521-19007-7 – ISBN 978-0-521-13812-3 (pbk.)
1. International relations – Philosophy. 2. Power (Social sciences) – Case studies. 3. Realism – Political aspects – Case studies. 4. Neoliberalism – Case studies. 5. Cultural relations – Case studies. I. Title.
JZ1305.G35 2010
327.101–dc22 2010031763

ISBN 978-0-521-19007-7 Hardback
ISBN 978-0-521-13812-3 Paperback

Dedicated to

My sons Alessio and Giulio Christian

Contents

Preface

This book is the second part of a greater project on power. The first part culminated in a book entitled *The Power Curse: Influence and Illusion in World Politics* (Lynne Rienner Publishers, Inc., 2010). The two parts fit together as an analysis of the cycle of power in world politics. The first book analyzes how nations lose power. Paradoxically, many of the weakening effects that bring about this loss of power inhere in the very process of power augmentation itself. As nations grow stronger, they are systematically plagued with adverse consequences that undermine this strength. In this respect, as much as nations value power, power itself can be a curse. If decision makers are not sensitized to these consequences, and hence do not undertake strategies to limit the effects of these consequences, they may become victims of a power illusion (i.e., their nations will be far weaker than perceived). The present book is a natural corollary to the first. In a world where power is still a principal objective of nations, but the process of power augmentation is both precarious and plagued, how can nations optimize power? This book attempts to provide an answer to this important question. It does so by crossing paradigmatic boundaries to produce a theory of power optimization that combines compelling tenets of the three major paradigms in international politics: realism, neoliberalism, and constructivism. I refer to it as the theory of cosmopolitan power. Such a synthetic theory is necessary to produce a vision of power that best fits the modern world system. Although scholars have found such paradigmatic boundaries difficult to bridge, especially on the issue of power, changes in modern international relations have made such a bridge ever more necessary for the purpose of producing a theory of power that better accords with the state of world politics in our epoch and beyond.

Many individuals have been instrumental in the completion of this book. Their generosity and insightfulness contributed immensely to the content of these pages in one way or another, and hence this book represents a collective effort. I would especially like to thank a number of such individuals: David Baldwin, Lewis Bateman, Philip Cerny, Michael Cox, Douglas Foyle, Gemma Gallarotti, Richard Grossman, Christian Hogendorn, Robert Jervis, Ken Karpinski, David Kearn, David McBride, Joseph Nye, Nicholas Onuf, Peter Rutland, Gil Skillman, Jack Snyder, Elizabeth Trammell, Alexander Wendt, and the anonymous referees of Cambridge University Press and Oxford University Press. I would like to thank Wesleyan University for financial support. Finally, a special thanks goes to my wife Gem and my sons Giulio Christian and Alessio, for not only being constant inspirations, but also for the innumerable ways they have filled my life.

Introduction

This book develops a theory of power in international relations that builds on the idea of smart power.[1] I refer to it as Cosmopolitan power.[2] It is different, and in many circles even considered bold and iconoclastic, because it attempts to cross paradigmatic boundaries that previously were fairly impenetrable, especially on the subject of power. It attempts to construct some overlapping theoretical set from the three main paradigms in international relations on this subject of power – Realism, Neoliberalism, and Constructivism.[3] Because the paradigmatic boundaries have been

1 The idea of "smart power" suggests that a foreign policy based on the combined use of both hard and soft power can yield superior results to one that relies exclusively on one or the other kinds of power. The work on smart power has been limited both in its theoretical development and its historical/policy applications (being principally restricted to the analysis of contemporary U.S. foreign policy). Hard and soft power will be discussed in Chapter 1. On smart power, see Nossel (2004), *Report of the Center for Strategic and International Studies Commission on Smart Power* (2007), and Etheridge (2009).

2 Beck (2005) uses the term *cosmopolitan* to convey a broad view of the diffusion of power in a new global age from the state to civil society. My use of the term *Cosmopolitan power* is far more state-centric than Beck's vision. It has simply been chosen to denote a more modern and sophisticated view of power that better fits changes in the world system and their impact on the nature of national influence. The vision of Cosmopolitan power does not position itself in any one paradigm; rather, it proposes to represent an overlapping set of tenets across paradigms that could be conceptualized as logically consistent. Thus, it represents a distinct vision of power forged from all three of the major paradigms in international relations – Realism, Neoliberalism, and Constructivism. This is the reason I use the term *Cosmopolitan* rather than more cumbersome synthetic terms such as *Cosmopolitan Realism* or *Realist Liberal Constructivism*.

3 By presenting these paradigms as single entities, this analysis obfuscates the great diversity of theories within each paradigm, each of which is a battleground. The citations in the last chapter are useful sources for clarifying the competing strands within the respective paradigms.

so imposing, such syntheses have remained elusive at best. Moreover, attempting a synthesis among the three paradigms in the context of the issue of power appears even more imposing because power may be the most salient point of conflict among the paradigms. Realism has been known as the paradigm that embraces the idea of power seeking, whereas Neoliberalism and Constructivism have been viewed as antithetical (even subversive) to the idea of power seeking. However, such attempts to balance various strands among competing paradigms may prove fertile ground for building more useful theories of power – theories that hold the key to enhanced influence for nations.[4] Greater power may be achieved through balance than through paradigmatic parochialism. Moreover, the synthesis proposed by Cosmopolitan power suggests that not only does a common intersecting set emerge among the paradigmatic tenets, but that the various paradigms actually rely on each other to achieve the important goals each espouses with respect to national influence.

There have been attempts to integrate some or all of these paradigms at both specific and more general levels. These have come principally from the Neoliberals and Constructivists. There has been little interest from the Realists (Sterling-Folker 2002, 74; Copeland 2000). Whereas Constructivists and Neoliberals appear to overlap significantly by embracing institutions (i.e., principles, norms, rules, regimes, and other phenomena undergirding cooperation among nations), the two paradigms traditionally have been seen by Realists as antithetical (Barkin 2003, 325).[5] Yet even the limited forays into the quest for paradigmatic syntheses have failed to venture into the very issue that, as Berenskoetter (2007, 1)

[4] In following Baldwin (2002, 177), this book will not make cumbersome distinctions between power and influence. Hence, the two terms will sometimes be used interchangeably to convey common elements gravitating around the capacity of a nation to attain its objectives in international politics.

[5] Wendt, in a personal correspondence, notes that attempts to integrate Realism and Constructivism come almost exclusively from the Constructivist side. On attempts to synthesize Realism and Constructivism, see Wendt (1999), Barkin (2003), Williams (2003), Sterling-Folker (2002), Johnston (2008), Onuf (2008), and Hall (1997). Some works from scholars who have demonstrated a more Realist orientation come from Jervis (1970), Copeland (2000), and Walt (1987), although such works are somewhat more crypto-attempts at bridging the gap. Fukuyama (2006), Kupchan (2004), and Ikenberry and Kupchan (2004) have issued representative attempts to synthesize Realism and Neoliberalism (using terms such as *Realistic Wilsonianism*, *Real Democratik*, and *Liberal Realism*). On this synthesis, see also Niou and Ordeshook (1994). On the relation between Realism and Neoliberalism, see Keohane and Nye (1989), Baldwin (1993), and Niou and Ordeshook (1994). On the relation between Neoliberalism and Constructivism, see Sterling-Folker (2000). On Constructivism, see especially Onuf (1989), Wendt (1999) and Adler (2002).

notes, holds the study of world politics "together" – that of power. As noted, power has been seen as the point of greatest divergence among the paradigms (Wendt 1999, 114).[6] Because the theory of Cosmopolitan power marshals an integration of power relations among the three paradigms – the issue thought to be least likely to bridge the theoretical gap – these findings could be considered both compelling and "crucial" from a scientific point of view (Eckstein 1975; Gerring 2004, 347; King, Keohane, and Verba 1994, 209–12).[7] Moreover, Cosmopolitan power generally supports important tenets of Realism; the augmentation of power, the optimization of power, and the quest for security are all legitimate goals of the state, and power relations unfold in what is fundamentally an anarchic environment. In this respect, the paradigmatic integration represented by Cosmopolitan power will potentially generate greater interest for Realists who previously have been reluctant to consider a theoretical interfacing with Constructivist and Neoliberal categories.

Continuing the search for alternative visions of international power, such as Cosmopolitan power, and how their implications can enhance national influence, is an especially important venture today. There is a need to better understand processes of power in international relations for scholarly and practical reasons. Even more importantly, the world today is experiencing an especially tumultuous and sensitive period, with greater dangers, but also greater opportunities for the augmentation of national influence. This situation promises to be with us into the future. Although the issue of power is at the very core of interactions among nations, the study of international power is still (notwithstanding the volumes of scholarship) underdeveloped relative to its importance in international politics (Baldwin 2002; Berenskoetter 2007). Moreover, the traditional theories of power in international politics are poorly suited to understanding the modern world system; there is a significant need for a more complex or "polymorphous" theory of power in world politics (Barnett and Duvall 2005, 40). The global system is in flux, while the power of nations continues to be the principal instrument for determining our collective fate as a planet. In terms of an historical time line,

[6] In fact, various scholars have proclaimed that there is much more convergence among Realists and Constructivists on the centrality of power than has been traditionally acknowledged (Wendt 1999, 97; Barkin 2003, 327).

[7] In that integrative properties appear in an area considered to be least fertile (i.e., a least likely case) for theoretical synthesis, the idea of more general integration of the paradigms becomes all the more compelling.

there has been a greater transformation in the lives of human beings during the last hundred years than in the preceding twelve thousand (since the emergence of farming communities). We are presently caught in this breakneck wave of change. In a sense, the modern world system has placed us in an environment in which everything is occurring more dramatically and faster than ever before. With this speed and magnitude of outcomes, we are faced with greater threats and opportunities involving national power.[8]

Technology continues to evolve, bringing with it manifold possibilities for both dangers and opportunities. Weapons of mass destruction (WMD) continue to develop in ways that increase the speed and magnitude of threat. It may be the case that the level of national power and the capacity to use it are outpacing the ability of nations to control it. The world politic demonstrates both processes of splintering (i.e., movements for independence) and collectivization (regional and global integration). Shifting political boundaries and identities continue to present a potential source of instability both between and within nations. Forces and processes that previously were under the public and scholarly radar (environment, demographics, disease) have reared an ugly head and demonstrated that the dangers facing us in the twenty-first century are far more extensive and pernicious than we perceived just several generations ago. New dangers from non-state actors in the form of terrorism and their potential access to WMD have made it all the more difficult to assess, monitor, and manage threats to national security. Shifts in power among the great nations of the world promise a different configuration of influence in the future. Globalization and growing interdependence have continued to reshape relations among nations, resulting in great opportunities as well as instability. The changing fates of democracy and capitalism have generated points of convergence as well as points of conflict in world politics. The income gap has increased between rich and poor, even after decades of concerted efforts on the part of nations and institutions to address such asymmetries. Beck (2005) has noted that the changes in the world have created a far more "hazy power space" than has previously been embraced by scholars and decision makers. National power itself has been transformed by the principal changes in world politics, and these

[8] On a theoretical level, Guzzini (1993, 445) identifies a period of "crisis" in the study of international relations due to the advent of new research areas and subdisciplines. The resulting disciplinary "disarray" has created a greater need to reconceptualize the process of power in ways that better fit this transformation in prevailing scholarship.

changes have made it far more difficult to gauge and consequently manage power. This hazy power space requires new questions about power and its changing role in international politics.

In this dangerous but opportunity-laden new world, no more influential means exist to shape international relations in the modern world than national power. Thus, leaders will continue to be animated in pursuing national strength. In light of this power quest, the principal lessons of this book about power appear even more relevant to the national interest. The problem of power augmentation in the face of a dynamic world polity requires the utmost vigilance and perspicacity among national leaders. The quest for power requires a far more enlightened and sophisticated vision of the process of power accumulation and the pervasive threats inherent in the process itself, one that matches the challenges of a complex and changing world. Cosmopolitan power holds much promise for generating such a vision.

The Argument and Plan of the Work

Cosmopolitan power is a theory of power that envisions the optimization of national influence deriving from a balance among sources of power underscored within the three leading paradigms of international relations. The sources of power have been synthesized within two general subsources – hard power and soft power.[9] Hard power draws from common tenets of Realist theory. This source of influence relies on the ability of nations to compel other nations to act in a manner consistent with the interests of the former (i.e., the target nation is pushed to do what it otherwise would not do without coercion or bribes). Soft power derives from Neoliberal and Constructivist visions of power. This source of power emanates from the admiration and respect garnered by nations acting in accordance with appropriate behavioral modes posited in the paradigms – nations with soft power endear themselves to other nations. Such endearment causes other nations to voluntarily act, without being compelled, in the interests of the nations with soft power. In this respect, hard power extracts compliance, whereas soft power cultivates it. The process of cultivating influence through soft power is referred to as soft empowerment, one of Cosmopolitan power's three main signature processes. In being wedded to a vision of hard power, the Realists have effectively missed the boat. The exclusive use of hard power is risky and often self-defeating.

[9] Both hard and soft power will be more fully defined and analyzed in Chapter 1.

Attempts to gain influence only through hard power sources can actually weaken a nation (what is referred to as hard disempowerment – another of Cosmopolitan power's three main signature process). This has always been a limitation of Realism, but changes in the world system have promised to raise the effectiveness of soft power relative to hard power, so the Realist approach to influence in the modern world will be even more frustrated. The Realist lexicon of power requires greater reliance on soft power if Realism's prime prescriptions – the optimization of power and the quest for security – are to be attained.

Conversely, both Neoliberals and Constructivists, to some extent, have threatened to throw the baby out with the bathwater. In reacting to Realist claims about prevalent power relations in international affairs with such counterpoised categories, they have failed to embrace the potential usefulness of hard power sources. In this respect, they have been equally guilty of missing the boat in producing a viable alternative of power. Like the Realists, Neoliberals and Constructivists also require help from the other side (in this case, hard power) to achieve their most treasured objectives: peace, stability, justice, prosperity, and national autonomy. Moreover, all three paradigms have missed opportunities to embrace soft power in ways that would attend to all of their goals: the use of soft power to empower rather than simply restrain behavior (soft empowerment). Neoliberals and Constructivists have underscored the use of soft power as a means of restraining the actions of nations but have failed to embrace the ways in which soft power can increase the influence of nations. Realists have been equally guilty of under appreciating the empowering effects of soft power and how those effects might contribute to increasing national influence. Ultimately, diversification among soft and hard power resources will be the only effective means of optimizing national influence (the third of Cosmopolitan power's main signature processes). This diversification, however, will prove challenging because of its requirements in the face of the pervasiveness of a power curse (of which hard disempowerment is an element) and because of common cognitive limitations on the part of decision makers. In this respect, decision makers will have to be ever vigilant and perspicacious by employing five fundamental strategies in assessing and monitoring national power.

Chapter 1 builds a theory of Cosmopolitan power by analyzing its component parts (soft and hard power) and how they coalesce, articulating its fundamental principles and prescriptions for its operationalization as a policy, and demonstrating the mechanics of the theory's signature processes of soft empowerment, hard disempowerment, and diversification. A more formal model of power optimization in the context of the hard and soft power nexus is relegated to the Appendix.

A compelling testament to the importance of soft power, and to the importance of a Cosmopolitan theory of power as a bridge for all three paradigms, is provided in analyses of the great books of the founding fathers of Realism: Thomas Hobbes, Thucydides, Niccolò Machiavelli, E. H. Carr, and Hans Morgenthau. Close textual analyses of the works that inspired contemporary Realist theory in international relations strongly attest to the importance of the signature processes of Cosmopolitan power, notwithstanding these writers' famous arguments about the utility of hard power. An acute awareness of the importance of these processes (soft empowerment, hard disempowerment, and, ultimately, the need to diversify between hard and soft power resources), in fact, pervades the great inspirational works of Realism. In this respect, these authors could more accurately be referred to as Cosmopolitan Realists. Although the sources of soft power vary among the respective authors, there is a pervasive theme that actors that endear themselves within their environments – even within anarchic environments – can leverage such assets into enhanced influence and safety among the actors with which they interact (soft empowerment). Concomitantly, they exhibit an acute awareness of the influence that may be lost when such endearing qualities are compromised by excessive reliance on hard power strategies (hard disempowerment).

Finding such a pronounced awareness of the virtues of soft power and the dangers of hard disempowerment in the most inspirational texts for contemporary Realist theory serves as a crucial-case testament to the importance of the vision of Cosmopolitan power. More specifically, the theoretical and prescriptive value of the vision of Cosmopolitan power is enhanced, given that is has been located in less likely places (i.e., the great works of Realism). Thus, the textual analyses serve as crucial-case studies that generate important inferential qualities about the importance of the theory of Cosmopolitan power in a scientific context.

Chapters 2 and 3 marshal crucial-case textual analyses of the great works of these founding fathers of Realism: *The Leviathan*, *The History of the Peloponnesian War*, *The Prince*, *The Twenty Years' Crisis*, and *Politics among Nations*.

The manifestations of Cosmopolitan power also can be seen across time, geography, and issue areas. To this end, case studies of the components of Cosmopolitan power are undertaken. Four case studies analyze the soft side of Cosmopolitan power in demonstrating the process of soft empowerment. A fifth case study looks at the hard side of the theory by analyzing the process of hard disempowerment. All five cases illuminate the need for nations to attain some golden Cosmopolitan mean between the extreme poles of hard and soft power. They attest to how both sources of power can work together to optimize influence and show that failure to embrace such joint sets ultimately leads to inferior outcomes.

The first three cases look at the economic and political benefits of soft empowerment as manifested through a process of emulation. One of the manifestations and empowering effects (i.e., soft empowerment) of the endearment generated by soft power, principally as a result of admiration, is emulation. There is no greater testament to the influence generated by such endearment than one nation emulating the policies of another. The benefits are numerous and manifold; ultimately, they translate into greater influence for these role-model nations in the world at large. However, few case studies have been completed on the precise benefits of being emulated. The three cases I present are attempts to fill this gap. First, the rise of free trade in Western Europe in the mid–nineteenth century, to a large extent, was driven by admiration of the British economic miracle. Early and vigorous industrialization was a potent force in driving other European nations to emulate Britain's policy of freer trade and open up their markets. Britain came to enjoy a myriad of benefits from other nations pursuing more liberal trading practices. Second, Britain also proved to be a financial role model a bit later in the nineteenth century, in the 1870s, when developed nations followed its lead and adopted gold standards. As with trade, many leaders were compelled by the British economic miracle and attributed such success to its early adoption of a gold standard (other nations being either on silver or bimetallist). Thus, emulation was perceived as a vehicle to similar economic gains. Convergence on gold, like free trade, produced a number of benefits for the British economy and the British state. The reversion to gold bolstered the benefits that Britain was already reaping from the fact that sterling had become the leading international currency for clearing trade, investment, and bank reserves. Third, many nations more recently have chosen to adopt the American dollar as a currency (i.e., dollarization). This financial emulation, like the adoption of gold standards and sterling among developed nations in the nineteenth century, attests to the soft power of modern America as a role model. Emulation in this regard manifests admiration of economic characteristics such as a sound financial system and a dominant economy. It also manifests faith in the stability of the American financial system. Dollarization has produced benefits for the United States quite similar to those enjoyed by Britain from gold standards and the use of sterling, in that all of these represent a form of monetary and financial convergence. In all three cases, emulation significantly raised the economic and political influence of both Britain and the United States in the world political economy in the respective issue areas during the respective historical periods.

These three cases of soft empowerment illuminate a Cosmopolitan process. They show endowments of hard power being supplemented by soft power in the augmentation of economic and political influence. In all three cases, the principal sources of soft empowerment were the endearing qualities of the economic policies of the United States and Great Britain. These endearing qualities, which resulted from the admiration and respect generated by the economic primacy achieved by these nations in specific issue areas, caused other nations to emulate the policies of these role-model nations. Emulation created a greater political-economic milieu that was favorable to the interests and goals of the role-model nations. In each case, already powerful economic actors found their economic and political influence augmented by economic and political opportunities provided by the cultivation of soft power. This enhanced influence, in turn, generated even greater economic primacy and political influence. This reflects a Cosmopolitan compound reinforcement effect between hard and soft power, in that a source of admiration and respect augmented the preponderant hard economic power resources of the role-model nations (i.e., their economic primacy and political influence). Emulation fundamentally created expanded opportunities for the role-model nations to achieve even greater economic primacy and political influence. This enhanced primacy fed back to reinforce the soft empowerment enjoyed by the role-model nation through emulation.

These three case studies in soft empowerment through emulation are undertaken in Chapter 4.

With respect to the hard side of the power continuum, there is great danger and risk, especially in the modern world, in strategies that are founded on the enhancement of national influence through excessive reliance on hard power. Such strategies will be counterproductive and ultimately self-defeating because they will often diminish rather than augment national influence (i.e., hard disempowerment). American foreign policy under the Bush Doctrine of 2001 through 2008 is a case in point. Bush's quest to achieve his three most cherished goals (limit terrorism, spread democracy and capitalism, and limit the spread of WMD) was founded on perceptions of American primacy in the world. Such primacy was conceptualized as a preponderant arsenal of hard power resources with which to coerce and compel. Inspired by the Bush Doctrine, the administration attempted to deliver the big three foreign policy goals through the use of force and coercion. In doing so, the administration deviated from a more effective Cosmopolitan mean in conducting foreign policy. Such excessively hard strategies proved counterproductive and ultimately self-defeating across all three goals. Invasions and coercion raised the specter of terrorism, as vituperation against the United States grew across the global spectrum, swelling the ranks of prospective terrorists and making states less enthusiastic to cooperate in America's war against terror. The threat of WMD was raised all the more, as these tactics gave nations an incentive to develop or increase their stockpiles as deterrents against America's threatening posture. Similarly, the prospects for regime change were set back, as vituperation against U.S. aggression and coercion undermined indigenous political elements in nations that would champion transitions to democracy and capitalism. In relying fundamentally on such resources in pursuing his crusade to achieve his goals, Bush rendered the United States weaker and more vulnerable to the dangers he feared most. Moreover, such a strategy made the attainment of such goals even more difficult. In the end, Bush's quest for enhanced influence delivered only a disempowered nation.

More than anything else, the failures of the Bush administration were failures in decision making. The administration was deficient in following important prescriptions about assessing and monitoring national influence. It proved rigid and unimaginative in managing the means of foreign policy. These deficiencies led the administration to rely excessively on hard power solutions to the exclusion and detriment of important soft power solutions.

Chapter 5 is a case study of hard disempowerment under the Bush foreign policy.

Soft empowerment also has been visible in the compelling nature of modern American culture. Perhaps no greater example of soft power exists in the modern global system. The pervasiveness of American culture is a dominant characteristic of our present age, and the forces of globalization have served as an effective chariot for compounding such soft empowerment. America's ideas, products, educational systems, lifestyles, institutions, and even the English language have disseminated an allure and magnetic endearment that have enhanced the opportunities for both

American civil society and the state. In this respect, the power of American culture has raised the economic, social, and political influence of the United States significantly in the world at large. Because of the allure of American culture; American society, businesses, and the state have enjoyed significant access to the global system, and that access has been accompanied by a myriad of opportunities and benefits. On a general level, the power of American culture has had definite manifestations for enhancing the influence of the United States in the greater global system. American citizens, organizations, businesses, and the American state have enjoyed enhanced influence in a world that has, because of American cultural penetration, increasingly come to function in the image of the United States. On a more specific level, this cultural penetration has been instrumental in facilitating some of the United States' most important foreign policy goals: spreading democracy and capitalism, combating terrorism, and limiting the spread of WMD.

As with the case studies on emulation and hard disempowerment that precede this case, the Cosmopolitan vision of power is also illuminated in the power of culture. In this respect, hard and soft power have interacted in ways that have enhanced the culturally driven political, economic, and social influence of the United States. American cultural penetration has been marshaled on hard primacy in world affairs, and the hard vehicles of American cultural penetration have been reinforced by the power of cultural penetration they have carried. Furthermore, the influence generated by American culture has served to increase the effectiveness of hard resources and strategies employed to promote America's foreign interests. U.S. primacy in world affairs has been buttressed on conterminous manifestations of both sources of power, each compounding the other.

Chapter 6 is a chronicle of how this cultural allure has functioned as a fundamental source of American empowerment.

The Cosmopolitan theory of power suggests some strong foundations on which to develop a new and integrated paradigm in international politics. Although the theory is restricted to one issue area (power), success in this issue area is inspiring because traditional paradigmatic cleavages have appeared to be strongest on this particular issue. If some common ground can be forged in one of the most divisive issues among practitioners of the competing paradigms, the prospects for theoretical interfacing on less contentious issues appear promising, and the possibilities for a new and more integrated paradigm are enhanced.

Chapter 7 concludes the book with some thoughts about using Cosmopolitan power as a foundation for greater theory building that integrates the three leading paradigms of international relations – Realism, Neoliberalism, and Constructivism – into a new paradigm I call Cosmopolitik. The analysis here involves only pre-theory: I discuss the possible building blocks of such a paradigm. I do not attempt to construct such a theory.

Theoretical Contributions and Methodology

Theoretical Contributions

The development of a Cosmopolitan vision of power relations comprises the principal theoretical contribution of this book. It is important for several reasons. First, it attempts to provide a synthesis among the three leading paradigms of international relations – Realism, Neoliberalism, and Constructivism. Second, such a synthesis is uncommon because it was developed in the context of a subject that previously was the principal point of contention among them – international power. This, in turn, raises the potential for a greater integration of the competing paradigms, given that some common ground has been forged in what previously was considered the most divisive issue underlying paradigmatic cleavages. Third, the theory provides a more viable synthesis on power because it embraces central tenets of Realist visions of power, and it traditionally has been the Realists who have been reluctant to consider a more integrated vision of power.

As noted just above in the Introduction, however, with respect to finding a common ground among these three leading paradigms, this book does not purport to construct a new paradigm of international relations. It merely attempts to provide an integrated theory of power. This theory of power can provide important building blocks for such a paradigm, but it does not represent such a paradigm. Such building blocks for a greater theory of international relations, which I call Cosmopolitik, are discussed in the last chapter.

Regarding the components of Cosmopolitan power, the book provides further contributions. It introduces the idea of hard disempowerment: nations can become weaker by attempting to augment national influence with strategies that rely excessively on hard power. In addition to filling a theoretical gap with the systematic development of this idea, the book also fills an empirical gap by providing a case study of hard disempowerment – foreign policy under the Bush Doctrine. In terms of soft power, whereas scholars have been attentive to the idea, their treatments have tended to be limited in theoretical development, testing, and historical scrutiny. This book also offers a more rigorous and systematic theoretical development, test and historical scrutiny of the idea of how soft power can contribute to national influence (i.e., soft empowerment), than have previously been presented. In addition to the theoretical development of Cosmopolitan power articulated in Chapter 1, a formal model of the theory is presented in the Appendix.

Finally, the idea of synthesizing the three paradigms through the use of power transforms common visions of Neoliberals and Constructivists in their conceptualization of power. Many of the elements of soft power that previously have been embraced by Neoliberals and Constructivists have largely been conceptualized as constraints. Norms, rules, principles, cooperation, beliefs, and legitimacy have been traditionally seen by practitioners of these paradigms as phenomena that have constrained nations from acting in certain ways. In this respect, the phenomena have been envisioned as disempowering. Embracing the richness of soft power leads to an acknowledgement that such phenomena can actually be empowering. Thus, such empowering qualities would bring them into greater harmony with Realist tenets involving the augmentation and optimization of power.

In all of these respects, the theoretical contributions of this book are intended to achieve the five principal goals of model building cited by Clarke and Primo (2007) – foundational, structural, generative, explicative, and predictive. The theory provides insights into a general class of problems – those associated with power accumulation (foundational). The theory is integrative in synthesizing disparate theoretical generalizations into a more general logic (structural). It produces novel directions for further study, such as analyzing the negative consequences of myopic power accumulation (generative). It explores causal mechanisms, such as the relationship between various types of power resources and the level of influence nations enjoy in the international system (explicative). Finally, the theory is capable of generating forecasts of events or outcomes that can be tested (predictive).

Methodology

The methodologies selected for assessing the explanatory value of the theory are that of the historical case study and crucial-case textual analysis. Given that such methodologies are often limited in their inferential power (i.e., representativeness) due to low N-settings and sampling constraints, the best one may aspire to is descriptive power given the richness of detail in the analysis of the relationship between the principal variables – that is, theory illuminated by history (King, Keohane, and Verba 1994; Gerring 2004; George and Bennett 2005). However, several characteristics of the case studies and textual analysis in this book raise the inferential value of the investigations. First, there are five historical case studies in all. These represent case studies on a variety of countries, on a variety of issues, and in a variety of historical periods. The historical continuum spans British trade and finance in the nineteenth century to American culture and foreign policy in the twenty-first century. The specific cases covered include the rise of free trade in Western Europe in the mid-nineteenth century, the emergence of the classical gold standard in the latter half of the nineteenth century, dollarization in the present age, U.S. foreign policy under George W. Bush, and the power of American culture in the present age. Thus, the sample has sufficient breadth to be at least compelling with respect to the inferential value of the findings it generates. More specifically, there are enough cross-unit reference points to at least diminish the inferential "boundedness" normally present in the case study method (Gerring 2004, 347; King, Keohane, and Verba 1994, 208).

Second, the processes that link soft power to enhanced influence and the process that links myopic hard power strategies to disempowerment are carefully traced in the case studies. This "process tracing" represents a vehicle for testing that can help to evaluate the inferential power of the theory, given the careful scrutiny of the modes of interaction among the principal variables (King, Keohane, and Verba 1994, 85, 86; George and Bennett 2005, 205–32).

Third, the theory of Cosmopolitan power is also tested through the use of crucial-case textual analysis of the great works of the founding fathers of contemporary Realism in international relations theory (Hobbes, Thucydides, Machiavelli, Carr, and Morgenthau). A textual analysis of these great works, which inspired present Realist thinking, reveals that these thinkers (who would be thought to be generally antithetical to ideas grounded in Constructivism and Neoliberalism – the components of Cosmopolitan power) embrace the importance of soft power. In this respect, we find affirmation for these ideas in places heretofore considered antithetical to such reasoning – in the terminology of crucial-case method, "less likely" cases (Eckstein 1975; Gerring 2004, 347; King, Keohane, and Verba 1994, 209–12). As "less likely" places to find support for these ideas, any significant support marshaled by these Realist authors for such ideas would carry especially compelling inferences about their value and theoretical implications.[10] Because the textual analysis is more of a crucial-case evaluation of the theory than most of the historical case studies marshaled in this book, it stands as a stronger test of the theory than the case studies themselves.

Fourth, the analysis contains elements of a structured-focused comparison in evaluating the impact of soft and hard power on national influence – the cases in Chapters 4 and 6 on soft empowerment and the case of the Bush Doctrine in Chapter 5 on hard disempowerment. Such a congruence in the analysis of the relevant variables across cases also enhances the inferential value in conducting case studies (George and McKeown 1985; George and Bennett 2005, 181–204; King, Keohane, and Verba 1994, 45). Moreover, looking at cases of both soft empowerment and hard disempowerment yields sufficient variation in the principal variables under scrutiny to limit problems of selecting on the dependent variable (King, Keohane, and Verba 1994, 129–49).

Finally, the case study of hard disempowerment in Chapter 5 carries especially salient crucial-case qualities, as the Bush Doctrine, which provided the principal impetus for the Bush foreign policy, was strongly grounded in a hard vision of power. As such, it presents itself as an especially valuable laboratory in which to observe the effects of strategies oriented preponderantly around hard power solutions to international problems (Eckstein 1975; Gerring 2004, 347; King, Keohane, and Verba 1994, 209–12).

Although a quantitative method of analysis has not been selected for this book, the theory presented here is sufficiently specified, and its historical manifestations sufficiently traced, that testable hypotheses can be generated and quantitative measures can be constructed to represent the relevant variables, thus creating possibilities for extensive empirical evaluation of the theory.

[10] The crucial-case method is normally carried out in the context of historical cases, in which one can look for validation of a theory in a "least or less likely" place (finding such validation would carry compelling inferential support for the theory) or scrutinize a "most or more likely" case for support of a theory (not finding this support would also carry compelling inferential aspects in the form of falsification). On the crucial-case method, see Eckstein (1975), Gerring (2004, 347), and King, Keohane, and Verba (1994, 209-12).

1

The Theory of Cosmopolitan Power

Cosmopolitan power represents an attempt to construct a more viable theory of power – especially in a contemporary context – by employing tenets from visions of power across the three main paradigms of international relations: Realism, Neoliberalism, and Constructivism. The main principles undergirding Cosmopolitan power carve out an intersecting niche for these tenets. The conventional vision of power that has traditionally dominated the study of international politics, and still reigns today, derives from Realism. This vision embraces the viability of hard power resources as the principal means of acquiring influence in the world system. Yet hard power alone is insufficient to effectively realize this objective, and if employed in excess, it can prove self-defeating and actually weaken a nation (i.e., hard disempowerment). Power-seeking can be made more effective by integrating the use of soft power into national strategies for acquiring influence (i.e., soft empowerment). Soft power demonstrates properties that are consistent with Neoliberal and Constructivist visions of power. The dominant vision of hard power has always reflected suboptimal qualities as a strategy for optimizing the influence of nations, but changes in international politics in the modern world system have rendered it still more deficient relative to strategies that make greater use of soft power. These changes have increased the effectiveness of soft power relative to that of hard power. Strategies that combine the two sources of power hold the potential to achieve results superior to those achieved with strategies that rely excessively on either one alone. These strategies revolve around the three signature processes of Cosmopolitan power, which challenge the dominant vision of power espoused by Realists. These include soft empowerment (the need to raise a nation's influence through the increased use of soft power), hard disempowerment (avoiding the dangers of overreliance on hard power, which carries self-defeating consequences), and the superiority of a prudent combination of hard and soft power over the excessive use of either one (optimal diversification between hard and soft power). Acquiring the best strategies for optimizing influence, even under a Cosmopolitan orientation, will continue to be quite challenging. Finding the right mix of hard and soft power will require leaders to be especially perspicacious in following a number of important decision-making strategies with respect to how national influence is evaluated and monitored.

The Conventional Vision of Power: Hard Power and the Realists

Contemporary Realists have tended to espouse a hard concept of power.[1] There are no greater spokesmen for contemporary Realism than John Mearsheimer and Kenneth Waltz. In *The Tragedy of Great Power Politics* (2001), Mearsheimer's treatment of national power stands as a compelling manifestation of the contemporary Realists' "hard" conceptualization of the menu of power among nations. To quote Mearsheimer (2001, 55), "[P]ower is based on the particular material capabilities that a state possesses." These material capabilities are essentially "tangible assets" that determine a nation's "military" strength. He divides state power into two types: latent and military. The latter is determined by the strength of a nation's military forces, whereas the former is conceived of as "the socio-economic ingredients that go into building military power" (Mearsheimer (2001, 55). The assets of latent power derive principally from population and wealth. As Mearsheimer (2001, 55) states, "Great powers need money, technology, and personnel to build military forces and to fight wars, and a state's latent power refers to the raw potential it can draw on when competing with rival states." The emphasis falls on the tangible power lexicon that determines a nation's capacities to employ force in pursuit of its goals. Military strength is not, then, the *ultima ratio* of power; it is the only *ratio* of power.

Waltz (1979, 131), in *Theory of International Politics*, demonstrates a similar "hard" disposition in defining power. Power is characterized in terms of capabilities, which consist in turn of "size of population and

[1] Barnett and Duvall (2005, 40) and Schmidt (2007, 61) contend that the common Realist visions of power are oriented around the idea of nations using "material resources" to influence other nations. Cox (1996, 92, 102) identifies Realist theory as reducing relations among states to "their physical power" capabilities.

territory, resource endowment, economic capability, military strength, political stability and competence."[2] Indeed, Waltz (1979, 113) contends that "[i]n international politics force serves, not only as the *ultima ratio*, but indeed as the first and constant one." Similarly, in his *War and Change in World Politics*, Gilpin (1981, 13) defines power as "the military, economic, and technological capabilities of states." National influence, in the final analysis, is dependent on the ability to threaten or marshal force.[3] Ultimately, it is this "muscle" that fundamentally determines a nation's power, which again is consistent with the Realist tenet that the ability to marshal force is the *ultimate asset* in anarchy (Hall 1997b, 592).[4]

This fundamental reliance on tangible power emanates from the purity of Realist interpretations of anarchy, which, in their most fundamental forms, derive from the conventional Realist interpretations of Hobbes' account of the state of nature. The sacred catechism of Realist tenets about the behavior of nations that follow from the condition of anarchy, defined "as no common power above actors to keep them in awe," leads actors to optimize tangible power resources (i.e., hard power) only because they are more certain to provide protection. Although even perceptions of power may reduce the vulnerability of an actor, they are no guarantee against victimization by force, nor are they guaranteed to be able to compel actors to behave in ways that make one less vulnerable. Tangible power resources can be used to repel acts of force, and they can be used to compel actors into submission.[5] Intangible sources of power carry no

[2] Waltz never clarifies the meaning of competence, but one could infer sound management of the tangible assets (i.e., leadership, policy, decision making).

[3] McNeil (1982) contends that the historical quest for power in human societies, especially after 1000 A.D., has been largely embedded in a vision that has raised the industrial-military complex above all other means.

[4] This is not to say that contemporary Realists completely negate any soft sources of power. Indeed, they are not barbarians, and even leading Realists such as Waltz (1959, 1979) and Mearsheimer (2001) cite the role of softer sources, such as cooperation and international organizations in influencing outcomes. However, these soft sources reside on the peripheries of their visions of power. Indeed, they are envisioned as far more modest in their contributions to national influence than hard sources of power. Also, contemporary Realists are not only interested in power. Their visions of international politics comprise a plethora of issues aside from power. It is, however, the case that power itself is a central and pervasive element in their visions because they believe that it plays a crucial role in international relations.

[5] Like that of Keohane and Nye (1985), this analysis will not make cumbersome distinctions between Realists and Neorealists. Ultimately, as Keohane and Nye attest, both would be characterized by a vision of international relations that derives from a condition of anarchy. And from this condition derives a fundamental emphasis on self-help as well as on the quest for tangible power as the ultimate means of statecraft in the world polity. This vision is consistent across the three strands of Realism identified by Doyle (1990):

guarantees that an act of aggression can be either repelled or perpetrated to eliminate a menacing actor.

The logic is akin to that of insurance protection in civil society. Although civil societies are not anarchic with respect to violence and crime ("9-1-1" is always available in the event of such victimization), there are anarchic elements with respect to other sorts of outcomes. Societies do not provide full and guaranteed remedies for all disasters, such as loss of property. In such cases, no guaranteed "9-1-1" remedies are automatically provided by civil society or the state that can compensate or protect individuals; thus, people are vulnerable to such outcomes. Individuals (especially those who are risk-averse) often choose to purchase insurance against specific disasters to guarantee recovery. Yet it is possible to be fully protected without such insurance by relying on sources of influence consistent with soft power (defined below in this chapter). For example, groups may form tightly knit social bonds that carry implications for individuals dealing with personal crises. In this case, acquiring friendships and goodwill may result in a more robust solution to victimization in one form or another than would an insurance policy.[6] In most societies, extended families serve as a sort of intermediate solution between ironclad insurance guarantees and reliance on goodwill solutions. In some cases, these are even bolstered by law (e.g., divorce law and wills). However, although expectations of goodwill remedies may be higher because of the familial connection, they nonetheless are not guaranteed like insurance compensation.

This argument does not propose that individuals will in all cases purchase private insurance against disasters even if they are available and affordable. It suggests only that remedies against disasters can in fact be guaranteed if individuals choose to invest in them, whereas no such guarantees apply to goodwill solutions. For the Realists, armies and control over other tangible resources with military applications serve an insurance function in that a response against some potentially disastrous outcome is guaranteed (i.e., one is not dependent on others, hence an actor is controlling his or her own fate).[7] Hence, for the Realist, every nation

Minimalism, Fundamentalism, and Structuralism. On the differing strands of Realism, see also Donnelly (2000).

6 Certain Amish communities in Pennsylvania adopt such communitarian crisis programs in lieu of private or public insurance. In this case, members devote some part of their labor and money for such programs.

7 Of course, a guaranteed response does not guarantee staving off disaster (e.g., your army might lose). But neither does the ownership of insurance always ensure full compensation in the case of personal disaster.

that can indeed field an army should do so, even though reliance on soft power may reduce the probability of a military attack vis-à-vis a purely military strategy. At least nations will have something with which to fight if goodwill fails to attract supporters.

This Realist vision of power has dominated scholarship on international politics since the inception of this field of study. This is a simple function of the fact that the Realist paradigm itself has dominated scholarship on international politics. It was not until the 1970s, with the inspiring work on Neoliberalism marshaled by Keohane and Nye, that paradigm-shifting challenges to Realism began to emerge. The other major paradigm that currently challenges Realism (i.e., Constructivism) is no more than two decades old. Realism is still the leading paradigm in international politics.[8]

Soft Power

Whereas Realists have traditionally looked at a nation's influence in the world as a function of these tangible resources (military strength, allies, bases, size of the economy, technology, raw materials, and so on), Nye has highlighted the influence that derives from a more intangible and enlightened source: a positive image in world affairs that endears nations to other nations in the world polity.[9] The principal vehicle for this soft empowerment emanates from the positive image deriving from a number of important sources: the domestic and foreign policies nations follow,

[8] The well-known and extensive TRIP survey (Maliniak et al., 2007) shows that Realism still wins out over its leading rivals in both the pedagogy and scholarship of international relations specialists today.

[9] Nye introduced the concept of soft power in "Soft Power" (1990b) and *Bound to Lead* (1990a), and further applied and developed it in Nye (2002, 2003, 2004a, 2004b, 2007). On soft power, both from supportive and critical perspectives, see especially a recent collection of essays in Berenskoetter and Williams (2007). See also Baldwin (2002), Gallarotti (2004, 2010), Yasushi and McConnell (2008), Kurlantzick (2007), Lennon (2003), Ferguson (2003), Fraser (2003), and Meade (2004). Also, Johnston's (2008) work on socialization introduces categories that reflect processes of soft power.

A central purpose for pushing the concept of soft power, which Nye calls a Constructivist concept because it relies on the influence of ideas and norms (his treatment of course also exudes a Neoliberal vision of power), is to vigorously introduce such a source of power into the prevailing menu that has conditioned debate about influence in the field of international relations. Because Realists have fundamentally constructed the traditional menu, the menu has naturally left out certain sources of power. In Nye's (2004a, 2) own words, these are aspects of power in "world politics that the Occam's razor of realism shaves away."

the actions they undertake, and/or national qualities that are independent of specific policies or actions (e.g., culture).[10] This positive image generates respect and admiration, which in turn make soft power nations more endearing in the eyes of other nations. When nations endear themselves to a significant degree, other nations may even attempt to emulate them (i.e., adopt their policies, domestic and/or foreign).[11] Thus, whether through respect and admiration or direct emulation, endearment can generate significant influence for a nation. Endearment serves to enhance the influence of a nation because others will more readily defer to its wishes regarding international issues and, also, avoid confrontations. Thus, decisions about issues affecting that nation will be bound within a more favorable range of options with respect to the interests of the respected and admired nation.[12] Emulation, specifically, creates a system of nations in which behavior and policies are consistently in accordance with the interests of a role-model nation. Consequently, that nation's potential confrontations with regard to international issues will be reduced because other nations will be less likely to propose drastic alternatives to its ways of conducting its affairs. Emulation also places second-party decisions within a bounded framework in which actions will not deviate significantly from a style that is consistent with the interests of the respected and admired nation. Soft power therefore shapes the social context within which other nations make decisions in ways that favor soft power nations (i.e., meta-power, discussed below in this chapter).

No single word perfectly describes the foundation of soft power, and I have chosen the term "endearment" as the one that is most representative, notwithstanding its connotations of personal affection. For the purpose of elegance, I strive to use a broadly representative term rather than an

[10] In some cases, the endearing qualities may emanate from hard power resources themselves, such as the admiration generated by great economic achievements or a large international presence. However, the hard power would have to be used according to principles undergirding the process of soft power. This is discussed below in the chapter.

[11] At a more general philosophical level, Adam Smith's *Theory of Moral Sentiments* (1759/2002) underscores how people want to be admired and are disposed to emulate those whom they themselves admire.

[12] Although such a vision recalls some of the categories relevant to Weberian charismatic authority, soft power differs significantly from charisma. Soft power generates endearment, but these qualities need not necessarily be "extraordinary" or "exceptional," nor are they perceived as "supernatural," as posited by Weber (1978, 242). Moreover, these qualities do not formally or directly endow a role-model nation with authority in a Weberian sense: the absolute ability to command and control. Rather, influence comes more as an indirect result of emulation and a direct/indirect result of endearment.

extended checklist. Ultimately, the concept undergirding soft power is one suggesting that nations will voluntarily support the wishes and interests of a soft power nation because the soft power nation has somehow cultivated their loyalty and support through actions, qualities, and/or policies that garner admiration and/or respect. The terms "admiration" and "respect" could be used instead, but they insufficiently capture the quality of being liked or esteemed (i.e., you can respect and admire a nation more than you esteem or like it). This does not mean that all the actions, qualities, and policies of soft power nations are endearing. Indeed, other nations may be repelled by a number of the actions, qualities, and policies of a soft power nation, but the preponderance of such "output" by a soft power nation should endear that nation to other nations in some form (notwithstanding how that output is distributed with regard to respect, admiration, and esteem).

Emulation (when nations adopt the policies of soft power nations) is an especially potent manifestation of soft power. Emulation can emanate from different sources of endearment. It may be the result of the soft power nation being liked or esteemed somewhat independently of its policies (e.g., the esteem of actions or the esteem of particular qualities, as when culture makes its policies alluring). Yet emulation may emanate from another source. Nations may like and esteem the policies of a nation far more than they like and esteem particular national qualities or specific actions of that nation (e.g., I like free trade and democracy more than I like some specific qualities of the nation pursuing such policies – the case studies in Chapter 4 illustrate this source of soft power). However, it will often be the case that even in such situations there has to be at least some (even if modest) esteem or affinity for the actions and many of the qualities of the soft power nations themselves if the emulating nations are to sustain such policies. It would be difficult to publically sell policies that emulate those of nations whose actions and/or various qualities are completely despised by that public. Yet national leaders may respect and admire the policies of nations whose actions and qualities are generally held in disregard by a large proportion of their populations and find ways to sell the policies to the public as policies that are of an indigenous origin and therefore independent of the nation that is held in disregard (e.g., in a number of nations where large proportions of their populations can presently be described as expressing anti-U.S. sentiments, significant proportions of their publics still largely admire a number of economic policies and political institutions in the United States) (Inglehart and Norris 2003; Pew 2003). In sum, whether nations are attracted to the actions and qualities of soft power nations or to their policies, the term "endearment" best captures most of these important factors for producing soft power and thus has been selected as a term for describing the process of soft power.

Rather than gain influence through direct confrontations of manifest or symbolic force (sticks) or through inducements (carrots), as hard power strategies dictate, nations may perspicaciously resort to the back door and maneuver other nations into actions that accord with their interests simply by endearing themselves as a result of this positive image that derives from their policies, qualities, and actions.[13] Thus, the difference between hard and soft power can be understood as follows: Whereas hard power extracts compliance principally through reliance on tangible power resources (either symbolic use through threat or actual use of these resources), soft power cultivates it through a variety of policies, qualities, and actions that endear nations to other nations.[14] Hard power contemplates nations compelling other nations to do what the latter ordinarily would not otherwise do (Dahl's 1957 classic definition of power). Soft power, on the other hand, conditions the target nations to voluntarily do what nations enjoying soft power would like them to do. In this respect, there is much less conflict of interests in the process of soft power.[15]

Within a relational power context, soft power itself represents a form of meta-power. Meta-power suggests that bargaining or power relations themselves exist within some greater constellation of social relations that affect the formation of preferences (i.e., condition the structure of the bargaining space) and thereby influence final outcomes that derive from the interactions. Preferences or the bargaining boundaries are endogenous rather than exogenous; they are determined by the processes taking place

[13] This relates to Lasswell and Kaplan's (1950, 156) process of "identification" in which rank and file members of a group adopt the values of their leaders out of respect and admiration. Interestingly, Waltz (1979) and other Realists argue that this identification manifests itself in the emulation of successful military strategies and preferences for certain hard power resources.

[14] Of course, actions and policies that deliver soft power are often exercised through the use of tangible resources; hence, the line between hard and soft power can sometimes be a bit fuzzy with respect to the employment of tangible resources. This is discussed below in the chapter.

[15] Soft power does not entirely eliminate conflicts of interests; rather, it promotes a process whereby interests merge more closely with one another.

in the greater social relations within which they are embedded. To quote Hall (1997a, 405):

> Meta-power refers to the *shaping* of social relationships, social structures, and *situations* by altering the matrix of possibilities and orientations within which social action occurs (i.e., to remove certain actions from actors' repertoires and to create or facilitate others). Meta-power refers to altering the type of game actors play; it refers to changing the distribution of resources or the conditions governing interaction [italics in original].

In this context, very little can be inferred about the balance of power in a bargaining process merely by simply looking at the position of equilibria within the existing bargaining space. Moreover, the interaction need not manifest itself in a conflictual process, nor do interests themselves necessarily have to demonstrate significant divergence. One actor may seem to be moving the other actor closer to his or her preferred position within the prevailing bargaining space without in fact enjoying much influence over the seemingly compliant actor. Because the preferences or interests are endogenous and therefore the result of some greater constellation of social relations, the bargaining space itself can be the outcome of some greater configuration of power that has set possible equilibria in a range highly consistent with the interests or preferences of the seemingly compliant actor. As Bachrach and Baratz (1962, 948) note, "To the extent that [an actor] succeeds in doing this, [other actors are] prevented, for all practical purposes, from bringing to the fore any issues that might in their resolution be seriously detrimental to [that actor's] set of preferences."[16] Hence, even losing a struggle for immediate power within the prevailing bargaining space may still be winning the bargaining game (i.e., losing a battle but winning the war) if some greater set of social relations can skew the bargaining space in favor of the compliant actor.

It is common to refer to meta-power as agenda control or power over an agenda. Nye (2004b, 9) himself describes soft power as control over the "political agenda" and attributes the genus of the concept to the work of Bachrach and Baratz (1962, 1963). Agenda control, in its more precise context, would indeed be one way of perpetrating such meta-power

[16] Bachrach and Baratz (1962, 1963) underscore the importance of non-decision processes as phenomena within which power relationships can unfold. In this case, power itself can be exercised before the actual competition over decision outcomes even begins by structuring the contexts within which the competition is played out. This serves as a challenge to the conventional scholarship on power that has evaluated power relationships based exclusively on the process of the actual competition over decisions.

outcomes. Agenda control, then, is a subset of meta-power. Within some collective bargaining process that is guided by a formal agenda, outcomes are circumscribed by the range of issues and strategic possibilities set by the agenda itself. The agenda defines which issues will be raised and, in doing so, sets the boundaries that define possible bargaining equilibria. If some actor can set the agenda or if the agenda itself is shaped by some greater constellations of social relations defined by prevalent rules or norms and procedures that favor that actor, then bargaining outcomes will merge toward the preferences of that actor irrespective of final equilibrium within the delineated bargaining space. This is the case because the delineation of the space is favorable to the interests or preferences of that actor. Thus, movement within the bargaining space itself is less indicative of the true balance of power than how the bargaining space is structured. Such outcomes would give an actor who can shape the agenda considerable meta-power.[17]

The work of Bachrach and Baratz itself has stimulated much thought and work on bargaining within a restricted agenda – what has been referred to in the power literature as the second face of power.[18] Conventional treatments of the second face process of power tend to be inconsistent with a process of soft power because such conventional treatments underscore a conflict of interests among actors; people set an agenda to favor their interests over the interests of others, and consequently, there are clear winners (agenda setters) and losers (those excluded). Such maneuvers will compromise rather than enhance the soft power of agenda setters. Soft power can, however, interface with a second face framework in a modified way. If certain nations endear themselves significantly to others, they may be trusted to set agendas. Such a privilege will place

[17] Although both Lukes (1974) and Isaac (1987) underscore fundamental differences between their work and that of Bachrach and Baratz (1962, 1963), all three visions of power in fact demonstrate an embedded social quality in which the direct interaction between bargaining agents is itself conditioned by some greater constellations of social relations.

[18] Four faces of power have been identified in the power literature. The first constitutes direct contests between actors, in which the outcomes from bargaining are reflective of the relative distribution of power (i.e., the conventional view of power relations). The other three faces of power constitute meta-power relations. Bachrach and Baratz' work has been designated as a second face of power. Barnett and Duvall's (2005) typology of international power conflates much of this second face into their concept of institutional power. For a good survey of the work on agenda control, see Mueller (1997, 2003). The other two faces will be described below in the chapter. For an explanation and comparison of the four faces of power, see especially Digeser (1992), Berenskoetter (2007), and Barnett and Duvall (2005).

them in a position to prevent decisions that sharply conflict with their own interests. Yet predatory agendas will compromise soft power. Agendas that best promote mutual gains will generate more soft power than predatory agendas, and the soft power in turn will allow agenda setters to keep their privileged position. Moreover, conflict regarding the agenda itself could be minimized by soft power because of the convergent interests created by respect and admiration. Thus, to the extent that non–agenda setters have adopted the policy orientations of agenda setters, agendas that are consistent with the interests of the agenda setters will also be consistent with those of non–agenda setters.

Although some elements of soft power could be consistent with a modified vision of the second face of power, the essence of the idea of soft power relates much more closely to the work of Lukes (1974) and Isaac (1987) – what the power literature refers to as the third face of power, insofar as it represents the manifestation of power through the process of co-optation. Lukes' idea of three-dimensional power, Isaac's idea of structural power, and Nye's idea of co-optation postulate that influence can be acquired if actors are able to mold the preferences and interests of other actors so as to bring them closer to their own preferences and interests. There is one fundamental difference, though. Both Issac's and Luke's (i.e., the radical vision of meta-power) logic is inspired by the idea of Gramscian (1988) hegemony, which in turn develops Marx's idea about the ideological legitimation of capitalism (i.e., the ideology of the dominant classes becomes the dominant ideology in society) (Marx 1972). For Gramsci (1988), effective control over any society could never be accomplished by brute force or threat alone; rather, it required an "intellectual and moral" element that undergirds an "historical bloc." This element represents control through what he calls "hegemony." In this respect, the radical vision of meta-power contains a strong element of conflict of interests in the social relations it contemplates because the process of co-optation imposes ideas that are against the objective interests of the groups being co-opted.[19] As with Gramscian hegemony of the state, Neo-Marxists posit that dominant nations also produce an "historical bloc" in the international political system: "[as] the hierarchical articulation of social forces that compose a society, [the historical bloc] is thus the objective basis of hegemony and is not merely a more or less structured set of social classes but a cultural, political, and moral phenomenon as

[19] Barnett and Duvall's category of structural power best conforms to this radical conception of meta-power.

well" (Pellicani 1976, 32). Thus, in the radical view, the modern capitalist political economy has created a prevailing morality and ideology that co-opts all nations into supporting the dominant mode of international political-economic relations that govern interactions in the world polity. This control is exerted through the venues of institutions that are portrayed as legitimate guarantors of collective interests in world politics, but actually are oriented around the interests and preferences of dominant nations. Neo-Marxists have envisioned these as the "institutionalization of hegemony" in the world polity.[20]

While this Gramscian hegemony, or the radical conception of the third face of power, would represent meta-power for dominant nations, it would nonetheless represent a kind of imposed control, although the imposition manifests itself through a co-optive indoctrination. Thus, it would not qualify as soft power because in such hegemony there is an element of adversarial manipulation (conflict of interests in the radical vision, which would be an illiberal means of generating compliance – i.e., fooling subordinate nations). The radical vision is based on the idea of false consciousness, which suggests that the objective interests of subordinate nations have not really merged toward the objective interests of dominant nations, only that a concerted effort to sell a universal ideology has inculcated a false sense of interests on the part of subordinate nations (Marx 1972; Lukes 1974; Gramsci 1988). There is most definitely a strong conflict of interests in this radical vision of power.[21]

Soft power generally eschews a strict conflict of interests as posited in the radical conception of the third face of power, as well as in the second face of power. This is demonstrated in Nye's (2004b, 10) own identification of soft power in the Bretton Woods institutions, which refutes Neo-Marxist critiques of such institutions as modes of Gramscian hegemony in the workings of both second face and third face processes. This merely reflects a sincere disagreement on the part of Nye, who sees such liberal principles of economic relations as truly beneficial for all

[20] The Neo-Marxist literature is extensive, but especially valuable and representative works can be found in Cox (1980, 1987), Gill (1993), Sklair (1995), and Murphy (1994).

[21] Even Dahl's (1965, 1974) own conception of power is not necessarily grounded in a conflict of interests. Interestingly, Dahl's classic work *Who Governs* (1974), as influential as it has been, has nonetheless been given insufficient credit as a thorough statement about the faces of power. Indeed, in Polsby's (1980) well-known study of power, we glean some fairly compelling arguments suggesting that Dahl articulated three faces of power. Guzzini's (1993) fusion concept of power as agent power and governance proposes a vision of power that also integrates various faces of power.

TABLE 1. *Sources of Soft Power*

International	Domestic
Respect for international laws, norms, regimes, and other institutions	Culture
Fundamental reliance on cooperation and a reluctance to solve problems unilaterally	– Social Cohesion – Quality of Life – Liberalism – Opportunity
Respect for international treaties and alliance commitments	– Tolerance – Lifestyle
Willingness to sacrifice short-term national interests in order to contribute toward multilateral solutions to international problems	Political Institutions – Democracy – Constitutionalism – Liberalism/Pluralism
Economic openness	– Effectively functioning government bureaucracy

nations, so that the socialization of less developed nations into the liberal-capitalist mode is not false consciousness but is a true facilitator of their objective interests. Because not only external observers such as scholars but also national leaders themselves are able to come to the realization of the imperialist intent behind a more radical conception of hegemony in some longer run, Gramscian indoctrination will not qualify as soft power, but in fact it will diminish the soft power of the imperialist nations (Nye 2004b, 9). More generally, it is clear from the sources of soft power that Nye enumerates (see Table 1) that the compelling behavior modes would indeed be beneficial to any nation willing to adopt them. Although it is the case that Neoliberals (within which Nye's work can certainly be positioned) envision mixed games among nations (i.e., games that contain elements of both conflict and cooperation), the process of soft power itself represents a subset of Neoliberal logic that more emphatically embraces the convergence of interests among nations.

This also brings up the relation between Foucault's (2000) fourth face of power, which Barnett and Duvall (2005) refer to as productive power, and the idea of soft power (Barnett and Duvall 2005; Digeser 1992). In one respect, soft power is closer to Foucault's vision of power than the radical vision in that both soft power and Foucault generally eschew ideas of conflict of interests relative to radical and second-face visions. However, some fundamental differences place the two visions of power at odds. Foucault's vision is more Constructivist in terms of the derivation of interests (i.e., interests are far more socially and consequently subjectively constructed), whereas soft power is more oriented around the existence of objective interests. This suggests that nations influenced by soft power do indeed have the capacity to rise above the false consciousness encouraged by hegemonic processes of socialization (in fact, there is extensive potential for "resistance" – you can't fool most of the people most of the time). In a Foucaultian vision the possibilities for such resistance are extremely limited. This limited potential for resistance also highlights the far greater pervasiveness of a Foucaultian vision of power relative to the process posited in a soft power context – that is, for Foucault the process is "omnipresent," pervasive in every "background condition" underlying all social relations. Thus, it represents an all-encompassing undercurrent of norms and values that inspire the very processes of socialization at the most general levels of human interaction (Brass 2000; Digeser 1992, 981). In this respect, the manifestations of power are neither specifically contextual nor situational. Soft power manifests itself in more specific contexts and situations – that is, having to do with the relationship between the actions and policy orientations of particular nations on the one hand and the responses to these actions and orientations by other nations on the other (Brass 2000; Digeser 1992; Foucault 2000).

Soft power has become somewhat misunderstood. It has become all too common to equate the concept with the influence emanating from the seductive cultural values created by movies, television, radio, and fashion (Fraser 2003). Soft power is much more. Soft power can be systematically categorized as deriving from two sources: foreign polices and actions (i.e., international sources) and domestic polices and actions (domestic sources), with multiple subsources within each. It should be emphasized again, however, that all these sources ultimately contribute to a positive image that endears a nation with soft power to other nations, and this endearment enhances a nation's influence in the world community. Thus, the sources of soft power converge into one process of empowerment. The policies and actions that deliver soft power are enumerated in Table 1.

First, under international sources, nations must demonstrate a fundamental respect for international law, norms, regimes, and other institutions undergirding cooperation among nations. This commitment to "playing by the rules" in the service of the collective good generates an image of dependability, sensitivity, legitimacy, and a stance against violence. No more endearing posture can be contemplated in world affairs. This general orientation is the principal source of international soft power; the sources that follow are more specific manifestations of this general orientation.

Second, nations must abstain from a unilateral posture in the promotion of their foreign policies. Nye's work on American foreign policy is most engaged on this issue of multilateralism versus unilateralism. Nye (2002) issues a strong warning against the dangers that the latter foreign policy style poses to the American national interest. Gallarotti (2004, 2010) systematically analyzes such dangers, the greatest of which is referred to as "the vicious cycle of unilateralism." Disregarding multilateral regimes in favor of such independence carries manifold consequences that increasingly isolate the unilateralist nation, and in this respect serve to increasingly eliminate traditional sources of multilateral leverage in the international system. Unilateralism can be especially debilitating because in an interdependent and globalized world, unilateral solutions to international problems are often inferior to collective solutions.[22]

Third, respect for international treaties and alliance commitments are central to the creation of soft power. The logic pertaining to the previous two sources of soft power is fully relevant here. Forsaking erstwhile allies and international commitments in favor of unilateral solutions produces a maverick image that compromises traditional sources of power embedded in multilateral support networks. Without such networks, even preponderant national resources will fall short of the effectiveness of multilateral solutions in attending to foreign objectives, thus creating an unsupportable burden for the maverick nation.

Fourth, the willingness to forego short-term national interests in order to contribute toward substantive collaborative schemes that address important multilateral problems is a necessary component of soft power. Consistent with international commitments and fair play, nations will garner considerable respect by foregoing short-term national objectives for the sake of collective solutions to international problems. Conversely, there is much to lose by showing an unwillingness to "do one's part" and imposing sucker's payoffs on other nations that are indeed making sacrifices for the collective interest.

Finally, a nation must pursue policies of economic openness. This dictates a foreign economic policy orientation that relies on liberal tenets. The greater the openness, the more elevated will be the national image. Free trade in goods and open capital markets represent a commitment to maintaining opportunities for economic growth in other nations. This is the antithesis of a mercantilist orientation that neglects the needs of

[22] For similar arguments against American unilateralism, see also Jervis (2003a) and Calleo (2003).

other nations and concentrates only on domestic needs. But even more than open markets in goods and money, openness to people and ideas similarly generates a positive image. Such openness conveys concern for the plight of individuals in foreign nations who seek refuge from abuses, or seek socioeconomic and political opportunities that are missing in their nations. In this respect, admiration hoists an image of "champion for the needy and downtrodden."[23]

Nye (2004b, 55–60) also underscores the importance of domestic factors as another important set of sources for generating soft power. As he notes (2004b, 56, 57), "How [a nation] behaves at home can enhance its image and perceived legitimacy, and that in turn can help advance its foreign policy objectives." Domestic sources are broadly categorized under two rubrics: the power inherent in culture and that inherent in political institutions. Politically, institutions must reflect broad principles of democratic enfranchisement. The system must represent a set of rules that deliver democracy, pluralism, liberalism, and constitutionalism. In this context, a positive image that endears a nation to others is generated by political outcomes that demonstrate a respect for well-regarded norms concerning desirable styles of domestic governance. These styles will converge on the objectives of politically empowering civil society and reducing political gaps (Huntington 1971). Culturally, soft power is enhanced by social cohesion (limited social cleavages), quality of life, liberalism, opportunity, tolerance, and the intoxicating characteristics of a lifestyle that generates both admiration and emulation (Nye 2002, 113, 114, 119, 141).

Like international sources of soft power, domestic sources also reflect an emphasis on policies and actions that exude an aura of respect for legitimate institutions, justice, collective concern, and rules of fair play. In both the international and domestic sources of soft power, we therefore see pervasive principles of Neoliberalism and Constructivism.

Although the components of soft power demonstrate various qualities that would be associated with liberal democracies embracing international cooperation, this is not to say that other qualities or value systems will not generate admiration and even emulation. Indeed, the Soviet Union in the 1930s generated a good deal of soft power based on its

[23] James and Lake (1989) and Lobell (2008) have articulated a variant of this logic in their case studies of a "second face of power effect," in which nations used free trade policies to change domestic political dynamics in target nations so as to generate desired security and economic policies.

economic achievements and the emphasis of communism on economic equality. However, because the focus of this book is on forging a vision of power that interfaces Neoliberalism and Constructivism with Realism, it is the value systems embraced by the former two paradigms that are underscored as sources of admiration and emulation that deliver soft power.

More on the Relationship between Soft and Hard Power

Although the difference between hard and soft power revolves principally around the difference between extracting compliance with tangible resources and cultivating voluntary compliance through an image that endears soft power nations to other nations, there are some important complexities regarding their relationship. The following discussion of some of these complexities challenges the simple relationship I have underscored; nonetheless, it is meant more to clarify than to confuse, even though it stretches the concept of both sources of power and introduces manifold interaction effects. Exploring such possibilities renders a richer, even if a more complicated, understanding of the two sources of power and how they relate.

One such issue involves the possible decomposition of soft power with respect to its relevance across the global power structure. This leads to various possibilities with regard to the benefits of soft power. Endearment would appear to confer equal benefits across the power spectrum (i.e., to both great and small powers). Nations that have earned respect are likely to enjoy preferential treatment both in multilateral forums and in bilateral relationships. In this case, nations may increase their alliance prospects, win more votes in international organizations, or stave off menacing gestures from other nations. But even here, the benefits may not be fully equal but rather in proportion to stakes in the system, especially if larger powers enjoy economies of scale. In this case, such larger powers might turn a positive image into far greater gains through greater control in the international system, allowing them to compound such benefits. Emulation might also produce differing outcomes depending on stakes and circumstances. So imagine emulating a liberal trade regime or even a democratic form of government. Such might benefit a greater power more than a smaller power according to stakes in the system. As large trading nations, greater powers may have a greater stake in the international trading system and thus benefit more from the emulation of liberal policies, all the more so if they are efficient producers. Concomitantly, emulating democratic governments may render similar stake-proportion benefits if democracies cause less conflict in the international system. Conversely, smaller nations can gain proportionally more from free trade if their trade sectors are relatively bigger in proportion to their economies (and they usually are) and they are highly efficient producers. Concomitantly, smaller nations may gain more from emulation if their prior political environment was chaotic relative to that of larger nations. Moreover, drawing on Dahl's (1957) concept of negative power (i.e., actors may react negatively to the actions of other actors), it may be the case that actions and images on the part of certain nations generate negative soft power. In short, not all compelling images in the world garner soft power.

The relationship between hard and soft power is complex and interactive. The two are neither perfectly substitutable nor rigidly complementary. In many cases, the exercise of one kind of power may enhance the other kind. It will often be the case that each set of power resources requires at least some of the other for maximum effectiveness (i.e., the very essence of Cosmopolitan power). Thus, some hard power resources will compound the effectiveness of soft power, and vice versa. For example, giving arms and economic aid to allies fosters reciprocity and bonds that can enhance a nation's image and hence its influence with the recipients. Gilpin (1975) underscores the extent to which the global economic primacy enjoyed by the United States in the postwar period was based on the Pax Americana, which American military primacy has sustained. Furthermore, the possession of hard power itself can make a nation a role model in a variety of ways. Even Realists such as Waltz (1979) underscore the attractiveness generated by large military arsenals and successful military strategies. In the case studies on soft empowerment in chapters 4 and 6, it is clear that economic primacy (i.e., economic hard power) generated significant soft power for certain nations, and that this soft power translated into enhanced influence in the global political economy for these nations. As a symbol of national success, extensive hard power certainly generates significant soft power by generating respect and admiration. However, these hard power resources cannot be used in ways that undermine that respect and admiration. In other words, they cannot be used in ways that deviate from the principles undergirding soft power (see Table 1). So even the employment of force can generate soft power if it is in the service of goals widely perceived as consistent with these principles (e.g., protecting nations against aggression, peacekeeping, or liberation from tyranny). Similarly, soft power can enhance hard power. A strong image can generate hard power for a nation if that nation can translate such an image into an enhanced industrial military capacity (e.g., trade agreements with nations that export important natural resources, access to strategic locations for new military bases, joint development of weapon systems).

In the case studies on soft empowerment in Chapters 4 and 6, we see precisely how these interaction effects led to a cycle of mutual reinforcement between hard and soft power. The case studies in Chapter 4 show how the economic primacy of the United States and Britain (extensive economic hard power) actually endeared their policies to other nations. This endearment led others to emulate the policies, and the emulation opened manifold opportunities for the two nations to prosper economically and politically to an even greater degree, and consequently enhanced their hard power. Their greater hard power in turn raised their economic soft power by making their policies all the more respected and admired. Similarly, the allure of American culture (analyzed in Chapter 6) has created manifold opportunities for the United States to enhance its hard power (socially, economically, militarily, and politically). And this hard power has in turn made American culture all the more alluring.

Of course, the use of one kind of power may also detract from the other kind of power. Uses of hard power carry obvious disadvantages for image if they are carried out in an aggressive, unilateralist style: invasion, imperialism, economic sanctions, and threats. Yet actions that enhance soft power can perhaps be equally costly in terms of sacrificing hard power. This is the position of many American unilateralists who presently look askance at being bound by international agreements; for example, Kyoto will stunt American economic growth, the Law of the Sea will limit the United States' access to important resources, and the International Criminal Court (ICC) may crimp the conduct of military operations overseas. A critique of soft power from a Realist perspective might cite the tendency of soft power to detract from the influence generated by hard power resources. For example, nations with reputations for being extremely cooperative and highly respectful of international law might lose some credibility when issuing threats.

Furthermore, the separation of the two types of power resources is somewhat arbitrary and imperfect categorically. International aid, for example, may increase soft power through an enhanced image but may also provide liquidity to purchase donor exports or pay back debts to banks in donor nations. Similarly, even the use of aggressive military force can generate a positive image with the nations that benefit from such an initiative – for example, the United States in liberating Kuwait and protecting Saudi Arabia during the Gulf War. Moreover, the exercise of each type of power resources has complex consequences for the specific power positions themselves. The use of hard power resources may diminish the hard power position of a nation in many ways (hard disempowerment). For example, military atrocities may stiffen resistance in a manner that weakens an aggressor nation if the victims either grow to hate the aggressor or sense that such atrocities can be withstood. Also, the use of threats that are never carried out may diminish the influence of the nation issuing such treats (Bachrach and Baratz 1963, 636). Similarly, the use of soft power resources may adversely affect a nation's image no matter how innocuous the resources. A clear example is the contempt that many people in less-developed countries (LDCs) hold for international development organizations such as the International Monetary Fund (IMF) and the World Bank because they see these institutions as promoting economic relations between North and South that are neoimperialistic. In the same vein, whereas some embrace Western cultural penetration, others see it as cultural imperialism and contamination that should be resisted.[24]

The issue of interaction effects between soft and hard power raises the issue of economic power, and economic power is indeed another testament to the complex and interactive relationship between hard and soft power. Economic power has often been mistaken as soft power, although it would fit more squarely into Nye's definition of hard power because it is based on tangible resources that can somehow extract compliance. As a set of tangible resources, economic power does constitute hard power in its most direct manifestations. It can be used to coerce or bribe nations into doing what they otherwise would not do. Yet economic power could generate soft power through both direct and indirect effects. In a direct context, foreign aid and investment may be promoted for the purposes of endearing a donor to recipients, but it can also generate indirect effects that cultivate soft power. For example, technological and economic primacy themselves may generate great admiration among the community of nations that translates into responsive actions and policies that enhance the soft power of the nations that enjoy such primacy (soft empowerment). In this respect, economic power can serve an important

[24] A testament to this adverse effect of dissemination is evident in national laws that limit the foreign content of media transmissions. On cultural imperialism, see Sklair (1995) and LeFeber (1999).

role in cultivating soft power.[25] Yet, as noted previously, the relationship between economic power and soft power depends on how the economic resources are used. As long as they are used in accordance with the principles undergirding soft power (see Table 1), they have the capacity to generate significant soft power. Conversely, if they are used in ways that are antithetical to these principles, they can significantly compromise a nation's soft power.

Another interesting interaction effect between the two kinds of power is that the use of one set of resources may either economize on or enhance the need for another set of resources. A positive image may create outcomes within such favorable boundaries for a nation that it actually reduces the nation's need to use "carrots" and "sticks" to gain compliance on important issues. For example, a nation's reputation for loyalty may garner allies whose own loyalty will eliminate the nation's need to expend unilateral resources to achieve its goals in international politics. Moreover, a nation's acceptance of restraints on its unilateral actions by ratifying a treaty (e.g., arms reduction) may not adversely affect its relative hard power position if such an action fosters similar restraints by other nations. A loss of hard power has been offset with a soft effect; others have accepted similar losses. However, intransigence to multilateralism may reduce a nation's hard power position even though it frees that nation from restraint. This would occur if reactions to such intransigence resulted in a more antagonistic international system. In such cases, the intransigent nation would have to compensate in other ways (both hard and soft) to restore its former position of influence (Nye 2002, 9, 10; 2004b, 25–27).

The issue of comparing the two types of power based on tangibility is also problematic. [26] Nye's language highlights a distinction between tangible and intangible resources (2002, 8; 2004b, 5). He speaks of a nation using hard power as "throwing its weight around without regard to its effects" (2004b, 26). Although much of Nye's analysis contemplates hard power principally as a source of influence grounded in tangible resources and soft power as grounded in intangible resources, tangibility is not a strict source of differentiation between the two categories.

25 The case studies of soft empowerment presented in Chapter 4 largely manifest such a process in which hard power resources (in this case economic primacy in various issue-areas) proved important sources in generating soft power for nations abundantly endowed with such hard power.

26 Indeed, critics of soft power highlight this problematic distinction between hard and soft power based on tangibility. See Baldwin (2002) and Meade (2004).

Nye's own logic would allow for intangible applications of hard power. For example, although a threat is intangible, it forces a mode of action onto another nation involuntarily, thus violating liberal rules of fair play (Baldwin 2002). In this case, compliance is being extracted rather than cultivated. Furthermore, hard power resources can generate attraction effects through "perceptions of invincibility" (Nye 2004b, 26). Nations may show deference and even admiration because they want to be associated with a winner, especially if the winner nation is using its hard power in the interests of the former.[27] Conversely, soft power has a tangible element in that it may take tangible resources to institute the policies and actions that deliver an endearing image.

Ultimately, although the two sources of power are quite interconnected and thus could share many qualities (e.g., tangibility and intangibility, international effects), the real differentiation of power is, as noted, in the context of its use. Nye's conceptualization of soft power suggests that the context of actions (whether tangible or intangible) be a manifestation of principles of fair play, cooperation, and respect for the rights of domestic populations as well as the rights of other nations (see Table 1). In this vein, hard power itself can be used in a manner that engenders the respect and admiration of other nations if it manifests itself in ways consistent with these principles (e.g., peacekeeping, protecting against aggression or genocide, providing economic aid on terms favorable to recipient nations). Hard power itself will be counterproductive to enhancing influence when it is used in a less enlightened manner – that is, in a manner antithetical to the principles undergirding soft power. Yet Nye's own view of hard power is much more neutral. There is no incrimination of hard power as necessarily evil. Ultimately, tangible resources can deliver both hard and soft power. However, tangible resources are merely instruments and are no better or worse than the manner in which they are used. One is reminded here of Khrushchev's famous response to the accusation of having offensive missiles in Cuba; he noted that a gun is either an offensive or defensive weapon depending on where it is pointed (Kennedy 1969).

The fundamental distinction that differentiates hard from soft power is the difference in the principles which dictate their use. Resources expended to cultivate compliance in the context of liberal principles,

[27] An example of the soft power garnered through an extensive military presence would be the goodwill promoted by American military functions abroad: education, political stabilization, provision of public goods (Hartman 2007).

whether tangible or intangible, can generate soft power. Those resources, both tangible and intangible, that are expended in the context of principles that envision the extraction of compliance or tangible resources that are illiberal generally fall into the category of hard power. Moreover, nations may certainly become stronger by relying on hard power, but they can become all the stronger by developing soft power resources as well. The use of both kinds of power is the "smart" policy (*Report of the Center for Strategic and International Studies Commission on Smart Power* 2007). In this respect, both soft power and hard power demonstrate their limitations when used exclusively. Too hard a policy may generate a pariah or brutish image that compromises international support and even generates countervailing processes that obstruct the attainment of foreign policy goals. Alternately, too soft a policy creates the image of a paper tiger and renders soft nations a target for aggressors. The idea of smart power suggests that influence can be optimized only by combining hard and soft power resources. This is the essence of the vision of Cosmopolitan power.

The Growing Importance of Soft Power

Greater attention to soft power itself reflects the changing landscape of international relations. It is no coincidence that such sources of power have been hailed by proponents of Neoliberalism and Constructivism, paradigms that have underscored the changing nature of world politics. In this case, theory has been influenced by real events. Although history has shown soft power always to have been an important source of national influence (certainly the case studies in this book do), changes in modern world politics have raised its utility all the more (Gallarotti 2010).[28] It has become and is continuing to become a "softer world." World politics in the modern age has been undergoing changes that have elevated the importance of soft power relative to hard power. In this transformed international system, soft power will be a crucial element in enhancing influence over international outcomes because it has become more difficult to compel nations and non-state actors through the principal levers of hard power (i.e., threats and force). The world stage has

[28] In case studies on power-seeking that span history and issue-areas, Gallarotti (2010) demonstrates that soft power could have significantly enhanced the influence of nations whose leaders were predominantly swayed by the allure of hard power (i.e., victims of a power curse in the context of a hard–soft power nexus).

become less amenable to Hobbesian brutes and more amenable to actors well aware of the soft opportunities and constraints imposed by the new global system. Nations that comport themselves in a manner that disregards the growing importance of soft power risk much. Even gargantuan efforts to increase influence may be rendered self-defeating if they rely exclusively on hard power. In such cases, the strength or influence a nation is acquiring through hard initiatives may be illusory. The changes in world politics that have raised the importance of soft power relative to hard power have been pervasive and compelling.

First, with the advent of nuclear power, the costs of using or even threatening force have skyrocketed. Keohane and Nye (1989) have long called attention to the diminished utility of coercion in a world where force can impose far greater costs on societies than they are willing to bear. The Neoliberal catechism has concluded that such diminution has destroyed the former hierarchy of issues that traditionally preserved the status of security atop the list of national interests (i.e., security's primacy has been challenged by other issues). Jervis (1993, 1988, 2002) has proclaimed a new age of a "security community" in which war between major powers is almost unthinkable because the costs of war have become too high. The nuclear threat is certainly compelling in this regard, but attitudes regarding war have also changed. Mueller (1988, 2004) reinforces the role of changing attitudes and modifies the nuclear deterrent argument by introducing the independent deterrent of even conventional war in an age of advanced technology. That conventional war can devastate nations is another reason for the disuse of force in the modern age. Moreover, greater governmental control over war, as opposed to the more idiosyncratic "criminal" sources of war, has reduced the incidence of war. In short, a synthesis of this logic suggests that warfare is definitely on the decline and possibly on the road to "disappearing" (Mueller 2004, 1). In the light of this logic, the importance of respect, admiration, and cooperation (i.e., soft power) have increased relative to that of coercion among the instruments of statecraft. Moreover, the dangers that the hard resources of military technology have produced require an ever-increasing commitment to the instruments of soft power for humans to achieve sustainable security.

Second, hard power also functions within a specific political, social, and economic context created by modernization – the context of interdependence (Herz 1957; Osgood and Tucker 1967; Keohane and Nye 1989; Nye 2004a). Using "sticks" and threats generates considerable costs among interdependent actors. As social and economic interpenetration increases, punishing or threatening other nations is to some extent self-punishment. Given nations' increasing economic and social stakes across each other's borders, surely some part of the perpetrating nations' interests will be compromised, e.g., their companies and citizens may suffer from punitive acts intended to harm the target nation (Cerny, forthcoming). In such an environment, strategies for optimizing national wealth and power have shifted from war and competition to cooperation. Yet even more elusive than the quest to contain damage within the target nation in such an environment is the quest to impose some specific outcomes on target nations and actors. In an interpenetrated world, targeted nations and actors have much room to maneuver and many avenues of escape. Transnational actors can avoid being compelled by carrots or sticks because of their access to the international political economy. They can escape coercion or bribes merely by taking refuge in their many international havens. This modern-day "economic feudalism" is shifting the nexus of power from the territorial state to transnational networks (Nye 2002, 75). In such an environment, transnational actors are ever more elusive (multinational corporations [MNCs]) and ever more dangerous (terrorists). The ineffectiveness of sanctions is also a testament to how targeted regimes can avoid the deleterious consequences of punitive actions by taking advantage of the international marketplace, both above and below ground. In such an environment, neither economic nor military strength will guarantee the capacity to compel or deter. Instead, favorable outcomes can often be delivered more effectively through the respect and admiration garnered through soft power instruments.

Compounding the increasing utility of soft power relative to hard power generated by military technology and interdependence are four other factors: democratization, globalization, the rise of the guardian state, and the growth of international organizations and regimes. The growth and consolidation of democracy compounds the disutility of coercion as the actors bearing the greatest burden of such coercion (the people) acquire political power over decision makers. This democratic peace phenomenon has shifted the power equation considerably (Doyle 1997; Russett and Oneal 2001; Ray 1995). As people become more empowered, they consolidate stronger political impediments to the use of force and threat. Furthermore, democratic political cultural naturally drives national leaders toward the cannons of soft power, which are grounded in respect for the democratic process at both the national and international levels. Thus, national leaders are much more constrained to work within acceptable policy boundaries – boundaries that increasingly discourage force, threat, and bribery.

Globalization has compounded the effects of interdependence by enhancing the process of social and economic interpenetration among nations. The information age has given civil societies the capacity to receive and transmit information across nations in a manifold and speedy way. Better links enhance networking among transnational actors. As the international stakes of these actors grow, so do their incentives to expend political capital within their own domestic political systems to reinforce the economic ties among nations (Milner 1988). Other technological manifestations of globalization magnify and solidify these links, so that transnational networks become pervasive forces in world politics. Nye (2004b, 31) states that these networks "... will have soft power of their own as they attract citizens into coalitions that cut across national boundaries. Politics in part then becomes a competition for attractiveness, legitimacy, and credibility." This access to foreign governments and citizens also compounds the effects of democratization in creating political impediments to the use of hard power (Haskel 1980). These forces have both diminished possibilities of political conflict and shifted the nexus of competition away from force, threat, and bribery (Rosecrance 1999).

The rise and consolidation of the guardian state in the twentieth century have worked through the political vehicle of democracy to further diminish the utility of hard power relative to soft power. Social and political changes have made modern populations more sensitive to their economic fates and less enamored of a "warrior ethic" (Jervis 2002; Nye 2004b, 19). With the rise of this welfare/economic orientation and the consolidation of democracy, political leaders have been driven more by the economic imperative and less by foreign adventurism as a source of political survival (Gallarotti 2000; Ruggie 1983). This has shifted not only domestic but also foreign policy orientations. The economic welfare concern has put a premium on cooperation that can deliver economic prosperity and stability, and has worked against hard power policies that might compromise these goals. The guardian mentality has served to socialize national leaders to a greater extent (more docile and respectful of legitimate means of statecraft) compared with their nineteenth century predecessors, and consequently has reduced incentives to extract compliance through force, threat, and bribery. For Jervis (2002), this diminution of the warrior ethic represents a fundamental change in values that has consolidated the new security community.[29] Moreover, Jervis underscores how these new economic imperatives have augmented the benefits of peace, another crucial factor contributing to the rise of the security community.

Finally, the growth of international organizations and regimes since 1945 has essentially cast nations more firmly within networks of cooperation, a fundamental component of soft power (Krasner 1983 and Keohane and Nye 1989). As the size and stature of these networks have increased, so too have the power of the norms and laws they represent. More precisely, with the growth and consolidation of cooperative networks, unilateral actions that disregard such institutions are becoming costlier. In effect, cooperative networks have ratcheted up the minimum level of civil behavior in international politics and consequently raised the importance of soft power dramatically. Expectations have gravitated toward the sanctity of such institutions, and as a result, actions that cut against these expectations generate greater fallout than they did in an environment in which no such institutional superstructure existed. To a large extent, the spread of networks of cooperation has somewhat civilized nations to a greater extent, which in turn has made them less likely to extract compliance in what are considered illegitimate ways (i.e., through coercion or bribery). But beyond the role of international regimes and organizations as constraining agents, their growth and strength have made them desirable because of the opportunities they provide. As Keohane and Nye (1989, 37) note, the "... ability to choose the organizational forum for an issue and to mobilize votes will be an important political resource [in the modern world system]."

The Principles of Cosmopolitan Power

A number of the venerated tenets of Realism need not conflict with some of the fundamental tenets of Neoliberalism and Constructivism with respect to the concept of power. The Realist tenets about the optimization of power and the quest for security are consistent with objectives posited by Constructivists and Neoliberals. In interdependent and complex communities like the international system, especially in the contemporary

[29] McNeil (1982, 307) notes how the martial "cult of heroism" became especially strong in the late nineteenth century, fueled by an educational system that underscored patriotism and the study of the classics.

period, truly optimizing the goals underscored by Realists for individual nations can be accomplished only by conceptualizing individual actions within frameworks that embrace elements of Neoliberalism and Constructivism. Not doing so can lead to consequences that debilitate rather than empower nations. By embracing the interdependent and complex nature of international politics, Realist visions of power can more easily interface with those of Neoliberalism and Constructivism.

Principle 1: The optimization of both absolute and relative power can be a legitimate goal of statecraft

This proposition is consistent with both the Realist prime directive of power optimization and Constructivist and Neoliberal beliefs that individual capabilities can effectively coexist with collective harmony (i.e., individual strength is not inconsistent with group welfare if individuals conceive of their interests in terms of group utility).[30] In this respect, all three paradigms can embrace the idea of power augmentation and optimization (Barkin 2003, 327). Being both absolutely and relatively strong can benefit individual nations in a variety of ways without necessarily imposing adverse outcomes on the group. Moreover, if nations

30 This proposition brings up the complex issue of how much power Realists prescribe. There is disagreement in the literature. The conventional catechism of "maximization" (i.e., getting all the power one can) does not apply to all strands of Realist thought. In his *Scientific Man*, Morgenthau (1967, 194) does refer to a "limitless lust for power." However, in his magnum opus of Realism, *Politics among Nations* (1978, 35–37), he uses terminology that does not necessarily convey an insatiable quest or maximization, saying that nations "strive," "struggle," or "aspire" for power. Although Mearsheimer (2001, 35) posits a tendency for a nation "to amass as much power as it can," he follows by saying that once hegemony, or primacy, is acquired, nations may become status quo powers. Mearsheimer (2001, 19–22) and Snyder (1991, 11, 12) draw a useful typology distinguishing Realists on this question. Offensive Realists (Mearsheimer, Morgenthau) prescribe an aggressive quest for primacy, which in some cases entails maximization. Defensive Realists on the hand (Waltz 1979, Walt 1987, Snyder 1991, Jervis 1978, Van Evera 1999) argue that nations defend their places in the structure of power (i.e., exhibit a status quo bias) rather than seek primacy. Realists do, however, agree that "security is normally the strongest motivation of states" (Snyder 1991, 11; Schmidt 2007, 55). Hence, if one wants to use a term with the broadest relevance in describing Realist theory of power seeking, the term "optimizing power" appears superior to the term "maximizing power." It is more accurate to say that Realists in general prescribe the optimization of power for the given level of security desired. On optimization, see also Baldwin (1997).

The question of optimizing absolute versus relative power is also problematic. However, given that most Realists accept the validity of the zero-sum proposition, optimizing absolute power will be tantamount to optimizing relative power because any gains will come at the expense of others.

conceive of their fates as inextricably tied to the collective structures in which they operate, individual strength can enhance the goals of other nations.

There is nothing in Constructivism or Neoliberalism that proscribes power augmentation or even optimization. The more important question involving power is, power for what purpose? Constructivists and Neoliberals do not object to nations being powerful. The difference between Constructivists and Realists with regard to this issue is that for the former, the perceptions of what constitutes power are intersubjective and driven by cognitions about sources of influence in international relations. These cognitions are created through socialization in the international arena. Realists see power as a more objective phenomenon, principally composed of hard sources (military, land, and other material assets). Neoliberals conceptualize power in a broader context of the political economy; in this respect, power resources are not strictly limited to hard resources with direct military applications. Nations may amass many economic resources and undertake strategies of cooperation that enhance their international influence. For Realists, there is little distinction among the power-seeking strategies that nations follow, something Constructivists deny. Moreover, the objective hierarchy of national goals for Realists puts power augmentation at the very top. For Constructivists and Neoliberals, the hierarchy is subjective and does not place the acquisition of hard resources in a venerated position in all cases. Yet Constructivists and Neoliberals both embrace the value of power augmentation and optimization if the power can be used in support of varied goals (not just in the context of military capacity in an anarchic world).[31] The idea of soft power is a manifestation of a more Constructivist and Neoliberal concept of the utility of power. But before the emergence of the idea of soft power, Constructivists and Neoliberals emphasized institutions and phenomena that constrained nations – that is, norms, rules, laws, and cognitions that drove nations to limit their power-seeking behaviors (Wendt 1999, 114).[32] With the idea of soft power, Constructivism and Neoliberalism

[31] Even here there is no real difference among the paradigms in the idea of attaining security. Constructivists and Neoliberals merely disagree with Realists on the precise strategies and power resources that will deliver that security. There is nothing in Constructivism and Neoliberalism that proposes to compromise a nation's safety.

[32] Exceptions to this have come in the work on the empowerment of ideas and norms through moral authority and principled beliefs. See Hall (1997b) and Goldstein and Keohane (1993).

can embrace institutions and phenomena that empower nations rather than merely restrain them. In this framework, Realists, Neoliberals, and Constructivists can agree that nations have an incentive to be powerful. However, empowerment through the use of soft power is also consistent with a Realist conception of power optimization in that diversification among hard and soft power resources is the best way to optimize power and consequently attain security. Only through such diversification can power and security truly be optimized.

Even if power is conceived as a zero-sum game, augmenting relative power need not delegitimize a Constructivist or Neoliberal vision of power. The question of power for what? is most relevant in this context. Growing relatively more powerful than another nation need not be menacing to the weaker nation if the stronger nation is acting consistently within Constructivist or Neoliberal behavioral boundaries (i.e., the nation is not growing stronger for the purpose of dominating or exploiting the weaker nation).[33] It would be consistent with such behavioral boundaries that this greater strength could trickle down to weaker nations through benign hegemony or support through, for example, stronger alliances and greater aid (Kindleberger 1986; Ikenberry and Kupchan 2004). Yet if this power is used outside the behavioral boundaries prescribed by Neoliberal and Constructivist visions, nations are not naïve and can defend themselves against brute aggression.[34] Such aggressive behavior has a built-in feedback mechanism that can significantly compromise the influence of nations acting with such impunity (Gallarotti 2010). Even the most animated Realist would not condone self-destructive aggression. This is a compelling theme of both Carr's and Morgenthau's major works, as demonstrated later in chapter 3.

Principle 2: National power is endogenous

National power is not determined simply by the isolated actions of any given nation (i.e., it is not exogenous). Because the effectiveness of a nation's power can be determined only in the context of interactions with other nations, power itself is a social phenomenon. Power is defined by the social context in which it is developed and exercised – that is, contingent

[33] In this context the interrelation of norms and power structures would be most visible, hence marking a compelling tribute to the co-existence of a Realist and a non-Realist vision of international change (Barkin 2003, 337).

[34] In this respect, the quest for and use of power suggests a flexibility built on an integrated vision of power that takes into account the actions and motivations of other nations.

or endogenous. Whereas the theoretical trademarks of Neoliberalism and Constructivism are proclamations of this "social" context within which international relations unfold, Realists have nonetheless been adamant about the importance of social effects. This social context is marshaled on a logic about complex system effects (Jervis 1997). Even for Realists, power relations are neither exogenous nor linear. More weapons need not give you more security in the face of feedback effects (e.g., security dilemma, balancing, stability-instability paradox). Moreover, the nature of the power game can vary even for Realists. Because of complexity, it is possible for power to be a zero-, positive-, or negative-sum phenomenon, depending on the context within which that power arises and evolves. If an ally gains greater power, power can be a positive-sum phenomenon. If an enemy becomes more powerful at a nation's expense, then power can be zero-sum. If both nations match in competition, then power can be a negative-sum phenomenon as money is spent but only parity can be achieved. All three paradigms would embrace the idea of power as an endogenous phenomenon.

Principle 3: Nations will optimize their security

People understand that although there are no external impediments preventing them from reaching mutually beneficial outcomes, so also there are no external impediments guaranteeing that nations will not act in ways that are detrimental to the interests of other nations. Therefore, all nations bear the risk of being victims of large-scale violence and consequently must take measures to protect themselves. In this respect, nations will wish to optimize their security. This is consistent with the Realist assumption of anarchy, and that in the face of such anarchy, security must be optimized (Mearsheimer 2001, 30). Yet such protection must be administered in ways that prevent misperceptions about intentions if security dilemmas or other deleterious feedback processes are to be avoided. In this respect, protection must be conceptualized within the context of the social structures averred by Constructivists and Neoliberals. One must protect oneself in a manner most conducive and sensitive to group interests because in an interdependent world, individual safety is contingent on collective safety (i.e., security is indivisible). This collective vision of security is a manifestation of the importance of soft power: a nation's power and safety derive significantly from the attitudes and perceptions of other nations. Indeed, Baldwin (1997) shows that there is sufficient flexibility in the concept of security to accommodate an integrative paradigmatic vision of national security.

Above and beyond this argument, a compelling paradox in Realism's ontology suggests possibilities for further interfacing Constructivist, Neoliberal, and Realist approaches to security. Paradoxically, Realism's ontology of human behavior ultimately predicates conflict and competition on the ability of humans to act collectively; people within a nation, and often nations themselves in the form of alliances, coalesce to protect themselves in an anarchic environment. Sterling-Folker (2002) identifies this ontology as a manifestation of a pervasive Darwinian element in the Realist logic. Yet such Darwinian logic would suggest that the associational or collective action on the part of actors would be selected in terms of the imperative of attaining security. In this context, the in-group versus out-group argument that Realists have marshaled in defense of the paradox (i.e., in-group cooperation perpetrates out-group competition) certainly becomes problematic. From an evolutionary standpoint, selection proceeds both within groups and between groups to arrive at optimal capacities for survival (Sterling-Folker 2002). But even from a purely institutional context, the capacity for optimal group selection is conterminous with the dictates of security. In this respect, even a Realist prime directive of attaining security would involve extensive intergroup (i.e., international) cooperation. This has been articulated across numerous decades by some of the field's leading Realists. For example, Herz (1957), in discussing possibilities for the demise of the territorial state, argues that sovereignty has historically been determined by the imperatives of delivering maximum security to the actors involved. Some forty years later, Jervis (2002), in a partial validation of Herz, embraced the advent of security communities as the optimal response to security in the modern age. Indeed, the quest for security across all three paradigms interfaces well in this respect.

Principle 4: Anarchy is still pervasive in the international system

Neoliberals fundamentally assent to the Realist proposition about the pervasiveness of anarchy and the quest for security. Although Neoliberals differ with Realists with respect to the hierarchy of issues, they nonetheless assent to the Realist emphasis on security as a principal goal of nations. They differ, however, with regard to their visions of the level of vulnerability and threat that nations face in the modern international system (Keohane and Nye 1989). Constructivists concede that anarchy does in fact exist, but they believe that perceptions of anarchy and the behavioral manifestations of these perceptions will differ according to individual mind-sets – that is, they will be socially constructed (Wendt

1992). Yet although security in anarchy may be socially constructed and so seemingly conflict with Realists' objective visions of security, Williams' (2003) analysis of the Schmittian foundations of the Copenhagen School's idea of securitization suggests strong elements of compatibility between Realist and Constructivist visions of national security. Williams (2003) shows that even constructed visions of security demonstrate consistent elements (enmity, decision, threat, and emergency) that render images and goals that merge toward common understandings of security in a Realist vein. In this case, images of vital national interests develop through discursive legitimization and the practical ethics of discourse.[35] Deudney (2007) shows how both Realist and Liberal traditions in political theory have demonstrated far more convergence on the sources of human security, in expounding a republican security orientation, than has heretofore been embraced by traditional scholarship. Baldwin (1997) reinforces the potential for paradigmatic convergence by noting that greater conceptual specification on all sides carries the potential to generate more integrated concepts of security.

Principle 5: Power optimization and security can occur only through the combination of both hard and soft power resources

Hard power is required at some level for protection, but hard power alone is ill equipped to optimize influence. The optimization of national influence requires both hard and soft power resources. This is the mantra of the work on smart power (Nossel 2004; *Report of the Center for Strategic and International Studies Commission on Smart Power* 2007; Etheridge 2009). Soft power is the antithesis of a menacing posture and therefore breaks down adversarial elements among other nations that might restrict a nation's influence in the community of nations. Moreover, the endearment garnered through the respect for prevailing social structures renders a nation's influence all the greater, as others will more willingly follow its lead. Because diversification facilitates a goal embraced by all three paradigms (power optimization and security), the inclusion of soft power need not conflict with Realist logic. Even Realists would not condone hard power strategies that are clearly self-destructive, and many of the processes they underscore suggest such a concern: adverse balancing, security dilemmas, and paradoxes of power (Jervis 1997; Maoz 1989; Baldwin 1989; Walt 1987; Preble 2009; Yarmolinsky and Foster 1983).

[35] On the Copenhagen School of security studies, see also Guzzini and Jung (2004).

Also, Neoliberals and Constructivists have attested to the optimality of a diversified portfolio of power resources (Hall 1997b; Keohane and Nye 1989; Nye 2002; Goldstein and Keohane 1993).

The Signature Processes of Cosmopolitan Power: Soft Empowerment, Hard Disempowerment, and Optimal Diversification

Soft Empowerment

Soft empowerment can raise the influence of nations in the world polity in many ways. Endearment predisposes nations to the interests and goals of soft power nations. Endearment, of course, can range from low to very high in terms of the favorable dispositions it can cultivate among nations. At the low end, nations may be moderately predisposed to the requests and goals of soft power nations, such that a limited effort to honor these requests and goals is forthcoming. At the upper range of endearment effects, other nations will be most enthusiastic about honoring such requests and goals. A pronounced form of soft empowerment comes through direct emulation of the soft power nations' policies.[36] Adopting the policies of soft power nations fundamentally diminishes points of conflict between the two sets of nations, which in turn makes the actions of a set of nations more amenable to and compatible with the specific interests of soft power nations.

The manifestations of soft empowerment can be quite extensive and diverse. The actions and policies of soft power nations carry consequences, which can unfold in a myriad of direct and indirect effects on the goals and interests of the soft power nations themselves.[37] Direct effects are numerous and obvious. Specific requests for assistance in any number of foreign policy ventures will more likely be granted. For example, nations may grant greater landing rights for military exercises to soft power nations. They may undertake more extensive alliance commitments

[36] As noted above, this may result from a soft power nation endearing itself to other nations so strongly that other nations adopt its policies. In this case, emulation results from great direct esteem for the soft power nation itself. Alternatively, the policies themselves may be highly esteemed, so much so that they are copied by other nations. The most pronounced endearment effect would be one in which both the soft power nation itself and its policies are highly esteemed.

[37] Complexity theory labels such effects as feedback. Actions by one set of nations create reactions on the part of other nations that in turn affect the former. In this respect, actions always generate consequences for the nations undertaking them (Jervis 1997).

and logistical support in those alliance commitments. They may grant preferential trading privileges. Also, in a direct context, they may vote to support proposals in international organizations that are favorable to the foreign interests of soft power nations. Moreover, they may oppose unfavorable proposals. In this respect, there are any number of direct avenues through which nations may respond to soft power nations in ways that enhance the influence of the latter.

Indirect effects also abound. For example, emulation among a number of nations may consolidate a greater community or confederation of nations that embrace similar foreign policy goals, the goals of the soft power (in this case, the role-model) nations. This would create a more favorable global milieu that benefits soft power nations, as other nations are pursuing policies consistent with the policies of these soft power nations (e.g., a monetary union based on the currency of a soft power nation or a free-trade area in which the role-model nation is the more efficient producer). There are also indirect effects through favorable third-party actions. The endearment effects within a specific set of relations may spill over into another set. Nations may come to esteem soft power nations and/or their policies as a result of other nations' esteem for them (i.e., jumping on the bandwagon). Also, rapprochement with one set of nations may indirectly result from direct diplomatic initiatives that improve relations with another set of nations (i.e., the friend of my friend is also my friend). In all such cases, soft power translates into a greater ability to attract more supporters and allies in the international community.

Domestic soft power represents another indirect source of influence. In this case, internationally endearing actions and policies may also endear themselves to the populations of soft power nations. Hence, national leaders of soft power nations would enjoy that much greater internal support for foreign policy initiatives.

Soft empowerment essentially entails enabling actions that enhance the influence of soft power nations. In this respect, they represent compliance with the desires of these nations. Sometimes that compliance is directly requested by the soft power nations. At other times, the compliance is voluntarily extended without such formal requests. Moreover, with respect to both types of compliance, the level of compliant behavior can vary a great deal, especially with respect to the intensity with which it is carried out. This is the result of the fact that even formal requests lack the specificity to encompass all possible actions relevant to the actual enactment of compliance itself.[38] For example, soft power nations may ask for more military support, but there will be much leeway as to how the military support is instituted (e.g., supportive nations may send their best troops and military technology, or air sorties may be of extended duration). Also, a soft power nation may ask for support for an initiative it is sponsoring in an international organization, but such support may vary greatly in form and intensity (e.g., lobbying may be more animated than is usually the case).

With respect to this tendency toward the imperfect specification of requests and desires, soft power appears to have some clear advantages over hard power. With regard to voluntary compliance with the preferences of soft power nations, because such compliance is largely self-motivated, we can expect such compliance to be carried out at a higher level of intensity than compliance coerced by hard power methods against the will of the target nations (target nations will have every incentive to carry out coerced compliance in the most lax manner possible without incurring the wrath of the coercing nation).[39] In the case of compliance with direct requests from soft power nations, we would expect far greater intensity in the enactment of compliance because of the latitude created by the imperfect specificity of the requests themselves. Conversely, decrees founded on coercion will be carried out with the least intensity within the range of latitude generated by imperfect specificity and monitoring. Given the imperfect specificity with which nations request compliance and express their desires for compliance, and given also the limitations on monitoring, a great many actions will take place under the radar. The

[38] Aside from the costs of specification, which are high (with perfect specification being impossible), imperfect specification is also a function of the fact that all actions pertaining to compliance cannot be effectively monitored; hence, a great many such actions stay under the radar.

[39] The advantages of soft over hard power in this respect are linked to the level of specificity achieved in particular demands and requests. When requests or demands are specified at a very low level and monitoring is also limited, thus giving substantial latitude for compliance, soft power will have clear advantages over hard power. However, where they are specified at a very high level and possibilities for monitoring are greater, we can expect hard power methods to generate a higher level of compliance in a more timely fashion relative to soft power (nations will respond more readily to coercive methods than endearing overtures if specificity and monitoring are high). Even in this latter case, though, whatever imperfections in specificity and monitoring that exist (and they always do) will work in favor of soft over hard power. Moreover, in the longer run, the adverse feedback effects of the hard extraction of compliance can generate significant weakening effects for the hard power nations (i.e., hard disempowerment).

fact that soft power will encourage those actions to enable the interests of soft power nations makes soft power itself an especially important source of international influence.[40]

In essence, both through direct and indirect effects, the world becomes a place more amenable to the interests and goals of soft power nations. Even when such nations fail to leverage positive sentiments into favorable outcomes through formal and specific requests, it is still likely that the outcomes will be forthcoming because such sentiments will motivate nations to honor the interests and goals of soft power nations beyond any formally specified requests or prompts.

Hard Disempowerment

Hard disempowerment is a manifestation of a more general process in which the augmentation of power, from the use of all types of resources (soft and hard), will generate weakening effects. This process is called the power curse. Nations that are not cognizant of such weakening effects, and thereby do not compensate for them, will find themselves the victims of a power illusion – a condition in which the nation is far weaker and more vulnerable than it believes itself to be.[41] Specifically in the context of hard power, the power curse process suggests that power augmentation through the use of hard power resources can generate significant weakening effects. These become more severe as nations come to bank more excessively on hard resources as a means of wielding greater influence. Decision makers have a tendency to overinvest in

[40] It is useful to think of such enabling possibilities of imperfect specification and monitoring in terms of what Leibenstein (1966) called x-efficiency effects. X-efficiency effects describe differing levels of productivity that result from factors other than the structure and application of inputs (i.e., allocative efficiency). Even with similar input allocations, efficiency among firms may still vary greatly because of factors unrelated to the application of inputs (e.g., motivation, incentive schemes, differing managerial styles). Much of this potential for variation is a result of the fact that labor contracts cannot be perfectly specified and monitored. Hence, there is much room for variation in the employment of human capital on the part of employees; unspecified and poorly monitored actions can either enhance the productivity of employees (x-efficiencies) or diminish that productivity (x-inefficiencies). To the extent that employees are more favorably disposed to their employers (this can be thought of as employers enjoying soft power over their employees), they will be more efficient (x-efficient) in the application of their human capital (e.g., work faster, encourage other workers to do so, share ideas about improving morale in the workplace). Employees unfavorably disposed (whose employers lack soft power) may feature work habits (e.g., work slowly, not inform on deficient workers) that diminish productivity (x-inefficient).

[41] The power curse will be discussed more fully below in the chapter. On the power curse and power illusion, see Gallarotti (2010).

hard power resources relative to soft power resources (the reasons will be discussed later in this chapter). Nations overly reliant on hard power actions and policies based on force, coercion, or aggressive bribery will face manifold negative consequences. Some of the most pernicious consequences emanate from the tendency for such excessive reliance on hard power to weaken nations by undermining their soft power. These consequences, like those of the process of soft empowerment, will be both direct and indirect. In this case, unlike soft power, which generates reactions more favorable to the requests and goals of the soft power nations (favorable feedback), hard power will cause other nations to react less favorably to the requests and goals of the hard power nation (adverse feedback). For example, using force or coercion to extract compliance in selected issues can generate countervailing postures and actions on the part of target nations that neutralize the effectiveness of the initial use of force or coercion (e.g., security dilemma or the creation of adversaries). Such unfavorable countervailing reactions, if extensive enough, can actually make the initial attempts at coercion completely counterproductive and result in a diminution of the influence of perpetrating nations. Yet this is merely a reflection of the hard disempowering process in a direct context.

The manifold consequences go well beyond the direct countervailing effects and involve a plethora of variables that can indirectly compound the self-defeating effects of exclusive reliance on hard power. Third-party actions can compound the direct negative effects of such hard strategies. Countervailing coalitions against coercive nations may proliferate as nations become alienated (i.e., the enemy of my friend is my enemy). More robust balancing may result when new nations join an alliance or confederation, or present members increase their stakes in the alliance. Yet such effects merely represent a particular security manifestation of hard disempowerment. The adverse reactions to such strategies can manifest themselves indirectly in all constellations of foreign relations. Current allies and erstwhile supporters of such hard power nations may be more reluctant to maintain support and commitments to them across a variety of institutions and issues. Alienated nations will be less likely to vote favorably in international organizations. Also, these nations may seek to revise past commitments so as to reduce their formal obligations to hard power nations. Furthermore, newly forming organizations or regimes that might benefit hard power nations may be more reluctant to include such nations as members. These adverse reactions across organizations and regimes may reinforce a greater disposition toward unilateral action that well-endowed hard power nations must face, leading to a pernicious outcome in the form of a vicious cycle of unilateralism. Overreliance on hard power strategies may drive well-endowed nations to engage more frequently in unilateral action to solve their problems, given the constraints that arise in multilateral arrangements as a consequence of their actions. Yet this unilateral impunity in conjunction with reliance on hard power methods will likely alienate members from these institutions such that outcomes from the institutions will cut increasingly against the interests of hard power nations, which in turn will lead them to withdraw even further from the institutions in attending to their foreign objectives. The institutions will be undermined all the more if lack of support from hard power nations undercuts their logistical and financial endowments. However, such institutions have been and will always prove to be important means of statecraft for even the most powerful nations; thus, losing their support can only compromise an independent-minded nation's strength.

Moreover, other adverse indirect effects may emanate from domestic sources. In this respect, hard power strategies may alienate the very populations of the perpetrating nations themselves, thus undermining the domestic political support required to sustain specific foreign policies.

Moral hazard is another major manifestation of hard disempowerment. In this case, abundant hard power can undermine incentives to prudently stay at the cutting edge of power-seeking strategies. Nations may become lax in contemplating and exploring the consequences of present power sources and strategies for gaining influence. This may actually serve to compromise a nation's hard power (i.e., a fat cat syndrome that inhibits the development of more effective hard power resources). But more generally, such moral hazard will manifest itself across the hard power–soft power continuum. Great hard power resources will often make a nation lax about developing soft power resources (i.e., the belief that the strong do not have to work as hard to cultivate friendships and a positive image in world affairs). [42]

[42] The conceptualization of moral hazard in this book takes a broader view of risk-encouraging behavior than the more restricted use of the term, which is often equated with the risk-encouraging effects of owning insurance against specific disasters. This conceptualization encompasses characteristics or factors that actually insulate actors from risk in the broadest sense, hence diminishing the incentives against acting recklessly. In this respect, this broad conceptualization of moral hazard encompasses numerous processes characterized by overconfidence and complacency in the face of risk.

With respect to compliance, it may be true that harder methods (to extract compliance) can generate faster and more thorough formal compliance (especially those actions precisely specified and successfully monitored) with specific decrees relative to softer methods because of the looming threats undergirding those methods. Decrees or requests can be extensively specified and monitored, covering and scrutinizing many actions relevant to the enactment of compliance. However, even though formal compliance may be forthcoming according to the level of specificity and monitoring potential of the requests or decrees, nations whose compliance is being extracted or coerced have every incentive to enact such compliance with the least possible precision and intensity with respect to the loopholes created by gaps in specification and monitoring. They will take every opportunity allowed by imperfect specification and monitoring to comply in ways that do not serve the interests of the perpetrator or hard power nations (i.e., be x-inefficient). Given that so many actions will not be specified or effectively monitored and remain under the radar, hard power appears to carry especially extensive dangers for nations that choose to rely only on such strategies to encourage compliant behavior on the part of target nations. Moreover, as noted, negative feedback manifested in vituperation on the part of targeted nations will generate both direct and indirect weakening effects for the hard power nation in the longer term.

In essence, through both direct and indirect adverse consequences, the world becomes a more adversarial environment for hard power nations. Where countervailing reactions are sufficiently broad and robust, hard strategies carry the potential for undermining the influence of those nations, rendering the strategies counterproductive and ultimately self-defeating. Even in cases in which sufficient muscle can be activated to extract timely and extensive compliance, leeway created by imperfectly specified and monitored decrees or requests carries significant opportunities for target nations to undermine the quality and intensity of the compliance sought, such that these strongly coercive strategies themselves may ultimately become counterproductive and self defeating.

Diversification

That soft power can enhance a nation's influence in world politics is clear. It is also clear that the excessive pursuit of hard power at the expense of the exclusion of soft power can severely compromise a nation's influence in world politics (i.e., hard disempowerment). Most of the scholarship on soft power has been inspired by the weakening effects of strategies that elevate the importance of hard power above all other instruments of statecraft. But inspecting the other side of the power equation highlights the crucial role of hard power in the lexicon of influence. The true optimization of power suggests some desirable diversification of both hard and soft resources. In his work on soft power, Nye is careful to aver that although soft power is important, it is not to be pursued excessively at the expense of hard power. Soft power has its limitations. It would, for example, have limited success against expansionist regimes motivated only by the prospect of acquisitions through the use of force and coercion.

The optimization of power for any nation, great or small, requires some balance between the two sources (Nye 2002, 12).[43] Even in the most celebrated critique of hard power, Keohane and Nye (1989) point out that in the modern world, military power still plays an important, albeit diminished, role. But it is also clear that, as Keohane and Nye (1989, 224, 225) stress, in an interdependent world order, "... the resources that produce power have changed... [and that] the minimal role of military force means that governments turn to other instruments." A number of these instruments comprise soft power resources. Unfortunately, this balance remains unspecified in the existing scholarship on power, aside from statements giving precedence to either one or another set of power sources depending on the paradigms involved. Nye (2004, 1) himself suggests a mix that is weighted somewhat in favor of hard power. But the relationship is more complex than a simple model of complements in the production of influence.[44]

Skewing the balance excessively in either direction can erode influence and leave nations weaker. Clearly, complete reliance on image and diplomatic goodwill makes a nation susceptible to the ultimate threat, as insufficient hard resources to create deterrence will create vulnerability to the use of force. Respect and goodwill without the muscle to resist aggression can be dangerous in anarchy. Disregarding the merits of hard power in an anarchical world presents significant dangers. In this respect, nations that pursue the saintly route at the exclusion of muscle may

[43] Interestingly, this is a manifestation of his own mixed intellectual orientation. In a biographical note, Nye (2004a, 1, 2) refers to himself as a precursor of Constructivism. Yet he also states that the "simple propositions of Realism are still the best models we have to guide our thinking."

[44] A formal model of optimal diversification among soft and hard power resources is presented in the Appendix.

fall into the trap of soft disempowerment.[45] Influence based on goodwill alone is fragile. Nations may lack the muscle to defend themselves against brutish actions or policies, or they may be unable to secure outcomes that are beneficial. Lacking such resources may also prevent a nation from correcting injustices against both itself and other nations, thereby allowing more sources of danger in the international system. In a related vein, a lack of hard power may prevent a nation from forcing other nations to do the "right" things (e.g., refraining from aggression or atrocities), which would have the same effect in terms of allowing more sources of danger in its foreign relations.[46] The logic that identifies ways in which reliance on hard power alone can be self-defeating could be relevant to a strategy that is overreliant on soft power, although the self-defeating processes would manifest themselves in a different form, principally in making nations more vulnerable in an anarchic world rather than in processes in which misguided or excessive attempts to empower nations actually generate negative consequences that serve to weaken these nations. Optimal strategies for power acquisition will require some diversification between muscle and goodwill. To recall a famous quote attributed to Al Capone: "You can get much further with a kind word and a gun than with just a kind word alone."Moreover, after some optimal mix of hard and soft power resources has been achieved so as to augment the power of a nation, there is still the general and pervasive problem of the power curse mentioned above in this chapter (Gallarotti 2010). Power augmentation itself, with respect to all types of power resources (hard and soft), generates inherently weakening effects. If nations are oblivious to the effects of this power curse and do not compensate for them, they can easily fall

[45] Too much soft power could have adverse effects independently of making nations more vulnerable to aggression. For example, would a world full of liberal democracies necessarily be more advantageous for the role-model nations? Certainly, the role model nations would lose the distinction of being in a select group, so their image would be compromised. Furthermore, could it also have an adverse effect on the democratic peace process, given that cooperation with like-minded states would become less salient?

[46] Indeed, even hard power used in a coercive way can bring substantial benefits if it is used in the cause of what are perceived internationally to be legitimate objectives: force in the cause of protection against aggression, in the service of peacekeeping, or in the prevention of genocide. Even here, however, force can still be disempowering by generating direct effects, manifested in the negative feedback from the targets of aggression (i.e., you make a greater enemy of the nations or actors you are fighting against). However, in such cases the disempowering third-party indirect effects are limited in that other nations will not despise a nation using force in what is perceived to be a just cause. Of course, even in a just cause, excessive force can indeed generate disempowering third-party and other indirect effects. On the right of might, see Temes (2003).

into a power illusion trap – that is, they are in fact weaker than they perceive because the weakening effects have diminished the power they believe themselves to have achieved through optimal diversification. As noted, hard disempowerment is a more specific manifestation of this more general power curse process.

The power curse at a general level has four sources and becomes all the more pernicious as the power of nations grows (i.e., its intensity grows in proportion to a nation's power level). First, there is a complexity effect. As the power of nations grows, they will find themselves managing relations in a more complex environment: more points of interaction because of a growing international presence. Complexity is difficult to deal with even at modest levels, and all the more so as power increases. More complex relationships are more difficult for nations to manage, so they more often fall prey to adverse outcomes in the international system that undermine their power. Complexity makes it difficult to foresee such outcomes and to manage them so as to ensure that national power is augmented (or at least not diminished). To compound the complexity effect, stronger nations will have less incentive to carefully monitor the complexity that surrounds them because in growing stronger, they are more resilient to adverse outcomes. Strength makes them less vigilant about avoiding the adverse effects of complexity. This would be a moral hazard effect in the context of complexity.

Yet moral hazard, a second element of the power curse, has a more extensive adverse impact on national strength beyond the complexity aspect. In general, greater power makes nations more complacent about managing their foreign relations. In this respect, the greater their power, the less nations need to worry about perspicaciously monitoring and controlling outcomes in their foreign relations. At the most extreme level, nations enjoying primacy have acquired enough power to make them invulnerable to a plethora of adverse outcomes in their foreign relations (i.e., they are too strong to worry). Thus, strength creates an inherent complacency about outcomes that can potentially diminish a nation's power.

A third element is the problem of overstretch. As nations grow in power, their stakes in the international system also increase. Greater power resources generate a greater presence in international affairs. It is in the nature of this growing presence to become self-reinforcing as nations come to rely on many of its benefits (e.g., military bases, economic partnerships). The other self-feeding process emanates from mission creep: greater international involvement is self-reinforcing as expansion calls for ancillary functions to support that expansion (e.g., greater military involvement in a region invariably generates the need for greater economic support functions). Such a growing presence can be pernicious if the growth generates weakening effects that are greater than the empowering effects of the expansion.

The final element of the power curse is a tendency to fall into a vicious circle of unilateralism. As noted above in this chapter, when the power of nations grows, they have more of an incentive to manage their foreign relations unilaterally (their power making it possible to work outside the constraints of the entangling commitments created by their cooperative arrangements with other nations – regimes, international organizations). As this penchant grows, those nations may undermine the institutions as important means of foreign policy. This cycle can generate potentially pernicious outcomes for maverick nations because in an interdependent world unilateral strategies are often inferior to multilateral strategies for attending to foreign objectives, i.e., no nation can achieve all of its goals alone. Hence, such institutions will remain, even for the most powerful nations, important means of statecraft. Compromising such means can only render a nation weaker.

The problems of the power curse and hard disempowerment will be difficult to solve. History has shown that the dangers of the power curse and hard disempowerment are both pervasive and pernicious. Historical case studies of power seeking have attested to the fact that decision makers tend to fall victim to the power illusion, and very often this manifests itself in a tendency toward hard disempowerment (Gallarotti 2010). Much of this is a consequence of the fact that decision makers have a tendency to overinvest in hard power resources relative to soft power resources. There are systematic reasons for this tendency. First, more tangible (hard) resources are far easier to count and monitor than are intangible (soft) sources of power. Cognitive limitations tend to select that which can be counted more than that which cannot.[47] Second, the use of tangible sources can generate more direct and short-term effects. Soft power policies are more likely to generate indirect and longer-term effects. Quick results are preferred to waiting for outcomes, and it is far easier to assess direct rather than indirect effects because, once more, of cognitive limitations. Such limitations also select hard power for a third

[47] The cognitive limitations referred to in this paragraph are chronicled in Jervis (1976) and are further discussed below in the chapter in the prescriptions for instituting strategies of Cosmopolitical power.

reason: tangible resources are more easily evaluated than outcomes. The ultimate test of influence is the extent to which outcomes in the international system conform to the objectives of nations. Both hard and soft power can bring about such outcomes, but outcomes are far more difficult to evaluate than are arsenals of hard power resources. Decision makers and the public will often disagree about the significance of outcomes and how they bear on national influence. Soft power can best be measured in terms of such outcomes. Hard power, however, maintains a cognitive advantage in this respect: perceptions often equate influence with the possession of tangible resources that nations can use to generate outcomes. Thus, a nation may be the loser in numerous diplomatic and even military confrontations, but if it possesses military primacy in the world, people may very well continue to perceive it as highly influential.

Aside from cognitive limitations, this tendency also reflects manifestations of a pronounced moral hazard effect. A large arsenal or great wealth may lull decision makers into a false sense of security that makes them feel less vulnerable to adverse outcomes. In the case study in chapter 5 that analyzes the Bush Doctrine, it is clear that perceptions oriented around the military and economic primacy of the United States led the Bush administration to sustain policies that were self-defeating with respect to the administration's most treasured foreign policy goals. Case studies across issues and historical periods have shown that leaders are overly tolerant of adverse foreign policy outcomes when they possess military and/or economic primacy (Gallarotti 2010).

The role of complexity in the face of cognitive limitations also confers advantages to hard power (Jervis 1997). Hard disempowerment often fails in ways that are not easily perceived and appreciated – complex and indirect feedback loops that work themselves out over longer periods of time. Soft power often succeeds through similar processes, but in this case through very different complex feedback loops that work themselves out over time. In effect, cognitive limitations in processing complex information will tend to make decision makers more obtuse to the failures of hard power and to the successes of soft power.

Hence, hard power relies on processes and sources that are easily monitored, understood, and evaluated (tangible resources, short-term results, and direct effects). Soft power is manifested through processes and sources that are not so easily understood, evaluated, and monitored. Thus, hard power will have an advantage over soft power in framing foreign policy.

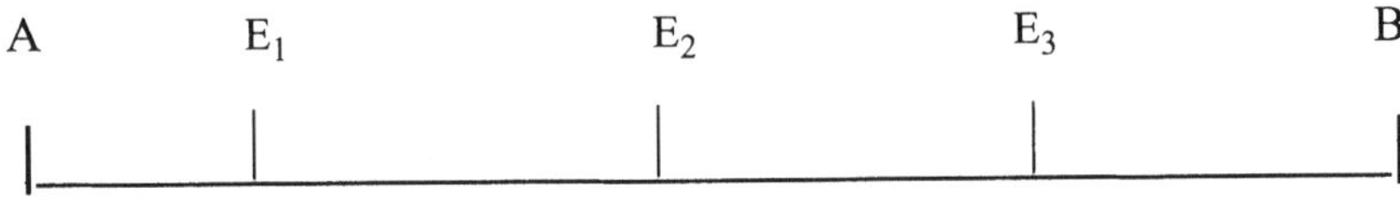

FIGURE 1. Unembedded Power Relations

Consequently, decision makers will have to be especially enlightened, perspicacious, and vigilant in overcoming such pernicious tendencies because such tendencies encourage power illusion.

Whereas diversification between hard and soft power promises greater opportunities for optimizing influence and attaining security, such an objective will be challenging for decision makers to pursue because of the cognitive advantages of hard over soft power, and more generally because of the pervasiveness of the power curse. A number of strategies will be especially important to avoid hard disempowerment and the power curse. These strategies are presented in the last section of chapter 1 in the form of several prescriptions.

The Mechanics of the Signature Processes: Soft Empowerment, Hard Disempowerment, and Optimal Diversification

Soft Empowerment

We can model soft empowerment within the context of a relational bargaining space or spectrum. This is a simple relational model of soft empowerment, with another more complex and formal treatment presented in the Appendix. Figure 1 represents a bilateral bargaining space between nations A and B with several possible equilibrium points. This model represents an unembedded power (i.e., non–meta-power) contest in which hard power is solely responsible for determining the bargain outcomes or equilibria.[48] National goals or objectives on the bargaining space are defined continuously over equilibria outcomes ranging from point A, which represents nation A's preferred outcome (i.e., that bargaining outcome completely consistent with A's national goals – A's point of bliss), to point B, which represents nation B's point of bliss with respect to outcomes. This power contest or bargaining process could be consistent with either a relational or a proprietary model of power, in that outcomes

[48] For simplicity, we assume a one-dimensional bargaining space, but as will be demonstrated, this depiction of bargaining need not preclude mutual gains under assumptions of soft power.

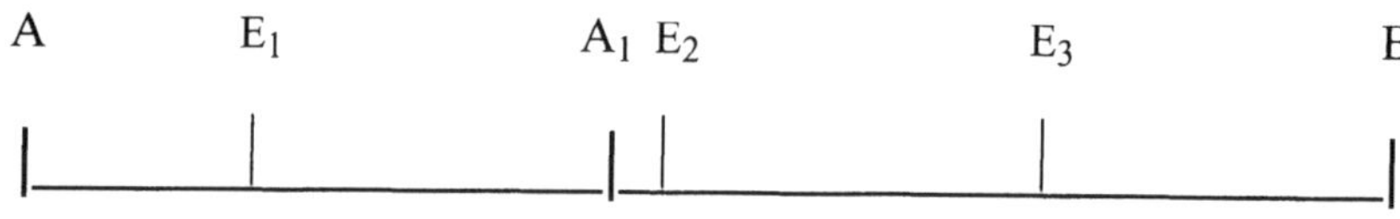

FIGURE 2. Soft Empowerment I

could be modeled as functions of the strict balance of power of material resources or as functions of a more complex balance of influence within the relationship between nations A and B. National goals or objectives are completely exogenous or given. They are not shaped by any greater constellation of social relations and so are static. Equilibria will converge toward consistency with some balance of resources and relational factors (tangible and intangible) among the respective actors. Thus, E_1 would reflect an outcome strongly beneficial to nation A and antithetical to the interests of nation B. In this case nation A has a strong superiority in the relational balance of resources. E_2 would show greater equality in the power contest, with an outcome that shows an equilibrium that roughly divides the spoils. E_3 would be the antithesis of E_1, with nation B being the superior nation with respect to the relational balance of resources and therefore getting the lion's share of the spoils in the bargaining contest.

Figures 2 through 4 represent embedded power (i.e., meta-power) contests. In these representations, nation B enjoys the benefits of soft power. Now national goals are endogenous in that they are embedded in a greater constellation of social relations and thus are variable according to the effects of this greater constellation of meta-power. Figures 2 and 3 represent only a change in the goals or objectives of nation A. In both representations, the goals of nation A have shifted closer to the point of bliss for B as a result of B's soft power, thus shrinking the bargaining space.[49] This shows that bargaining outcomes will fall into a range that is closer to the preferences of nation B. In Figure 2, the new space is A_1-B. In Figure 3, the new space is A_2-B. Thus, nation B enjoys soft power in Figure 2, but even greater soft power in Figure 3, as the bargaining space is more constrained in the latter.[50] In addition to manifesting itself

[49] Again, as noted, soft power does not entirely eliminate conflicts of interests, as is evident from the fact that points of bliss do not entirely overlap; rather, it is instrumental in promoting a process whereby interests merge more closely with one another.

[50] This should not suggest a conflict of interests in the shifting of national goals as a result of soft power. Adopting the goals of the role-model nations may in fact work better in terms of the objective interests of the nations that have shifted their objectives. On the other hand, all such shifts do not necessarily represent a convergence of interests in the short run (i.e., there may indeed be an element of false consciousness in the manifestation

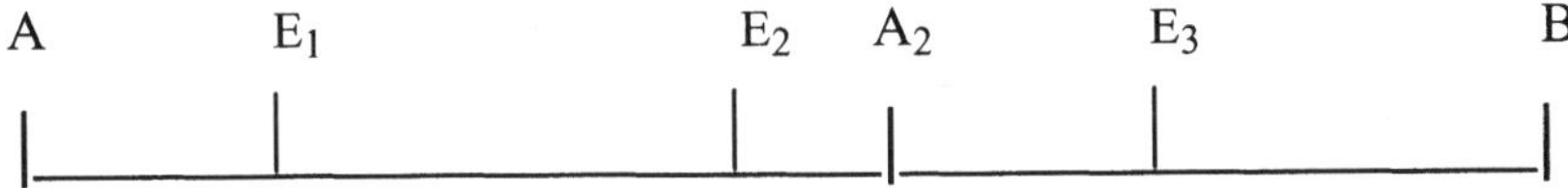

FIGURE 3. Soft Empowerment II

in an endogenous manner (changing the goals of nation A), soft power can manifest itself in an exogenous manner through deference. In this case, given the new bargaining space, B can make additional gains by shifting the equilibrium closer to its point of bliss through A's accommodations within the prevailing bargaining space. This would be represented in Figure 2 by a movement from equilibrium E_2 to E_3. In this case, B has enjoyed a compound benefit of soft power: not only did the bargaining space shift in its favor, but the bargaining equilibrium within that space also shifted closer to point B.

In moving from a power relationship represented in Figure 1 to Figure 2, in addition to the manifestation of soft power giving nation B an advantage over the structure of the bargaining space, we could also envision a situation of mutual gain. Let us assume that with the introduction of soft power (in Figure 2) from some previous state where the bargaining equilibrium was E_1 (in Figure 1), there is also a change in the bargaining equilibrium to E_2. In this case, under the structure of preferences (A_1-B), both parties would have made gains from their previous state. The new equilibrium is now closer to both points of bliss. It is closer to point B and closer to point A_1 than equilibrium E_1 was to points A and B. Of course, this occurs only as a function of the shift in nation A's goals.

Figure 4 shows a bilateral manifestation of soft power, in which both nations enjoy some of the benefits of soft power by shifting the goals of the other nation closer to their respective points of bliss. The new bargaining space is A_3-B_2. The effects of soft power on bargaining strength would depend on the previous state or point of reference. If the actors were previously at a bargaining structure defined in Figure 1, then nation B would be the preponderant beneficiary (i.e., have greater soft power vis-à-vis nation A). In this case, nation A's goals would shift far more than did nation B's toward the other's point of bliss. But if the previous state suggests a bargaining structure defined by Figure 3, then there would be

of soft power). In the long run, however, this adaptation of soft power approximates Nye's own vision, which generally tends to embrace the presence of a convergence of interests in the manifestations of soft power. In the long run, false consciousness is difficult to sustain. Hence, nations adopting the objectives and goals of others should tend to benefit from those adoptions.

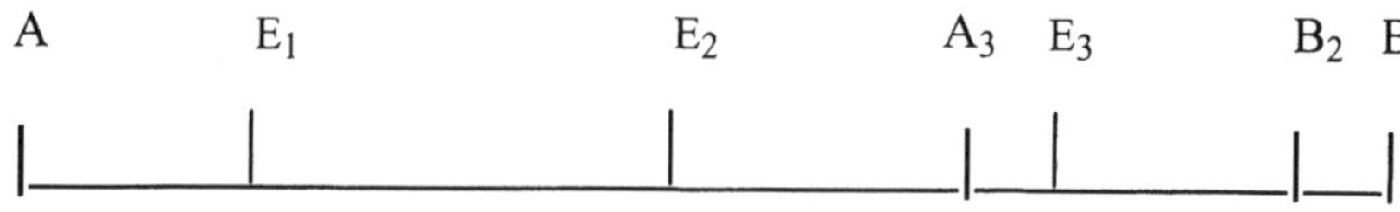

FIGURE 4. Soft Empowerment III

a much more balanced outcome, with both nations enjoying equal gains from soft power in the bargaining structure because of equal movements of goals away from the former points of bliss (A_3-A_2 = B-B_2). Such a situation could also generate mutual gains if the nations stayed at equilibrium E_3 from one state to the next. In this case, the equilibrium is now closer to each nation's respective point of bliss.

As with any relational power context, all parties may enjoy some advantages and successes in the bargaining process. There is no need to think that soft power is of a proprietary nature, no matter how great asymmetries are in power. Even if B is indeed the stronger actor in terms of both hard and soft power, respect and admiration may in fact run both ways. Although such respect and admiration may cause nation A to be more animated in adhering to the interests and values of nation B, a similar disposition may cause nation B to also shift its own goals in a manner consistent with the interests and values of nation A. The process of reverse globalization is an example. Although the United States may be the principal exporter of culture in the age of globalization, its own culture is somewhat modified through cultural importation. In this case, the preponderant cultural shift occurs in other nations, but American culture also shifts marginally toward the values and practices of other nations (Barnet and Cavanagh 1996 and Pieterse 1995). But even for dominant nations, we would expect some shift just from the nature of the process of accumulating soft power capabilities itself. Garnering respect and admiration depends in part on a willingness to cooperate and accommodate the preferences of other nations. These could be conceived of as the costs of creating soft power, but this would not be an entirely accurate representation of what this process entails. Costs could be expended without shifts in preferences or goals on the part of dominant nations. However, in the creation of soft power, the cooperation and accommodation itself is largely a manifestation of adopting a more communal sense of national interest and thus evaluating national utility as a joint rather than an exclusive or autarchic phenomenon. Such a preference shift would likely garner more soft power than mere accommodations in bargaining without any actual changes in goals because the former is a more salient testament of the sensitization of dominant nations to the needs and interests of other nations. Bargaining accommodations without adopting a more communal national interest would be perceived as a more superficial commitment to such needs and interests, and so would generate less respect and admiration.

The shift in national goals depicted in Figures 2 through 4 represents the adoption of the interests and values of other nations. As these shifts occur, bargaining outcomes will naturally be circumscribed within more limited ranges. This is a trivial derivation from a convergence of interests and values. Such convergence may take place at a more general level (e.g., adopt a capitalist orientation) or at a more specific issue level (financial liberalization). But we would expect bargaining to unfold within a more limited range if the actors involved shared similar orientations, ideologies, and interests. Differences will still exist but will play themselves out in a more bounded manner. Within the General Agreement on Tariffs and Trade (GATT)/World Trade Organization (WTO), for example, after members accepted the dominant norms of liberalization and reciprocity, bargaining played itself out within the parameters set by these expectations. Thus, the issues addressed, although controversial and highly contentious, have been the precise processes of liberalizing trade and reciprocating trade concessions rather than whether nations should attempt to liberalize or reciprocate concessions at all. What tariffs should be reduced? By how much should they be reduced? What is fair reciprocity? Which non-tariff barriers should be addressed? How should retaliation be instituted? What exceptions should be made for underdeveloped or distressed economies? All of these questions fall within the boundaries of norms dictating a liberal trade regime based on reciprocity and most-favored-nation privileges. Thus, the bargaining unfolds within a greater ideology of free trade that circumscribes the agenda governing which issues are raised and which solutions are viable. Questions or issues that challenge those boundaries are simply marginalized or excluded. Such an issue might be whether to model trade policy on principles of subsidized export promotion behind high import barriers (Finlayson and Zacher 1981).

Similarly, within the IMF, after nations bargaining with the fund over debt management accept the prevailing model that monetary and fiscal excesses are fundamental contributors to chronic debt problems, the bargaining process itself merges toward a more restricted menu inspired by such an economic orientation. How should the money supply be managed? What is an optimal target for inflation? To what extent should

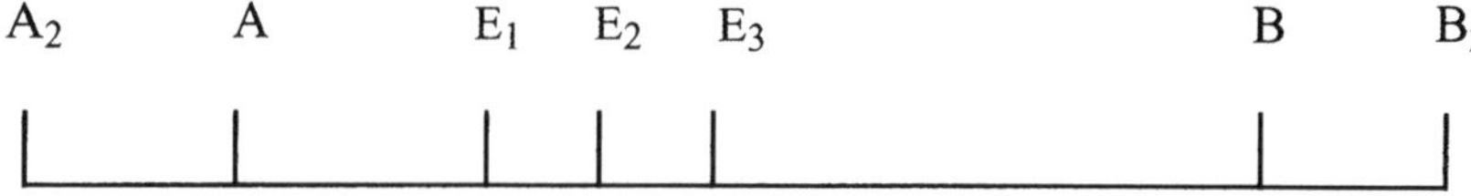

FIGURE 5. Hard Disempowerment

trade be liberalized? By how much should a currency be devalued? What subsidies will be cut, and by how much? What tax loopholes will be eliminated? Where will the tax burden principally fall? What industries will be privatized? Issues that question the fundamental nature of adjustment (whether it is generated by temporary macroeconomic excesses or is more of a structural nature), thus questioning the very viability of macroeconomic adjustment itself, would remain outside the principal bargaining space. Bargaining in both instances will unfold within the normative and ideological parameters of these regimes rather than challenge the parameters themselves (Bird 1987).

Hard Disempowerment

Having modeled the process of soft empowerment, we now look at the process of hard disempowerment more systematically. In this case, excesses on the hard side can compromise national influence by undermining a nation's soft power and thus drive other nations to take a more adversarial posture toward the perpetrating nation. Such a process is depicted in Figure 5. First, a simple case of hard disempowerment in the context of exogenous bargaining (i.e., no changes in the national goals) might manifest itself in the form of shifting equilibria within a fixed bargaining space. Let us assume a beginning state of bargaining space A-B and equilibrium point E_2. National goals are given and thus remain stable throughout the interactions. A situation in which B attempts to coercively impose an equilibrium more favorable to itself, such as E_3, might generate such vituperation and alienation that A responds with a countervailing effort in response to such an outcome and moves the equilibrium to E_1. In this case, an augmentation and greater application of hard power resources would have been counterproductive and actually diminished the influence of nation B with respect to imposing outcomes within the bargaining space.

An endogenous process would manifest itself with actual changes in the national goals themselves (i.e., a changing bargaining space). Let us assume the same starting point as in the previous case, as well as a similar bargaining strategy on the part of nation B (coercively trying to impose a favorable equilibrium). We can envision several manifestations of hard disempowerment within such an endogenous context. First, let us say that the equilibrium remained unchanged; in this case, both the pressure from B and countervailing response by A led to a neutral outcome and the equilibrium remained at E_2 (a standoff). If the actions of B so alienate nation A that nation A shifts its own goals farther away from the point of bliss for B (to point A_2), then B compromises some of its influence by extending the bargaining space to include a range of possible equilibria farther from its preferred point (A-A_2). An attempt to impose a more favorable outcome has failed, but the consequences of such an action extended the bargaining space into a more unfavorable range for nation B.

In this case, vituperation has caused nation B to become a negative role model. Nation A will set its goals farther away from a perceived pariah, both attempting to distance itself from the policies of nation B and manifesting a natural retaliatory response in an attempt to punish nation B by opening up outcomes that are further against B's interests. In this case, nation A appears to have suffered a loss because the new point of bliss is farther from the equilibrium. Yet such an outcome will surely push nation A to bring the equilibrium back closer to its new point of bliss, such as E_1. Thus, not only did the bargaining space open up in a way that is averse to the preferences of B, but incentives were created for adversarial nations to shift the point of equilibrium farther away from B's point of bliss (a lose-lose situation for nation B).

Such a shift in the goals of nation A could generate a net loss in influence for nation B even if nation B is successful in moving the equilibrium in a favorable direction. Let us say that nation B's use of hard power is able to move the equilibrium from E_2 to E_3. But nation B would still be a net loser of potential influence if the shift in goals increases the bargaining space to a length greater than the movement from E_2 to E_3. In this case, nation B would be winning a battle but risking losing the war. However, excessive hard power could lose both battles and the war if goals keep shifting on the part of nation A and its resolve to respond with countervailing pressure allows it to shift the equilibrium to point E_1. Another possibility would be for nation B to lose influence through its own shift in goals, from B to B_2 without a change in the equilibrium. This could be a result of various factors. Nation B may take a more unilateralist position that shifts its own goals to purge itself of any communal or cooperative orientation, thus moving to a more autarchic or particularistic sense of national interests. Or, responses in kind on the part of nation A to the actions of nation B may engender mutual vituperation, thus compromising some of the soft power of nation A, especially if nation B feels nation A has responded in an overly aggressive manner or nation B does not perceive its own attempts as being aggressive. In a case in which the equilibrium E_2 does not change, the shift in preferences to B_2 delivers an inferior bargaining outcome for nation B under the new bargaining space as it is farther from the new point of bliss. Assuming also a shift in nation A's point of bliss, this scenario would represent a mutual loss. Both are worse off because the bargaining space has expanded and so increased the set of possible inferior equilibria facing both.

Continuation of such a bargaining scenario in which nation B tries to coercively impose a favorable equilibrium on nation A could very well lead to a counterproductive vicious cycle of reliance on hard power. As nation B continues alienating nation A by trying to ruthlessly impose some bargaining outcome, nation A continues to set its goals farther from nation B's preferred outcome and will continue to try to push the bargaining equilibria closer to its own point of bliss, which could lead nation B to increasingly raise its own accumulation and use of hard power to keep outcomes within its own desired range. The situation will of course deteriorate if nation A responds in kind, promoting an increasing expansion of the bargaining space. Continuation of such actions on the side of both nations can lead them into a vicious cycle of conflict or competition. Such a situation might lead to quite deleterious outcomes, such as an arms race or a security dilemma, or even war itself.

Optimal Diversification

As noted, strategies overly reliant on any one set of assets will be suboptimal for enhancing national power. Overly soft nations will be paper tigers, whereas impresarios of hard power only will evoke countervailing responses that undermine national influence across issue areas. The perils of hard disempowerment and the advantages of soft power, especially given changes in world politics that have raised the value of the latter relative to the former, suggest that soft power should play a greater role than has been traditionally the case. However, there is an optimal mix of hard and soft power that can optimize influence and best promote security. Theoretically, because soft and hard power resources represent different factors of production in generating influence, we would expect some diversification between the two sources to produce possibilities for greater levels of influence than would otherwise be attainable through exclusive reliance on either one. Moreover, theories of investment show that assets whose returns are not strongly-positively correlated can produce some combination of risk and return that is superior to the risk and return of any single asset. Thus, as both factors of production and assets invested in the production of influence, soft and hard power can be optimally combined to deliver the greatest possible national influence given a nation's resources.

Because the modeling of optimal diversification produces a more formal mathematical model (versus the simpler model undertaken above), I have chosen to present it in the Appendix, to which I refer readers interested in such an articulation of the diversification process.

Prescriptions for Instituting Strategies of Cosmopolitan Power: Promoting Soft Empowerment and Avoiding Hard Disempowerment

Even with an acknowledgement that power optimization and security can best be achieved through the use of both hard and soft power, achieving such goals will still be especially difficult because these goals will depend on decision makers' abilities to determine the optimal mix of hard and soft power resources. Decision makers will have to be especially perspicacious in evaluating and monitoring their portfolios of power to arrive at such optima. Such optima would be directed toward embracing opportunities for soft empowerment, and avoiding the dangers of hard disempowerment specifically and of the power curse more generally. History has shown that the dangers of the power curse in general, and hard disempowerment specifically, have been especially pervasive and pernicious. Thus, decision makers will have to be especially vigilant in breaking away from a long historical legacy (Gallarotti (2010). Toward this end, several prescriptive strategies will be crucial.[51] Such strategies will be especially challenging because of cognitive limitations common among humans, and hence decision makers will have to be especially savvy and perspicacious in the ways they assess and monitor national power.

First, theories of power must be continually questioned and power audits continually undertaken with significant sensitivity to the changing face of power in world politics. This would mean constantly assessing and reassessing the effectiveness of a nation's principal sources of

[51] Gallarotti (2010) has applied these strategies at the more general level of the power curse and power illusion mentioned above. Because this book contemplates the manifestation of the power curse specifically within the nexus of hard and soft power, the application of the curse here will be more focused on how decision makers can avoid being victimized by hard disempowerment, how they can better embrace opportunities to acquire soft power, and so become more adept at achieving an optimal mix of power resources.

influence in world affairs. Sources that perform poorly need to be reevaluated, and possibly reconfigured or scraped. This holds true for both soft and hard power resources. Sources that perform well should be augmented, while those that do not should be reconfigured or diminished. Moreover, national leaders need to maintain a keen sense of changes in world politics and how they affect the risks and returns generated by traditional sources of power. Changes may render some sources no longer viable, whereas the effectiveness of other sources may increase. Changes may cause leaders to conceptualize and rely on completely new sources of power previously neglected as important means of influence in world politics. This is an especially effective strategy for enhancing soft empowerment and breaking down tendencies toward the power curse in the context of hard disempowerment. Continuous auditing will be a necessary vehicle for appreciating alternative power resources often neglected by conventional visions of power. Many such sources are in the soft power category. Thus, all such alternatives should be valued by decision makers willing to experiment in enhancing national influence. However, such a strategy is absolutely necessary for placing decision makers in a position to shift their reliance away from hard power resources. This is important because hard power resources can exude a hypnotic allure. As noted, they are easy to count, given their tangibility. Moreover, a large arsenal of such tangible resources can generate a moral hazard that makes decision makers lax in pursuing alternative soft strategies; for example, an imposing military force may lead decision makers into a false sense of invulnerability and influence. Such perceptions may make them lax in considering changes in the composition of power resources. These tendencies raise the potential for victimization from the power illusion as manifested in the form of hard disempowerment.

Such a strategy will, however, be difficult because it is inconsistent with common tendencies of human psychology that are manifestations of cognitive limitations above and beyond the tendencies to value tangible over intangible resources. People generally do not as a rule spill the apple cart on preexisting beliefs and theories. In this respect, people are more paradigmatic than exploratory (i.e., cognitively rigid). Theories or paradigms that people use to understand the world are fairly stable and compelling. Moreover, it is uncommon for people to perform frequent empirical tests of their theories and critically scrutinize facts that support these theories (Jervis 1976). Thus, although such strategies will be essential to optimizing power and security, they will prove challenging and require leaders to be vigilant, proactive, open-minded, and highly perspicacious.

Second, decision makers should consider the manifold consequences of power-enhancing strategies. This prescription pertains principally to the problem of complexity and suggests extensive perspicacity in estimating the manifold consequences of one's actions. As noted above in this chapter, because international politics is a complex system, relations among nations are not simple, linear, predictable, or exogenous. Feedback and indirect effects are pervasive, and such effects generate consequences for any action undertaken (Jervis 1997). Power is neither exercised nor accumulated in a vacuum. Power-seeking behavior always generates manifold consequences that feed back onto the original actions and ultimately alter the conditions within which these actions unfold. Often, such consequences create self-defeating or counterproductive outcomes with respect to national influence. Policies intended to enhance influence in fact often have the opposite effect and compromise a nation's influence. The power curse and hard disempowerment, as noted, emanate directly from such complex processes.

Complexity has important consequences for soft power specifically. Many of the benefits of soft power are indirect and longer-term (two signature characteristics of complexity). This, in turn, makes the benefits of such soft power (i.e., processes of soft empowerment) that much more difficult to discern and evaluate. However, such benefits are pervasive. Thus, soft empowerment strategies require more thorough evaluation and a pronounced commitment on the part of decision makers. This makes a more complete assessment of power necessary, one that covers the manifold possibilities for soft empowerment.

Like the first prescription, this one will also be challenging, given common cognitive limitations. The cognitive costs of dealing with complexity are high, which explains why people are more paradigmatic than open-minded in analyzing the world around them. This suggests the primacy of bounded rationality based on limited information and simple models in making decisions (Jervis 1976). However, in the face of complexity, such models are ripe for neglecting the potential of soft power and victimization from hard disempowerment specifically, and the pernicious effects of the power curse in general.

Third, decision makers should think in terms of net rather than nominal power. This is a corollary of the previous strategy, as complexity entails the evaluation of net effects (i.e., the outcomes one is left with after all the consequences of the initial uses of power have played out). Embracing the idea of net power is effective as a means of confronting the power curse and avoiding victimization from the power illusion because it encourages decision makers to take into account the negative consequences of power enhancement, and these negative consequences embody the power curse at the most general level. Such a tendency can be especially instrumental in confronting the problem of hard disempowerment. Perhaps no factor contributes as greatly to victimization from hard disempowerment than a tendency to evaluate power in nominal terms. Hard resources are nominal and infinitely quantifiable. In accumulating power resources, decision makers should be especially careful about assessing the costs of acquiring and using those resources, and then factoring those costs into their estimates of the nation's overall influence in international relations.[52]

This also will be a challenge to decision makers. First, as just noted above, the cognitive costs of dealing with complexity are high. Decision makers will therefore find it difficult to make policies that effectively integrate the full net effects of their power strategies. It is much more tenable to associate levels of influence with measures of nominal power, and in this case hard power resources will dominate over softer resources because their greater tangibility makes them more quantifiable. This will also introduce an element of moral hazard if nominal accounting reveals pronounced levels of resources. This, as noted above, may lead to perceptions of invulnerability that discourage decision makers from considering the net effects of the activation of such resources. In doing so, however, there will be a bias in perceptions against the limitations of hard power and against the potential for soft power.

Fourth, decision makers should judge power based on outcomes rather than resources. One of the stark lessons from case studies of the power curse is that decision makers appear to be especially tolerant of ongoing failures in attaining their most vital objectives. Much of this owes to the blinding effects of hard resource moral hazard; because they were well endowed with significant material resources, setbacks in terms of outcomes did not generate the same sense of urgency and panic that might have arisen in the face of more modest stocks of hard power (Gallarotti 2010). Assessing power based on resources rather than outcomes makes decision makers especially vulnerable to victimization from

52 Karl Deutsch (1966, 155) underscored the importance of a "net" conception of power more than four decades ago.

hard disempowerment. Again, hard power resources are more easily quantified and evaluated relative to soft power. However, they are especially advantaged in this respect relative to outcomes. It is far less problematic to agree on the size of a military arsenal, for example, than it is to agree on the meaning of specific outcomes in international relations and just how such outcomes are reflective of national influence. Thus, decision makers may remain confident about national influence even in the face of disconfirming outcomes if their hard power resources remain high. However, this could also effect evaluations on the soft side. Decision makers may be emboldened by what they perceive to be a strong image among fellow nations, such that even outcomes that cut against the national interest are not equated with an abatement of national influence. In this respect, moral hazard elements (i.e., blinded by resource endowments) cut both ways, in a hard and a soft context.

A simple analogy to personal savings appears useful. People find it far easier to assess their potential influence by counting their money than by assessing just how much people are conforming to their wishes. Indeed, one may have great influence without money, but a large bank account is far easier to quantify. Even here, though, problems of moral hazard appear compelling and pernicious. Although large bank accounts may ensure some level of influence, they can also significantly compromise such influence if feelings of invulnerability make people callous or insensitive to adverse outcomes. For example, the idea of "who needs friends when you have money" may leave a person with few people who he or she can influence significantly in important ways (i.e., you can't buy loyalty, nor can you buy love).

Like the previous strategies, this strategy will be difficult to institute because of information asymmetries. Again, given a human tendency to limit cognitive costs, the evaluation of power will be biased in favor of resources that are quantifiable or clearly assessed (Jervis 1976). This will give resources (both hard and soft) an advantage over outcomes as measuring sticks of influence. In this respect, the more general problem of a power curse is most pervasive. Moreover, it will give hard power resources an advantage, as noted, over soft power resources as measuring sticks.

With respect to outcomes, the issue of interpretation is also important. And this suggests an especially difficult problem for building effective strategies for optimizing influence. Because people deal with cognitive complexity through paradigmatic thinking, they tend to understand outcomes by filtering them through preexisting theories that they use to make sense of the world around them (i.e., the perception and assessment of outcomes is theory-driven). But given that outcomes are filtered through the perceptual screen of such preexisting theories, it is often likely that the significance and even the nature of the outcomes themselves are misinterpreted or misperceived. It is often the case that such cognitive rigidity distorts incoming information about occurrences in the world to conform to the preexisting beliefs and theories themselves. In this respect, people tend to be rationalizers rather than rational (Jervis 1976). Evidence that might disconfirm such paradigms or pre-existing theories may be distorted in ways that make it less salient as a source of falsification, or even distorted to the point of being transformed into something that actually confirms such paradigms or theories. There is ample evidence in case studies of power accumulation that such cognitive rigidity distorted perceptions of outcomes in ways that limited the ability of decision makers to institute policies that effectively enhanced national influence (Gallarotti 2010).

Fifth, decision makers should emphasize diversity in power resources and flexibility in their use. This is a natural corollary to the first strategy. Decision makers must be willing to institute changes dictated by their continual power audits. Case studies of the power curse suggest that decision makers tended to use a limited set of power resources to obtain vital objectives in the face of ongoing failures to attain those objectives, even though alternative resources were readily available (Gallarotti 2010). In such cases, there was also a lack of flexibility in applying resources to the realization of these objectives. Often, this was manifested in a deficient use of soft power options. At a more general level of the power curse, the cases demonstrated limited diversity and flexibility, even within each of the respective contexts of hard power and soft power themselves. There is no more important prescription than for leaders to contemplate policies that embrace a full range of resources, both hard and soft, that are amenable to change. Changes in the power resources themselves and in the greater system of world politics will encourage decision makers to consider a full range of options and be willing to entertain shifts in policies when outcomes suggest policy failures. The entire idea of optimal diversification among sources of power in a dynamic world, on which the theory of Cosmopolitan power is based, relies on such diversity and flexibility.

Again, such a strategy will test the perspicacity of decision makers. Once more, as with the previous strategies, the quest for flexibility and diversity cuts against common cognitive tendencies and so will require a pronounced effort to be realized. Diversity may be limited by the problem of information asymmetries; things that can be easily counted (hard power resources) may win out over resources than cannot (soft power). The bias will be all the greater against diversity if moral hazard effects of large hard resource endowments make decision makers reluctant to consider soft alternatives or render them insensitive to adverse outcomes. Such tendencies make nations ripe for victimization from hard disempowerment. And the quest for flexibility will face similar hurdles. Paradigmatic thinking and other cognitive rigidities will make changes in policies difficult to contemplate and institute. This rigidity, again, will be all the more enhanced in the face of hard power moral hazard and the subjectivity of evaluating outcomes as indicators of national influence.

Although all the strategies delineated above will be difficult to realize owing to common psychological tendencies in monitoring and evaluating power, they nonetheless will be necessary if leaders are to implement strategies that optimize influence and security for their nations. In this respect, decision makers will be challenged. However, this is consistent with the human drama, as human excellence is nothing more than the ability to rise above the natural limitations that confront us. Decision makers are constantly confronted with pervasive obstacles to effective policies, obstacles that are inherent both in psychological tendencies (cognitive rigidness, moral hazard, paradigmatic thinking) and in the social environments in which they function (political opponents, constituent pressures). Nevertheless, they are often able to carve out policies that deal successfully with important collective needs and problems. So too should decision makers have the capacity to overcome the obstacles to power strategies that optimize influence and security.

2

Crucial-Case Textual Analysis of the Founding Fathers of Realism

The Classical Inspirations

In the next two chapters, a crucial-case textual analysis is undertaken to shed light on the potential value of the theory of Cosmopolitan power for the study of power in international relations. In this application of a crucial-case test, I selected the very texts that have served as the greatest inspirations to contemporary Realist thinking in international relations: Hobbes' passages on anarchy in chapters 13 to 15 of *The Leviathan*, Thucydides' *The History of the Peloponnesian War*, Machiavelli's *The Prince*, E. H. Carr's *The Twenty Years' Crisis* 1919–1939, and Hans Morgenthau's *Politics among Nations*. In this respect, I selected the great works of the founding fathers of Realism as less likely candidates for embracing the signature processes of Cosmopolitan power (soft power, hard disempowerment, and the optimality of integrating both sources of power), given the Constructivist and Neoliberal character of these ideas. If we find that these great works, as less likely cases, somehow testify to the importance of such processes, we have some compelling evidence for the importance of these ideas for the study of power in international relations.

The least likely cases would be found in the works of contemporary Realists such as Mearsheimer, Waltz, and Gilpin. Such contemporary writers do in fact show a complex and pluralistic rather than a singular barbaric vision of international politics – that is, not everything is driven

The section on Hobbes is a revised version of "More Revisions in Realism: Hobbesian Anarchy, the Tale of the Fool and International Relations Theory," originally published in *International Studies* 45: 167–92, in 2008 by hard power politics and conflict – and they include processes in international relations that embrace soft power, such as cooperation and economic exchange. Contemporary Realists and their followers, however, do neglect or significantly downplay the role of soft power (Nye 2004a, 2). But contemporary Realists did not create their visions anew; their work has been built upon the shoulders of the venerated scholars who preceded them, those whose works are analyzed in this book. Thus, with respect to the leading contemporary Realists and their followers, the crucial-case tests undertaken here are intended to make more of a statement about the lessons they learned and applied in their own visions of international politics. Indeed, had they remained true to the lessons of the precursors from whose works their visions derived, their own visions would have embraced more of a Cosmopolitan orientation then has proved to be the case.[1]

A close reading of the great texts that inspired contemporary Realist theory suggests that although contemporary Realist theory itself has not granted the ideas of soft power and hard disempowerment significant roles in its vision of influence, the great works that inspired contemporary Realists themselves have indeed done so. Careful scrutiny of the great works of those who have become hailed as classical and more modern founding fathers of Realism suggests a greater diversity than conventional interpretations have acknowledged. Whereas the language and thrust of contemporary Realist logic underscore the central role of hard power, the great works that inspired contemporary Realism in fact reveal an appreciation of soft power as an important foundation of influence and an awareness of the dangers of excess reliance on that hard power. There is no doubt that these great and inspirational works are in large part testaments to the pervasiveness of hard power politics, and the interpretation in this book does not purport to turn the founding fathers of Realism into Constructivists or Neoliberals. This interpretation merely attempts to demonstrate a greater richness and diversity in their visions of power than has heretofore been embraced, a richness and diversity that acknowledge the importance of soft power and balance in pursuing influence.[2] In this respect, the most revered and inspirational Realist texts

[1] On crucial-case analysis and the less likely case scenario, see Eckstein (1975), Gerring (2004, 347), and (King, Keohane, and Verba 1994, 209–12).

[2] A number of works that have looked at the compatibility of Realism and Constructivism attest to the relevance that elements of soft power in a broad sense (in this case sources of power that derive from institutions) could have for Realist thought. See Wendt (1999), Barkin (2003), Williams (2003), Sterling-Folker (2002), Copeland (2000), Goldstein and Keohane (1993), and Hall (1997).

suggest that their authors were Cosmopolitan Realists, as their attention to hard power, appreciation of soft power, and awareness of the dangers of hard disempowerment converge to embrace the optimality of some middle ground between the poles of soft and hard power. Because so much has already been said in previous scholarship about the hard side of their Cosmopolitan vision, the analysis in this book will concentrate on revealing the more neglected and underappreciated soft side.

The Classical Realists

It would be too easy to challenge conventional visions of the Realist orientation of the iconic precursors and muses of contemporary Realist thought in international relations if we looked at writings other than their great works – or in Hobbes' case, looked beyond his discussion of anarchy (chapters 13–15 in *The Leviathan*). Hobbes' *The Leviathan* is not principally about anarchy but more about the commonwealth. Anarchy is an unpleasant state of transition that must be superseded to arrive at a civilized state of existence. Culling passages about moral and legal obligations of citizens of the commonwealth, as well as about religious restraints against monarchical tyranny, would hardly be a valid condemnation of scholars who have embraced the compelling logic of Hobbes' Realism in discussing anarchy. Similarly, in the work of Machiavelli, revisionism based on works other than *The Prince* would garner similar criticism. Should we deconstruct the political symbolism in the sex-capades of *La Mandragola* or highlight selected passages in his various other works, such as the *Histories*, to reveal something other than the reputed Realist vision of power? The arguments presented in those passages or books considered great works have been designated as the sources of greatest inspiration for Realism. Indeed, a strong indication of the value of the Cosmopolitan ideas of soft empowerment and hard disempowerment would come from testaments to their importance in these less likely places: the crucial cases themselves. In this case, it would be Hobbes' *The Leviathan* (chapters 13–15), Thucydides' *The History of the Peloponnesian War*, and Machiavelli's *The Prince*.[3]

All three of the classical Realists embrace a Cosmopolitan middle road between the extremes of the hard and soft power continuum by proclaiming the benefits of both soft and hard sources of power and acknowledging the dangers of excessive reliance on hard power (i.e., hard disempowerment). Although the sources of soft power vary across these

[3] Of course, no such exercise can be contemplated with Thucydides because only one of his writings is extant.

authors, a common strand oriented around the benefits of endearment (and, concomitantly, the dangers of compromising that endearment) is visible across their arguments. For Hobbes, even in a state of nature, if actors are to avoid a "nasty, brutish and short life" (i.e., enhance influence and avoid danger), they must endear themselves to other actors by abiding by expectations regarding reciprocity to cooperative gestures. For Thucydides, city-states endear themselves, and through such endearment enhance their influence and avoid ruin, by honoring well-respected norms and other institutions pertaining to interstate relations in the ancient Greek world. Machiavelli's vision of Cosmopolitan power is oriented around the need for princes to endear themselves to their people by honoring norms of civil republicanism in ruling their city-states – that is, domestic sources of soft power in a domestic context. Yet Machiavelli vigorously demonstrates how such domestically grounded soft power also has definite implications for interstate power relations. In effect, for all three authors, actors and states endear themselves to others by abiding by well-regarded expectations, rules, and norms that prevail in their interactional environments (even if those environments show strong elements of anarchy), and this endearment can be leveraged into greater influence and security (soft empowerment). Not doing so carries grave risks and, in some cases, may ultimately lead to ruin (hard disempowerment).

We step out of chronological order in beginning with Hobbes because his treatment of anarchy occupies the very core of the Realist paradigm. Moreover, as noted, the Realist preoccupation with hard power over soft power is a central component of what Realists consider the principal behavioral manifestations of anarchy. There is no more compelling place at which to begin a crucial-case analysis of Realism's founding fathers. The other cases unfold chronologically.

Thomas Hobbes

In the passages in which Hobbes most thoroughly discusses anarchy (chapters 13–15 in *The Leviathan*), we see clear testaments to the importance of endearment and, concomitantly, the dangers of compromising such endearment even in what has been traditionally considered an environment that punishes attempts to achieve such qualities. This testament to the benefits of soft empowerment and the dangers of hard disempowerment are manifested in the tale of the fool, articulated in chapter 15. Although this passage has traditionally received little attention from scholars of international relations, it nonetheless provides an important crucial-case testament to the processes of Cosmopolitan power. Therefore, this section on Hobbes serves a dual purpose: to illuminate a heretofore unappreciated passage in Hobbes that contributes to a revisionist interpretation of Hobbesian anarchy and, of course, to conduct a crucial-case textual test of the theory of Cosmopolitan power. Whereas traditional interpretations of Hobbes' state of nature embrace lessons that venerate the exigencies of hard power politics, a careful analysis of his vision of anarchy as developed in this tale of the fool shows a much more Cosmopolitan orientation.

Hobbes' work on anarchy has been hailed as the very foundation of modern Realist theory in international relations.[4] The elegance of his passages on anarchy in chapter 13 of *The Leviathan* is no doubt moving, especially the literal precision with which Hobbes purports to convey its behavioral manifestations. From a simple premise ("men live without a common power to keep them all in awe" – i.e., no 9-1-1), human interactions will devolve into a sort of chaos in which no one is spared the risk of death or violence (L, XIII, 8, 9).[5] Morality and ideas of right have no place here; instead, "force and fraud" become the "two cardinal virtues" (L, XIII, 13).[6] Under anarchy, even a group of inherently ethical people will soon devolve into a gang of brutes.

A slew of critiques have come from both Realists and non-Realists who have underscored the problems of using Hobbesian anarchy as a platform on which to construct a theory of relations among sovereign states (Hoffman 1981; Waltzer 1977; Beitz 1979; Bull 1977, 1981; Vincent 1981; Williams 1996, 2005; Milner 1991; Hanson 1984; Malcolm 2002).[7] Most of the revisionist literature fundamentally accepts the conventional interpretation of Hobbesian anarchy among individuals and is more concerned with marshaling arguments about why it is a poor analogy for understanding international relations. Even critics who have underscored possibilities for cooperation among individuals in a Hobbesian state of nature have themselves fallen well short of chronicling precisely how Hobbes' own logic about individual behavior in a

4 Bull (1977, 24, 25), Wendt (1999, 252), and Milner (1991, 69) locate Hobbes' treatment of anarchy at the very core of the Realist paradigm. On Hobbes as intellectual precursor of Realist theory in international relations, see also Johnson (1993).

5 References to *The Leviathan* will be in the form (L, I, 2): *The Leviathan*, chapter, section. The 9-1-1 metaphor for anarchy was suggested in a lecture by John Mearsheimer.

6 This introduces the famous Realist reversion of morality in anarchy, in which vices can become virtues and vice versa. This will also be seen in the work of Machiavelli, discussed later.

7 Much has been said about the limitations of Hobbes' state of nature as an analogy for international relations. Hobbes in fact said little about international relations directly in his writings. For discussions on this point, see especially Bull (1981), Milner (1991), and Hanson (1984).

state of nature generates such possibilities for cooperation (i.e., there is insufficient process tracing with respect to how Hobbesian anarchy itself generates such possibilities). Vincent (1981, 96) speaks of elements in Hobbes' state of nature that fall "in between" anarchy and civil order but does not expand on the composition of such elements and how they came to emerge. Bull (1981) cites Warrender's pioneering revisionist work on the Hobbesian state of nature in suggesting that Hobbes' own logic of anarchy admits possibilities of moral rules, but he does not expand on this statement regarding the issue of cooperation in anarchy. Williams' (1996, 2005) and Malcolm's (2002) treatments attack conventional visions of Hobbesian anarchy that propose a structural-objective process that drives rational action, but they never sufficiently trace the specific ways in which cooperation among individuals can arise within Hobbes' own logic about the state of nature.

None of the revisionist works from an international relations perspective looks closely enough at passages recounting the tale of the fool in chapter 15, but it is precisely here that a clear idea of the mechanics of how possibilities for cooperation (i.e., covenants) can emerge within a state of nature (i.e., without a commonwealth) best manifests itself.[8] A careful evaluation of these passages demonstrates a greater continuity within the work of Hobbes (both in his logic of civil society as well as in his logic of the state of nature), a continuity that has been somewhat disturbed by the distinction that Realists have made between Hobbes' treatment of the state of nature and his work on the commonwealth.

There is no doubt that Hobbes' anarchy, notwithstanding revisionist onslaught, is a dangerous place, and no amount of reinterpretation can make it anything else. Thus, no one could ever deny the importance of "force" (i.e., hard power) as a requirement for ensuring one's safety. Yet a revisionist interpretation of anarchy, which is best illuminated by the tale of the fool, does shed some light on anarchy as a more moderated environment, one that produces significant possibilities for cooperation.

In moving toward such an interpretation of Hobbesian anarchy, we must begin with reason. For Hobbes, humans are born with and develop

[8] Interestingly, the revisionist literature from an international relations perspective has paid scant attention to the tale of the fool. Malcolm (2002, 438) cites a very short passage from the tale of the fool but does not concentrate on the tale as a manifestation of a Hobbesian rationale for cooperation under anarchy. Such a careful textual analysis would have further vindicated many of the arguments marshaled in this vein. This is not the case in the work of political theorists, however, who have done a careful textual analysis of the tale and discussed its implications for conventional visions of Hobbesian anarchy. On the latter, see especially Kavka (1986), Barry (1972), and Warrender (1957).

reason (L, V). Reason, for Hobbes, is a faculty through which people discover the means of self-preservation. These means of self-preservation are called "laws of nature" – essentially, behavior modes "by which man is forbidden to do that which is destructive of his life or taketh away the means of preserving the same" (L, XIV, 3).[9] Two laws of nature reveal themselves. The first drives humans to "seek peace and follow it" (L, XIV, 4). This first law leads to the second law of nature – "that a man be willing . . . to lay down his right to all things" (L, XIV, 5). Herein lies the famous Hobbesian contract that brings forth a Leviathan, as the right to all things is commensurate with human freedom under anarchy. Once that right is relinquished, humans live in a state of civil society and happily exit the chaos of anarchy.

Yet because men are endowed with reason even in anarchy, laws of nature dictating self-preservation are applicable in anarchy as well. Even in anarchy, the laws dictating that men "find peace if they can" are compelling. However, common interpretations of Hobbes suggest that such peace is unattainable in anarchy – hence the compelling nature of the corollary to the first law of nature: that when humans cannot obtain peace, they should "seek and use all helps and advantages of war" (L, XIV, 4). Is peace obtainable in anarchy? If the answer is "yes," then the entire logical structure of what we have come to understand as Hobbesian anarchy falls. This is because of the role of covenant in Hobbes, which essentially amounts to a contract. Peace in anarchy would be founded on such covenants (mutual promises of safety and protection), but such covenants are precisely what enables the emergence of civil society (in this case, it is the covenant or contract among people to give up their liberties to a Leviathan).[10] Covenants are founded on promises, promises invoke obligations, and obligations in turn are the foundations of law and morality: all of this, which conventional interpretations of Hobbes said could not exist in anarchy, in fact will exist (L, XV).[11] Thus, allowing the possibility of covenants in anarchy would create significant tension for

[9] For an illuminating treatment of Hobbes' logic about reason and how it leads to possibilities for cooperation among individuals in anarchy, see especially Malcolm (2002).

[10] Covenants can indeed emerge from anarchy, as the famous Hobbesian contract that delivers humans from anarchy (creating the commonwealth) demonstrates. The real question framed here is, do we need to be delivered from anarchy completely for cooperation among individuals to emerge and be sustained? In other words, can we have cooperation or covenants without a Leviathan?

[11] See especially Kavka (1986), Barry (1972), and Warrender (1957) on covenants in anarchy.

Realists with respect to their use of Hobbesian anarchy as an analogy for their visions of world politics.[12]

Text beyond chapter 13 in *The Leviathan* profoundly attests to the fact that *peace is indeed attainable in anarchy*. The logic derives from the tale of the fool in chapter 15 (L, XV, 4). The chapter begins with a note on the implications of covenants or contracts for human co-existence. They are the foundation on which the very existence of civil society thrives. From the idea of covenant derives all of the legal, moral, and ethical constraints that essentially create and preserve civil society: "[T]he definition of injustice is none other than the not performance of covenant" (L, XV, 3). Hobbes again proclaims the dependence of the possibility of covenants on the existence of a Leviathan: a common power to keep all humans from behaving like brutes, the antithesis of civil society. Without such a common power above all humankind, "there is no own, that is, no propriety, there is no injustice; and where there is no coercive power erected, that is, where there is no commonwealth, there is no propriety, all men having right to all things, therefore there is no commonwealth, there nothing is unjust. So that the nature of justice consisteth in the keeping of covenant" (L, XV, 3).

Hobbes, however, delivers a monumental shift in his logic of anarchy when he immediately follows with the story of the fool. The fool is a reference to the biblical Psalms that allude to a heretic who questions whether he should be constrained by the laws of a God who does not exist – a clear reference to a state of anarchy.[13] Hobbes presents the fool's logic: "[T]here is no such thing as justice [and hence] every man's conservation and contentment being committed to his own care, there could be no reason that every man might not do what he thought conduceth thereunto, and therefore to make or not make, keep or not keep, covenants was not against reason, when it conduceth to one's benefit" (L, XV, 4). Hobbes

12 A more comprehensive analysis of Hobbes' treatment of anarchy across his works would be beyond the scope of this chapter. Various well-regarded Hobbesian scholars do, however, explore the broader applications of his logic of anarchy across his works. This body of literature attests to the consistency of Hobbes' treatment of the state of nature as an environment in which cooperation can be achieved. For such a broader treatment, the reader is referred especially to Malcolm (2002), Kavka (1986), Barry (1972), and Warrender (1957).

13 In the editor's note on the passage, he cites the Hebrew definition of a fool as connoting moral rather than intellectual deficiency. Thus, there is a clear parallel to humans in Hobbesian anarchy: people who have full use of their reason, which is oriented around self-preservation, without being bound by nonexistent moral constraints. See Hobbes (1651/1994, 90, f.n. 2).

further quotes the fool: "The kingdom of God is gotten by violence; but what if it could be gotten by unjust violence? Were it against reason to get it, when it is impossible to receive hurt by it" (L, XV, 4).[14] After a passage in which Hobbes detests the argument on the grounds that such reasoning has heretofore validated a history of mass violence (e.g., religious wars), he goes on to say that "*This specious logic is nonetheless false*" [italics added] (L, XV, 4). Of course, if the critique of the fool stopped here, it would be easy enough to discard because of the allusion to religion that exists independently of the state of anarchy. Although God exists under conditions of both anarchy and civil society, religion is never introduced as a constraint against the brutish behavior characterizing anarchy. This is most likely a function of the brevity of anarchy for Hobbes.[15] So such a diatribe against the fool could be dismissed as a mere critique regarding some religious issue that is superimposed over, but not integrated into, his fundamental logic. But Hobbes continues, as his critique of the fool goes on to squarely confront this religious barbarism in the context of the logic of anarchy through Hobbes' emphasis on the impact of such thinking on the question of covenant, the very thumbscrew on which the logic of anarchy and civil society turns. The logic unfolds in section 5 of chapter 15, which is quoted here.

For the question is not promises mutual where there is no security of performance on either side (as when there is no civil power erected over the parties promising), for such promises are no covenants, *but either where one of the parties has performed already*, or where there is a power to make him perform, there is the question whether it be against reason, that is, against the benefit of the other to perform or not. *And I say it is not against reason.* For the manifestation whereof we are to consider: first, when a man doth a thing which, notwithstanding anything can be unforeseen and reckoned on, tendeth to his own destruction (howsoever some accident, which he could not expect, arriving, may turn it to his benefit), yet such events do not make it reasonably or wisely done. Secondly, that in a condition of war wherein every man to every man (for want of a common power to keep them all in awe) is an enemy, there is no man can hope by his own strength or wit to defend himself without the help of confederates (where everyone expects the same defence by the confederation that everyone else does); and therefore, he which declares he thinks it reason to deceive those that help him can in reason expect no other means of safety than what can be had from his

[14] The reference to violence for God's kingdom is an acknowledgement that war was not unlawful for Christians. See editor's note in Hobbes (1651/ 1994, 90, f.n. 3).

[15] The reason for this may be driven by Hobbes' own life experiences as a fundamental influence on his thinking. In framing his quest for a stable state in the background of civil war, anarchy was never considered to be a long transitional period. See Lloyd (1992) and Sommerville (1992) on Hobbes' political ideas in historical context.

own single power. He, therefore, that breaketh his covenant, and consequently declareth that he thinks he may with reason do so, cannot be received into any society that unite themselves for peace and defence but by the error of them that receive him; nor when he is received, be retained in it without seeing the danger of their error; which errors a man cannot reasonable reckon upon as the means of his security; and therefore, if he be left or cast out of society, he perisheth; and if he live in society, it is by the errors of other men, which he could not foresee nor reckon upon; and consequently [he has acted] against the reason of his preservation, and so men that contribute not to his destruction forebear him only out of ignorance of what is good for themselves [italics added].

Hobbes conceives of a situation in anarchy in which people may enter into a covenant that entails exchanging promises, thus creating bilateral obligations. It is clear such a covenant is possible in anarchy because the first sentence in the passage uses the word *or* in distinguishing between a state in which civil society exists (where there is a power to make him perform) and a state where it does not, as in anarchy (Kavka 1986, 138). However, it is clear that for Hobbes, reason, the element that discovers the laws of nature that in turn drive individuals to seek peace, is attributed a role that can indeed bring about some condition of peace in anarchy as well.[16] This is clear from Hobbes' forceful declaration that reciprocity within the context of mutual promises in anarchy is consistent with reason ("but either where one of the parties has performed already"). If this is the case, then the very logic applicable to relations in civil society is also relevant in a state of anarchy.[17] The reason for this is evident in analyzing why the fool should reciprocate.

No stronger admonition against the fool's choice (which is to defect) can be given by Hobbes than his use of the word "fool" to characterize his choice. The compelling nature of reciprocity begins with Hobbes' own

16 According to Hobbes' language, when he speaks of cooperative confederations in this passage, conditions of peace in anarchy are not likely to be conceptualized on the same grand scale that they would be in civil society under a Leviathan.

17 Both Barry (1972) and Warrender (1957) envision little difference in structure between a covenant that creates a commonwealth and other types of covenants that may arise in anarchy. This validates Williams' (1996) arguments that in fact Hobbesian anarchy, contrary to the lessons espoused by Realists, represents a set of ethical and epistemological problems. For Williams, cooperation is limited by differing visions of norms regarding orderly co-existence among individuals. The Leviathan actually produces order not by being a coercive presence but by supplying rules around which expectations can converge. In essence, Williams envisions anarchy more as a coordination game. But if certain norms could indeed become compelling in anarchy (i.e., without a Leviathan), then the epistemological problem could be overcome and covenants could form around those norms, as the tale of the fool suggests.

conception of covenant. Nonreciprocity is cast as breaking a covenant ("breaketh his covenant"). Reason reveals compelling laws of nature that consummate some system of peaceful co-existence manifest in a covenant (Malcolm 2002). Because such expectations reveal the compelling attraction of a covenant (reason and subsequently the laws of nature), the initial gesture of cooperation on the part of the first party to the covenant ("performing" in Hobbes' terminology) carries with it all of the moral categories applicable to civil society. Under these conditions, Hobbesian nomenclature in his treatment of covenants is demonstrative: "bound," "obliged," "ought," "duty," "justice" (L, XIV, 7). This is one of the many areas where Hobbes' political philosophy and religious beliefs converge. His penchant for reciprocity is highlighted in a biblical passage within the context of consummating a covenant. "This is that law of the Gospel: 'Whatsoever you require that others do to you, that do ye to them'" (L, XIV, 5).

Beyond these religious and moral elements driving reciprocity within covenants in anarchy, the passage clearly reveals a strategic element of cooperation among self-interested actors. This is quite apparent as his response to the fool continues. Toward the middle of section 4 in chapter 15, Hobbes lays out the logic of the fool.

> [B]ut he questioneth whether injustice, taking away the fear of God... may not sometimes stand with that reason which dictateth to every man his own good; and particularly then, when it conduceth to such a benefit as shall put a man in a condition to neglect, *not only the dispraise and revilings, but also the power of other men* [italics added].

Possibilities of obligation, and therefore moral elements, in anarchy are reinforced by the use of the terms "dispraise" and "revilings." The dispraise and revilings are functions of expectations of reciprocity in anarchy. Thus, there is an admission that cooperation could be forged in some strategic condition but that the fool sees any such cooperation as noncompelling because of the lack of divine sanction. In this passage from section 4, the term "the power of other men" appears to be tied into some idea of punishment for defection, as it closely follows the statement conveying that defection leads to negative consequences among those who think like the fool. It is this very defection represented by the logic of the fool that Hobbes castigates. Here Hobbes is introducing a human element of sanction but does not yet spell out the precise nature of the consequences of defection, as he does in the section (5) – quoted above – that follows.

The strategic context of the fool's thinking is even more evident in this section. In the passage that begins "Secondly," it is clear that survival in anarchy emanates from reciprocity resulting in what Hobbes calls a "confederation." This is a very different conceptualization of the idea of cooperative groups in anarchy than we see in chapter 13 – that is, the reference to "confederacy" appears to be far closer to some idea of alliance of convenience for the purpose of aggression. To quote Hobbes from chapter 13, "For as to the strength of the body, the weakest has the strength enough to kill the strongest, either by secret machination, or by confederacy with others who are in the same danger with himself" (L, XIII, 1). This alliance of convenience will break down according to Hobbes' descriptions of relations in anarchy in chapter 13 because the condition devolves into "a war as is of every man against every man" (L, XIII, 7). Clearly, the mutual "danger" that Hobbes refers to in chapter 13 never abates, even when alliances of convenience form, because such alliances are created and extemporized in accordance with the perpetration of violence rather than peaceful coexistence. In chapter 15, the thrust of the logic portrays confederacy instead as a vehicle for protection: "[N]o man can hope... to defend himself from destruction without the help of confederates." Reciprocity as a foundation for such a protective or defensive alliance is manifest in the terminology "where everyone expects the same defense by the confederation that anyone else does."

From here on, the logic in section 5 of chapter 15 exhibits common game-theoretic elements regarding cooperation in environments where actors have complete freedom of action (i.e., no Leviathan). Keeping the fool as the main protagonist, it is evident that his logic does not bode well for his survival in anarchy because even in a world without a divine presence or a Leviathan, there are consequences for defection that punish the transgressor. In this case, he can be excluded from the group and therefore be killed ("if he be left or cast out ..., he perisheth"). This suggests some intriguing possibilities about the process of cooperation in anarchy. The idea of noniteration (i.e., one-shot game) and mutual/symmetrical vulnerability in strategic environments (i.e., each actor is equally vulnerable to the other) that Realists glean from Hobbes in the form of the classic Prisoner's Dilemma appear to be absent in the logic of this passage.[18]

[18] The Prisoner's Dilemma game portrays a situation in which two or more actors face a choice among competing strategies and their choices affect what happens to both themselves and the group (e.g., deciding whether to clean the dirty dishes in a house

Defection on the part of the fool will not destroy the entire group, or even compromise its effectiveness because even after defecting he can "be left or cast out." Thus, the symmetry in vulnerability of the classic Prisoner's Dilemma game is compromised here (i.e., the fool is more vulnerable than the group). But Hobbes also introduces a temporal and informational dimension that undermines the pernicious consequences of anarchy that Realists have traditionally embraced (i.e., only one play of the game, and limited information about what others will do). It is clear from the ability of the group to cast out defectors that the game does not end there for either. The fool will go on to seek another group, which must by definition exist in anarchy because a commonwealth has not yet been formed; if the group Hobbes refers to were singular, then it would in fact be that very covenant that forms the commonwealth. But this is not the case, as Hobbes articulates the fool's dilemma within the context of anarchy. The fool's decision is about optimal behavior in environments void of punishment from an authoritative power. The iteration (repeated play) manifests itself in a somewhat modified way. If we think of iteration in strategic situations according to the classic articulation of Axelrod (1984), the socialization of defectors comes through iterated play between the same individuals over some period of time that is indeterminate. Thus, socialization takes place through the shadow of the future that infinite iteration generates. In Hobbes' case, there does appear to be some shadow of the future at work, but iterated play does not manifest itself in the games among the same actors. Indeed, the fool would have been cast out of his protective confederation and then would have had to look elsewhere. So assuming some repeated play on the part of the fool, which means moving from group to group, there is nonetheless a draconian shadow of the future imposed on a defector; continual defection will

shared by several roommates). This game is principally characterized by the fact that each individual faces incentives that would discourage him or her from cooperating with the other actors (i.e., in our example, cleaning the dishes), which makes such a game especially pernicious. The incentives are such that no matter what other people do (whether they clean the dishes or not), each actor is better off not cooperating (i.e., defecting). But if no one cooperates, the group consequently suffers (i.e., there will be no clean dishes to use). Using the notation of game theory, the preference ordering D>C (i.e., defection is preferred to cooperation) holds for all individuals for all possible actions on the part of others. Although mutual defection has become a trademark of a Prisoner's Dilemma game, such an outcome will depend on conditions prevailing in the game, which means that there will be situations when cooperation could emerge. On the Prisoner's Dilemma game and the various conditions that can change the outcomes of the game, see Axelrod (1984).

continue bringing him inferior payoffs because he will be unwelcome into other confederations (assuming he survives, which Hobbes believes will not be the case – "he perisheth"). This would serve the same socialization function as iteration in an Axelrodian context. The results would be similar in both contexts. Both those who are loyal to the group and potential defectors would continue to face incentives to cooperate (Kavka 1986, 140).[19]

Hobbes does admit to the possibility that such a defector might be retained in a confederation because of pure ignorance on the part of the members of the group ("all men that contribute not to his destruction forbear him only out of ignorance of what is good for themselves"). But even here, defectors are on thin ice according to Hobbes because it is an expectation that they should neither "foresee nor reckon upon." The term "reckon" is crucial here as reckoning connotes reasoning. Reason for Hobbes is oriented, as noted above, around self-preservation. This evokes not only a clear understanding of oneself, but also of how others will behave in response to one's actions. It would be clear to the defector by way of reason that others would not be so ignorant of his/her threat to them as they too have reason, and the defector's own reason would acknowledge this. In the Latin version of section 5, Hobbes' language is even more definitive. "So, either he will be cast out and perish, or he will owe his not being cast out to the ignorance of the others, which is contrary to right reason."[20]

However, the shadow of the future may not end with the boundaries of anarchy. Hobbes' use of the word "society" in the passage stating that the fool cannot "be received into any society" appears crucial. Hobbes now introduces the possibilities of the emergence of a commonwealth, and the fool's own prior actions in a state of anarchy will have consequences for his inclusion in the commonwealth itself.[21] Extending the shadow of the future will make cooperation even more appealing in anarchy if expectations of transition to a commonwealth raise the value of avoiding

[19] The strategic imperatives facing actors in anarchy may result in the emergence of norms as vehicles that solve problems of cooperation in game-theoretical situations. Hobbes' own language in the fool's passage, which connotes the existence of normative elements, suggests that the strategic and normative elements of cooperation in anarchy are indeed synthesized. On the emergence of norms as solutions to game-theoretical problems of cooperation, see Taylor (1987) and Ullman-Margalit (1977).

[20] See Hobbes (1651/1994), 92, f.n. 7).

[21] This assertion depends on consistency in Hobbes' use of the term *society* in *The Leviathan* (Kavka 1986, 141).

transgressions in anarchy. In this case, such a possibility might modify the payoffs in the iterated game but would not fundamentally change the form of the strategic interaction. Interestingly, the possibility of some end point in the iteration resulting in the commonwealth could introduce an element of "chain store" paradox into the process.[22] Recognizing finality in a process leading to mutual cooperation within a society may raise the incentives of cooperating at initial stages in anarchy, as there is some heightened expectation that cooperation in anarchy may deliver security – why take chances when complete safety is just around the corner in the form of the commonwealth?

That the logic propounded by Hobbes in his response to the fool proposes a drastically different process of strategic interaction from the one adopted by Realists is evident from his literal treatment of anarchy in chapter 13. This new game no longer demonstrates the structure of the classic Prisoner's Dilemma game, with extreme vulnerability and no time horizons. In Hobbes' response to the fool, the traditional process defining a Prisoner's Dilemma game (each actor does better by defecting no matter what others do) is thrown asunder, leaving an entirely different scenario of interaction. It is questionable whether it is even strategic at all, if the term strategic conveys the existence of viable choices that can be selected in response to the actions of others in a manner that can improve one's fate. In Hobbes' logic, is there an alternative to cooperation in anarchy? Given the argument proposed by Hobbes, it is difficult to answer "yes," even under a variety of scenarios. The possibility of fooling members of the confederation and exploiting them without bearing the consequences is vitiated by reason, as noted above. Of course, one could try to exploit some confederation so as to acquire some material gain that one could carry to another confederation. Here, Hobbes is silent regarding whether different confederations actually share information about defectors, so there may be a possibility of moving from confederation to confederation while accumulating the spoils from the suckers. Yet this would be a bold move indeed, as the spoils could not be greater than one could carry on his person, and doing so exposes one to the risk of death during transition between confederations (that for Hobbes is certain). But the possibilities of exploiting limited information will surely expire with Hobbes' commonwealth (society) end point, when groups will no longer be separated

22 Chain store paradox refers to the outcomes of an iterated Prisoner's Dilemma game on early moves when players are cognizant of the outcome of the final play.

and can communicate about erstwhile defectors and subsequently punish them. Clearly, then, cooperation will dominate over defection.[23]

What of a situation in which some of the members of the confederation exploit those cooperative individuals who subscribe to Hobbesian reason? Should reciprocity also be the rule here? Even in this case, the idea of opportunity costs makes defection a severe choice under expectations of reciprocity. In a case in which members of the confederation are exploiting one another, surely reason will compel the third-party members (not involved in the exploitation) to cast the defectors out to perish. Even as a reciprocal act, defection will still confer a reputation of being unreliable. But suppose the defectors are numerous enough to create their own protective confederation such that they can reduce individual vulnerability and thus be less fearful of being cast out of the confederation? This would be illogical, as cooperation must undergird a confederation for it to carry out its protective function effectively. Thus, this splinter confederation would either be killed off or kill itself off.[24] This makes defection a losing strategy regardless of what anyone else does.[25] Even facing the risk of exploitation within a confederation may be preferable to responding in kind and being cast out. One may indeed face death from such exploitation by defectors in the confederation, yet this is not certain. However, being cast out increases one's vulnerability even more, because the defector loses the support of the group and must rely solely on himself, which, for Hobbes, means certain death. But even if death within the confederation is not certain, response in kind may still be inferior because it brands one as a defector, which is sure to cause one to be expelled. Anything short of death introduces probabilistic thinking that should lead toward cooperation in this logic. Would I rather be wounded

23 As a result of the logic of Hobbes' response to the fool, Curley (1994, xxviii) proposes altering the payoffs in Hobbesian anarchy from a Prisoner's Dilemma game to a Stag Hunt, in which you have contingent rather than dominant strategies (i.e., in a Stag Hunt, you cooperate only if the other actor cooperates, as opposed to Prisoner's Dilemma, in which you defect no matter what the other actor does). But even this moderation of predation does not go far enough in characterizing the cooperative nature of the game that Hobbesian logic is propounding in chapter 15.

24 It would be difficult to get allies or other confederations to form a union. If the splinter group tried to aggrandize itself through conquest, then surely they could expect some countervailing coalition to form against them.

25 This assumes that defection is not perceived as just retribution for transgressions within the group. But surely Hobbesian logic would attribute functions of law and enforcement within confederations as such instruments are applicable under covenants, which confederations represent for Hobbes.

in a confederation or in the wilds of anarchy? Here, the choice would be clear. In a fundamental sense, then, the idea of differentiating between responses to within-group defectors withers from Hobbesian logic. An individual always fares better staying loyal to the confederation, regardless of what anyone else does.

The new game suggested by the tale of the fool is neither a Prisoner's Dilemma nor even a Stag Hunt (in which cooperation is contingent on the cooperation of others in the group), but a game of pure cooperation in which actors should cooperate with the group no matter what anyone else in the group does. If one were to decompose strategic thinking in actors according to different modes, as Kavka (1986, 142) does, differing strategies (e.g., maximin, maximization, and disaster avoidance) should all deliver the same incentive to cooperate. The parallels between confederations in anarchy and the commonwealth are most apparent here. In civil society, there can only be one strategy for Hobbes: the dominant strategy of cooperation. Any sort of defection, even as a response in kind to exploitation (assume one kills a person who stole from him), is punished through law. Thus, the idea of strategic interaction does not characterize life in the commonwealth as civil society restricts the choices of actors. In the final analysis, life in Hobbesian anarchy need not necessarily be "nasty, brutish and short," especially for individuals who are not fools.

This interpretation of anarchy in *The Leviathan* is permeated with opportunities for actors who have endeared themselves to others (soft empowerment) and concomitantly manifests significant dangers for those who fail to do so as a result of overreliance on strategies of force and coercion (hard disempowerment). Even in anarchy, soft empowerment manifests manifold benefits that are both direct and indirect and enhance the safety and influence of actors through positive feedback effects. Cooperation (in this case, the soft power resulting from abiding by well-regarded norms of reciprocity) generates endearing qualities, which in turn generate these manifold benefits. In this case, the principal endearing quality driving opportunities for soft empowerment is trust. Confederations can function only if members coalesce around mutual perceptions of trust. Trust is more effectively generated by reputations for cooperation (i.e., both initial gestures and strong tendencies to reciprocate initial gestures of cooperation). Reputations of cooperation within the confederation, given the logic of Hobbes, can solidify and stabilize any confederation in manifold ways. Actors will work that much harder to preserve the sanctity of the pact, given that it delivers safety in a dangerous world (through both x- and non–x-efficiencies). Actors attempting to undermine the confederation will be dealt with that much more quickly and harshly. Direct and indirect effects also will abound with respect to external relations. It will be much easier for confederations to recruit new actors and confederations to join theirs in attempts to form a greater union because other actors and confederations will find such alliances safer and more secure. Such a dynamic may generate a positive feedback process of growth, making the confederation all the more secure. Therefore, such soft power can produce more robust and less vulnerable confederations.

Such soft empowerment effects can be compounded by domestic sources of endearment (i.e., democratic and politically liberal practices of respect for law and individual rights). These have manifold consequences as well. Security and the quality of governance within the confederation can generate informal property rights (according to Hobbes, they would create a sense of "mine and thine" in anarchy), which will make the members of the confederation more prosperous. Such confederations are also likely to be attractive to individuals who can vote with their feet, thus expanding the size of the confederation. Such prosperity and size will increase their strength and make them less vulnerable to aggressive coalitions, which, according to Hobbes' logic, are vulnerable because of the likelihood of cross-confederation covenants. This is merely a continuation of Hobbesian logic beyond an individual level – that is, his sense of obligation and reciprocity shows no distinction with respect to composition.[26] All the same, consequences apply to relations among confederations; unilateral gestures demand reciprocity, as reason dictates. The power of endearment generated by respect and reputation for cooperation should also be strong assets in generating defensive alliances; confederations in anarchy certainly would not want to join an aggressive and expansionist coalition.[27] In fact, there are incentives to optimize the size of defensive alliances just to be safe from such rogue confederations.[28]

[26] Numerous scholars in international relations have embraced possibilities of cooperation in anarchy, even though they have not sought vindication for their ideas in Hobbes. See especially Oye (1985), Axelrod and Keohane (1985), Wendt (1992), and Jervis (1978).

[27] Confederations that are successful in maintaining their safety will likely generate emulation by other confederations. The same external and internal practices that make them desirable places in which to reside and desirable allies will be compelling because other confederations are above all seeking "peace" according to Hobbesian logic. It stands to reason that union would be more likely and easier to institute among confederations that are structured and behave alike.

[28] Game-theoretical work on the strategic advantages of magnanimity support the possibilities of gains through endearment even in games that present opportunities for

Conversely, in such an environment, exclusive reliance on hard power strategies would be far more dangerous. In terms of intra-confederation dynamics, no successful confederation could be built around actors who relied on force and fraud. A confederation based on force and fraud would be a contradiction in terms. But even if collective action could succeed to produce and maintain such a confederation, prospects for such confederations would be gloomy indeed if they relied excessively on hard power strategies. Such strategies would compromise the endearing qualities generated by soft power strategies and lead to victimization from hard disempowerment. If confederations use their hard power in an aggressive way, there will be obvious responses in kind that may in the end neutralize such quests for primacy and ultimately even destroy the confederations themselves (negative feedback). Such strategies would undermine the ability of the rogue confederation to endear itself to other confederations, limiting possibilities for alliances that might prove crucial to the safety of the rogue confederation. Even if a confederation were not an aggressor, but thought its prospects for influence greatest if it concentrated exclusively on hard power at the expense of soft power resources, it would nonetheless shoulder some of the burdens of an aggressor. In this case, the security dilemma would be ever-present (i.e., more negative feedback effects).[29] Unmitigated aggrandizement of hard power is threatening in itself (for both reasons of feedback and moral hazard), but without cooperative gestures (i.e., endearment through soft power strategies) to allay perceptions of fear among other confederations, the threats would be perceived as all the more menacing, as perceptions of threat are a function of both the size of the competing military capacity and the reputation of the actors (Jervis 1978).[30] However, to build such a hard power capacity, other domestic objectives would have to be sacrificed. Thus, individuals within the confederation may be asked

exploitation, like the Prisoner's Dilemma. In such games, sacrifices could very well be strategically rational if such actions mitigated adverse actions that might unravel more favorable group outcomes (Brahms 1994).

29 The security dilemma, a classic example of a negative feedback process, defines a situation in which even the buildup of military forces for the purpose of defense may cause other nations to respond by building up their own forces, thus neutralizing the gains made by the initial buildup (Jervis 1978).

30 The moral hazard effect comes from the fact that greater hard power would lead to greater complacency about developing both alternative hard and soft power functions, and this neglect of soft power would further feed perceptions that a nation may be a threat and magnify the negative feedback effect (e.g., greater formation of countervailing coalitions).

for greater sacrifices in terms of resources and military service. Surely a defensive confederation would have a competitive edge for individuals who could vote with their feet, which in turn would make it difficult for the power-hungry confederations to attract members. In this respect, the need for endearment permeates relations in anarchy, as confederations need to endear themselves not only to other confederations but also to their rank and file members.

Furthermore, military aggrandizement might destroy the internal system of governance as a result of economic decay brought on by the growing need to generate resources required to support this aggrandizement of hard power – the problem of overstretch (Gallarotti 2010; Kennedy 1987; Snyder 1991). Moreover, opportunities for union with other confederations would be minimized, one important reason being incompatibilities between internal practices of governance (e.g., a more liberal orientation versus a more authoritarian one), thus restricting opportunities for alliances and supportive associations. Alliances could be forged among actors that eschew soft power, but then each confederation within such alliances might feel at the mercy of the other confederations' capacities for exploitation, which would negate possibilities for extensive cooperation, as this would make each feel more vulnerable. Hobbesian covenants could diminish possibilities of a security dilemma in such a case because of the power of obligation. Yet even here, the shadow of the future cast by the commonwealth as a final equilibrium, as mentioned in chapter 15, would socialize coalitions into cooperation founded on soft power. To be part of coalitions that perpetrate menacing acts or policies would compromise any endearing qualities they might have forged in the past and permit fewer possibilities for becoming part of a greater security community.

In sum, anarchy is still a dangerous place for Hobbes, notwithstanding the tale of the fool and the utility of soft power. So hard power resources and their activation in the form of force and coercion still serve a fundamental purpose in Hobbes' state of nature, precisely because there is no 9-1-1 (Leviathan) to keep all in awe. The Hobbesian treatment of anarchy has justifiably become one of the great inspirations for a hard power vision of politics. In excess, though, such strategies enhance the dangers of anarchy all the more (i.e., disempower), as is clear from the logic of the tale of the fool. Moreover, even in such a dangerous place, dangers can be limited and adverse outcomes avoided with the inclusion of soft power strategies that generate endearing qualities. In the end, the Hobbesian vision of anarchy is inherently Cosmopolitan: hard power resources are necessary, but soft power is just as crucial to optimize influence and achieve security in an environment without any common power to keep all actors in awe. The foundations of influence and security lie in a reconciliation of both forms of power.[31]

Thucydides

As to Hobbes, Realists have shown much intellectual debt to Thucydides' interpretations of the great war (*The History of the Peloponnesian War*) between Athens and Sparta in the fifth century B.C.[32] Many classes in international politics assign the *Melian Dialogue* as the very exemplar of a Realist vision of international relations (H, V, 84–116), underscored principally in the famous quote issued by an Athenian diplomat: "[T]he strong do what they have the power to do and the weak accept what they have to accept" (H, V, 89).[33] In addition to this manifestation of Realpolitik, structural Realists embrace Thucydides' reflections on the Peloponnesian War as an inescapable outcome of rising Athenian hard power and fear of such hard power on the part of Sparta, which caused Sparta to go to war with Athens. The War was inevitable, or structurally predisposed (I, 23 and I, 44). But like those of Hobbes, the lessons of Thucydides have become somewhat distorted. The elegant deductive logic derived from Thucydides' *History* has led scholars to a simple vision of international relations that has underexplained the great text. Like that of Hobbes, Thucydides' great chronicle reveals an impresario of hard power politics. But, as with Hobbesian anarchy, there is far more to the story of the war than the crucial nature of hard power. A careful reading of Thucydides' work suggests a very rich appreciation of both the potential of soft power and the dangers of hard disempowerment and consequently (quite fittingly for an ancient Greek thinker) the importance of finding some golden Cosmopolitan mean between the pole of hard power and the pole of soft power.

Perhaps the dominant theme of Thucydides' *History* is that, although muscle is an essential ingredient for greatness, the ultimate fate of city-states is also heavily dependent on their soft power. To achieve and

31 Interestingly, at a stylistic level, Skinner (1996) underscores a textual synthesis in *The Leviathan* as a whole, suggesting that Hobbes' recourse to humanistic rhetoric might be a soft textual buffer to the hard character of his formal reasoning.

32 On Realism's debt to Thucydides, see especially Garst (1989, 3), Conner (1984, 3), Waltz (1959), Keohane and Nye (1985, 42), and Johnson (1993, 209, 210).

33 References to *The History* will be in the form (H, I, 2): *The History*, book, section.

maintain this greatness, city-states must endear themselves in the greater political system in which they function. In Thucydides' chronicle, this endearment comes through honoring well-respected norms and institutions pertaining to interstate relations in the ancient Greek world. Through such endearment, city-states enhance their influence and avoid ruin. The fate of Athens itself becomes the focal point through which this Cosmopolitan theme ultimately unfolds. Athens achieved greatness through pursuing a golden mean of power: its physical strength made it imposing, but its soft power greatly augmented that strength by making it a venerated and trusted leader among Greek city-states in the early years of the Delian League. But as it came to increasingly compromise this soft power through a tyrannical excess of hard power politics in its relations with Greek city-states, Athens embarked on a path that eventually delivered it to ruin. Hence, Thucydides' *History*, quite appropriately, reads like a Greek tragedy, with Athens as the protagonist. As long as Athens followed the golden mean and matched its great military and economic power with the cultivation of good will that endeared it to other city-states, it prospered. However, it ultimately compromised this goodwill by deviating from a Cosmopolitan balance (through the hubris of hard power politics that finally alienated other city-states) and in doing so brought about its own demise.

A number of scholars have already contributed to a revisionist literature questioning the conventional lessons derived from Thucydides' *History* about the empowering nature of Realpolitik and the compelling influence of structuralism. Classical scholars have led the way, inspired by Cornford's (1907) revisionist reading of Thucydides, by attributing a tragic quality to the text. According to this vision, rather than prospering from following the dictates of pure Realpolitik, Athens actually came to an unfortunate end from doing so. Romilly (1963); Connor (1984); White (1984); Orwin (1994); Williams (1998); Crane (1998); Cartwright (2000) all picked up Cornford's gauntlet. For these authors, traditional interpretations of Thucydides missed the softer side of his story – the importance of ethical behavior in political communities. Whereas readers have embraced Thucydides' references to Greek Realpolitik, they have failed to appreciate the importance he attributes to the elements of soft power: justice, morality, legitimacy, and norms. Thucydides' text forcefully demonstrates that the imperatives of ethics should trump the dictates of amoral necessity. A number of scholarly applications of this argument specifically to international relations have paralleled the work of the classical revisionists.[34] These scholars too have also been inspired by Cornford's (1907) tragic vision of the fate of Athens. More specifically, Athens' power derived in large part from its legitimacy as leader of the Greek world, which was bound up in honoring well-respected norms that dictated relations among the Greek city-states.[35] As it increasingly undermined its legitimacy by violating normative dictates in deference to the imperatives of Realpolitik and forsaking its golden Cosmopolitan mean, it continued to be victimized by a process of hard disempowerment that would ultimately lead to its demise. In this revisionist scholarship, the greatest lessons to be derived from Thucydides' work are far more closely related to the consequences of neglecting soft power than to the benefits of embracing the hard power orientation dictated by Realpolitik or structural Realism.[36]

In general, ancient Greek texts, and in this respect Thucydides is no exception, are not a promising place in which to look for the pure manifestations of Realpolitik and its vision of hard power politics. These can best be found in the post-Enlightenment intellect, where a greater disjuncture emerged between ideology, morality, and piety on the one hand and the rational/practical mind on the other. Such a disjuncture was foreign to the ancient intellect. The Greek intellect, of which Thucydides' *History* is quite representative, synthesized all of these phenomena within a single vision of human excellence – that is, virtue. Above all, Greeks sought virtue as the ultimate goal in life. Virtue was defined along the lines of a sacred golden mean in the human character and considered to be a balance among many qualities. Classical scholars have highlighted

[34] See Garst (1989), Forde (1992, 2000), Rahe (1996), Johnson Bagby (1996), Lebow (2001 and 2003), Lebow and Kelly (2001), Kokac (2001), Bedford and Workman (2001), Welch (2003), and Doyle (1990). Lebow (2001, 547) flatly states, "Thucydides should properly be considered a Constructivist."

[35] Garst (1989), Lebow (2001 and 2003), and Lebow and Kelly (2001) underscore the distinction between hegemony (legitimate leadership) and control (authority through force and threat). Athenian power was strongest when Athens was a hegemon, but its power progressively declined as it exerted more control over its allies and associated states with its increasingly imperialistic foreign policy.

[36] This section draws on this literature but seeks to make significant additions. The literature tends to concentrate more on interpretations of the dialogues and speeches, and less on the actual history of the Peloponnesian War and the events reported by Thucydides. This analysis looks at them both. Moreover, most of the scholars concentrate on Athens and have much less to say about Sparta. This analysis pays more attention to Sparta. Finally, although much of the literature refers to the social structures underscored in Thucydides, it generally fails to sufficiently specify what these social structures are. This analysis does so.

the expression of Greek virtue as a multifaceted phenomenon manifest through a plethora of commendable human characteristics. Many of the characteristics are principally grounded in elements of soft power, with others reflecting Realpolitik qualities: courage, practicality, intellectual curiosity, piety, morality, respect for oaths and agreements, respect for law, dedication to family, warrior virtue, hospitality, self-control, justice, prudence, preparation, wisdom, patience, honor, glory, prestige, and physical excellence.[37] All of these traits were supposed to be pursued with balance and moderation. Any life dedicated to one quality over the others was considered a life of excess and not virtuous. Pursuing strategies that forsook all other qualities in favor of practicality and the pursuit of hard power was considered a major human flaw in the Greek psyche (Williams 1998, 198; Woodruff 1993, xvi, xvii; Kagan 1991, 21).

With respect to the actual events and developments leading up to the Peloponnesian War, it is evident that factors relating to soft power were at least as important, if not more so, than hard power factors relating to structuralism and Realpolitik. First, the hard structural impetus leading to competition between Sparta and Athens was mitigated. They did not compete in similar avenues of hard power. Sparta derived its military strength from its army, whereas Athens derived its strength from naval power. Athens did not fear Spartan challenges at sea, and similarly, Spartans did not fear an invasion from Athens (Doyle 1990, 236; Romilly 1963, 68; Thucydides IV, 12). Thus, each was willing to relent to the other's quest for primacy in its principal military avenue.

Geopolitically, this difference manifested itself in the territorial interests of the two powers. Spartan associations were generally inland areas, whereas the Athenians sought coastal areas (Greece and Asia Minor). Even at the peak of Athenian imperialism, each side fundamentally respected the other's spheres of influence. Leading up to the Peloponnesian War, the controversies that arose between the two great powers were more often related to third-party complaints (Spartan and Athenian allies complaining of intrusions) than to direct confrontations between the two great city-states (Souza 2002).

The immediate events leading up to the Peloponnesian War in 431 B.C. demonstratively attest to the importance of soft power. In voting for war,

[37] It is also clear that a number of these qualities tend to fall outside conventional visions of both hard and soft power: piety, honor, curiosity, prudence, self-control, and glory. On the role of prestige and honor in the ancient Greek psyche and Thucydides, see Lebow (2008) and Onuf (1998b).

militants in the Spartan assembly appeared to be driven by anger over Athens' violation of the autonomy clause of the Thirty Years' Peace. Spartans were animated by what they perceived as a violation of legal and normative commitments of this treaty, as well as by a strong sense of obligation to their allies that derived from Greek norms of political confederacy (Kagan 2003a, 41). Both concerns appeared to support the primacy of soft power considerations (i.e., reaction to a violation of well-respected norms) over the hard power considerations of Realpolitik and hard structuralism in the actual vote to go to war (i.e., gains in relative hard power, strategic benefits, and geographic expansion). It also appears that a particularly crucial issue involved the relations between Athens and Megara, the latter a member of the Peloponnesian confederation that the Athenians were trying to pry away from Sparta and into their Delian League.[38] This was a further affront in violating Greek alliance norms. Interestingly, the importance of the Megara issue suggests that Athenian compliance on this point could have turned the Spartan assembly against war. But even before the advent of war in 431 B.C., Sparta had numerous opportunities to respond to Athenian expansion, although it never did.[39] Many exceptional opportunities arose from the very nature of Athens' imperial hubris in overexpanding beyond its ability to administer effective control, a manifestation of an Athenian power curse (overstretch) and ultimately a hard power illusion.[40] Hence, for a city-state supposedly hell-bent on responding to Athenian ascension and being driven by Realpolitik and hard structural imperatives, Sparta demonstrated extreme timidity and a pronounced concern for the sanctity of norms in its relations with Athens in the fifth century B.C. (Kagan 2003a, 45, 46; Welch 2003, 305; Johnson Bagby 1996, 174, 175).

Thucydides' own interpretations of the Peloponnesian War show more emphasis on the merits of soft power, and the dangers of hard

[38] This so-called Delian League (founded in 478 B.C.) began as a defensive alliance among the Greek states under the leadership of Athens during their wars against Persia, but evolved into an imperialistic network for Athens as the century progressed.

[39] Thucydides himself made a number of references to the rather timid and cautious nature of Sparta in the fifth century B.C. as a central characteristic of its foreign policy. In the face of Athenian expansion throughout the century, states Thucydides, "Sparta did little or nothing to prevent it, and for most of the time remained inactive, being traditionally slow to go to war" (H, I, 118). Even the Spartan King Archidamus reaffirmed this tradition about Sparta when trying to convince the Spartan assembly to vote against war in 431 B.C.) (H, I, 80–85).

[40] See Gallarotti (2010) on the manifestations of the power curse and power illusion in the context of Athenian imperialism.

disempowerment, than on pure homage to the hard power dictates of Realpolitik and hard structuralism. In his discussion of the dispute between Corcyra and Corinth over Epidamus (a crucial incident in precipitating the war), Thucydides (H, I, 44) reports that Athens chose to side with Corcyra at the risk being perceived as breaking the Thirty Years' Peace by interfering in the affairs of Corinth (Corcyra was a colony of Corinth). It did so, according to Thucydides, for reasons of Realpolitik and structure; Corcyra had a great navy and strategic location, and Athens preferred to be its ally rather than its enemy. Yet in the debate between the ambassadors in the Athenian assembly, Thucydides actually underscores the influence of factors relating to soft power on the outcome of the dispute. Corinth naturally argued for Athenian support based on legal and normative obligations (H, I, 40–42); both well-respected norms regarding colonial relations and the terms of the Thirty Years' Peace dictated that Corinth's dealings with its colony were to be left unimpeded. Greek norms required that Athens reciprocate Corinthian support in prior situations when Athens had dealt in an unimpeded manner with its own colonies. In doing so, Athens would gain Corinthian gratitude.[41] While the Corcyran ambassador played the Realpolitik card by suggesting that war with Sparta was inevitable and that it was better to fight in alliance with Athens' navy against Sparta (H, I, 36), most of the Corcyran justification was based on morality. Corcyra painted itself as a victim of aggression, and therefore Athens was normatively bound to help fellow Greeks against cruel acts (H, I, 33). Moreover, Corinth was accused of breaking another time-honored norm by reverting to war rather than agreeing to settle a dispute against a fellow Greek state through arbitration (H, I, 34). In actuality, the Athenian assembly first chose the Corinthian side in its initial meeting on the question but later changed its mind. It is unclear whether Realpolitik/structural or soft power concerns finally led to the change; Thucydides does not account for it. Moreover, it is not clear that the soft power rationale of the Corcyran ambassador was less important than Realpolitik and the hard structural rationale in driving the final decision. It is clear, though, that even after choosing to support Corcyra, Athens comported itself in a way (through limited Athenian military engagement) that tried to minimize the diplomatic fallout and not alienate Corinth and its powerful ally Sparta

[41] Here, the Corinthian ambassador suggests an x-efficient element of such gratitude by saying "an act of kindness done at the right moment has a power to dispel old grievances quite out of proportion to the act itself" (H, I, 42).

(i.e., damage control with respect to its soft power). It was hoped that a symbolic show of support would be enough to deter Corinth from attacking (H, I, 44).

Thucydides' description (in Book I) of the debate before the Spartan assembly in 432 B.C., when the decision to go to war with Athens was ultimately made, appears equally reflective of the tension between the hard structural/Realpolitik and soft power factors surrounding the decision for war. Notwithstanding the conventional claim that Thucydides' interpretation vindicates the influence of Realpolitik and structuralism in starting the Peloponnesian War, the passage does far more to support the importance of soft power factors in starting the war. *In fact, considerations of Realpolitik and structure would have led Sparta to choose not to go to war with Athens at that moment.* In drawing lessons from Thucydides' *History*, readers have been influenced far too much by some of the literal passages without sufficiently scrutinizing the substance of the debates leading to war. In actuality, Thucydides makes just a few references to the structural inevitability of war with Athens in recounting the episode (H, I, 23, 44, 87). All are fairly self-contained and very brief statements, and are not extrapolated or even developed within the context of the greater events and factors leading Sparta to choose war. In actuality, Thucydides' detailed account of the war cuts sharply against his own literal and cursory statements about what caused it.

Sparta had invited all aggrieved parties to come and voice their complaints against Athens. Thucydides reports on the speeches of a Corinthian representative (arguing for war) and an Athenian representative (arguing against war). The Corinthian rationale for war centered mainly on the Athenian violation of sacred norms, agreements, and religious practices. Most importantly, the Corinthian delegate accused Athens of breaking the terms of the Thirty Years' Peace (violating the autonomy of Aegina, interfering in the Corcyran war, and blocking Megaran access to its own port). There are few references in this speech to the structural advantages of siding with Corinth in a war. Much of the diatribe against Athens focuses on the moral outrage resulting from Athens' insolence in breaking agreements among fellow Greeks and in usurping the freedom of fellow Greeks through imperialism. In this respect, Athens was vilified for not using its "power in the cause of justice" (H, I, 71). Corinth's principal plea targeted Sparta's sense of obligation to its allies, playing on Greek alliance norms. To quote the representative, "From your fathers, was handed down to you the leadership of the Peloponnese" (H, I, 71). The violation of these norms and agreements took on an important religious significance, as alliance bonds, peace treaties, and relations among Greeks were consummated through religious rituals. Violating any such institutions was tantamount to sacrilege. Interestingly, the most vigorous Realpolitik/structural arguments were made against war by the Athenian representative and the Spartan king (Archidamus), and the arguments of both related to the deleterious consequences of negative feedback and overstretch (Gallarotti 2010).

The Athenian speech centered on a deterrent threat that underscored the costs of war (H, I, 73–78). The representative proclaimed that the great power of Athens threatened Sparta with an extremely costly war: "[See] what sort of city you will have to fight against" (H, I, 73). The threat was embellished with references to the ferocity and success of Athenian campaigns during the Persian Wars early in the fifth century B.C. Moreover, it was suggested that even if Sparta won the war, it would likely be faced with unacceptable costs of conquest – that is, the financial and military burden of maintaining the Athenian empire (Spartan overstretch). The concluding words of the speech reflected pure Realpolitik. The Athenian urged Sparta not to be moved by the cries of allies or by any feelings, opinions, or ideas that might move it toward an emotional rather than a practical decision; Sparta should make "sensible decisions" (H, I, 78). Archidamus, the Spartan king, himself reinforced the Athenian's Realpolitik and structural arguments discouraging Sparta to go to war at that time. The language in his speech recalled the Realpolitik rational orientation of the Athenian speech; Sparta was urged to be "cautious," "wise," "slow," and "sensible," and to aspire to "practical measures" (H, I, 80–85). Fighting the Athenians now would be unwise (Souza 2002; Kagan 2003a). In the end, the actual process of voting in the Spartan assembly was initiated by the Spartan Ephor Sthenelaides, who primed the assembly with a strong endorsement for war based on normative commitments ("do not... betray your allies") (I, 86). Thucydides' account of these speeches and events makes it clear that Sparta's ultimate decision to go to war was more ideological and emotional than practical.

The famous *Melian Dialogue* has traditionally been highlighted as the epitome of Thucydidean Realpolitik. Indeed, no passage in Thucydides' *History* has been more celebrated by Realists, who have identified the passage as a precursor of and inspiration for a hard power vision of politics. The famous passage stating that "the strong do what they have the power to do and the weak accept what they have to accept" has generated the most recognized quote in the Realist vernacular

(H, V, 89).[42] Melos had been one of only a few Aegean islands to remain outside the Delian League. In 416 B.C., Athens tried to convince Melos to come over to its side in the war. Melos, however, wished to remain neutral. The dialogue between the Melians and Athenians represents a bargaining process whereby each side is trying to convince the other of the merits of its respective position. The arguments exude impeccable practicality and are strongly grounded in considerations of hard power politics. In a literal sense, the passage hails the primacy of such hard power politics, but did Thucydides intend for the passage to convey such a lesson? Classical scholars disagree on this point and have identified various lessons in the *Dialogue* (Williams 1998, 195). However, a number of them have agreed that the *Dialogue* represents a vehicle through which Thucydides in fact conveyed the destructiveness of Athens' quest for hard power (and hence the victimization of Athens from hard disempowerment) during the war rather than the glorification of hard power politics (Garst 1989; Forde 1992; Rahe 1996; Finley 1985; Williams 1998; Cartwright 2000; Connor 1984; White 1984; Romilly 1963; Lebow 2001 and 2003).[43]

Whatever Thucydides' intention, when the *Dialogue* is considered within the context of the *History*, it is a manifestation of an imperial foreign policy that excessively embraced hard power (to the exclusion of soft power) and consequently was detrimental to Athens both before and during the war (Cartwright 2000, 220, 221; Connor 1984, 155–7; Romilly 1963, 308; Garst 1989, 16). Just as with the Melians, Athens perpetrated similar cruel acts against Scione, Mende, and Mytilene.[44] In these cases, similar obstinacy on the part of small states in joining or staying within the Athenian League drew a similar savage reprisal from Athens. Such acts were a clear violation of well-respected norms regarding relations among Greek states. The smaller states faced a rigged trial, no arbitration was called for after negotiations failed, and the decision was enforced through brutal military action (Willams 1998, 202). Thucydides

[42] Romilly's (1963, 304) highly respected study of the *History* in fact identifies only three references in the entire text to the idea that "might makes right": in the famous *Melian Dialogue* (H, V, 84–116), in the speech of the Athenians at Sparta (H, I, 76), and in the speech of Herocrates (H, IV, 61).

[43] Forde (1992, 384) perhaps puts it best: "The Melians may be fools for thinking that justice can prevail in the face of Athenian might, but Thucydides shows the Athenians to be equally blind to the consequences of living wholly by the law of power." In this respect, victimization through excessive reliance on hard power is poignantly conveyed in the *Dialogue*.

[44] Athens punished Melos for refusing to join its alliance by executing a great many of the island's inhabitants.

even goes so far as to portray the competing philosophical orientations of the arguments in the *Dialogue* as "right" (the Melian rationale) versus "wrong" (the Athenian rationale) (H, V, 104). Thus, in the case of Melos, the weak did indeed suffer, as the Athenians killed all the Melian men and enslaved the survivors. However, the powerful Athenians would also suffer throughout the century as a result of transgressions against Greek norms in both their treatment of Melos and other Greek states.

The *Dialogue* is crucial for Thucydides as a didactic platform on which to convey a more general lesson about Athenian hard disempowerment. The *Dialogue* manifests an Athenian imperialistic style that became more brutal and tyrannical as the Athenian imperial appetite and consequent foreign involvements grew across the century. Such a style derived from a need for effective methods in ruling and ensuring tribute in an ever-expanding empire. As the Athenian machine expanded and became increasingly dependent on expansion to fuel its empire (mission creep and dependence), the expansion itself became self-enlarging, leading to overstretch, and this in turn brought ever more dangerous burdens with it. The need to continue to squeeze colonies to sustain the Athenian war effort and concomitant expansion led to deterioration in its relations with both the colonies and non-colonial states (Gallarotti 2010). These territories and states became even more reluctant to support Athens in times of need and increased the burden of empire through recalcitrance (negative feedback effects) (H, I, 22; II, 8; III, 10, 37, 40, 46, 57, 68; IV, 54, 81, 105; V, 9, 92, 99; VIII, 37). This alienation would culminate in a devastating blow to Athens following its Sicilian campaign (discussed later). This ties into what is a pervasive theme of Thucydides' *History*: the greed and hubris of Athens in consolidating its hard power without much regard to sustaining its soft power ultimately led to its downfall. Thucydides notes how Athens could have been victorious in the war "if she avoided adding to her empire during the course of the war, and if she did nothing to risk the safety of the city itself." Athens did neither, the biggest "mistake" being the expedition against Sicily (H, II, 65).[45]

[45] As a representative episode in the *History*, another compelling manifestation of Thucydides' homage to soft power and the dangers of hard disempowerment is visible in his chronicle of the revolution in Corcyra in 427 B.C. (H, III, 82–85). In attempting to rebel from Athens, the city was devastated by a civil war that ensued. In his account of such conditions, Thucydides laments a deterioration of individual and civic character, developments that he essentially describes as a pure state of anarchy. It was an environment in which virtue was turned on its head, and all that was formerly unethical became acceptable behavior: aggression became courage, moderation became evil, fanatical enthusiasm was commended, treachery became wisdom, plotting was an asset, and violence reigned supreme. Thucydides is quite clear in locating the root of such

The Sicilian expedition appears to be a microcosm of all of the lessons oriented around soft power and hard disempowerment that pervade the *History*. In a sense, it embodies the perfect storm with respect to the convergence of all of the dangers of Athenian hard disempowerment across the fifth century B.C. Sicily was long a desired prize for imperial Athens. It was one of the great producers of grain in the ancient world, an entrepôt at the crossroads of the major trade routes, and a strategic platform to southern Europe. With its conquest and future alliance, Athenians would enjoy a springboard to territories well beyond the Greek world. Upon resumption of the Peloponnesian War after the Peace of Nicias (421–415), Athens fixed its sights squarely on Sicily. In expanding the war to a second front, the expedition was merely the epitome of Athens' perception of its invulnerability as a result of its hard power primacy in the Aegean. In Thucydides' own words, Athens was "over-confident" (H, II, 65).

The destruction of the Athenian forces in the Sicilian campaign marked a crucial turning point in the war and signaled the death knell of Athenian primacy in the Aegean. As Athens grew weaker, especially after the Sicilian defeat, both colonial territories and allies began abandoning it, and Athens was increasingly left to go it alone. This devastating process of negative feedback in the Athenian alliance meant that a weakened Athens now lost the muscle to keep the alliance together, and city-states abandoned Athens in droves, moving to the Spartan side. This was a clear manifestation of the deterioration of Athenian soft power, as erstwhile allies were primed to take opportunities to abandon Athens once its weakened condition limited its ability to impose retribution on defecting states. With its unilateral power declining and its allies flocking to the Spartan side, it was only a matter of time before Athens would succumb. All of the strength that Athens perceived itself to possess was in the end illusory as a result of its falling victim to a process of hard disempowerment. The ultimate illusion was the belief that it was strong enough to begin a two-front war and secure large colonial holdings in southern Italy, a feat it would have been unable to achieve even if its hard power resources had been significantly greater than they actually were.

In sum, scholars have embraced Thucydides' *History* as an iconic justification for the primacy of hard power politics. The two main lessons

a cataclysm in civic and human character – the unbridled pursuit of power. To quote Thucydides, "Love of power, operating through greed and through personal ambition, was the cause of all these evils" (H, III, 82). On this episode, see especially Forde (2000, 154).

traditionally drawn from the work are that Sparta was moved exclusively by considerations of structural power politics in going to war with Athens, and that Athens glorified the efficacy of Realpolitik in pursuing its foreign interests. Indeed, these lessons do emerge from a number of the passages in the *History*. Consistent with a common ancient Greek vision of virtue, hard power was indeed an essential ingredient of excellence, and this is clear enough in the *History*. Yet the lessons of Thucydides' *History* are more demonstrative of the merits and efficacy of soft power and the dangers of excessively pursuing hard power to the exclusion of such soft power. In the final analysis, the *History* of Thucydides reads like a typical Greek tragedy, with Athens as the protagonist. Athens lacked virtue in failing to pursue the golden mean (a more Cosmopolitan policy) in its foreign affairs and ultimately paid the price for such sacrilegious excesses, an outcome so common at the end of ancient Greek dramas – hubris leads to a ruinous end.

Machiavelli

If Thucydides and Hobbes have been hailed as inspirations for Realpolitik and its hard power orientation, surely Machiavelli's *The Prince* stands as its very literary embodiment.[46] Machiavelli's *The Prince* is conventionally portrayed as an attempt to codify Realist principles within an intelligible scheme for a head of state – a "how-to" book for aspiring princes in Renaissance Italy in the face of interstate conflict and domestic political challenges. One could hardly find a better, more likely crucial-case testament to hard power politics than *The Prince*, and concomitantly, one could hardly find a better less-likely crucial-case testament to the virtues of soft power (Eckstein 1975; Gerring 2004, 347; King, Keohane, and Verba 1994, 209–12).

There can be no doubt that *The Prince* is indeed a testament to the efficacy of necessity. And in the cause of necessity, hard power resources can be great assets.[47] No political theorist is quoted more with respect to the merits of hard power: "It is much safer to be feared than loved" (17, 91); a prince must "learn to be not good" (15, 87); "one who deceives will always find someone who allows himself to be deceived" (18, 94);

[46] The edition translated by William Connell will be used (Machiavelli 2005). References to *The Prince* will be in the form (P, 1, 23): *The Prince*, chapter, and page number. References to the *Discourses* will be in the form (D, I, 2. 3): *Discourses*, book, chapter, and section.

[47] This is reminiscent of the Hobbesian prescription in *The Leviathan* (chapter 13) that in anarchy, force and fraud become the cardinal virtues (i.e., the famous Realist reversion).

the "prince must have no other object or thought... save warfare and its institutions" (9, 84); and, of course, the most celebrated catechism, "the means will always be judged honorable and praised by everyone" (18, 95).[48] Within this Realpolitik catechism abound infamous accounts of treachery, which, as in Boccaccio's *Decameron*, lead to celebratory ventures of "pick your favorite story" – in this case, stories of the most treacherous acts.

It is remarkable that within this text, which was conceptualized in response to what Machiavelli perceived as an extreme condition of anarchy in Italy, and that is generally regarded as the greatest manifestation of Realpolitik, soft power plays such a crucial role. In fact, soft power can be described as the single most important source of strength on which a prince must rely to carry out the general mission envisioned by Machiavelli. Soft power, in short, is the very essence through which a prince can secure and maintain the loyalty of a civic population over time, and this of course is the key to building a political sphere of influence that can cast the foreign invaders out of Italy and orchestrate a peaceful co-existence on the Italian peninsula. No doubt, *The Prince* reveals its author to be an impresario of hard power politics, in one respect vindicating traditional Realist interpretations of this masterwork. But Machiavelli's vision of power is much more pluralistic than the Realpolitik interpretation. The strength of a state depends on strategies and resources that can deliver the effective use of force and coercion (the hard side of influence), but the lexicon of influence includes a number of important softer elements, most of which are oriented around a prince endearing himself to his people through strategies and actions that honor pervasive republican norms and expectations regarding civil governance. In this respect, Machiavelli, like his fellow classical founding fathers of Realism, can best be described as a Cosmopolitan Realist. He too expounds a more moderated philosophy that can be found somewhere along the continuum between the extreme poles of hard and soft power.

[48] In reality, the celebrated catechism of the means and ends is misunderstood. Machiavelli never actually states a personal belief that the ends justify the means, only that the masses are swayed by the ends and would therefore be more accommodating to the means that attained those ends. Interestingly, for Machiavelli, a wise prince should be aware of this popular predisposition in order to maintain his soft power. In this respect, Lincoln was far more Machiavellian (i.e., the logic commonly attributed to Machiavelli) than Machiavelli in directly espousing the legitimacy of violent means for a noble end (to preserve the union of the American states). See especially De Alvarez (1999, 90).

The soft power revealed in *The Prince* is primarily conceptualized within a setting of domestic governance, so it relates more to the domestic sources of soft power (embodied in liberal constitutional principles of governance) enumerated in Chapter 1 (see Table 1 in Chapter 1). Although these sources of power apply to a domestic political context (i.e., the objectives of princes within their domestic political regimes), they also have strong implications for an international political context. Thus, the lessons about soft power in *The Prince* also carry important messages for scholars interested in the international manifestations of power.

Machiavelli wrote The *Prince* to guide autocrats, but he was above all an ardent republican in terms of his political philosophy (Femia 2004; Bok, Skinner, and Viroli 1990; Rudowski 1992; Pocock 1975). This is most obvious in his *Discourses*, in which he engages in a monumental veneration of republican governance (Machiavelli 1996). This republican orientation does not disappear in *The Prince*, but it permeates the book. Whereas governance in the cases of principalities remains autocratic de jure, for Machiavelli the actual mode of governance by the prince *must* remain consistent with republican principals. In his own words, principalities must be run in a "civil tradition."[49] This involves a head of state endearing himself to his people through extensive and systematic regard for pervasive expectations about political rights and privileges among civic populations. Any deviance from such principles of civil governance that lead people to feel oppressed is to be avoided by the prince at all costs, because with the people as "adversaries, [the prince] has no remedy" (P, 9, 70). Indeed, the *Discourses* and *The Prince* are testaments to Machiavelli's belief that states can become great only through good laws, as highlighted by the numerous examples of Rome and Sparta (Skinner 1981, 59, 60, 72; Mansfield 1979, 46, 81).

Machiavelli proves to be above all an advocate of the separation of powers within a pluralist government (Mansfield 1979, 38–40, 1996, 23; Femia 2004, 67; Viroli 1998a, 117; Fischer 2000, 127–29; Skinner 1981,

[49] In chapter 9 of *The Prince*, Machiavelli refers to a principality governed through the "favor of the people" (P, 9, 68) as a "civil" principality. Although power can be attained without popular support, it is clear that to maintain such authority the prince must endear himself over time: "[F]or a prince it is necessary to have his people as a friend" (P, 9, 70). Above all, the prince must avoid "oppressing" the people.

73–76).[50] He believes strongly in checks and balances as a barrier to the advent of tyranny. In the *Discourses*, which as a didactic work embodies an attempt to inspire Florentine leaders to replicate ancient Roman governmental institutions, he praises the Roman constitution (D, II, 1) because it combined elements of monarchy, aristocracy, and democracy (Guarini 1990, 29; Viroli 1998b, 154, 184; Skinner 1981, 79). According to Machiavelli, the optimal government "shared in all [three], judging firmer and more stable [than a single type of governance]; for the one guards the other, since in one and the same city there are the principality, the aristocrats and the popular government" (D, I, 2, 5).[51] Hence, whereas Machiavelli occasionally distinguishes between nominal forms of government in both *The Prince* and *Discourses*, he essentially conflates them in thinking about how governments functioned in his own time and how they should function in an optimal sense. In this regard, there is far greater continuity between his two great works (i.e., with respect to a theory of optimal political institutions) than has traditionally been acknowledged (Skinner 1990; Femia 2004; Virioli 1990, 1998). Machiavelli's term *vivere civile* ("civil governance") embodies this idea of governance unfolding within well-defined laws and political norms oriented around the communal interests of a people, which for Machiavelli should become the principal goal of a head of state (Guarini 1990, 34; Viroli 1990, 153; Viroli 1998a, 47).

Machiavelli's de facto republican orientation is neither surprising nor historically exceptional. The idea that republican governance in Europe was a product of early modern democratic movements is a popular myth and a product of historical exceptionalism. The Roman republic may have fallen, but Roman republican political institutions remained and evolved in historical context. Civil governance in Renaissance Italian states was

[50] Machiavelli was part of a group of literati who were pronounced advocates of republicanism in Florence, some of whom were persecuted for their beliefs (Skinner 1981, 57, 58). For especially insightful biographical portrayals of how Machiavelli's life and work fused, see De Grazia (1989), Skinner (1981), and Viroli (1998b).

[51] Citing Rome specifically, Machiavelli hails its ability to fuse different loci of political authority (branches) to form a stable government: "[R]emaining mixed, it formed a perfect republic" (D, I, 2. 7). In the *Discourses*, he marshals especially scathing diatribes against tyranny. For Machiavelli, the excessive accumulation of power in a monarchy, a clear manifestation of hard disempowerment, leads to a dangerous power illusion. The greater the consolidation, the greater will be the civil and elite discord fomented (negative feedback), and so what appears to be an augmentation of power in reality devolves into a more fragile regime because of the countervailing actions of aggrieved citizens and aristocrats. See *Discourses* (D, I, 2; D, I, 45. 3; D, I, 58. 3).

very much the rule, except in the most severe circumstances, irrespective of the de jure systems of governance that prevailed. Machiavelli poignantly declares the supremacy of republics throughout the *Discourses*. No autocrat or oligarch exists above the law in his ideal political community (D, I, 9; D, I, 16; D, I, 10; D, I, 45; D, I, 58. 3; D, III, 34. 3).[52]

The title of *The Prince* itself is a testament to Machiavelli's strong affinity for such a tradition of civil governance. The Latin title of the work is *De Prinipatibus*. This is a direct reference to the Roman principate. It was Caesar Augustus who replaced the title of "dictator," used by Julius Caesar, with that of "prince." This idea of civil tradition appears early in *The Prince* (in chapter 2), when Machiavelli discusses hereditary principalities. Such principalities are easier to govern, easier to hold, and easier to reacquire if lost precisely because of a continuity of governance across generations. Machiavelli strongly prescribes such stability in governance, "not to break with the orders of one's ancestors," which will ensure that the prince maintains public support (P, 2, 43). In light of the argument he makes in chapter 3 ("On Mixed Principalities"), the logic of de facto civil republicanism, even under an autocrat, appears compelling (Pocock 1975, 163). Machiavelli notes that people only "change their lord if they believe they will be better off" and that if changes are made without their consent, "men will take up arms against [their prince]" (P, 3, 43). Continuity within and across generations suggests that civic populations are generally satisfied with a particular bloodline (*assuefatti* to a *sangue*) and thus are essentially ruled by consent. This suggests a strongly perceived contractarian element that functions as a de facto constitution; some set of perceived rights and privileges is to be preserved according to time-honored political norms and customs (Pocock 1975, 158; De Alvarez 1999, 12, 13). In short, political survival is strongly grounded in the soft power of civil governance and consent, rather than in the hard power embodied in weapons and the threat of violence. Tyranny or repressive political regimes that employ such coercive measures will cause civic populations to rebel against heads of state (i.e., hard disempowerment). Princes will risk losing their states when they forsake such political norms and customs – what Machiavelli calls *ordini* (Whitfield 1977, 199).

[52] On this republican political legacy and continuity through the Middle Ages, see especially Lindsay (1962, chapter 2), Poggi (1978, chapter 2), Pocock (1975), and Ganshof (1996). On Renaissance Italian republicanism, see Bock, Skinner, and Viroli (1990), Viroli (1998a), Butters (1985), Hay and Law (1989), and Pocock (1975).

Machiavelli's concept of soft empowerment and hard disempowerment as relating to civil governance exhibits central roles for feedback and x-efficiency effects. Civil governance can empower in manifold ways. Feedback effects can be strongly positive, and thus enhance the political position of a prince, if the prince fulfills his part of the contract. However, such contracts are not specified and leave much room for x-efficiencies in supporting the ruling regime (e.g., supporting the ruling regime in every possible way, whether or not it is expected by the prince). Conversely, both feedback and x-effects can work strongly against the ruling regime if the prince produces unfavorable political outcomes for the civic population (i.e., hard disempowerment). In this case, people will work against the ruling regime (negative feedback) in ways that contradict the direct requests of the prince (e.g., not carrying out explicit duties). These non–x actions will be further compounded by x-inefficiencies. People will, in fact, not miss any opportunity to weaken the regime through actions whose precise manifestations are not specified by a prince (e.g., not informing on insurgents or being lax in contributing to military and political initiatives supported by the prince).

The logic regarding the sanctity of political norms and civic consent is developed in the context of mixed principalities in chapter 3, which Machiavelli considers as a problem of political consolidation of new territories (such new territories were expected to be numerous if Lorenzo de Medici followed Machiavelli's plea to consolidate a northern Italian territory under the rule of Florence). Hereditary principalities are low maintenance if the prince has the good judgment not to "rock" the political boat, but acquiring new territories is a bit trickier. Even here, the soft power embodied in civil practices holds the key to acquiring and maintaining political influence over new populations. Acquisition is often a violent process, even if the war for acquisition is short (if acquisition is accomplished through military means). In the short term, the prince has to deal with significant adversarial elements; this is a simple function of "the injuries that a new acquisition brings with it" (P, 3, 43). Yet once the acquisition is made, a process of political consolidation must follow, which involves a transition from hard power (the power of the sword) to soft power (embodied in the institution of a civil political regime).

Machiavelli's discussion of acquisition continues in chapter 6, underscoring the value of virtue and using one's own arms. Machiavelli proposes two celebrated arguments about acquisition that seem to embrace a strong appreciation of hard power. One is his famous prescription that if subjects do not believe, "one can make them believe by force" (P, 6, 57).

The other is the glorification of the martial virtue of the armed prophets (Moses, Cyrus, Romulus, and Theseus), who, through the use of force, were able to secure great territories. However, both, when scrutinized, unfold within a logic that is actually consistent with Machiavelli's Cosmopolitan vision of balance between hard and soft power. The idea of imposing ideas by force is articulated within the context of acquiring territories where "new orders" are introduced. Here, Machiavelli reiterates the dangers and difficulties of regimes that discontinue old systems of governance that he underscores in chapter 3. Consistent with this logic, the use of force cannot be a long-term strategy for endearing a prince to a civic population. At best, force against a popular body may be threatened for a very short time. However, acquisition always produces some seeds of discontent (recalcitrance on the part of aggrieved minorities), as noted in chapter 3, so some form of force is necessary to police an existing regime. He cites the demise of Savonarola as an example of the dangers of trying to maintain a political regime without sufficient arms.[53] However, Savonarola's demise came as a result of external forces: Pope Alexander VI branded him a heretic, providing his opponents with the necessary support to overthrow him. Savonarola remained widely popular in Florence, with his followers continuing their activities well after his death. In this case, Savonarola lacked the minimal means (police and army) of defending himself against aggrieved domestic groups and external threats. Such a police/military function is not inconsistent with civil governance. On the contrary, it is a necessary part of governance. Here the Cosmopolitan idea of a balanced endowment of power resources is quite evident.

What of the armed prophets? Even here, the glorification of their accomplishments reinforces rather than undermines the need for soft power. Although the four prophets did acquire much through force, they are not portrayed as tyrants who ruled through threats and fear. Rather, they were "virtuous" men, not brutes, who were known for their wisdom and political savvy. They were great rulers because they were able to establish stable political orders ("ordini") for the public good (Whitfield 1977, 200). Arms helped them to acquire their kingdoms, but prudence and virtue were instrumental in maintaining those kingdoms (Pocock 1975,

[53] Savonarola was a cleric who was influential in the governance of Florence after the Medici exile in 1494, orchestrating numerous changes in the constitution and political practices in Florence. He was burned as a heretic after he came into conflict with the Papacy.

168–72).[54] In this case, consistent with the classical orientation of *The Prince*, Machiavelli proposes an ancient Greek, and hence Cosmopolitan, concept of virtue.[55] As noted above in the context of Thucydides, the Greek concept of virtue extolled diversity in character, a diversity composed of courage, practicality, intellectual curiosity, piety, hospitality, self-control, justice, prudence, preparation, wisdom, patience, and physical excellence (Williams 1998, 47). Above all, it extolled moderation. This Cosmopolitan golden mean is never forsaken in *The Prince*, even in its most heinous prescriptions. Machiavelli's prophets, like all of his heroes in the *Prince*, were very much men of such qualities and men of moderation. Otherwise, they would never have enjoyed such political success. The example of Cyrus is crucial here. In chapter 14, Machiavelli presents Cyrus as the epitome of a person whom a prince should use as a role model. Although Cyrus demonstrated the utility of hard power, he nonetheless achieved glory by combining muscle with the qualities of "chastity, affability, humanity, and liberality" (P, 14, 86).

Machiavelli's greatest hero in *The Prince*, Cesare Borgia, is especially exalted for his political perspicacity: a keen sense of how to build and maintain a stable regime in new territories. Although Borgia's chronicles in *The Prince* portray some dastardly deeds to gain and maintain power, he is most revered for his princely virtue in the use of soft power (Sasso 1977, 210; Whitfield 1977, 203). This is made quite clear in chapter 7. After taking the Italian province of Romagna, Borgia decided to secure an extremely unstable region with a strong-armed lord, Remirro de Orco. Eventually, however, Orco's repressive style became far more extreme than was necessary to maintain order in Romagna. Machiavelli recounts how Borgia "judged that such excessive authority was not necessary, because he worried that it would become hateful" (P, 7, 61). In this context, Borgia ordered Orco to be beheaded in a public square, thus rendering the people "satisfied" (P, 7, 62). This heinous act was perpetrated within the context of a political expediency grounded in the need to endear oneself politically by punishing what was perceived as a popular injustice, an act grounded in a civil conception of governance (Mansfield 1996, 187). The qualities he exalts in Borgia, in this respect, are based on soft power: "win friends for himself"; "followed and revered by his

[54] Soft power was instrumental in helping both Moses and Cyrus acquire their kingdoms. As Machiavelli notes, it was necessary for Moses to find the Israelites "enslaved and oppressed by the Egyptians" and for Cyrus to find "the Persians discontented under the empire of the Medes" (P, 6, 56).

[55] On Machiavellian virtue, see especially Pocock (1975), Plamenatz (1977), Mansfield (1996), and Viroli (1998a).

soldiers"; being "pleasing, magnanimous and liberal"; and "maintain[ed] the friendships of kings and princes" (P, 7, 64).

Chapter 8 follows, with Machiavelli's infamous discussion of principalities acquired by evil deeds and his prescription of perpetrating such cruelties "all at once" (P, 8, 68). However, we know that this way of acquiring territories, for Machiavelli, is the least preferred because it is the most hazardous. In recounting the story of Agathocles, who secured rule over Syracuse by ordering the execution of all the senators and many leading citizens in the town square, Machiavelli resoundingly condemns such acts: "[O]ne cannot call it virtue to kill one's fellow citizens, to betray one's friends, to be without faith, without compassion, without religion." Machiavelli goes on to state that such "methods may be used to acquire rule but not glory" (P, 8, 66). In this passage, he places the idea of virtue squarely outside a realm that calls for actions that violate well-regarded norms of civil governance. Agathocles and Livoretto the Fermano (who also perpetrated wicked deeds in gaining control over Fermo by killing his uncle and other leading citizens) may have gained "rule" over their territories, but they hardly attained glory because they acted in a non-virtuous manner. Machiavelli's prescription about perpetrating cruelties "all at once" to secure rule is evident in this context. Both men can be commended for disposing of such cruel acts quickly and simultaneously, but Machiavelli makes it clear that lasting rule cannot be founded on such cruelties (Sasso 1977, 210). In fact, such cruelties must be expedited and minimized by a prince "so as not to have to renew them every day, and to be able, by not renewing them, to secure the men and to win them to himself by benefiting them" (P, 8, 68).[56]

Chapter 9, "On the Civil Principality," represents an especially salient manifestation of Machiavelli's veneration of a prince endearing himself as the crucial source of political survival: "a prince can never secure himself against a hostile people" (P, 9, 69). Even in situations in which princes gain authority by way of nobles, it is still crucial for them to secure the support of the people. It is not enough to have only elite support.[57] A prince achieves this by winning "the people to himself"

[56] De Alvarez (1999, 41) underscores the political moderation in this infamous chapter, which seems to outwardly preach cruelty and wickedness in achieving political rule.

[57] This is an important testament to the necessity of public support, as here even the support of powerful elite groups is not enough to secure rule over a hostile public. Machiavelli has already ruled out the viability of rule by princely tyranny over a civic population, and now he rules out the only other viable alternative to a regime based on popular consent (oligarchic tyranny). As noted, no matter what the ruling structure, political rule cannot be sustained where people are "oppressed" (P, 9, 70).

(P, 9, 70). This, in turn, is accomplished when a prince "takes up their protection" (P, 9, 70). Yet protection has a strong internal component in terms of domestic governance – protecting rights and privileges that the public demands. As Machiavelli emphasizes, people "ask only not to be oppressed" (P, 9, 70). Avoiding oppression, however, is conceived as far more demanding than some minimal respect for civil rights and privileges. The prince must endear himself significantly if he is to prosper, and this certainly requires more than minimal republican practices and institutions. Machiavelli states, "[F]or a prince it is necessary to have his people as a friend, otherwise, in adversity, he has no remedy" (P, 9, 70). A "friend" connotes more than mere acceptance and tolerance; it connotes a political relationship that is perceived as beneficial to the public. To quote Machiavelli, "[A] wise prince must think of a way by which his citizens... have need of his state and of himself, and then they will always be faithful to him" (P, 9, 71). Machiavelli reaffirms his vision of civil populism by mocking the traditional absolutist proverb that "he who builds on the people, builds on mud" (P, 9, 70).[58] On the contrary, the people are the bedrock of political survival (Mansfield 1979, 79; 1996, 178).

Chapter 10 reinforces the need for such support but introduces an element of safety from external threats, which Machiavelli revisits more elaborately when he discusses the need for fortresses later in the text. In this sense, popular support is crucial to all threats to the political survival of a prince, both internal and external. In speaking about protection from external threats, Machiavelli does note that a prince needs substantial hard power (military) to "fortify and supply his own town," but even more importantly, the defense of a state relies on the loyalty and support of its citizens. Aside from "fortifying" a state, the prince should also have "managed himself concerning the other affairs of his subjects, as stated above and as will be said below" (P, 10, 72).[59] Managing these "other affairs" (i.e., affairs of domestic governance) entails gaining the favor of the people. Once such favor has been procured and the state fortified, the state and its prince become invulnerable: "[A] prince who has a strong city and does not make himself hated cannot be attacked" (P, 10, 72). In this

[58] This civil populism is strongly reaffirmed in the *Discourses*. See especially D, I, 16. 4; D, II, 28. 2; D, III, 6. 2; D, III, 19.

[59] The term "as stated above and as will be said below" refers to the plethora of prescriptions he has advanced throughout the text regarding the need for civil governance. This is an especially important statement because it is a testament to the pervasiveness within the text of Machiavelli's veneration of soft power based on endearment through republican institutions as the very essence of political survival.

sense, prospective attackers know well the perils of attacking a state where citizens will fight with passion to protect a favorable political relationship. Machiavelli underscores this point when he writes that "men are always enemies of undertakings that appear difficult, and it cannot seem easy to attack a man who holds his own town gallantly and is not hated by his people" (P, 10, 72). This logic is a strong manifestation of an explicit contract between citizen and ruler; each pledges to protect the other in a reciprocal fashion.[60] Princes provide a favorable set of political outputs in terms of implicit and explicit rights and privileges, while citizens support princes from both domestic and foreign foes as well as abide by their rules, according to both the letter (non–x-efficiencies) and the spirit (x-efficiencies) (Lukes 2001, 571; Pocock 1975, 200; Berridge 2001, 555; De Alvarez 1999, 48).

Even in discussions that are fundamentally of a military nature, in chapters 12 to 14 and later in the text, when he considers the subject of optimal fortifications, Machiavelli's logic underscores the importance of civil governance. He reiterates his Cosmopolitan prescription for both civil governance and sound defenses at the beginning of the principal chapters on preparing for warfare (12 to14): "The principal foundations that all states should have ... are good laws and good arms" (P, 12, 76). When engaging in warfare, states should be either represented by the prince himself, or by a "worthy man" in the case of a republic. Moreover, the soldiers should always be "his own" (i.e., citizens' militias). The latter prescription manifests the sentiment that citizens' militias have a greater incentive to fight for a prince (the contractual bond for political output and x-efficiencies), and they have no incentives to overthrow the prince if victorious (as they have a stake in the perpetuation of his rule in the said political contract). Sending another in his place and using mercenary soldiers would be "useless and dangerous" (i.e., very x-inefficient) (P, 12, 76).[61] It is in the context of this argument (i.e., reciprocal obligations under an implicit contract) that Machiavelli's famous aversion to hiring

[60] This also features an x-efficiency element in that in the face of imperfect contracts, popular affection will render the people more committed to defending the regime and contributing to its prosperity.

[61] This is an argument Machiavelli reiterates in the *Discourses* (D, I, 21). In this context, he evokes a recognition of the problem of hard disempowerment with respect to effects of moral hazard. Having the hard power to defend oneself (large armies and mercenaries) may lead to a false sense of security and thus to complacency in developing the soft power to effectively activate one's indigenous military capacity. If these armies are not backed up by civil principles that lead soldiers to fight gallantly, then the power and invulnerability deriving from great hard power resources are only illusory. He repeats such a recognition when talking about the need for fortresses in chapter 20.

mercenaries or using auxiliary armies for protection becomes most clearly understood (Mansfield 1996, 187).[62]

Chapter 14 articulates another famous prescription, that "a prince must have no other object or thought...save warfare and its institutions" (P, 14, 84). Machiavelli's hard power side is most visible here. But does this mean that Machiavelli envisioned his prince as merely a militaristic brute bent on unbridled gain through the use of force, as popular interpretations of *The Prince* maintain? The argument Machiavelli develops suggests something far different. First, military training was not conceptualized as independent from human development – an important ingredient in a classical vision of human virtue (P, 1, 85). But beyond this, preparation for war was consistent with the dictates of civil leadership. The prince was the "commander" and protector of the people. Deficiencies in his abilities to protect his citizens would naturally make a prince less of a leader, one who "cannot be esteemed by his soldiers nor trusted" (P, 14, 85).[63] Finally, the language regarding the military orientation espoused in this chapter is very much defensive rather than expansionist. As noted above, military excellence is cast as a means to "defend" a prince's citizens. Machiavelli puts forth the principal reason for such excellence at the end of the chapter, when he notes that such excellence is in the service of responding to "adversities." In this sense, it is defensive because adversities are brought about by external misfortunes (i.e., "fortune"); wise princes do not, as a rule, invite misfortune through reckless acts of expansionism. This is clear in his veneration of the Achean prince Philopoemen, who trained for war in times of peace. His strategic exercises involved speculations among his officers on how to respond to various assaults by their "enemies" (P, 14, 86). The decisive affirmation of the idea of enlightened commander marshaled by Machiavelli in *The Prince* appears in this chapter as well. He cites Scipio's imitation of Cyrus as bringing him glory, and the qualities most celebrated were (as with Cyrus) Scipio's "chastity, affability, humanity, and liberality" (P, 14, 86). That soft power is an essential component even in Machiavelli's own logic on military conduct is an exceptional testament to Machiavelli's Cosmopolitan orientation (De Alvarez 99, 139).

62 Machiavelli's distaste for mercenaries exudes the manifestations of x-inefficiencies; paid soldiers have little incentive to fight their hardest in the cause of their employer because they derive only pay and have no stake in the political benefits of his ruling regime.

63 Lukes (2001) demonstrates that even some of Machiavelli's most militant prescriptions in *The Prince*, like the metaphor of the "lion," fundamentally manifest normative elements suggesting a regard for the public good.

A high point in Machiavelli's veneration of soft power as a significant ingredient of princely virtue appears in chapters 15 through 20, with chapter 20 especially noteworthy. These chapters form a cohesive set of arguments founded on the optimal "qualities of the prince" (De Alvarez 1999, 139). No other portion of the text is as poignant an articulation of what Machiavelli thinks a prince should be and how a prince should comport himself. In Machiavelli's words, these chapters address "what should be the ways and conduct of a prince" (P, 15, 87). The idea of the imperatives of necessity as guidelines to action are very apparent here, especially in his famous prescription that a prince must "be able to be not good, and to use this faculty and not use it according to necessity" (P, 15, 87). Machiavelli appears to reveal the classic Realist moral reversion of virtues and vices that was expressed so clearly in chapter 13 of Hobbes' *The Leviathan* (De Alvarez 1999, 80). Thus, in a world where people "are not good," a good prince will come to "ruin" (P, 15, 87). Machiavelli goes on to list various qualities, each occupying opposite tendencies within specific behavioral continua (e.g., chaste versus lascivious, honest versus crafty, hard versus flexible). However, there is no objective sense of which serve as virtues and which serve as vices; it is completely conditional on necessity. Is this Realist amorality? In a literal and noncontextual sense, it appears to be. But in the context of Machiavelli's republican orientation, this is hardly the case. In this context, necessity itself is driven by a pervasive political morality founded on republican practices. For Machiavelli, a prince may indulge in many different kinds of actions that appear prima facie to be vices, but this does not mean he is functioning outside the political boundaries set by civil principles of governance. In fact, it is these boundaries that dictate which actions will prevail under specific necessities and how those actions will be judged. Ultimately, the definition of virtue versus vice will be determined by the compatibility of actions and principles of civil governance.

This becomes clear in chapter 16, in which he compares the opposing qualities of liberality (i.e., generosity in spending) and parsimony within a political context. He notes that in a noncontextual assessment, the quality of liberality is generally held to be virtuous and that of parsimony is considered to be a vice. Yet in a political context, Machiavelli's logic suggests that this nomenclature is deceiving. A profligate prince may produce great public works and effective military campaigns for the greater glory of his state, but in doing so, he must "burden his people extraordinarily" through taxation. With this so-called virtuous liberality, the prince "has offended the many" and consequently "is imperiled" (P, 16, 88).

Therefore, "a prince cannot use this virtue of the liberal man in such a way that it is recognized without harm to himself" (P, 16, 88, 89). And if he retreats from such liberality, he "incurs the infamy of [the name] miser" (P, 16, 88). Here, though, Machiavelli contends that in such a context, the prince ought not "to worry about the name miser.... for this is one of those vices that let him rule" (P, 16, 89). Machiavelli goes on to say, "For with time he will be thought even more liberal ... [because] his revenues are sufficient for him, he can defend himself from whoever makes war on him, and he can make campaigns without burdening his people" (P, 16, 89). Machiavelli nicely summarizes the dichotomy of virtue and vice within a political context at the end of chapter 15, in which he writes, "... if everything be well considered, something will be found that will appear a virtue, but will lead to [a prince's] ruin if adopted; and something else that will appear a vice, if adopted, will result in his security and well-being (P, 15, 88).

Machiavelli in fact mocks the objective distinction of virtue and vice when applied to a political context – that is, he facetiously interchanges the terms *vice* and *virtue* (Sasso 1977). In such a context, the nature of princely qualities is judged by the political consequences of the actions, and such judgment is driven by the necessities dictated by popular expectations of civil governance. Machiavelli thus attacks the idea of an amoral conflation of virtue and vice by placing the dichotomy within a fundamental political morality determined by republican principles. In essence, expectations driven by principles of civil governance dictate which qualities and actions a prince *should* adopt, which drive perceptions of necessity. Hence, the Realist conception of necessity is infused by Machiavelli with a deeper sense of political ethics.

Chapter 20, on the usefulness of fortresses, is the ultimate testament to the role of soft power and the dangers of hard disempowerment in *The Prince* and places the implications for Machiavelli's domestic soft power firmly in an interstate context. In chapter 19, he makes it clear that a prince is vulnerable to internal and external threats. The former are abated through civil governance, whereas the latter are dealt with through "good arms and good allies" (P, 19, 96). In chapter 20, the distinction between outer and inner security for a prince disappears (Mansfield 1979, 266). The source of internal security is also proclaimed to be the source of external security – a regime founded on civil principles. Machiavelli argues that a prince must arm his subjects for protection against outside threats. The prince would have no other choice, because in the absence of large standing armies (i.e., in an age of militias), the only other alternative lies in mercenaries (a cure worse than the disease). If there is any question about Machiavelli's affinities for principalities founded on republican practices (and his disdain for tyranny), it dies here. A prince is forced to deliver political outcomes in a republican manner, as this will cultivate the loyalty of those who determine his fate. In this vein, his argument about fortresses unfolds. Fortresses are for princes who are not secure – that is, they rely on walls rather than popular loyalty (an argument first introduced in chapter 10).[64] But in the absence of the latter, no wall can stand up to outside aggression. In fact, disloyal subjects will help outsiders topple those walls. He states that "the best fortress there is is not to be hated by the people" (P, 20, 108). Indeed, loyal subjects will defend a prince like no other army (x-efficiently), whereas disloyal subjects would create the greatest vulnerabilities (x-inefficiencies). He goes on to underscore this prescription (in chapter 26) in the context of his most important didactic goal in writing *The Prince* – the liberation of Italy.

The discussions of fortresses, and mercenaries versus loyal militias are the clearest references in *The Prince* to Machiavelli's concern for the dangers of hard disempowerment. What are perceived to be assets that increase a prince's strength and diminish his vulnerability (fortifications, paid soldiers, and weapons) become in effect manifestations of exactly the opposite outcomes. In fact, excessive dependence on such hard power resources may make a prince complacent about maintaining the soft power necessary for the protection of his state (i.e., moral hazard) and so compromise its security. This also mirrors an inversion process in which Machiavelli indulges when he treats the subject of virtues versus vices. What appear to be sources of strength could very well turn into afflictions (or symbols of afflictions) that weaken a prince, just as seemingly apparent virtues can become vices. The lessons in soft power marshaled by Machiavelli throughout *The Prince* are conceived as warnings to princes against falling into the trap of hard disempowerment.

After arguments have been presented throughout the text regarding the necessity of domestic support through civil governance as the taproot of political survival, chapter 21 specifies such conduct to a greater extent. Until this chapter, Machiavelli speaks in fairly vague terms about princely comportment, especially in chapters 15 and 16, in which he

[64] Machiavelli reinforces the value of people over walls in the *Discourses* (D, II, 24).

contrasts diametrically opposed princely actions. The only attribute with specific applications to political strategy is profligacy, which could lead to burdensome taxation policies. Chapter 21, in didactic fashion, spins an interesting strategic plan. The prince should "encourage his citizens to... practice their trades," allow them to "improve [their] properties [and] open a business [without fear that] they will be taken away [or] fear of taxes," provide ample "feast days and spectacles," meet with the various prominent political groups (neighborhoods, guilds), "offer himself as an example of humanity and munificence," give "hospitality to virtuous men," and "honor those who are excellent in an art" (P, 21, 111). Such a political recipe for governance was stereotypical of an Italian city-state during the height of the Renaissance, and it mattered little whether it was a republic or principality. In this sense, as noted above, Machiavelli was a loyal child of the Renaissance with respect to Italian political philosophy (Bock, Skinner, and Viroli 1990; Pocock 1975).

Even with the exaltation of force and cruelty in this chapter as vehicles to engender popular favor for a prince, civil principles are never compromised. Machiavelli notes that a prince can gain esteem through "great campaigns and giving rare examples of himself" (P, 21, 108). The examples he uses are compelling. In terms of military campaigns, he celebrates Ferdinand's push into southern Spain. But this was consistent with civil expectations; the campaign was considered one of liberation from non-Christians (a Crusade), and it was not financed in a manner that burdened the people, as the Church picked up a great many expenses. Machiavelli's example of princely spectacle centers on public displays of cruelty by Bernabo of Milan, who had a reputation for torturing and killing transgressors in public places. But even here, Bernabo's spectacles were generally hailed as just punishments for heinous and despicable crimes, so they exuded the appeal of a popular public hanging.[65] Moreover, in the context of spectacles, Machiavelli hails the other side as well, stating that "rewarding" great deeds was as important as punishing transgressions (P, 21, 109).

Bernabo's spectacles reflect a pattern in Machiavelli's political philosophy behind the princely use of cruel acts. Cruelty was a means of governance, but never the foundation of governance. Even as a means, Machiavelli shows that it should be administered within a civil context

[65] Connell (2005, 109) quotes Franco Saccetti's famous *Trecentonovelle* on Bernabo's reputation: "However cruel he was, still in his cruelties, he had very much justice."

(Sasso 1977; Mansfield 1996, 18). The dastardly deeds of cruelty that are chronicled and commended in *The Prince* tend to be isolated acts against either individuals or small groups (Lukes 2001, 572). They are never sustained abuses against larger populations within the princes' states.[66] Indeed, it is a compelling message of *The Prince* that such a style of tyrannical governance would lead to political suicide. Even the isolated acts of cruelty of Bernabo, Liverotto of Fermo, and Cesare Borgia are all perpetrated in a manner consistent with public consent. Based on Machiavelli's distinction between fear and hatred in chapter 17, cruelties need not make you hated if they are carried out in a manner consistent with civil principles (Viroli 1990, 169). Indeed, cruelties must be justified by popular expectations regarding such principles. According to Machiavelli, the prince "should do it when there is appropriate justification and manifest cause" (P, 17, 93). Hence, the idea of cruelty is a salient manifestation of the Machiavellian reversion – a conceptualization of a politically virtuous use of cruelty.[67] This also sheds some light on his famous quote "it is much safer to be feared than loved," which has been hailed as a classic Machiavellian vindication of hard power (P, 17, 91). Yet in the context of his logic, "fear" is cast more as a legitimate means through which authority is exercised. Indeed, this is quite distinct from acts that engender hatred (i.e., illegitimate uses of authority). Even here, Machiavelli underscores the optimality of the Cosmopolitan golden mean when he notes that a prince should be both feared and loved.

The Prince culminates with a call to liberate the Italian states from the "barbarians" that occupy them. Although the literal structure of *The Prince* suggests that the last three chapters (24–26) represent a break in continuity with the rest of the text, the logic within this exhortation to liberate Italy very much continues the general argument that permeates the text – the need for civil governance. The exhortation to free Italy is fundamentally an exhortation for such civil governance. First, the liberation will reestablish Italian regimes that practice a civil tradition of governance. But just as importantly, the very success of such a campaign, which Machiavelli encourages Lorenzo de Medici to undertake, will depend on

[66] As noted above, certain conditions such as war or newly acquired territories may warrant short-term deviations from civil governance, but such methods cannot be sustained over longer periods according to Machiavellian logic.

[67] This theme is picked up in the *Discourses*, in which he praises Romulus and Cleomenes for murdering tyrannical autocrats for the purpose of preserving a civil way of life in Rome and Sparta respectively (D, I, 9. 2–4). See also D, III, 3.

Lorenzo's ability to implement Machiavelli's recommendations for optimal governance in Florence and its associated states (Whitfield 1977, 2000). He implores the young Lorenzo to undertake the liberation of Italy with his own Florentine subjects, for Lorenzo could not find "more true or better soldiers" as long as they "are honored and treated warmly" (i.e., x-efficient subjects) (P, 26, 122). Additionally, the campaign would be perceived as "just" by all of the Italians who take part in the liberation. And because of this perception of a just war, "there is a greatest readiness, and where there is great readiness there cannot be great difficulty" (P, 26, 120, 121).

Interestingly, Machiavelli's condemnation of the atrocities of barbarian occupation recalls the protests marshaled by the founding fathers of the American Revolution. The affinities with Jefferson's (1774/2006) *Summary View of the Rights of British America* are striking. Jefferson's assault on Britain's unwarranted encroachments, usurpations, and tyranny precisely mirror Machiavelli's castigation of the barbaric cruelties and insolences perpetrated in Italy by foreign invaders.[68] *The Prince* ends poetically with a passage from Petrarch's famous poem *Italia Mia*, and the poetry nicely encapsulates Machiavelli's Cosmopolitan political philosophy. Machiavelli speaks of the "virtue" of Italian city-states in "taking up arms" against the "fury" of oppressive barbarians occupying Italy and he goes to say that the "struggle" will be fueled by the "valor . . . in Italian hearts" (P, 26, 123). This is the ultimate call to liberate Italy. In this case, valor will win over fury because the sword of valor is sharpened by passion, a passion that has been cultivated within Italians by a prince who has "honored and treated [the people] warmly." No opposing army could withstand such a cadre, for there could not be "more faithful, more true or better soldiers" (P, 26, 122). In essence, the soft power cultivated by the wise prince will give him the means to liberate Italian city-states, for there can be no force that could withstand an army that is fighting for the acquisition and retention of civil governance.[69]

68 In a sense, was Machiavelli really all that different from Cavour, who also preached severe measures for the liberation and unification of Italy? Yet one was idolized and the other vilified. A more resolute Lorenzo de Medici might very well have turned Machiavelli into a national hero.

69 This conceptualization of the international effect of domestic soft power recalls the work of Reiter and Stam (2002), who show that democracies can be more effective in attaining their international goals because dependence on public consent makes their foreign policy initiatives (especially war) more resolute and effective (i.e., more x-efficient).

In sum, Machiavelli has been most recognized for his veneration of hard power politics, but a careful reading of his manifesto, *The Prince*, attests to the richness and diversity of a more Cosmopolitan vision of political power. A prince needs a great deal of muscle, but he also needs to demonstrate a softer side. Each alone is insufficient to guarantee a prince's safety and prosperity, but together they prove a formidable combination.

3

Crucial-Case Textual Analysis of the Founding Fathers of Realism

The Modern Inspirations

Continuing in the crucial-case textual assessment of the theory of Cosmopolitan power undertaken in the great works of Realism, attention is now turned to the modern works that most inspired contemporary Realist thinking in international relations: E. H. Carr's *The Twenty Years' Crisis 1919–1939* and Hans Morgenthau's *Politics among Nations*. As in the cases of the classical Realists, it would be all too easy to cull passages from Carr and Morgenthau's other works and proclaim them anything but precursors to contemporary Realists that venerate the role of hard power in international relations. Assessing many of Carr's other works might brand him a flaming Utopian or an anti-Realist – the very ideologies he vehemently condemns as naive in passages of his famous *The Twenty Years' Crisis 1919–1939*. According to his autobiography (Carr 2000, xix), Carr became disillusioned with Realism with the advent of World War II and went on to write two books that he called "Utopian" in nature: *Conditions of Peace* and *Nationalism and After*. Yet this would hardly raise any questions about his acclaimed articulation of the need for national leaders to consider the importance of hard power (and not be blinded by the lure of Utopianism) in forging a stable peace in his magnum opus *The Twenty Years' Crisis 1919–1939*, which has remained a principal vindication of hard power politics.

Morgenthau too could be an easy target of drastic revisionism if his other writings were considered. His *Scientific Man Versus Power Politics* (1967) exhibits strong elements of post-positivism and theology. In many ways, his indictment of secularity, rationalism, and science cuts at the epistemological foundations of Realpolitik. He writes that the exaggerated hope in the social healing powers of modern reason and science "has left man the poorer and made the burden of life harder to bear" (125). Indeed, modernity has repressed the emotional and religious side of humanity, leaving it in an inferior state. Developing the logical implications of this book could easily make a case for Morgenthau as a Constructivist or Postmodernist.

Of course, as noted, neither Morgenthau nor Carr stand as least likely targets for crucial-cases textual evaluations of the merits of soft power. Few would be surprised by claims that each embraced the role of ethical phenomena within the relations among nations. Yet as Lynch (1994, 592, 593) notes, although Morgenthau and Carr embraced the possibilities of ethical actions, they are still unlikely supporters of a Constructivist or Neoliberal vision of world politics. Indeed, in large part, their great works still stand as indictments of the categories of action embraced by these paradigms.

However, like the classical Realists considered in chapter 2, both Carr and Morgenthau also prove to be consummate Cosmopolitan Realists in that they believe the essence of national influence resides at the intersection of a respect for well-regarded international norms and institutions, and the ability to marshal hard power resources. Ultimately, for Carr and Morgenthau, their principal sources of soft power (respect for international norms and institutions) coalesce to generate perceptions of endearment, which deliver manifold opportunities for influence to nations in the international system and concomitantly limit the dangers that are ever present in that system. In this respect, although their visions of politics are applied in very different contexts, and their specific sources of soft power show some variation from the classical Realists, they share the unifying theme manifest in the work of the latter in their visions of the empowering qualities of endearment and the disempowering qualities of excessive reliance on hard power. They, too, embrace the golden Cosmopolitan mean on the continuum between the extreme pole of hard power and its antithesis, the pole of soft power.

Edward Hallett Carr

Modern Realpolitik and its veneration of hard power politics in the context of international relations begins with E. H. Carr's masterwork, *The Twenty Years' Crisis 1919–1939* (hereafter referred to as *Twenty Years' Crisis*) (Evans 1975, 77; Kubalkova 1998, 26; Wilson 2000, 183). Gilpin (1986, 306) cites Carr as one of the "three great realist writers." Mearsheimer (2001, 14) hails the book as one of the three most influential

Realist texts of the twentieth century. International relations scholars have come to view Carr's *Twenty Years' Crisis* as a "masterly defense of Machiavellian Realism" (Cox 2000, 2). His warning in the preface to the second edition of the book marshals the mantra that so inspired budding sympathizers of a hard power political perspective in international relations. Carr divulges a principal reason for writing the book: to warn people and scholars of the dangers of the prevalent interwar ideology of indulging in Utopian hopes of peace in the interwar years while neglecting the influence of hard power on the course of world affairs (Carr 1964, viii).[1] Not only has it served as a taproot to modern Realist theory, but it also represents one of the first attempts to introduce a political science of international relations (Kubalkova 1998, Rich 2000, Wilson 2000). In Carr's first chapter, he extols the virtues of rigorously analyzing the state of affairs in politics, a call that mirrors a reaction to a heretofore dominant tendency among students and practitioners of politics toward "Utopianism" – the propensity to place aspirations and wishful thinking above systematic analysis of how politics actually unfolds in reality (Carr 1964, 8). The book begins as a vindication of the superiority of careful analysis of the "way things are" to the "naive" expectations of deluded Utopians. Regarding the latter, Carr states, "The course of events after 1931 clearly revealed the inadequacy of pure aspiration as a basis [for understanding the post-war world]" (Carr 1964, 9). The natural response to this misguided optimism, for Carr, was an appreciation of the role of hard power in shaping international outcomes. As Utopian prescriptions for a lasting and stable international political order failed, the world was confronted with a harsh reality. Carr notes that "the point is soon reached where the initial stage of wishing must be succeeded by a stage of hard and ruthless analysis" (Carr 1964, 9). It is through such analysis that people will discern the importance of hard power politics as the saving grace that the interwar period needed to bring people back to a reasonable understanding of the problems that beset them. And with that understanding, they would be better able to navigate the rough waters to peace and prosperity.

However, in the theoretical chapters that launch the book (chapters 1 and 2, "The Beginnings of a Science" and "Utopia and Reality"), we see Carr already distancing himself from the extreme pole of hard power politics and taking a firm Cosmopolitan position between two

[1] The edition of *Twenty Years' Crisis* used is a reprint of the second edition of 1946 that was published in 1964.

extremes. The purpose of the book (bashing interwar Utopians over the head with a Realpolitk hammer) unfortunately serves to obfuscate the more complex and Cosmopolitan nature of Carr's thinking. Summoning the Realpolitik brigade to fight the dangerous misconceptions of Utopians distracts us from the fact that Carr embraced both very strongly. What he called Utopianism and Realism, are, in fact, conceived of as dangerous extremes.[2] His call for more Realism merely conveys a belief that the interwar ideology had shifted to a Utopian extreme, and such "naïve" beliefs were dangerous because they shifted policy away from some healthy middle ground. Carr wrote that "there is a stage where realism is the necessary corrective to the exuberance of Utopianism, just as in other periods Utopianism must be invoked to counteract the barrenness of realism" (Carr 1964, 10). According to his biographer, Carr saw himself as a modern Machiavelli in that he brought the idea of power into an age dominated by ethics (Haslam 1999, 72).[3] His call was not to replace one extreme with another, but to interject some systematic understanding of power politics into the heads of the Utopian visionaries. Indeed, Carr is most vociferous about the dangers of being exclusively a Realist. He states that Realism "depreciates the role of purpose... [and engenders a disposition that one is] powerless to influence or alter events." Carr continues with the statement that "such an attitude... may be carried to the point where it results in the sterilization of thought and the negation of action" (Carr 1964, 10). He goes on to condemn each extreme as "immature" or "old age" and concludes, "Mature thought combines purpose (i.e., Utopian action) with observation and analysis (Realism's systematic understanding of actual events). Utopia and reality are thus the two necessary facets of political science.[4] Sound political thought and a sound

[2] Carr uses the terms *Realism* and *Utopianism* throughout *Twenty Years' Crisis* to convey extreme poles on a continuum. Realism is equated with considerations of pure power politics, wherein policies and visions of international politics exhibit exclusive reliance on hard power resources to shape international outcomes. Utopianism is equated with exclusive reliance on the power of ethics and institutions (regimes, international organizations) to shape such outcomes.

[3] On the life of Carr, see also Jones (1998), Cox (2001b), and Carr (2000).

[4] Dunne (2000, 224–6) argues that it was this didactic use of Realism as an "epistemic weapon" that led both Realists and Idealists to misunderstand *Twenty Years' Crisis*. Idealists branded it iconoclastic, whereas Realists "colonized" it. Dunne (2000) and Linklater (2000) situate Carr's philosophy more robustly in the Utopian mainstream of interwar intellectuals. After all, the book was dedicated to "the makers of the coming peace." Haslam (1999, 70) and Evans (1975, 95) identify a strand of Victorian liberalism (which Carr, in fact, criticized in *Twenty Years' Crisis*) in Carr that was consistently visible in his writings.

political environment will be found only where they coexist (Carr 1964, 10).[5] Haslam (2000, 23) notes that Carr exhibited "two hearts beating in the same breast." Linklater (1997, 323) credits Carr with finding a "third way" between Realism and Idealism.

Constructivists and Neoliberals might lament that Carr was born too late. Carr embraced Realism so vigorously in his magnum opus because, as noted, the period under analysis suffered from an excess of Utopian naiveté about the power of international law to be able to deliver a system of peaceful change independently of material power. In the nineteenth century, however, Carr's analysis would have been much more outspoken about the neglect of Utopianism in international relations. Hence, an earlier birthday without a career change might have delivered the first modern Neoliberal or Constructivist.

The synthetic nature of Carr's logic makes him most difficult to classify (Howe 1994, 277). Indeed, many labels have been marshaled: post-Realist, Utopian Realist, optimistic Realist, liberal Realist, post-positivist, reluctant Realist, proto-Constructivist, post-nationalist, liberal communitarian, and welfare internationalist (Evans 1975, 88; Booth 1991, 531; Kubalkova 1998, 25; Howe 1994, 279; Linklater 2000, 240). Not surprisingly, this synthetic vision of international affairs invoked harsh criticism from both Realists and non-Realists. From the Realist camp, Morgenthau attacked him on many fronts, not the least of which included accusations of moral relativism. Idealists of the period reacted with consternation at what they perceived to be a cynical escape to power politics. Even scholars in the middle (like Hedley Bull) took Carr to task for his proposed marriage of Realism and Idealism (Howe 1994; Johnson 1967; Evans 1975; Booth 1991; Rich 2000; Dunne 2000; Linklater 2000; Wilson 2000).

Carr's advocacy of a "science" of politics merges well with this idea of Cosmopolitan balance. Political science has a prescriptive goal in addition to the scientific goal of understanding reality: attend to the body politic by seeking a balance between extremes (Carr 1964, 3, 9). These extremes are cast as antitheses that Carr presents as manifestations of the fundamental antithesis in Utopianism and reality: free will versus

[5] The 1990s produced a number of scholarly works that would partially reclaim Carr from the legacy of a Realist "colonization" by underscoring the more progressive postmodern, radical, Neoliberal and Constructivist elements in Carr's Utopian sympathies. See Booth (1991), Lynch (1994), Howe (1994), Jones (1997 and 1998), Falk (1997), Linklater (1997, 2000), Kubalkova (1998), Cox (1999, 2000), Dunn (2000), Rich (2000), and Wilson (2000, 2001). An early revisionist was Evans (1975). For an extensive review of the literature on Carr, see Cox (2001a).

determination, theory versus practice, intellectual versus bureaucrat, left versus right, and, finally, ethics versus politics. The first elements in each pair are manifestations of Utopianism and thus are well grounded in soft power: Utopian ideology embraces these ideas as manifestations of the elements of prescriptions for social engineering (theories proffered by the left and intellectuals that are based on some ethical standards being realized through agents exercising free will). The second elements manifest Realism (politics takes shape in determined outcomes that must be tended to pragmatically through practitioners attending to hard power realities). The health of the body politic relies on both practitioners and visionaries; each provides a necessary solution to problems faced by the body politic. Yet if this is the case, then soft power in the form of ethics must assume some independence and significance as a catalyst for political action. In fact, conceiving of political science as a vehicle for attending to the body politic assumes some ethical foundations for political behavior. Certainly, prescriptions cannot emerge from some course of events deemed to be determined. They must, by definition, imply some value judgments about appropriate outcomes in the body politic that are independent of the common course of outcomes (which themselves may be considered undesirable). It is in this logic that both soft power and hard disempowerment make their first appearance in what many consider a bible of modern power politics.

It is appropriate that the last antithesis presented by Carr in chapter 2 of *Twenty Years' Crisis* is ethics versus politics. If anything, this embodies the other dichotomies and becomes synonymous with the antithesis of Utopianism versus Realism. Realism contains the instruments of hard power and an understanding of behavioral patterns that prevail among nations or people. Yet Utopianism's ethical elements (which are grounded in soft power) provide corollary instruments that both guide action and enhance the power of Realist instruments. Carr's quest for a "sound political life" can only be delivered by a synthesis of both sources of power. Thus, Carr's logic unfolds into a dialectic: diametrically opposed processes and ideologies must find a reasonable coexistence for optimal political outcomes to be delivered (Kubalkova 1998; Jones 1998, 54, 55).[6] In this sense, the soft power that emanates from ethics complements Realism's keen understanding of purely political action and its hard power

[6] Carr's epistemology and methodology owe much to the influences of Mannheim and Marx, and even though he continued to deny being a Marxist throughout his life, the manifestations of historical materialism and critical reasoning were pervasive in his work. See Carr (2000, xix, xxii), Haslam (1999), Jones (1997), Kubalkova (1998), Rich (2000, 202), and Dunne (2000, 225).

resources. Believing that a nation or actor can attain maximum influence solely through reliance on Realist instruments is to fall into the hard disempowerment trap. For Carr, ultimate power emanates from a fusion between politics and ethics. His call for a joining of reality with utopia "for a sound political life" embodies a call for the synthesis of hard power politics with the soft power of moral force.

The argument thus far for Carr unfolds in a theoretical and general context, as he is yet to delve into the state of actual events and relations in the world polity. He does this in chapter 3, specifically in the context of the League of Nations. For Carr, the League of Nations evolved into the very institutional manifestation of deluded Utopianism, with its emphasis on the superiority of law, the belief that nations could agree on universal definitions of peace and aggression, and the placement of morality and common interests (public opinion) above state sovereignty. This vision was, for Carr, illusory, given the anarchic state of world politics. Yet this did not vitiate the importance of soft power in providing a foundation for order in world politics. He praises the early League as a striking balance between Realism and Utopianism. In his cleverly dialectical prose, it was a "virtue of theoretical imperfection" (Carr 1964, 28). The qualities he underscores attest to its delicate synthesis of power politics and ethics. The early League shunned the unrealistic goal of prohibiting war in favor of the more reasonable goal of limiting war. Indeed, nations could be swayed by law and norms, but never definitively controlled by such phenomena alone. The early League also gave the great powers a majority in the Council, a vindication of the reality that institutions could not act in ways radically independent of the underlying hard power structure in world politics (Haslam 2000, 23; Linklater 1997, 323).

Alas, the League ultimately went awry. Before it could achieve, according to Carr, a "working compromise between utopia and reality," it lapsed into a Utopian illusion and instituted legal instruments that would create an absolute veto on war (in collective security) and a machinery for automatic sanctions (Carr 1964, 29). It is here that the fundamental hard power political prescriptive rationale for writing *Twenty Years' Crisis* makes its appearance in the context of actual events in world politics. Carr has already introduced it in the abstract prescription of "curing the ills of the body politic." In this case, the abstract prescription is reified in the context of contemporary history: a plan for peaceful change in world politics. Thus, curing the international body politic is conterminous with ordering international relations in a manner that allows evolution without resort to war (i.e., a system of peaceful change). Indeed, the titles of the book and of the last two chapters are manifestations of the book's didactic orientation: "Twenty Years' Crisis," "Peaceful Change," and "The Prospects for a New International Order." The "twenty years' crisis" (i.e., the interwar period) for Carr represented a failed attempt to create such an international order of peaceful change, and its failure emanated principally from the inability of the builders of the postwar order to construct institutions that endogenized sufficient respect for state sovereignty; on the contrary, they thought they could eliminate it.[7] Although the early League began in a promising manner, it unfortunately lapsed into deluded Utopian attempts to supplant sovereignty and hard power politics with the rule of morality and international law.

But rather than a Realpolitik diatribe against the roles of international organization and soft power in world politics, Carr's argument here embraces them (Wilson 2000, 192).[8] The critique of the League is not about the folly of international organization; rather, it is about how international organization failed.[9] In Carr's mind, there was a better way of doing it. In fact, his critiques of the mature League of Nations strike an amazingly prophetic tone by anticipating the structure of the future United Nations (UN). Indeed the warnings voiced by Carr were not lost on the builders of the UN, who learned from the lessons of the failures of the League and instituted rules and practices that recognized the need to buttress the soft power of norms and law on prevailing hard power structures and respect for state sovereignty. "The present generation," notes Carr, "will have to build from the foundations. But before we can do this... we must examine flaws in the structure that led to its collapse... [so we can ascertain] what can be salved from the ruins" (Carr 1964, 62).

[7] In the preface to the first edition, Carr underscores the importance of the need for a better postwar "settlement" than in fact was devised. He casts a challenge to the "peacemakers of the future" to build on better foundations (Carr 1964, xi).

[8] Reiterating his theoretical critique of Realism, Carr states that "pure realism... makes any kind of society impossible" (Carr 1964, 93). But it would be precisely this "society" that would usher in a system of peaceful change and avert another "crisis."

[9] Carr's support for international organization was a manifestation of his own advocacy of social engineering based on central planning at the national level. This advocacy developed into a more pronounced call for regional integration buttressed by such planning at the international level (Haslam 2000, 28). Such is clear in his later publications, such as *Conditions of Peace*, *Nationalism and After*, and *The Future of Nations*. In this respect, he revealed a disposition toward welfare internationalism (Linklater 2000, 247; Rich 2000, 211).

Carr goes on to underscore the problem of the dialectic in international relations by following his critique of Utopianism with a scathing censure of hard power politics as a foundation for world order. Carr affirms that "we cannot find a resting place in pure realism" (Carr 1964, 89). Realism fails across the board; it lacks a goal, emotional appeal, the right of moral judgment, and grounds for action. It is an arrested philosophy that cannot transcend its own pessimism about peaceful coexistence to deliver a viable plan for change. Yet here, the dialectic on philosophic orientations evolves into a dialectic on power, and this recalls the soft-hard power dialectic that originates in Chapter 2 – in Carr's terminology, the "pole of power" (hard power) versus "morality" (soft power). The fundamental logic is restated in slightly altered prose. Just as Utopianism and Realism are pervasive in international politics, so too are coercion and consent. Moreover, any hope for avoiding another "crisis" rests on the ability to integrate these forces: "[P]olitical action must be based on a co-ordination of morality and power.... It is as fatal in politics to ignore power as it is to ignore morality" (Carr 1964, 97).[10] The interplay between soft and hard power here becomes strikingly evident as Carr attacks nations that have taken refuge in the extremes in pursuing their national interests. Carr states, "[T]he utopian who dreams that it is possible to eliminate self-assertion and to base a political system on morality alone is just as wide of the mark as the realist who believes altruism is an illusion" (Carr 1964, 97).

Carr's Cosmopolitan Realism is poignantly manifest in his chapter 8, "Power in International Relations." His hard Realist bent is evident in the first two elements of his lexicon of national power: military and economic power. The material resources of a nation form a major core of national power. But the third element, "power over opinion" (i.e., the need for public support), adds a soft power element to the lexicon. Interestingly, he begins his discussion of power over opinion as not distinct from hard power: "power over opinion cannot be disassociated from military and economic power" (Carr 1964, 141). In this vein, he initiates his discussion of the power over opinion in the context of propaganda. Indeed, states require public support to effectively employ their hard resources, and they obtain it through conditioning public opinion. He notes that even democracies are not "altogether innocent" of such measures (Carr

[10] His intellectual debt to Niebuhr is evident here, as Niebuhr is hailed as having conceptualized politics at the intersection of "ethical and coercive factors" (Carr 1964, 100).

1964, 134). But as his logic develops, he goes on to place the role of public opinion squarely in a soft context in discussing the issue of "truth and morality in propaganda" (Carr 1964, 143). He acknowledges that leaders and states may have at times been successful in molding opinion through propaganda, but sees the idea that public opinion can always be controlled as "untenable." Such is the case because the "power over opinion is limited in two ways" (Carr 1964, 144). First, the truth will ultimately prevail: states and leaders will never be able to cloak their societies from the truth in the long run. In this context, the public will have definite desires that are independent of attempts to condition their thinking and will at some point clearly ascertain if the policies followed by their leaders deliver on those desires. Second, power over opinion is limited by the fact that human nature is inherently utopian. It is in this context that Carr interjects the idea of international morality into the lexicon of national power. For Carr, there are pervasive attachments across national populations to elements of such an international morality, and these elements must interface well with national objectives and policies if those populations are to support such objectives and policies. In this respect, the soft power of the public's support interfaces with and modifies the hard power of material strength. To quote Carr (Carr 1964, 145),

> International politics are always power politics; for it is impossible to eliminate power from them. But that is only part of the story. The fact that national propaganda everywhere so eagerly cloaks itself in ideologies of a professedly international character proves the existence of an international stock of common ideas... that... stand somehow in the scale of values above national interests. This common stock of ideas is what we mean by international morality.[11]

Carr proceeds to delve into the nature of morality in international politics in chapter 9. Notwithstanding his label as a Realist, in his life's work, Carr always reflected a deep sense of right and wrong, even in politics (Haslam 2000, 23; Linklater 1997, 333). First, he establishes that morality can, in fact, operate at the level of the nation-state and, second, that there is some social structure in international politics that activates this moral power. He justifies the attribution of moral obligations and rights to nation-states by "personifying" the state, as he calls the state the moral equivalent of the "group person" (Carr 1964, 148). Carr notes that it is necessary to indulge in this "fiction" based on a fallacy of composition,

[11] The term "power" here is used in reference to military and economic, hence, hard power.

because people attribute such qualities to nations and have expectations that nations will behave according to those qualities. Carr states that "the idea of certain obligations automatically incumbent on civilized men has given birth to the idea of similar... obligations incumbent on civilized nations" (Carr 1964, 154). However, this idea of political ethics is buttressed by the widespread perception, and consequent expectation, that nations reside in an international community. Carr claims that morality must apply to the nation-state as an actor "because there is a world community." This community owes its existence to the fact that "people talk, and within certain limits behave, as if there were a world community" (Carr 1964, 162).[12] Yet from a prescriptive standpoint, no international order can exist without the acceptance of and respect for norms. Carr explains that "it is difficult to see how orderly international relations can be conducted [unless people believe that states] have moral duties to one another and a reputation to be enhanced by performing those duties" (Carr 1964, 151).[13] In such a community, nations must endear themselves to other nations by respecting pervasive norms and institutions if they are to achieve the levels of influence they desire (i.e., soft empowerment). Disregard for such dictates of soft power can only compromise national influence (i.e., hard disempowerment).

As he goes on to develop his logic of the role of ethics in international relations, Carr exudes a strong sense of the role of soft power and hard disempowerment in the context of the international configuration of hard power. This strongly manifests his Cosmopolitan orientation in that Carr's Constructivism and Neoliberalism unfold in a category that occupies the inner core of the vision of power politics. For Carr, all configurations of international power are "hegemonic" in the respect that they are all asymmetrical (Linklater 2000, 251). Carr never differentiates systematically between differing polarities in discussing such power structures. He conceptualizes hegemony or domination "like the supremacy of a ruling class within the state" (Carr 1964, 168). Thus, it may be one or a few powers, but the structure of influence within any system is skewed

[12] Carr anticipates Bull's anarchical society (1977) in deriving moral obligations and rights from the existence of a world community and conceptualizing that morality as coexisting with elements of power politics.

[13] The Realist in Carr makes him circumspect to imprint individual morality onto states. He is clear about the limitations of morality among states, noting that vital national interests will generally dominate ethical expectations and constraints. But this is a far cry from saying, as Realists do, that norms are not significantly compelling in the face of national interests (Carr 1964, 158–62).

in favor of the great powers. For Carr, "any international moral order must rest on some hegemony of power" (Carr 1964, 168). Although he acknowledges the interplay of hard power and morality as reflecting possibilities for Gramscian hegemony (i.e., the norms of the ruling powers become the ruling norms), he nonetheless sees the viability or orderly longevity in such systems as depending on objective (as opposed to inculcated) consent on the part of weaker nations (Carr 1964, 234 and Cox 1980). For Carr, it is difficult for dominant powers to fool weaker powers much of the time because the presence of an international community generates "an international stock of common ideas" about fairness and justice in international relations (Carr 1964, 145). This requires status quo nations to legitimize such skewed power structures by respecting norms of fair and satisfactory accommodations to weaker powers (which are revisionist in nature and therefore seek change). Carr states, "[H]egemony is itself a challenge to those who do not share it; and it must, if it is to survive, contain an element of give and take, of self-sacrifice on the part of those who have, which will render it tolerable to members of the world community" (Carr 1964, 168). Thus, hegemonic systems legitimize themselves when status quo powers effectively endear themselves to revisionist powers by addressing needs for change in a manner that is perceived as consistent with widely held norms of international justice and fair play.[14] It is in this process, Carr argues, that "morality finds its surest foothold in international... politics" (Carr 1964, 168).

In this respect, dominant nations have a widely perceived moral obligation to render due respect to the revisionist sentiments of weaker nations. Yet this obligation also empowers dominant nations because they endear themselves to the larger membership of the system, thus generating the consent they need to maintain a stable system that delivers abundant benefits with respect to the particularistic goals of these dominant nations. Hence, such compliance to ethical expectations garners significant influence or soft empowerment for powerful nations. Herein lies the foundation for Carr's theory of a viable system of peaceful change. But without the soft power of endearment that in turn cultivates consent, even extremely skewed hard power structures are not guarantees of stability for nations enjoying primacy. Banking only on hard power provides a false perception of influence over outcomes in the international system. In fact,

[14] Carr states that "... those who profit most by [an international] order can in the long run only hope to maintain it by making sufficient concessions to make it tolerable to those who profit by it least" (Carr 1964, 169).

pursuing the pole of hard power excessively can generate enough countervailing actions so as to diminish the influence of the nations that indulge in such strategies, making them classic victims of hard disempowerment.[15]

This argument is historically reified in Carr's analysis of the Versailles Treaty, which assumes a central role in *Twenty Years' Crisis*. It is the central historical manifestation of the logic underlying his dialectic. It would not be an exaggeration to say that, for Carr, the treaty itself created the twenty years' crisis (i.e., the inability of the West to arrive at a legitimate system of peaceful change after the war).[16] Versailles was indeed the historical lynchpin of the crisis. The crisis, importantly, was for Carr both an ethical and political crisis. The treaty failed on both ends, and the Utopian institutions built to preserve a system of peaceful change could not overcome the political and ethical failures of Versailles. For Carr, it was not simply a problem that Versailles was signed by Germany under duress, as all treaties are. It was, rather, "the severity of its contents [and the fact that the allies broke with common norms when they] refused to engage in oral negotiations with the . . . defeated Power" (Carr 1964, 188). The treaty, for Carr, violated a central international moral code: "the obligation not to inflict unnecessary death or suffering on other human beings" (Carr 1964, 154).[17] The reparations imposed excessive burdens on Germany, a critique that was most famously averred by Keynes in the *Economic Consequences of the Peace* (1919/1988). Although the matter is still debated among many economic historians, the reparations problem and consequent disruption of international and domestic capital markets were fundamental causes of the length and severity of the great depression (Kindleberger 1986). In addition to the excessive financial burden borne by Germany, the boundary and disarmament clauses were generally perceived as "unjust," even among populations of the allied nations who had just finished fighting a war against Germany (Carr 1964, 221). In this respect, Carr saw Versailles as an ethical failure. Hence, the twenty years' crisis that Carr lamented in his avowed masterpiece of Realism was actually conceptualized principally as a product of moral deficiency (Carr

[15] Here there is a strong parallel to benevolent strands of hegemonic stability theory, as articulated in Kindleberger (1986). See Wilson (2000, 187), Linklater (1997, 332), and Jones (1998, 65).

[16] The principal didactic purpose of *Twenty Years' Crisis* was to push British elites to more skillfully manage power relations with revisionist nations like Germany so as to avoid war (Falk 1997, 41).

[17] In an autobiographical note, Carr (2000, xix) states, "I was outraged by French intransigence and by our unfairness to the Germans."

1964, 222). Indeed, it generated the antithesis of endearment: alienation. And this alienation made a stable and peaceful international system ever more elusive.

The consequences of this ethical failure were unfortunate but hardly unexpected. The burden of reparations and consequent economic crisis in Germany brought some of the most radical elements of politics to the fore.[18] Restoring Germany economically became concomitant with restoring it to its rightful international position of hard power (herein lay the political failure of the treaty). Ironically, Germany now was armed with the soft power of being in a revisionist position that was perceived as legitimate in the eyes of the world. With German popular opinion galvanized in support of resurrection and international opinion lending legitimacy to the resurrection, Germany was primed to restore itself. However, the political and moral failures of Versailles placed this resurrection on a violent path. Germany was unnecessarily abused by instruments of international law and had been cast from the "comity" of nations. This had the effect of estranging Germany from the comity by destroying "common feelings" between German and the Versailles powers. Consequently, Germany "adopted a completely cynical attitude about the role of morality in international politics" (Carr 1964, 221).[19] Ironically, one could again place Germany's own aggressive posture of impunity (actions independent of international moral codes) in a legitimate context because Germany was reacting to injustices instituted in legal instruments of the postwar settlement.[20] Oxymoronically, one could say that Germany was

[18] Carr shared pervasive ideas about the rise of militaristic/totalitarian regimes and the instability of the interwar years. Ruthless dictators and the regimes they orchestrated were, according to Carr, a "symptom" rather than a "cause" of the twenty years' crisis (Carr 1964, 225). Interestingly, Carr goes on to exhibit a Wilsonian flavor in his vindication of a democratic peace logic. He casts blame for World War I on the secret treaties and insecurities generated by the balance of power. Domestic political checks against war might have emerged if people themselves had been more involved in the contemplation and execution of foreign policy.

[19] This argument divulges a clearer view into Carr's own support of Chamberlain's policy of appeasement. Although he supported the allied policy position of the late 1930s with respect to Germany, he was not an unconditional advocate of appeasement. German requests of the 1930s were seen as grounded in legitimate demands, with a German majority in the Sudetenland seeking association with a Germany that was mistreated and alienated (Jones 1998, 62). Indeed, such accommodations in response to threats of force would not have been necessary if the Western powers had not pushed Germany to redress its grievances outside diplomatic channels (Wilson 2000, 173, 184; Evans 1975, 78, 93).

[20] Indirectly, this generated other advantages for Germany's unilateral resurrection, as the moral high ground allowed it to carry out violations of the boundary and disarmament

perfectly ethical in its unethical reaction to the Versailles provisions (Jones 1998, 62). Carr concluded that the moral and political failures of Versailles would "lead to war" (Carr 1964, 222). Guided by an absolute dictator, Germany was primed to bring about a series of violent changes.

Carr's views on the moral failure of Versailles stand as the most pronounced manifestations of the compelling relevance of soft power and hard disempowerment in world politics in *Twenty Years' Crisis*. The postwar settlement lacked legitimacy; hence, the abusive instruments that the Versailles powers tried to use to limit the resurrection of Germany compromised their soft power over Germany (the antithesis of endearment) and ended up being counterproductive (disempowering). In generating vituperation among Germans and engendering a perception of Germans as victims, Germany took a much more aggressive posture in reentering the community of nations. Furthermore, the impunity of Germany's expansionist/aggressive posture was allowed to germinate all the more because Germany's perceived international legitimacy in redressing the provisions of Versailles limited countervailing responses by the Versailles powers. France and Britain did not react more strongly and quickly to Hitler's remilitarization because they lacked confidence in the moral grounding of the Versailles settlement. Another manifestation of hard disempowerment for the Versailles powers was the moral hazard generated by the harsh economic conditions that the terms of the treaty imposed on Germany. Such terms initially led the powers to become more complacent about both Germany's resurrection and their diplomatic relations with a weakened nation. In this respect, moral hazard had hard power effects as well.

Conterminous with the deterioration of the soft power of the Versailles powers, the perceived victimization of Germany actually gave Hitler greater soft power, which provided essential leverage for Germany's resurrection.[21] Thus, an expansionist power was functioning in a more passive environment. This consequently skewed the configuration of

clauses of the treaty because international public opinion sided with Germany (thus making armed reprisals by France and Britain less tenable). Moreover, German victimization made it easier for Mussolini to justify an alliance with Hitler. Mussolini justified the alliance morally as a quest to restore "justice, security and peace" (Carr 1964, 155).

21 Of course, Hitler would completely compromise this soft power in his quest for domination; thus he was both a beneficiary and a victim of soft power in the course of a decade. In this respect, contrary to Carr's erstwhile critics, he was not a fan or supporter of Hitler, but only an advocate of fair and just treatment of Germany in the postwar order (Haslam 1999; Jones 1998).

power significantly in favor of Germany. In this respect, the Versailles powers were strongly victimized by hard disempowerment, as their neglect of soft power in solving the German problem generated adverse outcomes in the global balance of power. The influence and security that the victorious powers perceived in the clauses of Versailles were, in the end, illusory, setting the stage for a stronger and even more menacing Germany. Instead of solving a problem through the avenues of hard power, Versailles only succeeded in creating a bigger one. In an autobiographical note, Carr (2000, xix) states that "... the Western powers had asked for what they got."

Carr's critique, however, is not restricted to Versailles. His discussion of Soviet foreign policy also provides a poignant view of the impact of soft power and hard disempowerment. He notes that Soviet Leaders compromised their soft power by refusing to honor treaties made by previous regimes. They also were delinquent in not pursuing robust security regimes with their European neighbors, who in turn were less than animated in resurrecting such regimes after the war. This unilateralist disposition hurt the Soviets and Versailles powers in several ways. First, it gave Hitler greater justification in breaking Versailles statutes and other agreements limiting Germany's rise (Locarno). Second, the poor reputation effects generated by this untrustworthiness made it harder for the Soviets to build more robust security communities among their neighbors. This left the Soviets and the other powers more vulnerable to German aggression because there were fewer countervailing coalitions (i.e., they were caught in a vicious cycle of unilateralism). Moreover, limited countervailing coalitions emboldened Germany even more (i.e., adverse feedback effects) (Carr 1964, 151, 156).

It is fitting that Carr ends the book by marshaling a vision for the future. The vision emanates from the failures that led to the crisis of the interwar years. Carr promotes a vision of a "new international order," one that (unlike all preceding orders) could be founded on peaceful change. Developing his dialectic in this context, he conceptualizes peaceful change as founded on allowing hegemonic systems to generate just and equitable outcomes for weaker (revisionist) powers. In this respect, such systems should be flexible in allowing change without violent reprisals by disgruntled revisionist nations. The changes would be orchestrated within an ethical superstructure of well-regarded norms and laws of international relations, but would also be congruent with underlying hard power structures. Not only would this marriage of hard and soft power be beneficial for the system as a whole, in avoiding violent eruptions, but it would also provide each nation with a means of optimizing its influence in world affairs. Thus, each nation would be a microcosm of the system: hard power would give it the foundations of strength, but that strength would mean little if it was not complemented by the moral strength generated by endearing oneself through soft power policies. Without both, real influence would be only illusory. In a clearly Cosmopolitan tone, Carr states that "every solution of the problem of political change... must be based on a compromise between morality and power" (Carr 1964, 209).

In sum, the conventional reading of Carr's magnum opus has attributed far too much importance to the later part of this equation: hard power. Carr's attention to the empowering qualities of soft power and the enervating qualities of hard power throughout *Twenty Years' Crisis* actually demonstrates a far more balanced vision of influence in international politics. Indeed, pure naked power gave nations the material means to achieve their objectives and could pave the road to a stable peace. Yet this naked power necessitated a complementary veneration for the soft power of endearment, which manifested itself through the respect for pervasive norms and institutions in the international system. In this respect, Carr strongly vindicated the desirability of a Cosmopolitan golden mean.

Hans Morgenthau

Along with Carr and Thucydides, Gilpin (1986, 306) cites Morgenthau as one of the "three great realist writers." Mearsheimer (2001, 14) hails *Politics among Nations* as one of the three most influential Realist texts of the twentieth century. Lebow (2003, 216) calls Morgenthau "the intellectual father of postwar realism."[22] A number of the passages in *Politics among Nations* have become legend among students of international relations. International relations can best be understood as being based on the belief that nations act in their "interest defined in terms of power" (Morgenthau 1978, 5). Also celebrated in the Realist catechism of international relations is the famous quote "International politics, like all politics, is a struggle for power. Whatever the ultimate aims of international politics, power is always the immediate aim" (Morgenthau 1978, 29). Power, then, in a system of sovereign states void of an overarching power (like force and fraud in common visions of Hobbesian anarchy) becomes the ultimate source of influence and must be raised above all other means

[22] The fifth edition (1978) of the book was used for this textual analysis, as it was the last revision completed by Morgenthau as the sole author.

of statecraft. This power, of course, has been traditionally equated with "hard" power.

Although Morgenthau barely cites Carr in his book, *Politics among Nations*, in structure, spirit, and logic, could be called a true progeny of Carr's *Twenty Years' Crisis*. Like Carr, Morgenthau begins with an emphatic quest for a more positivistic approach to international relations. In the first of his famous six principles of Realism, he purports to identify "objective laws" that will produce a more "scientific" as opposed to a legalistic or humanistic understanding of the subject (Morgenthau 1978, 4, 14). Also like Carr, after disposing of some methodological preliminaries (in chapters 1 and 2) that attempt to elevate the work in the hierarchy of ontological value above previous work, he emerges breathing fire and wielding a hard power rhetoric that has long inspired the community of Realists. Such a convergence is not surprising, given that their ideas crystallized in a period when appeasement failed and people were struck by how force had triumphed over diplomacy.

A look at Morgenthau's precise definition of national power reveals that the list of factors indeed reflects a poignant veneration of hard power. Morgenthau cites geography, natural resources, industrial capacity, military preparedness, and population first. The conceptualization of the first five factors closely parallels Measheimer's (2001, 55) and Waltz's (1979, 131) visions of power as tangible assets. Yet as we proceed through the list of factors comprising national power, we see a deviation from an exclusively hard power focus that brings in soft power as crucial to foreign policy. For Morgenthau, the manifestations of power themselves can feature effective soft elements, because he has a very elastic vision of how power can be used. He notes that although his mantra about power (national interest being always defined as power) is "universally valid," its meaning is not "fixed once and for all" (Morgenthau 1978, 8). This variability exists because power is ultimately contextual: "Its context and its use are determined by the political and cultural environment" (Morgenthau 1978, 9). Hence, effective power can emanate from across a spectrum that is bounded by the pole of morality on one end and the pole of force on the other (Morgenthau 1978, 9; Murray 1996, 81). Also like Carr, Morgenthau's fundamental vision of soft power is oriented around nations endearing themselves in the international community by honoring pervasive norms and institutions that influence the relations among states. Only when his inventory of hard sources of power is joined with such endearing qualities can nations truly enjoy optimal opportunities to wield influence in the international system. Hence, like all the founding fathers of Realism preceding him, Morgenthau ultimately carries a Cosmopolitan banner of power. Morgenthau's Cosmopolitan vision finds the golden mean between the pole of a world of "untamed and barbaric force" and its antithesis, a pole of a world "disciplined by moral ends and controlled by constitutional safeguards."[23]

Like Carr once again, all of his intellectual energies in propounding such a compelling vision of power are for the purpose of building a peaceful and stable plan for coexistence among nations. Thus, the didactic purposes of the great works of these authors share a common grounding.

Morgenthau's softer side is apparent when he begins introducing "intangible" factors that fill important roles in the activation of power. In his chapter 10 on the evaluation of power, Morgenthau issues a strong reference to the perils of hard disempowerment in warning against the "equation of national power with material force [alone]" (Morgenthau 1978, 168). Indeed, he cautions leaders about the "paradox that a maximum of material power does not necessarily mean a maximum of overall national power" (Morgenthau 1978, 169). Morgenthau offers a poignant negative feedback logic about the manifestation of hard disempowerment by stating that the nation that "throws into the scale of international politics the maximum of material power . . . will find itself confronted with the maximum efforts of all its competitors" (Morgenthau 1978, 169). He goes on to assert that no nation, regardless of its material power, has ever succeeded in imposing its will for any length of time over the rest of the world with its hard power alone. This is a theme that manifests itself across Morgenthau's works (Cox 2007a, 175). He continues by noting, "Without [these intangible factors] a powerful nation may frighten other nations into submission or it may conquer by sheer overwhelming force, but it cannot rule what it has conquered. . . . In the end, the power of militarism must yield to a power tempered with self-restraint" (Morgenthau 1978, 169).[24]

23 Like Carr, he embraces a Cosmopolitan vision of human action; thus, aside from purely hard power seeking, actions also manifest economic concerns, morality, religion, and art. There are no pure types in behavior, as people are neither "beasts" (completely amoral) nor "fools" (completely moral) (Morgenthau 1978, 14). The international playing field features "supranational forces" and an "international morality" that have limited "the aspirations of power" among nations (Morgenthau 1978, 337, 338).

24 This reference arouses ideas of the disempowering effects of x-inefficiencies generated by coercion and force. Subjects in the conquered lands will take every opportunity, created by the imperfect specification of decrees, to undermine the interests of the aggressor nation.

After introducing his first intangible factor (national character), which contemplates certain foreign policy traits as based on national culture (i.e., there are pacifist cultures and more militaristic cultures), he proposes what he calls the two most important components of national power: national morale and diplomacy. Morale is a lynchpin of national power in that it impacts all of the hard power (i.e., tangible) resources listed by Morgenthau. As Morgenthau notes, without such morale, "national power is either nothing but material force or else a potentiality that awaits its realization in vain" (Morgenthau 1978, 146). Indeed, morale is the "soul" of national power (Morgenthau 1978, 146). Without it, no government is able to "pursue its policies with full effectiveness... [because] it pervades all activities of a nation" (Morgenthau 1978, 140). National morale is defined as public support of policies (Morgenthau 1978, 154).

With respect to governmental policies, two important factors condition morale: the quality of domestic government and foreign policy. In terms of the quality of governance, liberal democratic governments are cited as possessing superior morale: "[A] government that is truly representative... has the best chance [of generating national support for foreign policy]" (Morgenthau 1978, 145). Indeed, a people "permanently deprived of its rights and of full participation in the life of the nation will tend to have a lower national morale" (Morgenthau 1978, 143). The argument suggests an x-efficiency logic, where the performance of a populace has great elasticity with respect to political support. This contemplates a process of domestic sources of soft empowerment similar to that envisioned by Machiavelli (soft empowerment through civic support).[25]

The domestic quality of government is compounded by the particular types of foreign policies that are chosen. Morgenthau suggests that foreign policies that demand excessive sacrifices or burdens on the part of civil society will cut sharply against national morale and deprive ruling regimes of popular support. He discusses the devastating effects that excessive war losses have had on national morale throughout history. Nations have been weakened significantly by the "overtaxing" of their populations in funding expansionist and bellicose policies and have caused "ruin" from attempts at "unlimited conquest" (Morgenthau 1978, 139, 150).

[25] The international effect of domestic soft power developed in this vein recalls the arguments of Machiavelli regarding the utility of fortifications, as well as the work of Reiter and Stam (2002), who show that democracies can be more effective in attaining their international goals because dependence on public consent makes their foreign policy initiatives more resolute and effective.

Morgenthau marshals an important hard disempowerment element in this context when he decries the policies of leaders who cannot construct a satisfactory balance among power resources. For example, nations that attempt to build a military capacity far greater than an industrial capacity to support such a goal (overstretch) will cause a decay in morale that could generate a crisis of the state. He calls such a plan one of "national weakness rather than power" (Morgenthau 1978, 152). This ties into the quality of government argument in embracing a democratic peace logic that suggests that national strength is dependent on foreign policies that are fundamentally in keeping with the domestic priorities of populations (Lebow 2003, 230). These policies are, in turn, founded on a disposition of moderation in foreign aspirations (to avoid overstretch) and public accountability with respect to foreign policy. Nations will only be at peak power with foreign policies that are consistent with domestic priorities, and these priorities are derived from popular predilections.

With his final ingredient of national power, diplomacy, Morgenthau underscores the contribution of soft power to national strength. He calls diplomacy the "most important" ingredient (Morgenthau 1978, 146). Indeed, diplomacy "combines [all the ingredients] into an integrated whole, gives them direction and weight" (Morgenthau 1978, 146). If morale is the soul of national power, then diplomacy is its "brains" (Morgenthau 1978, 146). In a strongly Cosmopolitan tone, he contends that all of the tangible resources he lists make up the "raw material" of national power, but diplomacy and morale are the "catalysts" that are responsible for making those resources effective (Morgenthau 1978, 146, 148). Hence, the realization of national influence is dependent on national morale, but above all on the practice of diplomacy.[26] Morgenthau defines diplomacy as a process of "compromise, persuasion and threat of force" (Morgenthau 1978, 531, 543). The process, as defined, appears to be sufficiently elastic to allow the kinds of swaggering and power play that would indeed validate a typically Realpolitik vision of coercive diplomacy. In very Carrian fashion, Morgenthau regards material power as a fundamental element of diplomacy when he describes the four tasks of diplomacy (Morgenthau 1978, 529, 530). Diplomats must assess the objectives of their nations as well as those of other nations in light of the power available to realize such objectives (one and two). They should

[26] This emphasis on diplomacy also manifests itself in his applied work on U.S. foreign policy and the Cold War (Cox 2007a, 175; Goodnight 1996, 143). See especially Morgenthau (1951, 1969).

then assess the compatibility of these objectives (three) and, finally, use the appropriate means suited to these objectives (four).[27] Does this mean that raw material power drives the process? In fact, it is just the opposite. Morgenthau is very clear in his vision of how diplomacy plays itself out as a civil interactional process. He states that "a diplomacy that ends in war has failed in its primary function: the promotion of the national interest by peaceful means" (Morgenthau 1978, 529). Coercive diplomacy may manifest itself from time to time, but it has little survival value as diplomacy in the way Morgenthau envisions it. Although the structure of hard power resources must be correctly perceived and acknowledged (the Carrian condition), it cannot drive the process of diplomacy. Consistent with a Cosmopolitan vision, the factors of power work as a symbiotic whole.

More generally, Morgenthau's vision of national morale cuts sharply against coercive diplomacy (Good 1960, 610). As noted, popular support is a necessary condition for effective foreign policy. Diplomacy oriented around bullying, swaggering, and threat would diverge from the sort of liberalist principles of democratic societies.[28] Such diplomacy would garner limited support in such regimes. More autocratic regimes might be able to engage in such diplomacy, but it would ultimately have to be marshaled on potential sacrifices (e.g., requiring significant arms buildups that would thwart social objectives, thus causing populations to face deprivation), and Morgenthau is clear that such sacrifices could not be sustained if one were to maintain popular support.[29] Moreover, according to task three, the objectives between the nations involved must be "compatible," which means mutual satisfaction with the outcome – otherwise, the outcome will be unstable, as it would be imposed on some nations. In light of Morgenthau's logic, coercive diplomacy would eventually crumble because the requisite arms buildups would undermine the ruling regime's

[27] The first two recall the Carrian diatribe in *Twenty Years' Crisis* against Utopians, who sought peace without considering underlying material power structures.

[28] In this respect, his vision of diplomacy exhibits true elements of soft power, rather than just an instrumental quality that could be consistent with a purely Realist vision of diplomacy. Although instrumental diplomacy, geared toward achieving particularistic goals without regard to the welfare of other nations, may placate nations for a while, it would certainly have limited survival value, because other nations would eventually resent arrangements that are strictly self-serving. In other words, diplomacy would eventually lose the legitimacy that, in the eyes of Morgenthau, made it so effective in stabilizing international relationships. Moreover, Morgenthau sees effective diplomacy as a necessary stepping-stone to a world state.

[29] It would, however, be consistent with rule four that regimes marshaling coercive diplomacy must support it with appropriate muscle (i.e., muscle is the appropriate means of enhancing the effectiveness of threats); otherwise, the threats would be empty.

policies (sacrifices that cannot be sustained); would devolve into arms races (which would no longer be a purely diplomatic solution because it would eliminate the functions of compromise and accommodation); could leave one of the parties feeling that the outcome was illegitimate because it was forced to comply against its wishes (which would violate the mutual satisfaction condition); or would end in war (which is the antithesis of diplomacy). In this respect, Morgenthau's logic underscores a compelling warning against various potential sources of hard disempowerment. Indeed, national leaders must undertake a type of diplomacy that endears their nations to other nations, rather than one that alienates. It is only with the former that nations can wield significant influence over other nations.

Diplomacy is a poignant manifestation of Morgenthau's soft side, and it plays a crucial role in his vision of the evolution of world politics. It does so because it is the very means by which the world can escape the potential cataclysm of a nuclear war among the superpowers (Algosaisi 1965, 242). Morgenthau's Utopian side, (as with Carr in *Twenty Years' Crisis*, a prominent component of his master work) is manifested in this very discussion of diplomacy (Speer 1968, 207). Morgenthau laments that diplomacy in his epoch has lost many of its stabilizing functions relative to the way it operated prior to the twentieth century. This is a result of several factors.[30] Yet the effectiveness of diplomacy must be revived in this dangerous world – a world where "technological developments" have made war a cataclysmic event that must be avoided (Morgenthau 1978, 541). Improved diplomacy holds the key to peaceful coexistence in the international system. In the short run, conflict can be "mitigated and minimized" through a more vigorous diplomacy that avoids the pitfalls of the past century (Morgenthau 1978, 525). But in the long run, it is the only means by which the lasting solution to peace can ultimately be constructed. Morgenthau argues that lasting peace can only be achieved by moving out of an anarchic environment: "[T]here can be no permanent peace without a world state" (Morgenthau 1978, 560). Yet in order for a world state to be constructed, the foundations have to be forged, and these foundations are constructed through diplomacy (Morgenthau 1978, 560; Speer 1968, 215). The essence of effective diplomacy is grounded

[30] Communications technology has diminished the need for diplomats; diplomats have been held in disrepute as spies rather than as peacemakers; diplomacy has been transferred away from nations to international organizations; the two superpowers are newcomers to diplomacy; and, finally, the crusading ideologies of capitalism and communism have eliminated moderation in foreign relations among the superpowers.

in soft power elements: respect for norms and institutions, penchant for fair play, and respect for multilateral solutions. This recalls the strand of Utopian vision with which Carr ended *Twenty Years' Crisis*.[31]

Politics among Nations, like *Twenty Years' Crisis*, unfolds as a compelling testament to a Cosmopolitan vision of power. The fire-breathing prescriptions for hard power politics are balanced and integrated with extensive references to the utility of soft power. Above and beyond diplomacy, Morgenthau is generous in hailing the contributions of these soft elements to national influence throughout the book.[32] For Morgenthau, these soft elements are pervasive, and their importance should be apparent to national leaders (Morgenthau 1978, 7).

In chapter 3, "Political Power," he identifies three sources of political power: expected benefits, fear of punishment, and respect or love for men and institutions (Morgenthau 1978, 30, 31). The latter strongly manifests a conception of soft power in that cultivating an endearing image as a result of respect and esteem generates influence in the international system.[33] He goes on to consider the force of "legitimate power," a source of influence that draws its strength from being "legally and morally justified" (Morgenthau 1978, 32).

In chapters 4 through 6, he discusses three ways in which nations manifest their power (through the status quo, imperialism, and prestige). Each manifestation illuminates the significance of soft power. Status quo empowerment is manifest to a large extent in existing regimes. These are legitimate sources of power in that they comprise institutions that are legally and morally justified (Morgenthau 1978, 42–44). Although imperialism has a strongly hard power element, Morgenthau nonetheless warns against the unmitigated use of such means of power. He notes that influence over other nations cannot be founded on military domination alone. All such attempts in history (he cites Hitler, Napoleon,

[31] Murray (1996, 88) traces an Augustinian vision of humanity that runs through Niebuhr and culminates in Morganthau. It embraces a natural human tension in which spirituality must coexist with a baser lust for power. In Niebuhr's (1932, 4) famous words, politics is a place "where conscience and power meet."

[32] Morgenthau reflects a moral vision of politics that manifests itself throughout his lifelong body of work, sometimes more starkly in some works (e.g., *Scientific Man*, 1967) than in others. Revisionist scholarship on his theory of politics highlights the vigorous ethical orientation that permeates his body of work. Indeed, although national interest is compelling, it must always be accountable to "strict moral limitations" (Murray 1996, 81). On Morgenthau's moral vision of politics, see especially Murray (1996), Lebow (2003), Smith (1986), Russell (1990), Speer (1968), Good (1960), and Algosaisi (1965).

[33] This logic is further developed later in chapter 9 (Morgenthau 1978, 154, 155).

and British India) have led to unfortunate outcomes for the perpetrators in the form of excess victimization caused by hard disempowerment. In a later discussion of great power politics, he reaffirms this risk of hard disempowerment, noting the deleterious consequences of attempts at "unlimited conquest" and "overtaxing" national resources (Morgenthau 1978, 150). Yet possibilities for significant weakening effects of negative feedback are abundant in environments where indulgence in hard power resources may lead other nations to perceive that aspiring nations are on an imperialistic path, even if they are not. In this respect, he recalls a security dilemma logic in talking about the possibility of deleterious power dynamics emanating from such outcomes (Morgenthau 1978, 71–73).

With respect to prestige, he notes a propensity of nations to seek recognition for the hard power they possess. However, prestige also has a compelling soft element in that restraint in asymmetrical power relations can garner an image that enhances influence on the part of the moderating powers. This links up nicely to Carr's idea of a self-effacing hegemon (Morgenthau 1978, 87, 88). Ultimately, in each of the principal vehicles through which power is manifested, an essential precondition of influence is that nations use strategies that endear themselves to other nations.

Surprisingly, one of the most salient acknowledgements of soft power emerges in his evaluation of the old (pre-1914) balance of power system. For Morgenthau, the old balance of power worked well because it was founded on a "moral consensus" (Speer 1968, 215). This consensus was the result of "shared values and universal standards of actions" that manifested an "international community" (Morgenthau 1978, 221, 228, 525; Koskenniemi 2001, 438). Outcomes derived from the activation of this consensus on the part of leaders and diplomats, and did not simply derive from automatic processes inherent in structures or systems. Stability and peace were the results of leaders and diplomats following clear and universally respected norms of international relations: a quest for peace, independence, sovereignty, moderation in foreign policy aspirations, and the reintegration of defeated foes (Morgenthau 1978, 224–7; Lebow 2003, 228).[34] In this respect, it was the existence of an international moral community that allowed the balance of power mechanism

[34] Deviations from the peace norm were legitimate to the extent that they countered illegitimate uses of force (responses to imperialism or expansionism). In this context, Morgenthau notes that European states generally approved of the Balkan and Belgian revolts, as well as the Prussian and Sardinian aggression to unite Germany and Italy, respectively. Here, he refers to the legitimacy of force in the service of self-determination (Morgenthau 1978, 226, 227).

to effectively serve the purposes of peace and stability. Without such a community, Morgenthau will later write in his book, the prospects for lasting peace among nations are slim.[35]

However, after spending the first half of the book (chapters 1–14) developing a vision that embraces this community in international relations, he returns with Realpolitik vengeance in the next nine chapter (15–23). In these chapters, he revives the Carrian hammer used to bash the visions of Utopians in the first part of *Twenty Years' Crisis*. Indeed, he goes on to argue that fundamental changes in international politics have served to weaken this community and thus have undermined erstwhile constraints against pure hard power seeking, these constraints being international morality, international law and institutions, and public opinion.[36] The most conspicuous and powerful of these forces of change is the rise of nationalism. Although nationalism existed before the twentieth century, according to Morgenthau, it was not of a kind that undermined the existence of the moral community that nurtured the factors that abated the tendency toward pure power seeking, so it maintained peace and stability. The present nationalism, for Morgenthau, has weakened a "moral consensus" and replaced it with a quest to transform national ideologies into international ideologies. Morgenthau refers to this as "universal nationalism" (Morgenthau 1978, 337–40).[37] Because of this new and Messianic nationalism, continues Morgenthau, "the international morality that in past centuries kept the aspirations for power of the individual nations within certain bounds has . . . given way to the morality of nations" (Morgenthau 1978, 337). Morgenthau also highlights two other changes that have weakened the communitarian limits on the struggle for power: the advent of total war and the new balance of power. Morgenthau's greatest concern with respect to these developments is their impact on prospects for peace and stability in the present world.[38] The old balance of power functioned well and delivered

[35] It is with this concept of moral community of nations as a necessary condition for lasting peace that Morgenthau comes closest to Carr's Utopianism.

[36] In these chapters, however, he does nothing to undermine his arguments that soft power factors are crucial elements in the nexus of national power.

[37] This is one of the many poignant manifestations of the specter of the Cold War on Morgenthau's thinking. His idea of universal nationalism reflects the evangelical battle between liberalism and communism.

[38] This fear is the driving force behind the book itself. The specter of all-out war between two superpowers in a nuclear world is the very challenge inspiring Morgenthau, as both a social scientist and a human being. Indeed, it is for Morgenthau (1969, 207) "the issue that overshadows all others."

satisfactory results. But the changes in international politics have challenged it and its underlying foundations (Koskenniemi 2001).

According to Morgenthau, both nationalism and total war have undermined the normative foundations of the moral consensus undergirding the old balance of power. The norms of protecting human life and condemnation of war have depreciated because of the advent of total war and nationalism. Nationalism has undermined what he calls the "cosmopolitan" attitudes of old diplomats and leaders, attitudes that were instrumental in forging and sustaining peace, and replaced them with more rigid and particularistic goals. Total war has legitimated all-out conflict (i.e., involving all facets of society) and the exorbitant casualties of war. The restraints of the old balance of power norms on national actions have consequently weakened (Morgenthau 1978, 244–56). Moreover, in addition to the normative changes, the balance of power itself has changed in ways that have rendered it less stable. Morgenthau contends that the present balance is less flexible because of the existence of fewer great powers (a bipolar configuration), the absence of a balancer, and the disappearance of the colonial frontier – that is, there is no outlet for competition (Morgenthau 1978, 348–55).

However, in subsequent chapters, when Morgenthau discusses this new balance of bipolarity, which has been proclaimed deficient, he more vigorously embraces its stabilizing elements. In doing so, he proclaims its soft power elements and underscores the dangers of hard disempowerment. He notes that bipolarity carries potential for "enormous good" and that it is "the ideal system of the balance of power" (Morgenthau 1978, 550, 551). Much of his argument anticipates Waltz's (1979, 170–76) arguments about the stability of a bipolar world. Morgenthau quotes the French philosopher Fenelon on competition among few nations: that it encourages "wise moderation [in] maintaining the equilibrium and the common security." Indeed Morgenthau sees the bipolar structure as producing "moderate competition"(Morgenthau 1978, 364).[39] The moderation emanates from shared convictions and objectives that generate normative behavior.[40] In this respect, notwithstanding Morgenthau's previous statements about the depreciation of balance of power norms under

[39] Morgenthau's (1969) discussions of U.S. foreign policy reaffirm the idea of common interests among the superpowers.

[40] Murray (1990, 104) identifies a pervasive view in Morgenthau's works that suggests that national interest incorporates "an obligation to self-limitation and tolerance." Lebow (2003, 233) argues that Morgenthau always believed that influence and power ultimately depended on wisdom and ethical sensibility.

bipolarity, he ascribes to bipolarity an integrated set of norms similar to those undergirding the old balance of power (Speer 1968, 209). It appears that for Morgenthau, the quest for stability and peace is compelling in bipolarity as well. Morgenthau is adamant throughout the book about the fact that "war has always been abhorred as a scourge"; hence, the predisposition for peace is overriding even among superpowers in a bipolar world (Morgenthau 1978, 391).[41] The status quo, and hence stability, is reinforced by shared convictions about dangers of reckless expansionism and adventurism, and in this respect Morgenthau ascribes mutual vigilance among superpowers about avoiding excessively provocative foreign policies. For Morgenthau, superpowers are aware of the dangers of hard disempowerment in both of these respects: the adverse reaction to attempts at "pronounced superiority" (negative feedback) and to the "short lived empires... and the ravages they cause" (overstretch) (Morgenthau 1978, 364). Wise leaders therefore are pushed to seek "a kind of equality" with erstwhile competitors. In the end, Morgenthau affirms an even more robust moral consensus undergirding the new balance of power in that he underscores the continuing power of the "old norms" (peace, independence, stability, and moderation) in conjunction with a more stabilizing structure of power (the stability of bipolarity) and greater deterrent threats against adventurism (nuclear weapons). Consequently, his previous assault on international morality as a weakened constraint against power seeking is significantly revised with these arguments.[42] In the final analysis, the bipolar balance of power is also capable of generating a constellation of relations that promotes a moral community in the international system.

Rather than view such contradictory arguments as inconsistencies in the work of a great thinker, one can see that Morgenthau's caveats put such disjunctures into perspective. It is a perspective that often reflects

[41] The norms promoting peace and stability are raised to a far greater extent under the new balance, according to Morgenthau, because of new "technological developments" that have enhanced the destructiveness of war (nuclear weapons) and also have enhanced the need for cooperation among states to solve national problems (he cites the environment, food security, natural resources, and population control) (Morgenthau 1978, 541). See also Goodnight (1996, 149).

[42] As a counterweight to the destabilizing effects of nationalism and total war, Morgenthau cites the rise of liberalism and the enlightenment as new developments that have generated an enhanced "intellectual and moral energy [that has sustained the] search for alternatives to war and international anarchy" (Morgenthau 1978, 393). Indeed, post enlightenment society has shown an "increased humaneness and a civilized disposition toward human relations" (Morgenthau 1978, 392).

the compelling influence of the idea of a Cosmopolitan mean in Morgenthauian logic. In each chapter in which he wields his Carrian hammer (15–18) to assault the viability of constraining or soft elements in international politics (morality, law, and public opinion), he underscores a "warning against extremes." He emphasizes that it is just as dangerous to "underestimate" the influence of these elements as it is to "overrate" them (Morgenthau 1978, 236, 264, 279). Thus, his own attack on these soft elements of power gravitates toward Carr's treatment of these same issues in *Twenty Years' Crisis*. Both thinkers are wielding a didactic hammer against the excesses of Utopian thinking in these arguments (Goodnight 1996, 144). That they often flip-flop among positions reflects their passion against dangers of immoderate behavior as well as a didactic quest to make an impression on the reader about avoiding excesses.[43]

In the chapters comprising the final three sections of the book, Morgenthau concludes with a search for the means through which world peace may be forged. After lukewarm praise of arms limitation as such a means, he fixes on what is for him the only viable foundation for a lasting peace in a nuclear world: supranational organization. Yet such a "transformation" can only be built on the pillars of a more extensive international community that is not as vigorously manifest as of yet. The only way to build that community, as noted, is to develop closer webs of cooperation among nations through diplomacy. He therefore ends with diplomacy (peace through accommodation) as something that can deliver peace directly in the short run but is the only way to forge the conditions of a lasting peace in the long run – a strong international community. Like Carr's masterwork, Morgenthau's *Politics among Nations* starts with a passionate plea against the excesses of Utopian visions and the utility of hard power resources but ends with an expression of a Utopian desire to dig the foundations for a lasting peace, one that will (for Morgenthau) help humans avert the cataclysm of nuclear war (Speer 1968, 215). It is this fear that charges the work with its prescriptive thrust, one that manifests Morgenthau's own humanity and morality and ultimately renders him a much more Cosmopolitan thinker about the role of power seeking (Morgenthau 1978, 529). We are reminded of this by the subtitle of the book, *The Struggle for Power and Peace*.

In the final analysis, Morgenthau, like Carr, embraces a moral vision informed by an understanding of the reality of international relations. As

[43] Murray (1990, 96) sees this vacillation as an "expedient to clarify the issues."

Murray (1996, 88) aptly summarizes the Morgenthauian vision of politics, it combines "a transcendental morality with a realistic appraisal of conditions." The transcendental morality in conjunction with the realistic appraisal is a vivid manifestation of the value of soft and hard power and ultimately a testament to the Cosmopolitan character of Morgenthau's vision of power.

4

Case Studies of Soft Empowerment

Free Trade, the Classical Gold Standard, and Dollarization

The next three chapters present case studies for the purpose of illuminating and partially testing the theory of Cosmopolitan power. By carefully tracing the benefits generated by soft power (soft empowerment) and the weakening effects of strategies excessively oriented around hard power (hard disempowerment), these chapters render a testament to the desirability of a diversified foreign policy that embraces some Cosmopolitan balance among the two sources of power. As with most case studies, there is a natural "boundedness" in the inferential power of the results because of limited observations. In this respect, they fall short of being "strong" tests of the theory. However, there are several qualities of these case studies, enumerated in the Introduction, that render the findings somewhat more inferentially compelling, thus raising their value as tests.

The three cases of soft empowerment considered in this chapter illuminate a process in which soft power enhanced the economic influence of actors that had already attained economic primacy (i.e., largely through hard power) in their respective spheres. All three cases show endowments of hard power being supplemented by soft power in the augmentation of economic and political influence. In these cases, the principal source of soft empowerment was the endearing qualities of the economic policies of the United States and Great Britain. These endearing qualities, which resulted from the admiration and respect generated by the economic primacy achieved by these nations in specific issue areas, caused other nations to emulate the policies of these role-model nations. Emulation created a greater political-economic milieu that was favorable to the interests and goals of the role-model nations. In each case, already powerful economic actors found their economic and political influence augmented by economic and political opportunities provided by the cultivation of soft power. This enhanced influence, in turn, generated even greater hard power for the respective nations (i.e., greater economic primacy and political advantages). Hence, the cases reveal a Cosmopolitan interaction process between hard and soft power resources.

One of the principal manifestations of soft empowerment is the state of being emulated. Nye underscores this aspect as one of the most important benefits of soft power, but he offers limited analysis of how emulation can serve the interests of nations with soft power (i.e., limited process tracing). Other case studies of soft power are also limited in systematically chronicling the specific benefits derived from emulation.[1] In attempting to provide more systematic and analytical structure to the process of soft empowerment and a Cosmopolitan theory of power, this gap should be filled. This chapter attempts to provide case studies that help to fill this gap.[2] Emulation brings other nations into behavioral modes that mirror both policies and interests of role-model nations. Such a specification better clarifies the relational consequences of soft empowerment by revealing a more precise view of the congruence between the structure of state actions and the structure of state interests. As such, it provides a more systematic and vivid vision of the functioning of a soft power dynamic.

Great Britain and the Rise of Free Trade in the Nineteenth Century

Kindleberger (1975) chronicles the proliferation of free trade in Western Europe in the mid-nineteenth century as a direct manifestation of

1 Lennon (2003) analyzes how soft power in general (i.e., in multiple aspects rather than just emulation) can be used to combat terrorism. Fraser (2003) addresses some of the benefits of emulation for the United States but focuses more on how American media and culture serve as vehicles for raising the appeal of the United States among foreign populations. Yasushi and McConnell (2008) look at soft power primarily in the context of the United States and Japan. Kurlantzick (2007) analyzes how China has recently embraced the value of soft power in promoting its foreign and domestic interests. Johnston (2008) analyzes the impact of socialization on Chinese security policy but does not directly employ the theory of soft power. In evaluating the theory of soft power and recommending avenues of future research into the concept, Lukes (2007, 97) offers several leading questions, but never asks for a greater clarification of how emulation actually benefits a role-model nation.

2 As demonstrated in Chapter 1, the concept of soft power is broad, and emulation is merely one of its important components. This chapter concentrates on this component because of its importance and also because of the paucity of case studies on such an important component.

national elites admiring the prosperity of Britain as well as its early industrialization.[3] Kindlebeger (1975, 51) uses the terms "precept" and "example" to convey the soft power of British policies. Fielden (1969, 85) supports this view: "Western European states wished to emulate Britain industrially." Much of the credit for such outcomes was attributed to the twin policies of free trade and the gold standard (Gallarotti 1995b, 145; Bairoch 1989, 23). The French diplomat Michel Chevalier noted at the time how keen nations were to adopt British economic policy innovations in hope of also achieving its economic ascent (Gallarotti 1995b, 145). In this case, it was Britain's free trade policy that "should also be copied" (Fielden 1969, 85).[4] The idea of the transformative power of free trade was more tenable and obvious than the gold link, but both were compelling nonetheless. The attraction reflected an extreme admiration of economic conditions in Britain that was deeply rooted in the merits of the Cobdenite ideology that influenced British politics during the mid-century. Although various nations began moving toward the British example in the 1840s and 1850s, it was not until the advent of the Cobden-Chevalier Treaty (1860) between Britain and France that the free trade chain gang manifested itself. The period from 1860 to 1879 marked the most robust period of tariff reduction, both legislated and negotiated in line with the system of trade reciprocity featured in the Cobden-Chevalier Treaty.[5] This is generally considered the high point of free trade in the nineteenth century. Although most of Europe and the United States drifted toward a more protective posture after 1880, various developments, even in that period, maintained fairly fluid trade until World War I. First, the innovation of negotiated tariffs (wherein multischedule tariffs that could be negotiated replaced single-schedule

[3] Nye (2002, 10) cites the emulation of British policies of free trade in Western Europe as a manifestation of emulation emanating from Britain's soft power, but does not elaborate on the example.

[4] Bairoch (1989, 23) underscores how advocates of free trade in Europe played up the link between British economic primacy and its free trade policies, but he holds that, in fact, causation actually ran in the opposite direction. It was economic development that led to a disposition for free trade in Great Britain. Fielden (1969, 97) cites this belief in free trade as an engine of economic growth as a major reason accounting for why the British did not shift to protectionism after 1880.

[5] The famous German tariff of 1879 engineered by Bismarck (which raised agricultural and manufactures tariffs across the board) for political-economic reasons is generally cited as the event that moved Europe back in a protectionist direction (Bairoch 1989, 52). Of course, Britain continued to trade freely until World War I.

tariffs that could be changed only by legislation) made famous by the Cobden-Chevalier Treaty gave nations far greater flexibility in setting lower tariffs. The tariff schedules generally reflected a double-tariff system in which nations could choose to trade at either a maximum or minimum level. A preponderant amount of trade was carried on at minimum tariff levels, effectively carrying on the unencumbered trade of the 1860s and 1870s.[6] Second, transport costs decreased significantly after 1850, especially in the period from 1880 to 1910 (by 60 percent). The great decline in transport costs made up for the increases in tariffs, in many cases even superseding them. Given that protection was instituted almost entirely through tariffs (quotas and other non-tariff barriers were much less visible), changes in transport costs, as well as cost-reduction strategies, gave traders effective means of overcoming existing tariffs and penetrating markets. It is therefore no surprise that the growth of trade in the period after 1880 remained robust, and economic growth on the Continent was even greater than it had been before 1880 (Bairoch 1969, 50, 70).[7]

Indeed, once reciprocated, British free trade promoted a highly desirable environment for British industry and the British economy. The structure of protection in Europe had been oriented strongly around protecting against British goods, as early industrialization made British goods the principal targets of protectionist European states.[8] Even when Britain's lowered tariffs were not reciprocated before the 1850s and 1860s, and protectionism in Europe was partially revived in the United States and

[6] The dual tariff system employed tariffs as bargaining chips that were used to pressure other nations into keeping trade at minimum schedules. Bairoch (1989, 36) refers to the process as "tariff disarmament." This period saw a plethora of treaties granting most-favored-nation status, thus effectively creating a network of fairly free trade. In 1908, the number of treaties among leading trading nations was as follows: Great Britain, 46; Italy, 45; United States, 30; Germany, 30; and France, Spain, and Japan, 20 to 30 each (Saul 1960, 135).

[7] Of course, British growth slowed in the period after 1880 but still remained consistently positive, with low unemployment until the war.

[8] Although some have questioned the advantages Britain gained through free trade, such as McCloskey (1980), who argues that free trade shifted the terms of trade against Britain and hence lowered economic growth, the advantages were nonetheless impressive, especially in a political-economic context. Of course, such terms-of-trade losses must have been moderated because of reciprocity treaties on the part of other nations. Hence other nations were not oppressing British growth through a highly redistributive optimal tariff, if indeed they enjoyed such an advantage at all with the spread of free trade (Kenwood and Lougheed 1999, 68).

Europe after 1880, reducing British prices on both manufactures and agriculture raised British consumer welfare considerably.[9] Lowering the price of food was all the more essential to the isles, whose people were oppressed by high food prices, and British manufacturers were also oppressed by the difficulty of obtaining affordable inputs. In some cases, vital inputs such as sand, ship timbers, and silk were difficult to obtain even at high prices. Whereas historians have generally seen the rise of free trade in Europe as being contemporaneous with a slowdown in the industrialization of the British titan, they underestimate the extent to which availability of more and cheaper inputs kept British industry going at a greater intensity than otherwise might have been the case (Saul 1960, 29–32). Even at mid-century British manufactures were still highly competitive and the British workforce was still the most productive in the world. A major theme of one of the most respected studies of British trade in this period, S. B. Saul's *Studies in British Overseas Trade 1870–1914* (1960), is that Britain reaped great benefits from the fluid trade it maintained with the rest of the world throughout the nineteenth century.[10]

Even very early initiatives at free trade in Britain demonstrated not only an ideological attachment to Richard Cobden and Adam Smith, but also an acknowledgement of the benefits that might be reaped in an economically advanced nation promoting free trade in Europe. The

[9] Kindleberger (1975, 32) and Bairoch (1989, 26) highlight the immediate benefits of Britain's unilateral reductions (especially those of the abolition of the Corn Laws): lower food prices, higher real wages, a declining cost of capital, greater economic growth per capita, greater consumption per capita, and increased manufacturing profits. Much is made about the devastation of agricultural free trade on the British farming sector, but this was mitigated by several factors. First, by 1846, Britain was already importing a large amount of foodstuffs. Second, much of the agricultural sector was able to transition to "high farming" products that kept incomes in the agricultural sector up. In fact, incomes to landlords remained robust for thirty years after the repeal of the Corn Laws. Finally, transition to manufacturing was least painful for Britain, as only 22 percent of British labor was involved in agriculture in 1846; compare this to agricultural labor on the Continent, which was closer to 63 percent (Bairoch 1989, 48, 49).

[10] In cases when the competitiveness of British products was suffering, it was not because of tariffs. In fact, the competitiveness of products of all nations after 1880 was not affected significantly by tariffs. Moreover, the lower tariffs in Britain gave British firms access to cheaper inputs that allowed them to compensate for tariffs in foreign markets with lower domestic production costs, thus enabling them to maintain their competitiveness. Although protectionism abroad did not lead to a significant transformation of British industry, traditional industries were still able to diversify somewhat in order to maintain their markets abroad. In the textiles industry, one of Britain's leading industries, Britain was able to maintain a competitive edge by shifting to higher-quality goods (Kindleberger 1975, 28; Kenwood and Lougheed 1999, 74; Saul 1960, 141, 142).

British were fearful of the growing power of Prussian manufactures. The rising Zollverein (a trade union among Germanic states) was perceived as a growing menace to Britain's economic position in Europe. Under the protection of such a bloc, Prussian machines might threaten Britain's lead in manufacturing on the Continent. Hence, lowering agricultural tariffs – the Corn Laws – was an attempt to disrupt the solidarity between iron and rye that consolidated the protective walls of the Zollverein. Undermining the Zollverein was a means to promote British economic primacy through free trade. The perception was a classical manifestation of hegemonic stability theory: free trade will benefit the economically largest and most productive nation in the world system (Krasner 1976). In this case, free trade fit British interests perfectly, as its manufactures were dominant in foreign markets, but Britain was forced to rely on the rest of the world for the supply of its raw materials (Kenwood and Lougheed 1999, 69).

But the free trade wedge was also useful with respect to other potentially menacing trade coalitions. A number of economic blocs crystallized in the nineteenth century, each comprising a preferential trading network. The Italian states and Austria were especially active in courting other nations for the purpose of establishing trade unions. Moreover, coalitions gravitating around monetary networks, although not formally customs unions or even trade blocs like the Zollverein, functioned as de facto blocs (even though they had no common external tariffs or even multilaterally negotiated trade policy). The Latin Monetary Union (franc nations practicing nominal bimetallism) and the Scandinavian Monetary Union (northern European nations using silver standards and having close trading associations with Germany) were just such blocs. Promoting free trade across these nations after 1850 served to soften the hard shell of the de jure and de facto preferential trading networks and gave British products freer reign among European nations (Fielden 1969, 88; Kenwood and Lougheed 1999, 61; Bairoch 1989, 31).

As the center of world commerce, Britain became the principal player in the service industries (commercial and financial) supporting trade. Furthermore, the spread of free trade, with Britain at the forefront, bolstered Britain's global position and global stake. Its technological capacity for commerce gave it the means to preserve and protect that stake. This essentially opened up the world political economy to British industry as well as to the state (Bartlett 1993, 76). Markets for exports and suppliers of needed raw materials could be secured with Britain's commercial power. This capacity placed Britain at the very center of the most important trade clearing networks that arose in the nineteenth century. The proliferation of multilateral clearing networks, with Britain at their core, carried a myriad of other advantages for Britain.[11] As the largest trading nation in each of the networks, Britain realized the greatest reduction in transaction costs emanating from having to dispense with direct payments for bilateral trade imbalances. And, of course, a core role in these networks increased opportunities for British service industries. British shipping and financial services became dominant as means of clearing world trade (Saul 1960, 53). In fact, much of world trade was cleared through interbank transfers in London. Moreover, as clearing increasingly took place through sterling transactions, the British came to enjoy some of the advantages of generating deficits without tears. Because interbank sterling transfers were responsible for clearing most trading balances, British traders could run up substantial debts without having to ship gold.[12]

The networks also served an especially important role in the structure of British trade as the century progressed. As nations moved in a somewhat more protectionist direction in the 1880s, Britain's trade within networks increased and more networks arose, providing Britain with a counterweight in its balance of payments as the markets on the Continent became somewhat less accessible. Moreover, the growth in services that the networks generated produced a significant rise in invisible earnings that compensated for declining manufacturing exports (Saul 1960, 43–64). Finally, the networks served to moderate demands on Britain's relatively meager gold holdings in the Bank of England because of their multilateral clearing arrangements. This lubricated the adjustment mechanism for Britain as well as for other nations involved, which in turn solidified the stability of the international economy and also kept economic pressures from boiling over into security problems. It was all the more important for Britain to have a fluid and resilient adjustment mechanism. As the world's largest creditor, it was the lynchpin for the stable functioning of the international political economy.

To a large extent, then, the promotion of free and flexible trade in the latter half of the nineteenth century delivered many of the

[11] Multilateral clearing replaced bilateral payment arrangements as trading relations proliferated to create a circular structure of payments. These structures were coterminous with principal trading groups (Saul 1960, 43–64; Kenwood and Loughheed 1999, 93–103).

[12] With respect to deficits without tears, there were also the added benefits that government debt did not have to be created and compensatory monetary policy did not have to be enacted for the clearing of trade balances. Deficits without tears is discussed later in the last section of this chapter.

expected economic gains through anti-monopoly effects, higher real wages, lower transaction costs, greater productivity, greater access to markets, increased opportunities for British industries, and allocative efficiency for Britain. The economic benefits of freer trade were highly significant, but the political benefits were also compelling. The expansion of trade had strong positive externalities for Britain's geostrategic position in the world. It is clear that throughout the nineteenth century, the security and geostrategic goals of Britain were always tied closely to its role as the leading commercial state (Fielden 1969). At the global level, it fostered the rise of a larger and more integrated world economy that enjoyed progress and economic growth, thus enhancing its political relations. As Saul (1960, 64) proclaims, the British policy of free trade "allowed the world trading system to grow remarkably rapidly and peacefully," generating political externalities that benefited Britain. Kenwood and Lougheed (1999, 68) highlight the general "atmosphere" of freedom and stability in European relations created by the freer movement of people, goods, and money. Furthermore, the British Navy was one of the principal beneficiaries of the rise of free trade in the nineteenth century. British supremacy in shipbuilding never waned across the nineteenth century (Saul 1960, 31). Given the limited disjuncture between commercial and military shipbuilding in this period (militarization of vessels could be done with little difficulty, and even retrofitting was much simpler than it would be today), Britain realized the ability to support the most important means of its global power: its navy. The global power of Britain was manifest in its power over the seas, compensating for a less-than-imposing land force (Bartlett 1993, 59, 63). British foreign policy was carried out most vigorously on coasts and across bodies of water, both in its most aggressive forms (Palmerston's gun boats) and its less militaristic forms (the imperialism of free trade).

The greater commercial and naval capacity of Britain also provided multiple avenues to escape political competition and conflict on the Continent. With the deterioration of the Concert of Europe system on the Continent, the balance of power was growing more precarious.[13] Naval and commercial access outside the Continent, whether to colonies or remote regions of the world economy, gave Britain a means of carrying on

[13] The Concert system was forged with the Concert of Europe in 1815, according to which the leading military powers sought to channel potentially destabilizing issues into diplomatic forums rather than having them end up in destructive wars. The Concert system weakened considerably after the Crimean War (1854), with the following decades revealing an inability of the great powers to work together as effectively in abating destabilizing problems. On the Concert, see Elrod 1976.

its strategic and economic goals without adding to the instability created by competition among Continental powers. In essence, its superior naval capacity gave it many more escape routes from the political competition engulfing the Continent. Of course, with this greater naval power and access to the world, the British were in a position to bolster one of its most important political functions on the Continent: the role of balancer in the European balance of power.[14] The greater global presence added extra weight to Britain as a potential ally (thus discouraging adventurism), and escape routes from Continental competition eliminated a source of friction. Both served important functions with respect to Britain's foreign policy interests in the nineteenth century.

Moreover, with respect to Britain's quest for stability on the Continent, the proliferation of negotiated trade after 1860 added an important layer of economic solidarity on top of an existing political framework. Trade agreements have long had political uses and implications in European history. The Cobden-Chevalier Treaty of 1860 between France and Britain, for example, was employed by France to buy British neutrality in France's war with Austria. Like the French in this instance, the British had a propensity to carry on diplomacy by commercial means. These commercial undertakings were important in keeping allies close but also in coercing recalcitrant states (Bartlett 1993, 59, 64). Furthermore, beyond Britain's own use of commercial diplomacy, the proliferation of trade treaties that had most-favored-nation clauses created an intricate web of commercial interdependence among the Continental powers that overlaid their security relations (Fielden 1969, 90; Kindleberger 1975, 45). Often, it was commercial negotiations that produced important security outcomes. This added another diplomatic filter for competition among Continental powers.[15] This, in turn, served manifold British strategic

[14] The balancer role called for Britain to be ready to throw its weight into any military alliance that was opposing aggression or the quest for primacy on the part of another nation or alliance (Bartlett 1993).

[15] Britain's relations with both Germany/Prussia and France, the two most important Continental nations, were placed on a better path through these trade strategies. First, the multilateral movement toward free trade slowed the manufacturing competition from France and Germany, thus keeping them behind in the military race. Furthermore, reinforcing Prussia's quest to take control of the Zollverein by using free trade policy brought the economic interests of Britain and Prussia into greater conformity. Moreover, the trade treaties forged with France from 1860 onward were important levers for solidifying alliance relations when France was more disposed to British interests, and also for reigning in French recalcitrance when relations were more turbulent between the two nations (Kindleberger 1975, 33, 34, 43; Gallarotti 1985, 181).

interests in keeping the balance on the Continent stable and fluent. In addition, Britain's strategy of not retaliating against protectionist measures after 1880 served some important geostrategic functions as well, two of the most important of which were to limit friction with Continental powers over markets and to mitigate Continental competition for colonies. Access to British markets made Continental powers more secure with Anglo-European economic relations.

The proliferation of trade diplomacy after 1860 was also an important stabilizing mechanism to compensate for the weakening of the Concert system in managing the balance of power. The additional diplomatic filter imposed on European diplomacy effectively brought back some of the elements of the Concert system. It served to "internationalize diplomatic questions" and reinforce the norm of "conferencing" in solving European political problems. The commercial diplomacy infused greater self-restraint into European politics in the latter half of the century, which the Concert of Europe had been so effective in achieving in the first half (Elrod 1976, 164, 168).

It is interesting, and quite characteristic of a Cosmopolitan process of power manifesting itself, to see how hard power politics played themselves out on the Continent in the latter half of the nineteenth century and how they were impacted by elements of soft power. Whereas the soft power consequences of British economic primacy were instrumental in contributing to the ongoing economic influence of Britain, Britain was facing much stiffer competition in military hard power on the Continent.[16] Interestingly, this came as a result of its rivals (that could not compete with Britain economically) undertaking hard military power strategies to combat Britain's hard and soft economic power. British soft power, in enhancing its balancer role and providing a countervailing wedge against such strategies, consequently served to diminish military threats that might emanate from such strategies. Thus, British soft power enhanced its influence over the course of security matters (hard power) on the Continent. Yet even more directly, the greater economic power rendered from growing soft power made Britain a more menacing foe militarily.

[16] There has been extensive debate about the course of British primacy during the latter half of the nineteenth century: was it a declining hegemon or not? Although there is no attempt to answer such a controversial question here, it is clear that whether or not its primacy was declining, the soft power generated through economic policy emulation served to make Britain stronger economically and politically than it would have been without such soft empowerment. On the question of British hegemony, see especially Gallarotti (1995b) and Krasner (1976).

Both manifestations of hard power ultimately allowed Britain to fight a war – World War I – against enemies that had embraced principally hard power policies. The British were strong enough to fight a war and were capable of forging a strong alliance in war. So whereas the war had turned Britain to hard solutions, soft power had been instrumental in cultivating that hard power.

In sum, under both reciprocity and moderated reciprocity in free trade policy during the latter half of the nineteenth century, Britain gained great economic and political benefits from its soft power as an economic role model. As the leading producer of industrial goods and the world's clearinghouse for trade in terms of goods and services, Britain came to enjoy a myriad of benefits from other nations pursuing more liberal trading practices. These benefits of soft power enhanced Britain's hard power (economic primacy and political influence) on the Continent even more, manifesting a Cosmopolitan interaction process of reinforcement between the two sources of power.

Great Britain and the Classical Gold Standard, 1880 to 1914

Sterling and the gold standard spread among developed nations in the nineteenth century for reasons similar to the appeal of free trade (discussed in the previous section) and dollarization (discussed later in the next section). Sterling had become the leading reserve currency in the world, far ahead of the proliferation of gold standards in the 1870s. This, as with modern-day dollarization, was a principal function of the position of Britain in the international economy (i.e., the hard power of economic primacy) and the stability of monetary policy in Britain that made sterling a safe bet. The growth of the British economy resulted in a manifold expansion of trade that made sterling a dominant currency in clearing trade transactions. Even as early as the first quarter of the century, sterling was estimated to be financing more than three-fourths of world trade (Gallarotti 1995b, 277). This was a compelling reason for sterling to become the dominant currency in nations' international reserves, but the confidence and admiration of Britain's industrial miracle that kept it economically preeminent in the world economy kept perceptions of risk in sterling positions extremely low (i.e., like betting on the dollar for modern-day nations pursuing dollarization). Just as such properties made Britain a trade role model, they also made it a monetary role model (Gallarotti 1995b, 145).

As with dollarization, seigniorage gains were enjoyed throughout the nineteenth century.[17] In addition to the direct seigniorage gains enjoyed by creating money, holding sterling amounted to an interest-free loan for Britain. The dominance of sterling provided a great advantage in orienting trade toward British products, and it enhanced all of the opportunities the United States now experiences with respect to opportunities for financial intermediation in foreign capital markets (discussed later in the next section). As much as technology and productivity drove the British industrial juggernaught in the nineteenth century, sterling tagged along as a very helpful handmaiden (Lindert 1969, 10–12).

The holding of sterling by other nations served important functions for Britain. The ability to run up commercial debt without tears relieved Britain from crucial pressures in its balance of payments position that potentially could have been destabilizing for maintaining convertibility. This actually proved to be a far less abused privilege than in the case of the United States under Bretton Woods, when the possibilities of financing trade without resorting to hard reserves (in this case, gold) allowed the United States to run large deficits without incurring significant burdens. Britain's external position had remained fairly strong throughout the century, and it was not prone to the inflationary tendencies of the United States under Bretton Woods, as monetary orthodoxy dictated a more responsible management of the money supply (Fetter 1965). Yet British balance of payments did show secular difficulties with respect to other leading nations as the century progressed. Although the colonies took up an increasing load of exports to compensate, the British balance of payments demonstrated a trend toward deterioration after 1870 (Saul 1960). The increased holding of sterling balances in foreign reserves helped relieve Britain of the monetary consequences of a deteriorating balance of payments. This manifested itself especially with respect to Britain's own gold reserves. Whereas specie in London was abundant, the gold reserves of the Bank of England were always scant, even with

[17] On seigniorage, see the last section on dollarization later. Although sterling circulated in various nations, it was not as pervasive as the circulation of dollars under dollarization in the current period. Sterling circulated informally in varying degrees, as national monetary systems were not subject to the same monopoly power of money creation that would manifest itself in the twentieth century. Hence, with respect to money in circulation, Britain enjoyed seigniorage gains primarily from informal dollarization. The circulation of sterling, of course, was much more formal and pervasive in the colonies and Portugal; hence, seigniorage gains there were more of a formal type.

respect to sterling liabilities within the British system, not to mention the size of Britain's international liabilities. Monetary experts and authorities throughout the century made quite a fuss about the destabilizing potential of the Bank's predilection to hold only a "thin film of gold" (Bagehot 1873/1921).[18] The abundant foreign use of sterling preserved the liquidity position of the Bank of England throughout the century, even in the face of this thin film.

The reversion to gold standards that took place among leading nations in the 1870s served to solidify and compound the advantages that sterling had reaped for Britain earlier in the century. This "scramble for gold" was a classic manifestation of Britain's soft power.[19] Monetary elites generally shared the belief that Britain's lead in industrialization was principally driven by adopting a gold standard.[20] In fact, Britain was the only leading nation officially on a pure gold standard before 1850. This prevailing belief was behind much of the pervasive movement toward gold in the latter half of the nineteenth century. Indeed, because of the British example, a gold standard became a highly prestigious system of monetary management for national economies (Keynes 1913/1971, 13, 14; Gallarotti 1995b, 154; Bordo and Rockoff 1996). As with the link between free trade and British economic primacy, this correlation between Britain's economic success and gold was hardly a manifestation

[18] In his famous *Lombard Street*, a diatribe on the irresponsible central banking policies of the Bank of England, Walter Bagehot (1873/1921) suggests that "a more miserable history [in managing a national reserve] can hardly be found." Yeager (1976, 302) estimates that the Bank's gold holdings through the period from 1880 to 1914 gravitated around 2 percent of the national money supply. Minimizing gold holdings reflected the private-banking priorities of the Bank of England, as gold reserves were non–interest-bearing assets, and thus holding excessive gold diminished profits. All leading central banks in the nineteenth century were also profit-making companies, so this was not an unusual posture for such banks. The Bank of England, however, surpassed all other leading central banks in its attention to its profit-making mandate (Gallarotti 1995b, 123–6).

[19] The scramble for gold commonly refers to the adoption on the part of developed nations of gold standards during the 1870s (Gallarotti 1993).

[20] The increasing use of sterling showed a somewhat different soft power dynamic relative to the scramble for gold that began in the 1870s. The attraction of sterling showed much of the same soft power attraction of modern day dollarization: a manifestation of the confidence generated by the reserve nation (in this case the United States now and Britain then). With respect to the attraction of the British gold standard, the soft power dynamic featured similar elements, but above and beyond this confidence, there appeared a perception similar to the one that fueled the movement toward free trade in the nineteenth century. This perception attributed a link between Britain's economic primacy and its early industrialization on one hand, and its use of a gold standard on the other (Gallarotti 1995b, 145).

of causation. Perceptions erred in that respect and perhaps attributed far more economic "glitter" to the standard than was merited.[21] Although the scramble in monetary regime transformations in the 1870s was also the result of some crucial short-term factors (especially the rapid depreciation of silver), the ideological appeal based on admiration of the British economic miracle served as an ongoing bias pushing elites in the direction of gold throughout the nineteenth century. The crucial conditions of the 1870s lent urgency to that bias and thus consummated monetary regime transformations in the 1870s (Gallarotti 1993, 1995b, 143–80).

Kindleberger (1984) notes that until the 1870s, Paris was emerging as a viable competitor to London for financial primacy. But with the reversion to gold on the part of developed nations, London solidified its place on top of the financial hierarchy. This was important in a number of respects that tied into Britain's national and global interests. On a micro level, it gave great advantages to London and British financial intermediaries, both inside and outside Britain. One of the principal reasons for shifting to gold standards was for nations to have greater access to the London market. As access was enhanced, demand for British assets and services followed. Using the gold standard gave nations preferential access to finance in Britain. Using gold allowed them to contract loans at more favorable rates because gold standards rendered a higher credit rating to borrowers (Bordo and Rockoff 1996). British financial houses, which specialized in financial services oriented around bills and gold (the two were ultimately interchangeable), provided the leading services in capital markets oriented around gold. This enhanced an already preponderant lead over foreign financial intermediaries in the diversity and quality of services they provided. The world financial markets were ripe for the picking, especially given that British banking continued to expand internationally, and foreign business in Britain proliferated concomitantly. The closest rival, France, fell ever shorter in terms of an international financial player. The link between national and international finance for Britain was strong, as it was the world's greatest financial and commercial power. A preponderant economic stake in the international system essentially made Britain a world banker. This placed British banks and the Bank of England in the principal role of clearinghouses for global

[21] Numerous monetary experts and statesmen of the period attested to the problematic nature of this perception, noting that the scramble for gold was predicated on faulty interpretations of history (Gallarotti 1995b, 145).

finance, giving London the greatest pulling power over capital of any financial center in the world. (Gallarotti 2005, 40).

Reversion to gold on the part of other nations also enhanced London's position as the leading gold market in the world. The holding of sterling balances on the part of foreign banks had always been an important factor for maintaining convertibility in England in the face of paltry gold reserves in the Bank of England. However, the greater primacy that reversion to gold rendered onto the London gold market enhanced the strength of British convertibility even more. It meant that the Bank of England and British finance could obtain more gold at a faster rate under periods of stress or high demand in Britain. London was the major conduit for gold in the world, which provided it with endless capacity to replenish gold stocks in need. With this pulling power came greater control over international capital flows. This had numerous advantages for both British finance and the British economy. On a macroeconomic level, it kept the British economy liquid throughout the nineteenth century. Because confidence in sterling and gold was vigorous, foreign traders and financiers were perfectly happy to clear payments exclusively through British banks. In terms of domestic finance, this made the British financial system more liquid, as confidence kept investment targeted on Britain. Moreover, there was an important international side effect to the power of British finance. Its power to attract capital allowed it to continue as the major capital exporter of the nineteenth century. This kept the international system sufficiently liquid as well, a major source of stability for the international economy in this period (Gallarotti 1995b, 193–200).

The economic advantages Britain reaped from the primacy of sterling and gold compounded the manifold effects of free trade in opening up economies and integrating the world economy to a greater extent, and in turn compounding the political benefits of free trade, as discussed above. Polanyi (1957) sees the emergence of an international financial system oriented around sterling as a lynchpin in preserving the "great peace" of the nineteenth century. It integrated nations into a web of economic interdependence that, in conjunction with the rise of trade diplomacy, undergirded security relations on the Continent. In this respect, the benefits of the extensive adoption of gold and sterling compounded all of the political benefits of the rise of free trade in the international political economy. Political stability on the Continent was enhanced, as were trans-Atlantic relations with the United States, which was also making extensive use of sterling and gold. The greater economic influence rendered by British financial primacy also enhanced the effectiveness of its balancer role in the European balance of power. But perhaps even more importantly, it negated the destabilizing effects of a reversion back to protectionism by keeping some semblance of an international economic regime oriented around the British economy when markets on the Continent were putting up barriers to trade.[22] Indeed, the reliance on sterling allowed Britain to remain a trading hub even though nations became more discriminating in their trading policies, and the British primacy generated a natural link among other nations. As in the case of a trading system, a stable international financial system was good in its particularistic opportunities for the British economy as well as for the stability of the international political economy collectively. This served Britain's vital national and foreign interests with respect to its role as dominant economy and balancer.

In sum, along with the other pillar of British soft power, the admiration of British trade policy, the attraction of sterling and gold rendered significant political-economic influence onto Britain in the latter half of the nineteenth century. The adoption of gold and the use of sterling created an international milieu that expanded Britain's opportunities, which compounded Britain's economic primacy and enhanced its political influence. Thus, as with trade, British influence also manifested a Cosmopolitan process of compound interaction between hard and soft power. British soft power emanated from Britain's hard power as an economic monetary hegemon (i.e., primacy), and this soft power reinforced the dominant monetary position of Britain, which in turn raised British stature as a role model (i.e., enhanced soft empowerment) even more.

Dollarization in the Modern Era

Dollarization is defined as the adoption of a foreign currency to fill the roles of money in an economy. Dollarization represents a more extreme solution to the problem of inflation. Nations that have dollarized have been unable to reign in inflation using more conventional means (more discipline in monetary policy, fixed exchange rates), and thus have drifted to more extreme measures of controlling the money supply, such as currency boards and dollarization.[23] Although many currencies could

22 As noted above in the first section, effective protection after 1880 was moderated by the use of trade treaties that created a network of nations trading at preferential tariff rates.

23 Currency boards (where official reserves are often held in dollars, but the dollar does not fill other roles of money in the economy) are also called quasi-dollarized systems (Altig and Nosal 2002, 1).

theoretically be employed as the basis for dollarization, the American dollar fills this role most extensively relative to other currencies in nations practicing variants of dollarization. The use of the dollar emanates from a shared confidence in and admiration of the American economy, and the management of the American money supply.[24] Because national money supplies are linked to the creation of dollars in the United States, only supreme confidence in the stability of the dollar would lead to such a choice. In creating a common currency area, the greater economic integration that results makes economic spillovers likelier. Hence, in selecting the dollar, nations are making a statement about their faith in the stability of the American economy and political system (Altig and Nosal 2002, 11). In this case, emulation is indeed the highest form of flattery for the United States.

Dollarization regimes range from unofficial dollarization, when a foreign currency is used both as a source of purchasing domestic goods, savings and investment (but in this case does not have full legal tender); to semiofficial dollarization, when the foreign currency has full legal tender but often plays a secondary role in a variety of transactions (such as paying wages, taxes, and household bills); to full or official dollarization, when the foreign currency plays the principal roles of money as a unit of account, a medium of exchange, and a store of value (while the domestic currency plays a secondary role). Variants of dollarization are practiced in many countries today, principally in transition, emerging, and developing economies.

The use of American dollars in foreign economies carries a myriad of advantages for the United States. Seigniorage is generally touted as the most glaring advantage (Cohen 2003, 229; Altig and Nosal 2002, 1; U.S. Senate 2000a, 3). The United States, by printing the money, earns what is referred to as seigniorage, whereas the domestic government relying on dollarization foregoes such seigniorage. Seigniorage is defined as the difference between the value of placing money into circulation and the cost of creating that money. Ultimately, nations obtaining dollars will have to purchase them with goods and services (Altig and Nosal 2002, 4). A dollar bill costs roughly 3 cents to create yet fetches 100 cents

[24] Of course, it is clear that the global economy has chosen the dollar as the principal key currency, both at the private and public levels. Individuals and firms have long used dollars in exchange and as investments. Central banks have held more dollars than any other key currency. Thus, dollarization is just another iteration (albeit a more extreme one) of a global predilection for using the currency of the United States (U.S. Senate 1999, 32).

worth of goods. Net nominal seigniorage amounts to the value minus the cost of production, hence 97 cents. A more accurate estimate of real seigniorage is the change in the monetary base (ˆM) of the recipient nation (or nominal seigniorage) divided by price level units (PLU) in the U.S., hence ˆM/PLU. So if the U.S. issues 200 million new dollars to country X, then the nominal seignorage for the U.S. is 194 million dollars (200 × .97). Dividing by price level units of 1.05 gives you real seigniorage in the amount of 184.76 million dollars. The seigniorage gains for any nation printing money are therefore considerable. Conversely, the losses in seigniorage that come from relinquishing this right are also considerable. The United States gains billions of dollars in net seigniorage from around the world each year. One estimate has suggested that if all of South America and Mexico were to dollarize, the seigniorage for the United States would amount to earnings between 0.2 and 0.8 percent of U.S. gross domestic product (GDP) (Altig and Nosal 2002, 5). The size of seigniorage redistribution is so large that the most salient issue between the United States and dollarizing nations has become the question of equitable seigniorage sharing (U.S. Senate 1999; U.S. Senate 2000a; U.S. Senate 2000b). Moreover, seigniorage enters into the American federal budget on the receipts side, which is especially crucial in the present period of large fiscal deficits (U.S. Senate 1999, 22).

Furthermore, financial gains to the United States from dollarization are also acquired in what amount to interest-free loans. Individuals whose national laws prevent them from holding wealth in foreign notes and coins will have to resort to assets to fulfill their portfolio preferences. Because a principal asset for investment is American Treasury securities, the individuals holding such securities will be extracting interest payments from the U.S. government. However, holding notes and coins carries no such claims to interest payments. Thus, if a dollarization currency is proclaimed legal tender in a nation, individuals can very well hold dollars rather than American bonds, relieving the United States from having to transfer interest payments. The gains here can, as with seigniorage, be considerable, as they would amount to the monetary base times either the interest rate or the level of inflation in the foreign nation. The gains here would also be especially important for the United States in a fiscal context. In this respect, dollarization functions as a subsidy or rebate to American taxpayers. Yet more generally, in terms of the federal budget, savings on debt service and the receipts from seigniorage together form a counterweight to the severe deficit spending of recent administrations (U.S. Senate 1999, 22).

Dollarization has a significant impact on the external accounts as well. The term "deficits without tears" has long been used to describe America's advantage from being the world banker under the Bretton Woods regime.[25] On the one hand, dollar reserve holdings in foreign banks relieve the United States from creating government debt that would burden its taxpayers. On the other hand, American deficits are being financed by holding American dollars, many of which will be deposited in the United States; thus, in effect, no compensatory monetary policy has to be instituted, so no contractionary effect on the American money supply is necessary.[26] This "sterilization effect" keeps the money supply stable when it normally should decline. Therefore, deficits can be run up without the burden of offsetting monetary policy (Bergsten 1994, 204; U.S. Senate 1999, 43). This has been especially important recently, as the United States' current account has experienced a period of significant deterioration, fueled especially by the burgeoning trade deficit with China.

The lowering of transaction costs, another important benefit of dollarization, would also carry manifold benefits for the United States. First, American multinationals would enjoy greater efficiency in their operations from such monetary standardization (U.S. Senate 2000a, 3). Similarly, there would be substantial benefits in terms of better portfolio investment opportunities; many of these effects would be the result of resources formerly used to hedge exchange-rate risk now being employed in more productive investments.[27] The other efficiency effects come primarily in the form of lower transaction costs created by standardization at a more general economic level than just the operations of multinationals (e.g., currency conversion costs of tourism) (Altig and Nosal 2002, 6).

The gains would also extend to trade and other investment opportunities. In terms of investment, dollarization would more closely integrate national capital markets. There would be less exchange risk (because of fixed exchange rates) and no financial conversion costs in those

[25] Financial gains through interest-free loans and deficits without tears can be considered benefits of indirect seigniorage, distinct from the more direct seigniorage benefits composed of the difference between the value of dollars placed in circulation and their cost.

[26] Depositing American dollars in the United States means that the money supply does not experience destabilizing swings.

[27] The reduction in exchange risk is one contributing factor to the decline in investment risk, but there is also the fact that monetary integration will place nations along convergent inflationary paths, thus promoting closer macroeconomic convergence (Barro 1995).

economies, which would significantly lower the costs of capital in those economies. This would open up many more opportunities for U.S. companies and individuals to invest and prosper in the dollarized nations and also would encourage far greater investment in dollar-denominated assets. Greater integration gives American financial intermediaries and complementary industries a significant wedge in penetrating foreign capital markets. Above and beyond the superior quality of their services, American financial firms would enjoy the "denomination rents" that result from increased demand for American financial services (Frieden 2003, 326). Aside from the greater opportunities for American private industry, the greater internationalization and integration of the foreign financial markets would produce greater transparency and regulation in those markets, which would enhance their stability and consequently deliver a more stable international monetary system (U.S. Senate 1999, 25). This would have manifold benefits for the United States as well. First, it would make it more difficult to fund terrorist activities as well as covert investments into the development of WMD, two of America's most important foreign policy concerns during the past decade. Second, greater stability in foreign markets would relieve the pressure on the United States of private and public bailouts in the wake of financial crises. America has indeed carried the burden, through its banks and its support of international financial institutions, throughout the postwar period. Third, greater stability would also relieve the debt overhang problems in least-developed countries (LDCs) that have plagued U.S. banks and public lending institutions during the past three decades. Finally, transparency is likely to spill over into other areas of public policy, such as fiscal policy. This would serve to give impetus to the structural reforms in developing nations, of which the United States and the IMF have been erstwhile advocates (U.S. Senate 2000b, 19, 69). Dollarization would ultimately provide more impetus for foreign governments to undertake greater regulatory changes consistent with practices in the United States (Frieden 2003, 328).

Trade effects would also amount to greater market penetration for several reasons. The absence of exchange risk would encourage greater trade between the United States and dollarized nations. Furthermore, the savings in the costs of foreign exchange transactions would encourage the dollarized nation to buy more goods from the United States. Non-dollarized currencies would still have to incur transaction costs in being converted to the currency of the dollarized nation, causing traders to shy away from the goods of non-dollarized nations. Trade diversion effects would benefit the United States in this case. Moreover, the greater integration of markets resulting from monetary consolidation would enhance the demand for U.S. products. In this case, the American dollar would be an ambassador and advertisement for U.S. goods, both of which would amount to enhanced competitiveness for American companies.

The political benefits of dollarization appear substantial as well (Cohen 2003; Frieden 2003). In this respect, greater dependence on the United States as the supplier of dollars bestows manifold political advantages. For one thing, the fact that foreign money supplies are held in dollars makes the United States the major source of liquidity and an important lender of last resort to these economies (Cohen 2003, 229; Frieden 2003, 327). The resulting political power has been clearly evident in the case of Panama. Panama has used dollars since 1903. This ongoing dependence has allowed the United States to influence the course of Panamanian politics throughout the century. U.S. influence drove Panama to secede from Colombia to build the Panama Canal, and its ongoing influence in Panama has allowed it to keep a tight leash on the canal throughout the century. An especially salient manifestation of this influence was evident under Reagan, when the United States tried to oust General Manuel Noriega. Initially, Reagan attempted to facilitate a coup through financial warfare. Reagan effectively tried to demonetize Panama by freezing Panamanian assets in U.S. banks and prohibiting dollar transfers to Panama. The resulting economic shock featured a decline of 20 percent in Panama's GDP. While it was the invasion that eventually brought down the Noriega regime, it was also clear that the monetary dependence created by dollarization gave the United States preponderant power over the Panamanian economy. On a global scale, the United States, as a banker for the world economy, gains disproportionate political influence as a function of its influence over national economies and monetary systems in similar ways (Cohen 2003, 230; U.S. Senate 1999, 56).

On a regional level, dollarization promises to be of significant political importance to the United States, mainly because variants of dollarization have been adopted in a number of Latin America nations. The United States has a strong interest in maintaining prosperity, stability, and close ties in its own backyard, but especially in Latin America (U.S. Senate 1999, 43). This region has historically been fraught with both political and economic instability that have threatened key U.S. interests – maintaining environments supportive of democracy and capitalism in the Western Hemisphere. Greater foreign dependence on the United States, as well as greater U.S. penetration in and integration with these economies, promise to enhance such objectives. Indeed, adopting the dollar as a currency serves to "import" a credible monetary policy immediately, allowing the dollarizing nations to experience the manifold economic benefits of such confidence-creating outcomes (Altig and Nosal 2002, 7). Greater integration, internationalization, and stabilization in these economies promises a more conducive environment for economic development. All of these outcomes enhance prospects for democracy and capitalism in the region.[28]

On a global scale, the greater linkages to the dollar can only enhance the political and economic influence of the United States, thus compounding the economic and political regional benefits enumerated above. Dollarization has placed the United States in a more authoritative position both politically and economically over dollar-dependent nations, enhancing U.S. leverage to realize its foreign policy goals. Much of this leverage emanates from the fact that greater integration through dollarization brings the economic and political interests of the United States and dollarized nations into greater convergence (U.S. Senate 2000b, 46; Altig and Nosal 2002, 9). Moreover, such a mechanism for stabilizing and developing the economies of dollarized nations has proved superior to the more conventional strategies of direct foreign aid.[29] But while aid has been costly, dollarization generates net benefits for the United States in promoting economic stabilization and development, such as seigniorage, deficits without tears, and opportunities for American businesses. It is also likely that enhanced growth in these economies will stimulate growth in the U.S. economy as well (U.S. Senate 1999, 29). Dollarization will be a win/win development and stabilization strategy for the United States in that the United States is being rewarded for promoting economic growth and stability in dollarized nations. In this case, the United States can "have its cake and eat it too" (U.S. Senate 2000a, 3).

Furthermore, there is a strong positive feedback effect between the prestige of the United States and the greater use of the dollar, each feeding on the other. A more prestigious image in the world community will

[28] Important American public servants such as Lawrence Summers and Alan Greenspan have underscored the importance of the stake that the United States has in the stability of its regional neighbors, and as a result of this stake, dollarization is of immense importance (U.S. Senate 1999). Such enhanced monetary integration would also serve to encourage an important U.S. trade goal in the region: to bring other regional players into the North American Free Trade Agreement (NAFTA) (Altig and Nosal 2002, 11).

[29] See especially U.S. Senate (1999); U.S. Senate (2000b); Salvatore, Dean, and Willett (2003).

pay dividends in everything from fighting terrorism to creating greater demand for U.S. goods. On social, political, and economic levels, this positive image will reap manifold gains for the United States and American citizens (U.S. Senate 1999, 44; U.S. Senate 2000a, 3).

Moreover, the more stable international global economic order created by dollarization promises to disproportionately benefit the dominant economic power in the system. In this respect, just as the United States has historically benefited from a free trade regime across nations, a stable economic order is a public good that rewards the United States commensurately. Fewer meltdowns relieve the United States from carrying the burden of stabilization programs; nations will be in a position to better embrace political and economic policies that mirror U.S. practices; and the world economy will be a more conducive place for American enterprise (U.S. Senate 1999, 53; Krasner 1976). Dollarization will also keep the United States ahead of the challenges of the Euro as a global key currency, thus staving off the monetary challenge marshaled by the European Union (EU) (Altig and Nosal 2002, 11). In the final analysis, dollarization is creating an international political economy that better accords with America's most important foreign policy goals.

Various arguments about the negative effects of dollarization on the United States have raised a number of key concerns. First, there is the concern that the dollar overhang from dollarization may produce some instability in the U.S. monetary system and dollar exchange rate. Second, there is concern that the Federal Reserve may face significant constraints that interfere with its domestic mission. A corollary concern is that the Fed will be forced to become a regulator of foreign banks in dollarized nations. Finally, there is a fear that adverse economic developments in those countries that are dependent on dollars will cause their people to blame the United States.[30] Estimates, however, show that the overhang from dollarization has been relatively small (circa 5 percent of external liabilities), so the potential for destabilizing both the exchange rate of the dollar and the domestic monetary system of the United States appear limited (U.S. Senate 1999, 61). With regard to the increased international role of the Fed, it is already the case that the Fed takes foreign economic developments into consideration when framing monetary policy. The limited levels of dollar overhang will not increase that sensitivity significantly. Furthermore, the Fed has for years functioned in a *de facto*

[30] On the concerns over the negative effects of dollarization, see especially U.S. Senate (1999), Altig and Nosal (2002), and U.S. Senate (2000b).

dollarized international economy without feeling the compulsion to go out and regulate foreign banks (U.S. Senate 1999, 61; U.S. Senate 2000b, 4). Finally, dollarized economies have been experiencing problems for years without much political backlash toward the United States. Transmission shocks have occurred even more frequently among nations not sharing a common currency (Altig and Nosal 2002, 8).

In sum, dollarization has carried extensive advantages for American citizens, businesses, and the state. As with the British experience with free trade and the use of sterling and gold, with the expanded adoption of the dollar, the United States has reaped, and continues to reap, great advantages that have enhanced its political and economic goals. Also, as with British trade and finance, dollarization has manifested a Cosmopolitan interaction process among hard and soft power. The great economic primacy of the United States has rendered opportunities for soft empowerment through dollarization, and the resulting emulation of U.S. monetary practices has fed back to enhance the hard economic and political power of the United States.

5

Case Study of Hard Disempowerment

U.S. Foreign Policy and the Bush Doctrine

U.S. foreign policy under the George W. Bush administration represents an especially crucial case laboratory for the analysis of the process of hard disempowerment. First, the United States enjoyed global primacy with respect to hard power under the Bush years. Although a number of naysayers identified a deterioration of the relative power position of the United States during these years, few have questioned whether the United States had enjoyed a preponderant position of global influence.[1] Moreover, because the Bush Doctrine vigorously embraced the use of hard power strategies at the expense of soft power strategies in promoting critical foreign policy goals, it is an especially critical case for assessing how an exaggerated dependence on hard power can be disempowering in the modern world system.

The Bush Doctrine and Hard Power

Although George W. Bush campaigned on promises of a "humble foreign policy," events that would confront the fledgling president called off all bets. After 9/11, the United States embarked on a new course in global affairs, one that painstakingly and autonomously sought to blaze a crusading trail that would leave those who menaced Americans charred in its path. According to Bush, the new threats to the American

[1] See Cox 2007b and citations to the literature on the subject of the "new American decline." Brooks and Wohlforth (2008), who have averred that rumors of American decline were greatly exaggerated, have issued a scathing critical response to this literature.

people ("radicalism" and "technology") created conditions that altered American foreign priorities (White House 2002a, 3). This, in turn, called for new solutions. Whereas grand diplomacy and alliances had been the appropriate methods to confront security threats in the old world of international politics, the new world of terrorism and proliferating WMD vitiated the effectiveness of these cumbersome and slow strategies. The new threats called for anticipation, speed, and resolve, none of which accorded with the lethargic processes of international organization or activation of alliance commitments in the face of threats. The strategy must be to "destroy threats before they reach [American] shores," which would necessitate that Americans "not hesitate to act alone, if necessary, to exercise [their] right of self defense" (White House 2002a, 6). Moreover, as Bush proclaimed in the National Security Strategy (2002a, iv) and reiterated in the preface to the National Strategy to Combat Weapons of Mass Destruction (White House 2002b, 1), "the only path to peace and security is the path of action." Indeed, the premise of Bush's national security strategy was that "America is at war," so it was a "wartime national strategy" (White House 2006, i). In war, the United States could not afford to be passive. The policy mandated an unapologetic imposition of U.S. will and thus was strongly grounded in an orientation of assertive nationalism. This strategy was dubbed the Bush Doctrine. The doctrine designated vigorous use of American power and unilateralism as the foundations on which to construct a more effective style of American foreign policy.[2]

Deriving from what was termed "roll back theory" in the 1950s, this updated Neoconservative version (first manifest under Reagan) strongly embraced the same fears of overly passive foreign policy in the face of ever-growing menaces (akin to the critique of containment in the 1950s).[3] This neoconservative view of U.S. foreign relations designated force, coercion, and assertive unilateralism as crucial means of effectively confronting the pervasive evil forces that threatened American interests. In this respect, the doctrine was fundamentally grounded in a hard power orientation.

The strategies dictated by the doctrine strongly exuded the hard power primacy of the United States as firmly buttressing the "action" these strategies entailed. In Bush's own words from the National Security Strategy (White House 2002a, iv), "Today, the United States enjoys a position

[2] The Bush doctrine has been spelled out in the National Security Strategy (White House 2002a) of 2002 and reinforced in the National Security Strategy (White House 2006) of 2006. For insightful descriptions of the Bush Doctrine, see especially Smith (2007), Jervis (2003b, 2005), and Monten (2007).

[3] On Neoconservatism, see Irving Kristol (1995).

of unparalleled military strength and great economic and political influence." This "strength" and "influence" should dictate how the United States' foreign policy strategies must be configured. Indeed, Bush proclaimed, "The great strength of this nation must be used to promote a balance of power that favors freedom" (White House 2002a, 1). Smith (2007) has concisely identified the neoconservative worldview that generated the beliefs driving the Bush Doctrine: the United States must remain dominant across global issues; it must maintain this primacy versus all competitors; U.S. enemies thrive in environments where American foreign policy is passive; and finally, the United States must foster its image across the globe (what he calls "liberal imperialism"). This brash and aggressive orientation in foreign affairs has, as would be expected, drawn differing responses from the public and intellectuals alike. Critics have condemned it as arrogant, parochial, and chauvinistic, whereas supporters have hailed it as redeeming.[4]

The consequences of the doctrine for the United States and its foreign policy have been pernicious. Rather than strengthening the United States in the face of new and old threats, Bush's foreign policy weakened the nation in many ways. The greater influence deriving from the United States' preponderant hard power, which was supposed to deliver the United States from the imminent dangers facing it, was illusory. The Bush foreign policy proved self-defeating even in promoting the administration's three major goals: abating terrorism, promoting democracy abroad, and reducing the threat of WMD. The policies of strength followed by the Bush administration delivered weakness instead. Kaplan (2008, 183) captures the nature of this victimization well in noting, "Bush and his top advisors began their administration believing that America was so peerlessly strong that it could impose its will unilaterally." The hypnotic allure of U.S. hard power as a strategic springboard produced a myopic and limited foreign policy based on force and coercion. Yet in being so myopic and limited to hard power, it fell into the trap of neglecting alternative soft policies that could have enhanced national influence and better promoted the administration's major foreign policy goals (Halper and Clarke 2004, 182). The administration failed to appreciate the advantages of being admired and emulated. And in doing so, it

[4] For representative arguments defending the Bush doctrine, see "Defending and Advancing Freedom" (2005), Kagan (2003), and Rice (2000). For diverse critical responses to the policy, see especially Kaplan (2008), Fukuyama (2006), Smith (2007), Nye (2002, 2003), Jervis (2003b, 2005), Kegley and Raymond (2007), and Calleo (2003).

undermined a great deal of the soft power the United States had come to enjoy as a result of its culture and the policies it had pursued under Clinton. In this respect, the Bush strategy proved self-defeating and ultimately disempowering for the United States.

In Gallarotti (2010), I analyze the weakening effects of the Bush Doctrine within the more general context of power dynamics encompassing the power curse and power illusion (discussed in chapter 1). Because the present book analyzes the manifestations of this more general dynamic specifically within the context of a soft-hard power nexus, this analysis will focus on the administration's victimization from hard disempowerment.

American Hard Disempowerment under the Bush Doctrine

After eight years of the United States flexing its muscles from a position of primacy, the state of world affairs at the end of Bush's tenure appeared worse with respect to American interests than it did before he took office. Politics in Latin America moved to the left, and anti-U.S. sentiment arose concomitantly. All of the U.S. posturing and coercion put little dent into the development of WMD in North Korea, India, Pakistan, and Iran.[5] The Doha Round failed. Peace in the Middle East was as elusive as ever. Both political instability and poverty increased in Africa. U.S.-Soviet relations were at a post–Cold War nadir. The new economic titans of Asia (China and Japan) were ever more recalcitrant and independent minded. Democratic state building in Iraq and Afghanistan was precariously held together through military occupation. The price of oil for most of Bush's second term was higher than ever and applied a chokehold on the American and global economies. The administration exited in the midst of the worst global financial meltdown since the Great Depression. Finally, polls showed that the United States and the Bush administration were held in very low esteem by the international community. The state of world affairs was a compelling reflection of the decline of American influence during the Bush presidency, its hard power notwithstanding.[6]

In terms of the big-three foreign policy goals of the Bush administration (limit the spread of WMD, spread democracy, and combat terrorism),

[5] The evidence of claims that in fact the Iraq War put Libya out of the nuclear business is at best ambiguous.

[6] Although Walt (1999) commented on the adverse state of world affairs before Bush took office, it is clear that they were worse with respect to U.S. interests when he left office after eight years of employing extensive hard resources to improve them.

the prevailing strategies for bringing about such outcomes in Iraq and Afghanistan served as poster cases for the self-defeating consequences of excessive dependence on hard power. There are striking parallels to the fight against terrorism under Bush and the fight against insurgency in Vietnam (Gallarotti 2010). In both cases, American tactics compromised the very soft power that might have undermined the ability of terrorists and insurgents to recruit new members. Furthermore, fighting the war against these menaces exclusively with hard power proved counterproductive because of the negative feedback generated by coercion.[7] Moreover, robust initiatives based on pacification strategies would have produced far better results against an enemy invulnerable to conventional military solutions. Even the U.S. military underscored the need for pacification strategies in Iraq (U.S. Military Index, 2008).

In Iraq, the invasion and occupation proved counterproductive in attending to the goal of terrorism abatement. As in Vietnam, the transfer of security functions to Iraqi forces (like Vietnamization) proceeded slowly, keeping the United States in the despised position of invasion and occupational force (Gallarotti 2010). The United States generated resentment not only because of its outright occupation, but also from all three major political groups in Iraq for other reasons. Debaathification made it an enemy of Sunnis; for Shiites, the insistence against popular elections linked the United States with the political and religious oppression of Hussein; and the Kurds continued to be acrimonious toward the U.S. failure to deliver true political autonomy and power to the group (Allawi 2007, 132–46). The problems facing the United States were compounded by indirect effects with respect to Israel. Preemptive operations by the United States emboldened Israel to also act preemptively against erstwhile threats. Both Shiek Yassin and Hamas leader Abdel Azziz al-Rantissi were assassinated in 2004, which in turn compounded the terrorist and Palestinian problems and set back Bush's Road Map for Peace in the Middle East (Garner 2005, 149).

This general resentment against American hard power strategies, which fueled terrorist sentiment in Iraq (as well as in other nations), was compounded by crucial decisions regarding the management of the transition to self-rule. Ali Allawi (2007, 83), former Iraq Minister of Defense, stated,

[7] Bush underscored the principal means of fighting terrorism in the National Security Strategy (White House 2002a, iv) as hard power resources. "To defeat this threat we must make use of every tool in our arsenal – military power, better homeland defenses, law enforcement, intelligence, and vigorous efforts to cut off terrorist financing."

"... the entire process of planning for a post-war Iraq was mired in ineptitude, poor organization and indifference." Decisions to disband the army and the policy of Debaathification put into motion a process that significantly fueled the causes of terrorism and insurgency. These decisions put hundreds of thousands of people – fifty thousand Baathist workers and about four hundred thousand soldiers – out of work (Kaplan 2008, 151; Allawi 2007, 150–60). The causes of terrorism and insurgency appeared especially appealing to Baathists and displaced soldiers, as they experienced both the anti-Western resentment and economic hardship that made them especially impressionable to the anti-American cause and led them into militia groups (Allawi 2007, 177). In addition to fighting the perpetrators of the economic hardship, these new insurrectionist recruits found militia groups to be essential to their economic welfare. The militia groups became all the more important given the refusal of the U.S. occupying forces to undertake police functions in the early months of the invasion. With no police, the Iraq army disbanded, and with American soldiers not policing Iraqi streets, a massive wave of looting developed that made the situation in Iraq all the more menacing. Hence, aligning with militias became essential, as they fulfilled a fundamental role of protection for displaced Iraqi soldiers/bureaucrats and their families.[8] The instability was compounded by the dismissal of thousands of experienced Baathist bureaucrats who were replaced by inexperienced counterparts (Kaplan 2008, 150, 151; Allawi 2007, 161). The environment created was a menacing one indeed. There emerged a situation of lawlessness in which militias could obtain resources and weapons. The militias were headed by ex-soldiers who knew the art of war well. State building to restore order was set back significantly through the dismissal of many competent public servants. To compound matters, all of the displaced and deprived parties were now targeting the United States as the principal villain.

Yet Debaathification and the disbanding of the army led to feedback processes that also thwarted the goals of creating a democratic Iraq in the Western style and the limitation of WMD. With respect to the goal of building democracy, the growing dependence on militias for economic welfare and safety placed major roadblocks in the path of a stable coalition and democratic government in Iraq. The proliferation of militias

[8] We see path dependence effects (i.e., non-linearities) in the evolution of the militia problem. Although police functions were beefed up with the development of new Iraqi armed units, the prior existence of militias made the militias difficult to uproot. Hence, dealing with the militia problem was best done preemptively (before they came into existence) or at a much earlier stage.

fueled rather than diminished sectarian divisions in Iraq. In effect, American strategies allowed a process of counterinsurgency versus a weak government to devolve into civil war (Allawi 2007, 233–48). The economic and social chaos resulting from very restricted military objectives led to the proliferation of sectarian militias that, because of restricted police functions, were able to acquire significant resources with which to perpetrate violence, both against each other and against the United States. At this point, rather than just facing insurgents, the U.S. forces had to be prepared to fight larger and better-endowed military units. In setting itself in opposition to armed indigenous groups, the United States effectively became an enemy to all.[9]

The strategy of Debaathification set back the pace of state reconstruction and effectively delegitimized American strategies for state building, as the Iraqi population equated American occupation with political and social chaos (Kaplan 2008, 185; Allawi 2007, 83). In this respect, as with Vietnam, the building of a stable government in the face of insurrectionist forces necessitated softer policies that were better sensitized to the need for effective pacification strategies based on political reform, institution building, and economic relief.[10] In both cases, an external presence intervened to promote political stability in the face of a vibrant insurgency and extremely difficult economic conditions for the population at large. But in terms of the indigenous political environment, Iraq appeared to be Vietnam on steroids. South Vietnam was not as seriously fractured politically from sectarian or ethnic divisions. Saddam Hussein overcame those divisions through brutal repression of the Shiites and Kurds. The United States has continued to hope that some coalition government will eliminate those divisions democratically, yet there is no historical precedent for such fractured societies being stabilized within a democratic environment (Walt 1999).

Finally, with respect to WMD, although the development of nuclear capacity may have been avoided in Iraq for the time being, there is no doubt that the aggressive and preemptive solutions used in Iraq have made the cause of the United States all the more difficult with respect to other

[9] An influential poll of one hundred foreign policy experts gave the Iraq campaign a score of 2.9 out of 10 points (The Terrorism Index 2007).

[10] Military elites vociferously criticized military operations in Iraq. Much criticism centered around the incompatibility between the needs of effective counterinsurgency and the large-force/apolitical strategies employed in Iraq. As with Vietnam, a successful campaign that would deter terrorism and promote democracy required far more vigorous civil-military solutions (Kaplan 2008, 49, 50, 84, 162).

nations. Thus, the net effects of shutting down some nuclear research and development in Iraq may in the end generate more actual weapons systems in Iran, North Korea, and other nations that perceive such systems to be the only viable means of averting an American invasion. In this respect, the coercive strategy of eliminating WMD has actually increased the deterrent value of such weapons for nations and has therefore made the development of WMD all the more desirable (Johnson 2004, 285; Kegley and Raymond 2007, 102; Jervis 2003a; Garner 2005, 12; "The Other Struggle" 2007, 16).[11]

Considering all three goals of the United States in Iraq (combating terrorism, limiting WMD, and promoting democracy), the shadow of hard disempowerment loomed large. Brzezinski (2007, 148) has identified the campaign as a "geopolitical disaster for the U.S." Rather than seek a balanced strategy that embraced elements of both hard and soft power, Bush attempted to achieve all three goals with a single hard strategy: a military invasion. In the end, actions targeted toward bringing about specific objectives actually made those objectives all the more difficult to realize, thus enervating American foreign policy in the region.

Beyond Iraq, the aggressive crusade of the United States to bring about these three goals proved self-defeating and disempowering in other ways. The militaristic and coercive methods used to root out terrorists even outside the Middle East broadened the cause of anti-Western militancy and alienated the governments of the target nations. Both Jervis (2005, 353) and Betts (2002, 19) contend that the use of U.S. power in the war against terrorism has actually increased "American vulnerability." Both feedback processes have energized terrorism and support of anti-Western movements among governments and societies at large.[12] In addition to creating new and greater enemies in the nations invaded, the web of fear and vituperation created by the United States' coercive solutions to terrorism has spread to other (especially Muslim) countries and consequently generated negative feedback processes that have undermined the U.S. global image and thus its influence. According to a Pew (2003)

[11] Jervis (2003a, 86) argues that attempts to force disarmament will actually speed up proliferation. In fact, a Pew (2003) survey shows that a great many people in Muslim nations fear a U.S. invasion.

[12] Although only five al-Qaeda attacks were documented between 1993 and September 11, 2001, seventeen more occurred during the next two years (Piven 2004, 6). The Terrorism Index poll (2007) shows that 91 percent of respondents see the world today as a more dangerous place for the United States than it was in 2001. Moreover, 84 percent believe that the United States is losing the war on terror.

survey, a majority in seven of eight Muslim nations see the United States as a military threat. Not only have countervailing coalitions hostile to the United States been created where fewer existed before, but the feedback in the key area of terrorism is even more devastating and self-defeating for the United States. Hostility breeds the rise of more martyrs among Muslim populations that are likely to perpetrate the very acts that the coercion was supposed to eliminate (Brzezinski 2007, 149; Halper and Clarke 2004, 313; Smith 2007, 198; Kaplan 2008, 184; Betts 2002, 26; Jervis 2005, 353; Calleo, 2003, 14).[13] In this respect, excessive reliance on hard power to deal with terrorism has been most counterproductive.[14]

In terms of spreading democracy in the wider global system, the coercion and aggressive posturing employed in marshaling the liberal crusade for democracy has taken on an air of "imperialism" (Smith 2007). Rather than generating domestic political dynamics favorable to democratic evolution, these methods have generated countervailing processes that stymie such an outcome. The crusade has often undermined the power of moderate and pro-Western regimes by fueling support for anti-West hardliners in politics. This has retarded possibilities for democratic state building and capitalist transition within a number of nations. In this respect, the American crusade to spread democracy has backfired because it has equated indigenous democratic movements with American pressure. However, even well before the invasion of Iraq, the hard line taken against other nations through menacing rhetoric and sanctions had polarized politics, with the balance of power skewed to the conservative side. Thus, the United States may have eliminated or attempted to force out more autocratic regimes, but in doing so, its coercive and interventionist actions have sown the seeds of discontent that undermined more democratic regimes (Gardner 2005; Nye 2003). The height of this deleterious process was visible in Bush's rhetorical campaign against autocratic regimes with the use of pejorative terms such as "axis of evil," "rogue states," and "outposts of tyranny." These alienated general populations not only in the target nations but also in other autocratic nations that had erstwhile problems with the United States. The pejorative rhetoric set into motion political shock waves that set back reformist politics across the globe (Kaplan

[13] The statistics on suicide bombings bears this out. In 2007, there were 658 reported attacks worldwide, more than double those of any other previous year. Of all such incidents over the past twenty-five years, 86 percent have occurred since 9/11 (Wright 2008).

[14] Brent Scowcroft proved to be quite intuitive in his warnings that invading Iraq would actually increase the terrorist threat (Halper and Clarke 2004, 227).

2008, 62). The anti-American sentiment generated by this confrontational style has served to raise the level of nationalism in the target states, and consequently both the rising nationalism and anti-Americanism combined to undermine indigenous liberal transformation processes within these states, as the populations and regimes have become less amenable to reform (Gardner 2005, 164, 165; Halper and Clarke 2004, 262).[15] Furthermore, the poorly tailored imposition of an American vision of democracy in Iraq and Afghanistan (i.e., without sufficient sensitivity to the particular sociopolitical conditions in the target nations) has resulted in setbacks that have delegitimized not only American-style democracy but also democratic transition in general.[16] This problem has been compounded by a tendency to overlearn from history and equate all forms of democratic regimes with the failed attempts to impose American democracy (Jervis 1976). Tragically, the United States has squandered significant opportunities to promote democracy and capitalism across the globe, as recent surveys (Inglehart and Norris 2003; Pew 2003) show that resounding majorities in many nations (even in autocratic Muslim nations) do support the idea of Western-style democracy and capitalism in theory (e.g., Indonesia, 64 percent; Jordan, 63 percent; Lebanon, 75 percent). It would appear that doing nothing at all would have been superior with respect to American interests than trying to coercively impose or promote Western-style governments and economies. Indeed, Smith (2007, 235) states that in promoting democracy through imperial aggression, the "liberal internationalism [of the United States] has seriously damaged its own cause." Although Bush, in his quest to spread democracy, did exhibit sensitivity to soft values at the domestic level by trying to create regimes that promoted popular rule, freedom, and individual choice, his hard foreign policy methods proved counterproductive to the goal.

[15] The Terrorism Index poll (2007) shows that only 3 percent of respondents believe that Iraq will become a beacon of democracy among autocratic states. Moreover, 35 percent of respondents believe that the war will actually discourage Arab heads of state from promoting liberal reforms.

[16] Interestingly, it is clear in the Iraq and Afghanistan cases that the United States has been more intent on building pluralistic political regimes (with competing political interests) than democratic regimes per se (i.e., popular determination). Indeed, democracy may produce outcomes that cut against U.S. interests if radical groups (e.g., Hamas or Hezbollah) win elections. The difficulty here is that pluralistic systems work well where competition is channeled into political institutions. But in these fractured societies, in which competing groups have competed through violence, pluralism is a recipe for civil war (Gardner 2005, 164, 165, 189).

In terms of WMD, the Iran effect has been seen elsewhere. North Korea has certainly vindicated the idea that the United States' coercive policy in dealing with WMD raises the utility of such weapon systems as deterrents, but in this case, it is clear that they also hold utility as bargaining chips (Jervis 2003a; Garner 2005, 12).[17] After the six-party talks concerning North Korea's WMD faltered in September 2003, the North Korean envoy announced that his nation intended to formally declare that it had tested, and would continue to test, nuclear weapons as well as its improved missile delivery systems. But he added that such weapons programs would be stopped if Washington agreed to an iron-clad nonaggression pact with North Korea. Shortly after that declaration, North Korea's parliament expressed support for Kim Jong-il's policy of maintaining a "nuclear deterrent force" to counter a potentially hostile United States. Although Bush perfunctorily pushed diplomacy through the six-party talks, he gave little leeway to negotiators, as he was antithetical to negotiating with militant autocrats like Kim Jong-il.[18] Bush saw the deal as "blackmail" (Kaplan 2008, 68). All the while, Bush never relinquished a coercive posture in dealing with North Korea. In fact, he reinforced this orientation by ordering the Joint Chiefs of Staff to prepare military operations against potential North Korean targets, some of which were suspected weapons centers (OPLAN 5030). When this was leaked to the press, North Korea pushed even harder to develop WMD in hopes of building a viable deterrent against military strikes (Kaplan 2008, 68).[19] In undermining the more positive diplomatic relations built with North Korea under the Clinton administration and with increasing tension between the two nations, Bush encouraged further development of a nuclear capacity in that nation.

The Bush posture had other feedback consequences that made the quest against WMD all the more difficult. In pushing the hard line against Kim Jong-il, Bush undermined diplomatic efforts by South Korea's Kim Dae Jung to bridge testy issues (including WMD) between the two nations on the Korean peninsula. Lack of U.S. support undermined a foreign policy

[17] Heisbourg (2004, 16) refers to this process as "precautionary proliferation."

[18] The six-party talks proved valuable in addressing the Korean problem because of the involvement of China and the multilateral legitimacy they created. It may be the case that these talks carry greater potential than the Security Council, which was turned in a more confrontational direction on issues of WMD by Bush.

[19] Kim Jong-il became more sensitized to the utility of WMD against American threats because of his belief that Iraq was invaded because it had failed to build a nuclear device (Gardner 2005, 153; Kaplan 2008, 74).

that was pitched as a focal point of Kim's political initiative for a new South Korea. Consequently, Kim suffered political setbacks that eventually led to his electoral loss to a new leader, Roh Moo Hyun. This hurt the United States' cause significantly because Roh harbored strong anti-American sentiments and proved more difficult to influence. A key to U.S. hopes of limiting WMD in North Korea has been to foster better relations on the peninsula, thus reducing tensions that contributed to Kim Jong-il's need for deterrence capabilities. Yet with a less amenable leader in South Korea, such designs have been dealt a serious blow. Although Kim Jong-il finally accepted American terms to curtail his nuclear energy program under international surveillance in 2007, Kim nonetheless had been able in the previous years' void of negotiations to acquire enough weapons-grade plutonium and weapons technology to build several nuclear devices. Moreover, because of U.S. insistence on what North Korea has considered overly intrusive verification measures, the agreement has broken down, and North Korea has once more restored initiatives toward reactivation of nuclear power and weapons programs, even engineering a missile test on April 5 and an underground nuclear test on May 25 of 2009. In the end, Bush's militant crusade to deliver the United States from the threats of terrorism and WMD have made the threats even greater because of the negative feedback generated by the United States' confrontational strategy (Gardner 2005, 154; Kaplan 2008, 68–76).

With respect to the administration's three major goals, one of the most devastating weakening effects of this hard power posture of the Bush Doctrine, which has diminished U.S. capacity to achieve these goals, emanated from inherent negative feedback elements that undermined the domestic soft power buttressing foreign policy. In general, coercive solutions, especially as manifest in preemptive war, generate elements that undermine the solutions themselves. First, such solutions often must be sustained to succeed, as what is being sought requires ongoing functions (rooting out terrorists, disarming WMD, and transforming political regimes). Preemptive war must be sustained if it fails to achieve specified goals. This requires exceptional support from Congress and the U.S. public. This domestic soft power, which is crucial to propagating such solutions, is often fragile, even if the public is convinced that the causes of American foreign policy are in the national interest.[20] But such

[20] Jervis' (2005) argument that public support for the Bush Doctrine would ultimately erode proved prescient. Indeed, it showed a continual decline, as approval ratings of the president and foreign policy polls demonstrated.

solutions, especially preemptive war, are by nature ill equipped to deliver assurances of success. Rationales for preemptive war are based on speculation regarding the future (what was expected to happen) and limited information about the past (because little has already happened, there is less of an informational base on which to predicate war). In conjunction with the natural fragility of domestic support for coercive foreign policy in democracies, the limited evidence for its rationales is an ongoing obstacle to public and Congressional support, thus undermining the very soft power required to sustain such policies (Jervis 2003b, 2005). Yet the weakening effects do not end here, as domestic political shocks from the policies, and possible backlashes if the policies ultimately fail, create a debilitating shadow of the future (i.e., syndrome effects). Indeed, developments in public opinion and in Congressional politics under Bush revealed a growing backlash against his policies. Approval ratings of the Bush policy deteriorated concomitantly with Congressional confrontation (Halper and Clarke 2004, 221, 237–40). The adverse manifestations of asymmetrical war processes (frustration about military campaigns that were expected to be "cakewalks") were heightened by broad perceptions of deception. The rationales used to invade Iraq were never corroborated, and the prognostications for the course and expense of the war diverged greatly from reality (Halper and Clarke 2004, 215–21; Piven 2004).[21]

Just as the Vietnam syndrome hamstrung the United States in conducting its regional geostrategies during the Cold War, a similar Iraq syndrome has already hamstrung the United States in effecting its three major goals in the future and also has acted as a debilitating factor by impairing U.S. foreign policy in general (Piven 2004). The hamstring effect has been raised all the more by a propensity to overlearn from history. In this case, the United States would be more restrained than it normally would be in pursuing its goals in the world polity because of perceptions that the Iraq case will be repeated in other scenarios (Jervis 1976). Indeed, the United States has had to backtrack from its position against Iran and North Korea; it has been far more restrained in its relations with Pakistan and the Palestinians in promoting democratic reform and political stability; it has retreated to a more feeble approach in dealing with Russia before the Georgia incident; it has been much less resilient in the face of the transition of Latin American politics to the left; and it

[21] A plethora of arguments have been made about the so-called true motivations of the war, from securing power over oil to war as a vehicle to promote the Republican right's domestic policy agenda. See Piven (2004) for a survey.

has relented in its pressure on China with respect to liberalization and human rights.[22] Clearly, the depreciation of political capital in the wake of the Iraq failure has enervated foreign policy (Kaplan 2008). This is all the more troubling considering that the military feels ill prepared to take on a significant campaign elsewhere in the world, even with full domestic support (U.S. Military Index 2008). Bush's shift in his second administration to a foreign policy that was somewhat less unilaterally coercive in promoting his goals, relative to his first administration, appears to have been a function of these hamstring effects.

Geostrategically, the shadow of hard disempowerment has revealed numerous menacing outcomes for the United States. In the Middle East, the dynamics generated by the Bush foreign policy was forging the United States' worst nightmare: political-strategic solidarity among Muslim nations. The lack of such solidarity over the years has been crucial to U.S. interest in protecting Israel and influencing the price of oil. Certainly, the confrontational posture toward Iran and Syria regarding WMD has forged bonds among those nations as sisters in the cause against American intrusion. Even more frightening is a potential bloc between Iran and Iraq forged in Shiite religious solidarity and anti-Western sentiment. Although Saddam Hussein had been demonized by the United States, he in fact served important functions in promoting American interests in the Middle East. His militarism and threats against other Middle Eastern nations (Kuwait, Iran, and Saudi Arabia) maintained a schism in the Middle East that blocked the formation of any grand alliance against the United States and/or Israel. His secularism promoted a political balance in the Middle East that prevented a religious solidarity that might also menace the United States and/or Israel. Removing Hussein loosened Shiite religious fervor, which could eventually produce the same outcome that occurred in Iran in the 1970s once the United States and its allies have unlatched the political shackles presently placed on restoring self-rule in Iraq. Ironically, the war for Iraqi freedom eventually may produce the very outcome that the Gulf War was fought to prevent: a bloc between two of the largest oil producers in the world. An Iraq/Iran block forged in Shiite politics would be even more troubling than an Iraq/Kuwait bloc

[22] In this respect, and ironically, hard power solutions served to undermine the very hard power resources necessary to carry out such solutions effectively. In this case, the failure of hard solutions caused the United States to backtrack on the development of various hard power resources. But, as noted in Chapter 1, it is as precarious to fall excessively short on hard power as it is to overindulge in hard power at the exclusion of soft power.

because of the greater strength of Iran. Hussein's removal seems to validate the American cliché "be careful what you wish for" (Brzezinski 2007, 148).

More generally, the invasion of a Muslim nation void of international legitimacy poisoned relations with all Muslim nations (as aggrieved populations placed pressure on the ruling regimes to withhold support – note the Pew survey cited above in this chapter), which has dealt a serious blow to American interests in the Middle East as well as in the world at large. One glaring manifestation of this was the difficulty in getting permission from even erstwhile supporters (Saudi Arabia, Turkey) to set up bases from which to conduct the invasion of Iraq. Similarly, Egypt and Pakistan, two major recipients of U.S. aid, proved quite aloof in the face of U.S. requests. This cold posture continued to turn negotiations sour in a variety of issues, from oil pricing to terrorism. In light of the feedback mechanisms that have obstructed American objectives in the Middle East, it is clear that the Bush Doctrine, rather than advancing the Middle East Project (i.e., hopes of a liberal transformation across Middle East nations), placed significant roadblocks in its path (Smith 2007, 208).

In Asia, of course, the menacing posture toward North Korea undid much of the progress for better relations on the peninsula, which has been a mainstay for stability in the region. North Korea has retrenched in a way that has thwarted American goals in Asia, which are to integrate Communist nations into the global economy and maintain a wedge against potential Communist alliances. China, which has shared some of North Korea's vituperation against American confrontation, may have been driven to better relations with North Korea than otherwise may have been the case. Certainly the fear of Taiwan coupled with the United States' aggressive unilateralism has placed China in a more defensive position. One manifestation of this enhanced feeling of vulnerability has been a campaign on the part of China to build security regimes across the globe, from the Middle East to the South China Sea. Although Bush's hard line may have generated more cooperation from Russia and China in some areas, potential backlashes could create a ripple effect that poses a major problem for the United States' principal allies in Asia, as they must carry a large part of the burden of strained relations in the region. Chinese relations represent an especially promising vehicle to stabilize relations in Asia, as China shares a number of goals with the United States on trade and North Korea. China, like the United States, seeks a politically stable Asian theater so that its economic relations can flourish. Both nations also wish to limit the proliferation of WMD in the region. Finally, both would welcome some liberal reform among autocratic governments in the region. However, Bush's neoconservative bent on confronting rather than working with autocratic states limited the possibilities for forging agreements on the greater geopolitical fate of Asia. Once more, the Bush Doctrine and hard power solutions only made things worse (Gardner 2005, 155, 156; Shambaugh 2004).

Regarding U.S.-Russian relations, what started as a positive relationship in the aftermath of 9/11 deteriorated significantly. After a warm start with a conciliatory phone call from Vladimir Putin in 2001, the Bush administration and Putin left office with some experts talking about a renewal of the Cold War, or at least the beginnings of a Cold Peace. In this respect, Bush's quest for liberal transformation in Eastern Europe and the fight against terrorism there have been dealt a blow as well. Once again, balancing U.S.-Russian relations with these broader goals required multiple and diverse solutions. Bush's myopic response, with his unilateral-confrontational style, generated feedback that soured the relationship. Bush's proposed missile defense shield to protect against Iranian attacks generated suspicion and a new fear on the part of Russia. Furthermore, the fallout with both Russia and Iran regarding the missile shield may have driven them even closer together, as both continue rapprochement based on oil, nuclear technology, and weapons sales (Gardner 2005, 140).[23] The United States' aggressive push to expand the North Atlantic Treaty Organization (NATO) and support of independence movements in Eastern Europe (mainly Kosovo) made Russia feel excessively isolated in orchestrating its foreign relations in Europe. Moreover, American criticism of Russian reversion to autocracy alienated Russia all the more. The backlash manifested itself adversely for American interests, with Putin suspending an arms control treaty, issuing menacing language (comparing the United States to the Third Reich), and even issuing more menacing threats, such as targeting missiles at U.S. allies (Gardner 2005, 130). Putin and Bush left office with a mutual gesture of extending olive branches, with bilateral talks about multilateralizing the missile shield so that Russia could oversee and manage it as well. However, the rift in U.S.-Russian relations once more flared up regarding the question of Georgia, heating up the U.S.-Russian rivalry. In this respect, nonlinearities in the form

[23] The missile shield has also reinforced an existing energy partnership between Russia and China and brought the two great powers together into a strategic front against the United States, as Medvedev and Hu issued joint protests against the shield. Brzezinski (2007, 168–71) is especially outspoken about the dangers a Russo-Chinese strategic partnership carries for the United States

of path dependence worked against U.S. efforts at rapprochement, as earlier strategies of confrontation under Bush placed relations on a less amicable path, and negotiated solutions to the problems facing the two superpowers even after Putin and Bush left office became all the more difficult.

Dealing with Pakistan will perhaps be the United States' greatest challenge. The hard disempowerment effect is especially visible in Pakistan, as the United States' quest to reduce the threat of terrorism and WMD has made these problems much greater there. A war against their ethnic Pashtun kin in Afghanistan and support for an unpopular Musharraf turned the general population against the United States, fueling support for anti-American activity. This, in turn, fueled the position of radical elements in politics, which manifested themselves in part in the assassination of Benazir Bhutto. The path blazed by the Bush Doctrine made the United States poorly equipped to deal with Pakistan. Yet in terms of the intersection of the three major goals of American policy under Bush, Pakistan represents the "perfect storm": it has fully operational WMD, an extremely large Muslim population that is pervaded by a plethora of extremist elements (it is reputed by many to be the new base of al-Qaeda operations), and it has become extremely unstable politically since the assassination of Bhutto. Instability has raised the dangers of WMD and terrorism all the more. And with the deteriorating image of the United States among Muslims, the United States will have limited leverage in reducing the threats from terrorist cells and WMD in Pakistan ("The World's Most Dangerous Place" 2008, 7; Halper and Clarke 2004, 210; Kaplan 2008, 167).

At the global level the anti-American sentiment generated by the Bush Doctrine has generated a "counter-Americanism" that has carried manifold adverse consequences for the United States and Americans. Halper and Clarke (2004, 237) lament that these consequences are pervasive in a complex international system. They are "diplomatic, commercial, educational, cultural, touristic." Nations and their civil societies will be less receptive to American overtures, which will serve to deprive the United States and U.S. nationals of resources, experiences, and agreements that would benefit them. These run the gamut from the EU's opposition to U.S. genetically modified food to Brazil's decision to discontinue using Microsoft Windows in government offices. In essence, the anti-American posture abroad has represented a pervasive deterioration of American influence in the world, a devastating weakening effect when considering the global scale of American activities (Halper and Clarke 2004).

The Moral Hazard of the Bush Doctrine and Soft Power

In the Bush case, great military primacy (i.e., hard power capacity) led the United States to bank on the efficacy of coercion in bringing about desired goals in the international arena. However, as a consequence, the reliance on coercion, both force and threat, caused other important power resources of the United States to deteriorate, as a result of both neglect and the counterproductive effects of coercion. In effect, the Bush Doctrine made the United States muscle-bound. The fundamental tenet of the Bush Doctrine, that the United States still enjoyed primacy in a plethora of international issue areas, led the administration to become victimized by moral hazard, in this case the tendency to be less than fully perspicacious in developing the flexible array of tools to effectively conduct foreign relations. Many of the adverse consequences of this muscle-bound effect created by moral hazard manifested themselves as a deterioration of American soft power. Yet, in undermining important soft power resources, these consequences carried significant disempowering effects with respect to U.S. influence. A trail of these moral hazard effects can be seen across the three major goals of the Bush administration: eliminating terrorism, promoting liberal transformation among nations, and limiting WMD. In analyzing the problems in achieving these goals, it becomes clear that soft power solutions were absolutely crucial for bringing about these goals. But in fact, the hard power allure of the Bush Doctrine squeezed such solutions out of the foreign policy agenda.

With respect to terrorism, primacy in hard power led the Bush administration to attack the problem using conventional weapons, which (as noted) generated a more hazardous position for the United States in a world fraught with potential terrorists.[24] Interestingly, even before the invasions and military occupations after 9/11, perceptions of military primacy led the United States to undervalue the threat of terrorism, even after several al-Qaeda attacks and Osama bin Laden's declaration of a holy war in his *fatwa* of February 1988. In this case, moral hazard had manifestations both for hard and soft solutions to terrorism.[25] Yet after 9/11, the Bush Doctrine introduced a different kind of moral hazard into

[24] Betts (2002, 20) states, "American global primacy is one of the causes [of the terrorist] war."

[25] Betts (2002, 22) notes that other events in the 1990s contributed to this false sense of security generated by primacy: winning the Gulf War easily, facing no casualties in Kosovo, and being able to disengage in Somalia so easily when military operations went awry.

the fold: invasions, military occupations, political intervention, and coercion. These had manifold consequences for compounding the threat of terrorism. In essence, the reaction to terrorism produced reckless policies in the form of solutions that proved overmilitarized, excessively coercive, imperialistic, authoritarian, and diplomatically injudicious (Betts 2002, 20–22). Directly, this hard assault actually created more targets for terrorist insurgents in occupied nations in the persons of the occupying forces and complementary-service personnel. Indirectly, as noted above in this chapter, it made Americans abroad and their allies greater targets of terrorism, as attested to by the greater incidence of terrorism after 9/11 (Piven 2004, 6). Moreover, as with Vietnam, military primacy and reliance on conventional military operations actually channeled global and local insurgencies against the United States increasingly into terrorist initiatives, which even the U.S. military admits is especially difficult to handle given prevailing military operations (U.S. Military Index 2008).

As Betts (2002) and Lambakis et al. (2002) observe, terrorism has a multitude of tactical advantages that render it a more elusive target of hard strategies like conventional coercive and military strategies.[26] In this respect, terrorism represents an asymmetric threat that occupies what Betts refers to as the "soft belly of American primacy."[27] Terrorism is rooted in civil society. Uprooting such a well-integrated and concealed phenomenon is challenging at the least. Globalization has provided it, furthermore, with a plethora of vehicles and opportunities to organize, strike, and disappear. Even in the case of state-sponsored terrorism or terrorist-friendly political environments, the networks and operational logistics of the initiatives have always proved to be well concealed within the civil societies of the host nations, as many failed attempts to uproot terrorists from such environments has consistently demonstrated (e.g., Pakistan, Lebanon, Syria, Egypt, Saudi Arabia).[28] This battlefield hardly lends itself to the weapons that have delivered military primacy to the United States, but in fact places greater currency in soft power solutions (Thomas 2008; Halper and Clarke 2004; Lennon 2003). Furthermore,

[26] Lambakis et al. (2002) underscores the general tactical advantages of "asymmetric" threats (i.e., threats against which conventional weapons are poorly suited to defend), terrorist operations being a subset of asymmetric war.

[27] In terms of military strategies, terrorism comprises a fourth generation type of warfare, far removed from the earlier generations oriented around conventional operations (Kegley and Raymond 2007, 59).

[28] The Terrorism Index (2007) suggests that policy experts envision a good many nations being possibilities for future al-Qaeda strongholds.

terrorism enjoys the tactical advantage of being the insurgent force in an asymmetrical war. This lowers the requirements for success (in that terrorists win simply by not losing, i.e., maintaining some capacity to inflict harm) vis-à-vis state actors who only succeed by winning (i.e., completely rooting out terrorism) (Betts 2002).[29] But a further advantage of inferiority in an asymmetric war is that the difficulty of winning a quick and decisive victory frustrates the domestic societies of the stronger parties, inhibiting the ability of the latter to effectively marshal a vigorous and sustained military effort.[30] Furthermore, terrorists have the tactical advantage of attack; that is, one cannot see them coming and they can make extraordinarily large impacts on nations with limited means (a small number of men who hijacked airplanes caused 9/11, and a small operation delivered anthrax). Finally, terrorism enjoys a targeting advantage. Terrorists are difficult targets because of their elusiveness and limited exposure, but their targets are infinite and cannot be fully protected: power plants, bridges, airports, stadiums, waterways, skyscrapers, and people (Betts 2002; Thomas 2008). Indeed, Kegley and Raymond (2007, 69) have reminded us that America's "preponderant power is not reducing global terrorism."

In this sense, terrorism requires a different cure: soft power is the key to addressing the weaknesses of the United States' soft underbelly (Kegley and Raymond 2007, 69). Yet it is precisely this more effective solution that has been compromised by the moral hazard of Bush's hard power solutions. From a military standpoint, the moral hazard emanating from conventional primacy has caused military operations to undermine the most effective means of promoting "sustainable security" (Thomas 2008; Halper and Clarke 2004, 281). Fighting terrorism through coercion and conventional military strategies (large-scale interdiction, troop deployment, occupation, and threats) has come at the expense of more progressive tactics. Moreover, such approaches at best have fared poorly and at worst have proved counterproductive.[31] To a large extent, Bush's

[29] This draws on Kissinger's famous statement about the war against insurgency in Vietnam; that is, insurgents win simply by surviving.

[30] The frustration effect emanates from the fact that primacy raises domestic perceptions of quick and decisive victory, but as this outcome is frustrated and the costs of carrying on the war mount, societies can quickly turn against the war, and hence hamstring the war effort. On the frustration effect and asymmetric warfare, see Mack (1975), Boserup and Mack (1975), Barnett (2003), Arreguin-Toft (2005), and Ewans (2005).

[31] In addition to the extremely poor results from the use of direct force against terrorism, Crenshaw (2003) notes that even coercive diplomacy has fared poorly in containing it.

reliance on conventional military operations delayed the recognition of the need for more effective counterinsurgency strategies. Thomas (2008) and de Wijk (2003) demonstrate that, in fact, sustainable security against terrorism can best be delivered by operations founded on prevention, indirect methods, disaggregation, and limited-scale engagement. Prevention requires civilian and military personnel working in potential trouble spots with domestic institutions and personnel to set up infrastructures for deterring or anticipating threats that might migrate internationally. This strategy highlights the benefits of indigenous constabularies that would interdict threats at the roots. Indirect methods would work through unconventional military channels and allied/partner nations that develop domestic security functions. These methods would feature pacification-type strategies that encourage better governance and the socioeconomic development of indigenous civil societies. Disaggregation would emphasize the need to frame security strategies based on local and regional conditions. Limited engagement would stress the use of small numbers of military and civilian personnel in developing indigenous security capabilities. The main functions of these personnel would be oriented around training, advising, intelligence gathering, and paramilitary and covert operations (U.S. Military Index 2008; Thomas 2008; Lambakis 2002).[32]

Such a sustainable security initiative would rely extensively on soft power in terms of implementation and success: it would require the access of American military, diplomatic, and civilian personnel to potential troubled spots. The joint-security operations would require extensive cooperation between the United States and foreign political entities (Newhouse 2003; Jervis 2005; de Wijk 2003).[33] Moreover, bilateral initiatives need to be complemented and integrated into a multilateral security network. This would rely on international regimes and international organizations to broker and participate in the security initiatives carved out by the United States and selected nations. Both bilateral and multilateral initiatives would be predicated on the receptivity of participating nations

32 An extensive survey of military officers has revealed a belief that the U.S. campaigns against Iraq and Afghanistan have not only debilitated the U.S. military conventionally, but have also served to undermine the development of more effective operations against terrorism (U.S. Military Index 2008).

33 Halper and Clarke (2004, 282) draw on the failure of Britain to contain insurgency in Palestine as a case reflecting the need for local cooperation as the fundamental means of combating terrorism. Jervis (2005) and Newhouse (2003) underscore the difficulty of effective intelligence when acting unilaterally to solve the terrorist problem. It has become evident that the kind of informational requirements to confront terrorism can never be delivered without such local cooperation.

to the American overtures for sustainable security. Bush's policies dealt a strong blow to this receptivity at both levels (Gardner 2005, 80). In this respect, the Bush solution to terrorism proved a double-edged sword in undermining sustainable security. First, it proved counterproductive by generating even greater security threats through terror. Yet it also undercut the soft power necessary for launching and maintaining such a sustainable security initiative, both in the United States and abroad: allies and partner nations proved to be a coalition of the unwilling; indigenous populations were repulsed by Americans and their initiatives for local security; and the American Congress and public showed bipartisan condemnation rather than bipartisan support for foreign policy (Jervis 2005; Kaplan 2008; Johnson 2004, 2006; Allawi 2007).

Above and beyond the soft power–military strategy link, the moral hazard effect of the Bush Doctrine compromised American security at an even more fundamental level (Halper and Clarke 2004, 280, 281). Enhancing soft power would have rendered many of the sustainable security initiatives less necessary because such soft power could have effectively addressed many of the root causes of terrorism. But this would require a multifaceted diplomatic campaign that aimed for regional political and economic stabilization. This would be based on a willingness to work with governments rather than beyond or above them, and would embrace multilateral engagement (Fukuyama 2006, 185). The United States should have worked in a multilateral context, both within and outside the Middle East, to bring about a resolution to the Palestinian problem. This would have required a normalization of relations with nations that Bush targeted as rogue states. The United States should have guaranteed the civil liberties of all who were being held under suspicion of terrorism in both the United States and foreign bases. The United States should have improved relations with the other major regional power brokers whose domains contained most of the asymmetric threats to the United States: China, Russia, Pakistan, and Saudi Arabia. These domains also featured many of the autocratic regimes holding back liberal democratic transitions. Finally, the United States could have more vigorously provided the economic public goods to deliver many parts of the world from deprivation. All such soft power initiatives would have addressed the problems of asymmetric threats at the source. Ultimately, such a preventive approach relies on x-efficiencies in civil society (i.e., the United States having allies in foreign populations). The Bush Doctrine, unfortunately, generated extensive x-inefficiencies in this cause (Gardner 2005, 3; Hapler and Clarke 2004, 279–82).

This soft war would be an entirely different kind of war in that it would aim to "win the hearts and minds" of populations in potentially dangerous regions (Lennon 2003). Interestingly, it has been the more radical elements, against which the United States has been fighting a hard war, that have done a better job in conducting such a soft war. Throughout the Middle East and the Muslim world at large (especially Afghanistan and Pakistan), radical Islamic groups have from the 1990s been actively engaged in providing public goods to populations in deprivation or turmoil. These groups often have been far better than the domestic governments of their states at providing general relief and public goods (welfare, education, health care, and food aid). The generosity on the part of Hamas, Hezbollah, and al-Qaeda has become legend among Muslim populations in a number of countries. It is little wonder that recruitment into the ranks of extremist organizations has been vigorous and has shown no signs of declining (de Wijk 2003, 20).

Like terrorism, the problem of WMD was also confronted by Bush with hard strategies. Again, military primacy led coercive strategies to squeeze out softer strategies in limiting the spread of these weapons. But like terrorism, WMD, as asymmetric threats, enjoy a plethora of tactical advantages against conventional U.S. security strategies. The geographic size and global presence of the United States creates a fairly indefensible network of targets. The freedom of American society and the level of globalization create manifold opportunities to obtain materials to build WMD, develop them through small numbers of perpetrators, hide them effectively, and deliver them with alarming speed and consequences (Lambakis et al. 2002; Ellis 2004). All of this is especially true of chemical and biological weapons. As we have seen in the past (with anthrax and the use of such weapons in the war between Iran and Iraq), only very small levels of input are required to produce devastating consequences.[34] The fact that such small levels of inputs are required to deliver such devastation makes the problem extremely difficult to root out from global civil society. Given the indefensibility of potential targets (especially agriculture and water systems) and the ease with which perpetrators can inflict damage, the United States is alarmingly vulnerable to such attacks.[35] But even nuclear weapons, given technological advances, have evolved

[34] The Terrorism Index (2007) shows that policy experts envision numerous nations as possible sources of nuclear technology.

[35] Response time to such attacks must be rapid in order to avoid extreme consequences, but many biological and chemical agents are not even easily detectable (Lambakis et al. 2002, 32).

to a point at which state-sponsorship is no long necessary to build and use such devastating weapons. Indeed, an especially vigorous market in missile and nuclear technology has been visible since the end of the Cold War, with the United States being a major player as well, albeit indirectly. Moreover, much of the trading is in the black market, where monitoring is almost nonexistent.

As with terrorism, sustainable security against WMD requires a soft power solution (Newhouse 2003). Regional security communities in which the United States had a strongly integrated role would have to be constructed. As with terrorism, the strategies of prevention, indirect methods, disaggregation, and limited-scale engagement would be required for a sustainable initiative. They would be implemented in fundamentally similar ways as in the war against terrorism. This, again, would rely on foreign receptivity to American involvement in national and local security initiatives, as well as receptivity among allied and partner nations in building multilateral initiatives to support bilateral plans for sustainable security. Again, as with terrorism, the Bush Doctrine, in undermining this receptivity among host and potential partner nations, also undermined sustainable security possibilities against WMD (Gardner 2005, 160). As with terrorism, reliance on big-war strategies generated moral hazard in developing the more viable soft strategies (Thomas 2008; Lambakis et al. 2002). Big-war mania under the Bush regime crowded out the more finely tailored operations required to confront such asymmetric threats. Effective intelligence initiatives are especially crucial. The problem of WMD, as an asymmetric phenomenon, is manifest at the undercurrents of world politics (terrorist activities, concealed activities in so-called rogue states). Thus, effective intelligence is the very lynchpin determining the success of counter-WMD operations (Jervis 2005; Newhouse 2003). However, the strong-arm methods of the Bush assault undermined the soft power required to deliver such initiatives.

Also as with terrorism, in addition to the soft power–military strategy link, the moral hazard effect of the Bush Doctrine in neglecting the soft power consequences of hard power strategies has compromised American security at the grassroots level. Enhancing this soft power would render many of the sustainable security initiatives unnecessary. The strategies for confronting terrorism through the multifaceted diplomatic campaigns, in a quest for geostrategic pacification outcomes (i.e., regional political and economic stabilization), would work well for WMD as well, given the asymmetric qualities they share with terrorism. Effective preemptive strategies against asymmetric threats, as noted, require strong x-efficiencies to root out the threats, which means having foreign populations favorably disposed to U.S. interests. Only soft power can effectively deliver such x-efficiencies at the grass-roots level (Halper and Clarke 2004, 281).

Furthermore, undermining the very need for WMD relies on multilateralism. Eliminating security threats, political instability, and economic deprivation are three essential objectives for reducing the incentives to rely on WMD. These objectives could only be delivered through multilateral venues. Such venues have shown far more success in delivering such outcomes than Bush's hard campaign. The Non-Proliferation Treaty (NPT), Biological Weapons Convention, Chemical Weapons Convention, Comprehensive Nuclear-Test-Ban Treaty (CTBT), and Nunn-Lugar Cooperative Threat Reduction Program for Commonwealth of Independent States have produced numerous positive accomplishments in the area of sustainable security in the context of WMD. Strengthening these initiatives and adding more of an economic relief dimension to them would hold far more promise than Bush's unilateral hard crusade (Heisbourg 2004, 17; Guoliang 2004, 79–83).

As with terrorism and WMD, American military primacy under the Bush Doctrine squeezed out softer strategies that could more effectively promote liberal democratic regime change as well. Overly militarized and coercive strategies for promoting regime transformation have, as noted, set back prospects for such outcomes. Indeed, the heavy-handed approach, which has generated perceptions of being victimized by "liberal imperialism," has discredited much of the ideological appeal and undermined the power of indigenous political forces attempting to consummate the change within the regimes (Smith 2007, 235). This has effectively undercut the soft power necessary for such a political transformation (Lennon and Eiss 2004). Thus, by relying on these methods for promoting change, the United States has failed to embrace the more viable means of effecting sustainable change, and in this sense, hard power has again victimized the United States through moral hazard in neglecting viable strategies for political transformation. In fact, there have been a number of empirical studies on the effectiveness of using force to promote liberal democratic regime change. The results across these tests strongly suggest that force consistently fails miserably in bringing about such change (Kegley and Raymond 2007, 117–19).

Sustainable political change has to be indigenous, as history has shown that stable and lasting institutions cannot simply be imposed on regimes without sensitivity to prior political culture and prevailing socioeconomic conditions. Sustainable change is founded on general ideological receptivity for regime change and a vigorous domestic initiative on the part of political leaders.[36] Both create the requisite soft power foundations for new regimes to flourish (Lennon 2003; Lennon and Eiss 2004). As with terrorism and WMD, U.S. goals for true regime change in the long run are better effected through strategies of positive engagement. This would mean regime enhancement through diplomacy, cooperation, economic partnerships, and disaggregated political engagement (local, regional, and national). In effect, these would be strategies of "political pacification" that would both promote and reduce the burden of political and economic transformation (Ansari 2004, 280).

Moreover, the United States should be more interested in state success than in democracy. Failing and failed states are the likeliest breeding grounds for terrorism and tyranny (Kegley and Raymond 2007, 59). Also, it is far easier to strengthen states than to rebuild them after they have failed or collapsed. In this respect, the major goals of American foreign policy are best served if the focus of American soft power is on helping to forge legitimate domestic institutions that deliver satisfactory political goods rather than on regime orientation specifically (Fukuyama 2006, 185). In fragile states, it is not externally imposed attempts at democratization that deliver a stable democracy, but rather political stability. This kind of stability can only be delivered multilaterally, as unilateral attempts can never generate the legitimacy needed to build legitimate institutions. Hence, the foundations of soft power initiatives are forged through political cooperation. But this cooperation must be pervasive, which the Bush Doctrine did not permit. Cooperation must include all relevant parties, irrespective of regime types and diplomatic legacies. In this respect, such political stability has required engagement with erstwhile enemies. Thus, rapprochement has remained one of the most important but elusive requirements. The moral hazard generated by the Bush Doctrine unraveled a significant diplomatic fabric that might have enhanced

[36] It is in this respect that analogies to the war-induced political transformations in Japan and Germany fail. The soft power foundations for such change were far more abundant in Germany and Japan, as compared with Iraq. The Nazi ideology was discredited, whereas in Japan, the emperor supported reforms that already had a long legacy in Japan (from the Meji Restoration). Moreover, both societies were highly structured and not ethnically or religiously fractured, and their military occupation was brief. In Iraq, however, the occupation has lasted and Western ideas have become targets rather than models for reform. Moreover, religious and ethnic divisions make a stable pluralistic political system tenuous at best (Rubin 2004).

such rapprochement, consequently setting back the cause of state building and state rescue (Rotberg 2003; von Hippel 2003).

The belief in the idea of incorrigible rogue regimes (i.e., that regimes are void of the indigenous progressive ideas and forces to support liberal transitions, and therefore such transitions must be imposed) is not only misleading, but also dangerous. It has in fact encouraged just the kind of imperialistic assaults that have set back the liberal democratic cause across many such perceived regimes. Globalization and economic progress have been instrumental in stoking progressive indigenous forces in all political systems. All such perceived regimes have a sizable number in their populations who embrace liberal political and economic ideas, and many of them are extremely influential political actors (Inglehart and Norris 2003; Pew 2003). Iran, for example, has headed this list of purported incorrigible rogue regimes for some time and has therefore remained a principal concern for those who have been pessimistic about the possibilities for indigenous reform. But Iran, in fact, has demonstrated a strong veneration for republicanism for more than a hundred years. Starting with a constitutional revolution in 1906, strong sentiments for democratic political institutions have remained strong in Iran. Ansari (2004) contends that the past century in Iranian political history reveals a vigorous process of "organic democratization." Iranian politics, according to Ansari (2004), have always reflected a dynamic and pluralistic nature. Even the crucial political events that eventually produced more autocratic regimes (under the Shah and Khomeini) began as democratic upheavals. The constitutional spirit of 1906 has never died and has in fact been compounded by the present-day forces that are continually modernizing Iranian society.

The economic need to deliver desirable outcomes (especially employment opportunities to the growing mass of educated young) in a globalized world has forced all modern regimes to make accommodations to political freedom and the market. Moreover, even the most autocratic regimes in the modern era have relied on an urban proletariat and bourgeoisie as important pillars of political support (Ansari 2004). In this respect, powerful indigenous forces for change are always fighting against the development of a political gap (Huntington 1971). These conditions are prevalent in all such regimes that have been branded as politically arrested. Saudi Arabia, Syria, Jordan, Libya, and Lebanon have been continuing to feel the pinch of a modern and materially grounded society facing economic difficulties and stagnation in a globalized world. This has led to economic, political, and educational reforms in all of these nations. Hence, the underpinnings of organic democratization have apparently manifested themselves across this rogue world (Alterman 2004).

Even in what might be the most repressive regime among the purported rogues, North Korea, progressive forces are promoting a "quiet revolution" in government and society at large (Lankov 2007). The Kim Jong-il regime has continued to face great internal pressure from these progressive forces and has found it increasingly difficult to repress a greater transformation emerging in North Korea. Irrespective of massive attempts to keep people and information under control, there is far greater freedom in North Korea today than has been the case in preceding decades. Less than airtight borders and greater elusiveness made possible by a globalized world have allowed markets to emerge, people to migrate out, and information to flow freely in. The levers of control have also been compromised by a debilitating corruption that has continued to delegitimize the regime among the greater population. Lankov (2007), in fact, sees striking similarities between present-day North Korea and the Eastern bloc nations shortly before the fall of the Berlin Wall. Whereas most would see the potential for political change in present-day North Korea as limited, the indigenous forces that can marshal a transformation in North Korea are nonetheless strongly manifesting themselves.

In sum, the Bush Doctrine's reliance on hard power generated a type of moral hazard that rendered the United States muscle-bound in its foreign policy. The use of coercion and force undermined the most important power resources for achieving its most vital goals (i.e., soft power) through both counterproductive effects and fundamental neglect. At a more basic level, the Bush Doctrine undermined the credibility and legitimacy that were necessary for building multilateral networks in pursuit of the United States' most treasured foreign policy goals. This was compounded by discarding such networks in favor of independent action (discussed more fully later in the next section). Thus, the Bush Doctrine limited the flexibility in the access to power resources necessary to marshal effective U.S. foreign policy. Brzezinski (2007, 147) is representative of a large cross-section of scholars who lament the hard disempowerment caused by this muscle-bound condition and call for a new and more flexible policy orientation that is founded on a softer core. Indeed, only through such change does the United States have a "second chance" to reclaim its international influence.

A Vicious Cycle of American Unilateralism

It is interesting that Bush hailed the invigorating benefits of multilateralism in his National Security Strategy (White House 2002a, v): "We are also guided by the conviction that no nation can build a safer, better world alone. Alliances and multilateral institutions can multiply the strength of freedom-loving nations." Regardless of this rhetorical support, the track record of the Bush administration has left much to be desired with respect to multilateralism. Indeed, the disposition toward unilateralism that has emanated from the Bush Doctrine was a clear manifestation of perceptions of U.S. hard power. Premised on the Neoconservative belief that the United States enjoyed primacy in the global power structure across issues, the Bush Doctrine embraced independent action as a necessary means of securing U.S. global interests (Smith 2007). In short, it was a clear rejection of the venues of soft power (power through cooperation) and a commitment to the instruments of hard power. Bush himself blazed a unilateralist trail both before and after 9/11, and even independently of national security issues. The trail was extensive: a recalcitrant posture toward the UN; withdrawal from the International Criminal Court; rejection of a UN agreement on enforcing a ban on germ warfare as well as a UN resolution designed to protect children against slavery and forced labor; refusal to sign the Kyoto Protocol; continued waffling on Law of the Sea negotiations; withdrawal from the Anti-Ballistic Missile (ABM) Treaty and pressing ahead with a missile defense shield in the face of worldwide opposition; reluctance to sign on to the Biological Weapons Convention; reluctance to participate in a grand UN initiative designed to address racism in member nations; remaining a lethargic observer with respect to the Ottawa Treaty (Mine Ban Treaty) and the CTBT; and taking an independent line at a UN conference on limiting the illegal trafficking in small arms by trying to water down resolutions. This abdication from multilateralism has far from vindicated neoconservative expectations.[37] The rejection of important soft venues for pursuing U.S. global objectives has in fact disempowered the United States. Moreover, the quest for independence has led the United States into a vicious cycle of unilateralism, which clearly revealed that unilateral U.S. hard power has not been sufficient to guard the national interests across global issues. In fact, these unilateral strategies emanating from perceptions of hard power proved far inferior to multilateral venues as levers to obtain the United States' most cherished goals. The influence perceived as deriving from this hard power alone was an illusion. This power illusion vindicated those who have averred that the United States, notwithstanding its primacy, was not strong enough to "go it alone" (Nye 2002, 158).

[37] For an especially insightful collection of essays on U.S. unilateralism under Bush and its consequences, see Malone and Khong (2003).

The United States' aloof posture under Bush generated manifold alliance effects that have compromised the U.S. global power position. Disregard for the UN Security Council and NATO, especially in dealing with Iraq, sent shockwaves through those constellations of relations, damaged the credibility of both organizations as important power brokers, and compromised the standing of the United States in both bodies (Gardner 2005, 129).[38] This rift has not been as inconsequential as some, like Kagan (2003b), believe because the United States has historically used both as important venues to pursue its global interests, especially when it has sought multilateral legitimacy as a seal of approval and direct logistical support for its actions (Jervis 2005, 354).[39] The United States has been critically dependent on both for its principal international goals: postwar stabilization in Iraq (with the Security Council now being invited to play a greater role), peace in the Middle East, the war against terrorism and WMD, and peacekeeping/state building throughout the world. With such bodies being adversarial rather than supportive, the United States can only have been rendered less able to attain its international goals, which required alliance or organizational backing. In this respect, the United States was left with fewer cards to play when protecting its interests. Such being the case, the United States faced a vicious cycle of unilateralism under Bush: as unilateralism alienated allies and supporters, it became even more necessary because of a diminished recourse to multilateral forums (Smith 2007, 198).

NATO support has been especially crucial, and given U.S. unilateralism under Bush, it has proved especially fragile as well. The United States has always been assisted by its allies in carrying out its most important international objectives. The United States chose a different path after 9/11 with respect to NATO. The NATO Summit in Prague in the following year was reflective of this vicious cycle. While the United States was pursuing its own conceptions of retaliation for 9/11 and already planning for war with Iraq, NATO was left on the margins of both efforts. Bush

[38] The acrimony not only arose because of an American posture of impunity in acting independently of its allies and international bodies, but also because of a failure to at least consult allies and international organizations of its plans, which suggests a complete disregard of alliance and legal commitments (Halper and Clarke 2004, 229).

[39] Ignatieff (2003) cites the "moral authority" international support lends to, and effectively bolsters through legitimacy, American foreign policy initiatives. The legitimacy creates greater x-efficiencies on the part of supporting nations that enhanced U.S. influence. In this respect, legitimacy has indeed proved to be, as Kegley and Raymond (2007, 121) note, "the ultimate force multiplier." Because this legitimacy influenced American public opinion, Bush found it increasingly harder to marshal his foreign policy without it.

focused on Britain as a key ally in the coalition of the willing but continued to alienate his other NATO allies by carrying on war and occupations without substantive consultation and accountability. As the disdain for American unilateralism grew, it became more difficult for NATO allies to muster either the popular support or elite disposition to help the United States when it found itself targeted as an imperialistic occupier. In this case, NATO reluctance to provide enough muscle to both lighten the burden for the United States and legitimize the occupations left the United States in a pernicious state of isolation in attending to its goals in Iraq and Afghanistan. Whereas the counterfactual suggests that more support from NATO nations might have been forthcoming without U.S. impunity, it is clear that whatever reluctance would have been created among NATO nations (even if the United States had dealt legitimately with NATO) was increased through both public and elite alienation, all of which undermined the alliance commitments that compelled NATO nations to support U.S. initiatives (Kaplan 2008, 179–83).

NATO has been intimately involved in the three major U.S. goals concerning terrorism, WMD, and liberal state transformation. But on a broader scale, a supportive and vibrant NATO has always been essential to American interests throughout the world (Smith 2007, 198). NATO is the principle instrument through which the United States is presently brokering and securing its geopolitical interests in Europe. Furthermore, its support is a boon to U.S. goals in every principal region in the global system. It continues to be the peacekeeper in Kosovo, but it has also allocated a large number of troops in Afghanistan and has been instrumental in training Iraqi security forces. It has even been engaged in African peacekeeping by providing airlifts for African peacekeepers. The United States seeks to even expand this peacekeeping role to obtain both logistical help and legitimacy for its foreign ventures. It has pushed NATO to develop a vigorous program against cyberterrorism, pushed it to undertake a greater role in long-term civil reconstruction in Iraq, and continued to beseech European allies to take over more of the peacekeeping operations in Iraq and Afghanistan. Furthermore, the United States has pushed for more European support in its dealings with Iran and North Korea. Yet the alienation resulting from American impunity has scarred the alliance, and NATO has been recoiling at the very time the United States needed it most, leaving the United States in a more isolated position in attending to its foreign policy goals.

Such a constellation of relations was clearly manifest at the NATO Summit in Bucharest in April 2008, where Europeans were contemplating a change in the alliance toward a more limited focus in operations. This is a symptom of a U.S.–EU rift that mirrors a splintering of the alliance in recent years.[40] There has already emerged in the alliance a two-tiered system in terms of which nations supply frontline troops versus which undertake less hazardous duties. Also, the joint operations in Afghanistan are hardly well coordinated, but have verged on a free-for-all. Moreover, the politics of NATO are absolutely crucial to American interests in Europe. The question of expansion is intimately intertwined with U.S.–Russian relations and hence of immense importance to the United States. The Bucharest Summit demonstrated the importance of NATO when the allies voted to endorse Bush's plan for a missile defense shield in Poland and the Czech Republic and agreed to send more French troops to Afghanistan, but nixed Bush's desire to expand the alliance by not announcing a plan to include the Ukraine and Georgia.[41] Clearly, the alliance still holds crucial leverage over important geostrategic interests of the United States in Europe and the world at large. And with associate status for Russia in the new cooperative council, NATO provides the principal multilateral forum for cooperation on European security matters with Russia. This is significant for the United States, as it provides a rare multilateral reinforcement venue for working on political issues between the two nations. Being marginalized in the alliance removes the United States from an important position of influence in the course of alliance politics and diminishes its ability to orchestrate its most vital European relations by pressing it to accomplish more of its objectives independently. Indeed, the United States' drift from grace in NATO under Bush left it increasingly isolated in facing some of its biggest challenges (McKinnon 2008). And as the United States increasingly adopted a more independent posture under Bush, it made such a posture more self reinforcing because of further alienation on the part of NATO and the bureaucratic drag of having developed a more independent style of foreign policy.

The UN and Security Council are even more essential than NATO in terms of maintaining American interests in the global arena, and a similar process of unilateral reinforcement has manifested itself in those forums

[40] The EU has continued pushing for a unified foreign policy at the same time that NATO has been pushing the development of a more European-based security function. Both of these threaten the role of the United States in the alliance, a role the United States should not forsake if it wishes to maintain its influence over important geostrategic issues (Gardner 2005, 25).

[41] However, European nations did state that they expected both countries to eventually join NATO.

as well. Forsaking them has significantly disempowered the United States across issues. Thus, whereas unilateralism may have given the United States more freedom to act without constraints in the very short term, it has weakened the United States and limited its sources of leverage in the longer term. Indeed, the United States has squandered significant opportunities to pursue its interests by resorting to meta-power in such well-respected multilateral venues that could have been cultivated through better U.S. engagement. It somewhat defies reason that the United States would spend decades building these institutions to promote its milieu goals and then abandon them when vital interests were at stake. Regarding the goals of WMD and terrorism, the institutional framework of the Security Council has provided a compelling problem-solving venue. The Council has passed sixteen major resolutions demanding Iraqi disarmament. Security Council Resolution 1368 contemplates a broad and effective mandate to hunt down terrorists throughout the world. More generally, the Council provides extensive latitude to the permanent members (the United States and allies) to manage security in the world at large.

With respect to nation building, decolonization has cast the UN in the leading role – a role in which the United States finds it difficult to compete in reestablishing political order in Iraq (Heisbourg 2004, 11). Although the use of meta-power through multilateral venues lacks the speed and directness of unilateral approaches, it will prove a greater source of influence in the long run, as lasting solutions to international problems must be grounded in legitimate and influential structures of governance. The imposition of illegitimate and/or weaker structures will be ultimately self-defeating.

In terms of global peacekeeping, the preemptive policy of the United States has threatened to unravel the legal fabric of the security regime contemplated under the UN Charter. The United States has relied heavily on this regime to promote its goal of limiting regional and ethnic conflict in the postwar period. Although Article 51 of the Charter expressly affirms the right of unilateral militarism, many interpret its language as precluding preventive attacks, allowing military action only in self-defense (i.e., after being attacked). The United States has made use of this clause in legitimating multilateral and unilateral responses to acts of aggression that opposed American interests, from the Korean War to the Balkan and the Gulf Wars (Wirtz and Russell 2003, 118). Setting precedents that undermine the clause can only enhance military action in the world at large as nations gain greater legitimacy for preemptive invasions. As a case in point, U.S. impunity, in breaking with Security Council and

NATO obligations in dealing with Iraq, unleashed a wave of actions on the part of other nations (a vigilante effect) that conflicted with American foreign goals (Guoliang 2004, 77). In the wake of Bush's national security statement in 2002, India, Russia, Iran, Israel, and Japan all issued statements proclaiming their right to perpetrate preemptive strikes for self-defense (Kegley and Raymond 2007, 102). Hence, the American desire for a world of fewer regional and ethnic conflicts will be increasingly frustrated to the extent that such a precedent is compelling. Moreover, the United States' preemptive posture in this respect is inconsistent with the milieu goal of enhancing respect for human rights and international law. At a more general level, U.S. policy appears to have been guilty of a "paradox of peace" in that it has sought to disseminate a commitment to peace through a preponderance of weapons and unilateral militarism (Yarmolinsky and Foster 1983).

By forsaking such multilateral forums in a quest to protect its vital interests, the United States has missed some extraordinary opportunities to galvanize and shape these forums in a way that is consistent with said vital interests. The lesson learned by the Soviets in the early years of the UN was somehow lost on the Bush administration. Early on in the history of the U.N. the Soviets responded to disagreeable votes in the Security Council by simply walking out and boycotting proceedings. Although this did not affect them on procedural issues, it took a heavy toll on one substantive issue. The Soviets boycotted Security Council deliberations on the Korean question because the Council had earlier voted to allow Nationalist China to keep its representative on the Council, even after the Communist Revolution. The Soviets were not there to veto the resolution calling for a multilateral response to the invasion of South Korea, giving greater legitimacy to the American cause against North Korea. The lesson was clear. Nations may gain independence by relinquishing multilateral obligations, but they also lose power over the proceedings in those organizations and thereby sacrifice opportunities to shape the agenda. Such organizations can have considerable influence over the vital interests of those nations. In the worst-case scenario, absence may cause outcomes in the organization to become more hostile to the interests of the recalcitrant nations, which introduces perhaps the most pernicious consequence of the vicious cycle of unilateralism: continued politico-strategic aloofness may create more enemies than it eliminates if the abandoned organizations take a confrontational turn. And such contests produce a very uneven playing field as organizations carry far more legitimacy for their causes, *ceteris paribus*, vis à vis individual nation states. Ergo, they are contests to be avoided. At a minimum, if not confrontational, the organizations may simply produce additional roadblocks for a nation's foreign initiatives. In this case, the old cliche holds true: "If you can't beat them, join them."

From a more general structural perspective, institutions that circumscribe and restrain sovereign actions in the international system tend to work in favor of dominant nations. This has been fundamentally acknowledged across the political spectrum of international relations theory, from Neo-Marxists to Neoliberals (Krisch 2003; Cox 1980; Keohane 1984). Yet the benefits of this "institutionalization of hegemony" are all the greater because the United States has been the most prolific international "legislator" of the postwar era (Krisch 2003). The possibilities for enjoying meta-power in these institutions are even greater for the United States because decision-making structures that have guided the institutions have been configured to a large extent by the United States itself (Krisch 2003). Hence, the status quo fundamentally has rested on institutions built and supported by the United States. Compromising the effectiveness and even the existence of these institutions will consequently undermine important traditional sources of U.S. leverage in the international system. Moving outside these arrangements for slightly more flexibility in the short term carries the risk of weakening the United States across most issue areas in the long term. If we look at all of the arrangements that Bush has forsaken in his quest for a more effective foreign policy, we see a trail of decimation in multilateral initiatives that have heretofore protected and promoted vital U.S. interests: the ABM Treaty (which enhanced the power of U.S. deterrence), Kyoto (which promised to deliver market-based solutions to environmental problems), the International Criminal Court (ICC) (which could export U.S. criminal law to the international system), the Law of the Sea (which establishes definitive property rights on uses of the sea), the Biological Weapons Convention (which limits possibilities for devastating assaults on American soil), and the Convention on Small Arms (which limits the resources for asymmetric strikes against the United States and Americans abroad).

When the United States alienates its allies within the context of existing arrangements, these allies may divert to alternative arrangements that do not include the United States and may even eventually generate competition for U.S. interests (Ikenberry 2001, 19). In this respect, the vicious cycle of unilateralism is compounded by a tendency to create competitive and even antagonistic institutions. There have been a plethora of manifestations of such a phenomenon under the Bush presidency. The United States' European allies have been animated in seeking out alternative and additional security arrangements outside NATO. European nations have been seeking to forge their own rapid deployment force because of dissatisfaction with the unwillingness of the United States to compromise on the management of NATO's deployment. France has reached out to Russia (Cooperation Council on Security Issues), North Korea, Iran, and Chechnya in search of new security arrangements. France and Germany have reached out to China to consolidate arms dealings. Russia has been seeking an alternative security arrangement with NATO outside the NATO-Russia Council. France, Britain, and Germany have been prompting Russia to form a multilateral security initiative to negotiate with Tehran over nuclear arms. Russia and China have joined the Shanghai Cooperative Organization, along with various Eurasian republics, to promote trade, limit drug trafficking, and fight terrorism. Russia has been seeking to bring China and India into an arrangement that would fight pan-Islamic terrorism. Even Israel has affronted its American connection by joining India to form a security pact against terrorism (Malone 2003, 23; Gardner 2005, 134–9). All such developments have diminished the multilateral support systems that the United States has employed to attain its foreign goals, leaving it in a more vulnerable independent position. This position has become more self reinforcing as the United States has had to adopt more unilateral strategies to attain its goals. In addition to the competition, and even confrontation, regarding security arrangements involving the United States, these cross-cutting commitments may create significant problems if non-U.S. regimes require U.S. allies to forsake their U.S. regime commitments. This is akin to the problem of cross-cutting vassalages (i.e., when vassals had more than one lord) that made feudalism such an unstable political system in the Middle Ages.

In the case that nations choose to remain in the present arrangements with the United States instead of seeking other venues, a corollary effect of alienation could manifest itself in another deleterious outcome for the United States. Establishing a reputation for impunity within multilateral forums may generate a backlash that leads other nations to impose greater de facto (if not de jure) restraints against the United States in order to counterbalance the inclusion of what might be considered a maverick nation. Consequently, the United States might find the "deck" increasingly "stacked against it" when pursuing its objectives within those institutions. In this respect, we witness a paradoxical effect of restraint. A history of restraint and cooperation under international agreements and legal instruments may accord greater net benefits in terms of flexibility than a history of impunity (Krisch 2003, 64). Ongoing loyalty will place a nation in a better position to ask for exceptions to rules when they accord most with vital interests. A disloyal and recalcitrant nation will have compromised the political capital to ask for such favors. One stark example of this was evident in the differential treatment by NATO allies in the Security Council with respect to the cases of Kosovo and Iraq. The United States' NATO allies were reluctant to give a Security Council mandate to justify U.S. military action against Iraq, even though Iraq was found to have been in breach of Resolution 688 for more than a decade. Yet the same nations allowed NATO air strikes against Kosovo without even requesting such a mandate. Legally, the basis for U.S. action against Iraq differed little from that of Europe against Kosovo, but U.S. allies raised the institutional barriers for the United States in reaction to what was considered a trail of unilateralist impunity (Heisbourg 2004, 10). Another example has been the manner in which nations in the ICC have been, during the Bush years, increasingly reluctant to grant the United States exceptions because of perceptions that the United States will never compromise on the statute (Krisch 2003, 64). The vicious cycle process is quite visible here. As a unilateral posture generates institutional limits to the flexibility of the United States in multilateral forums, such unilateralism becomes all the more necessary because of these institutional restraints.

There is no question that strong alliance relations are a key to American milieu goals of democratic state building, WMD, terrorism, economic transformation, and forging regional and ethnic harmony. Ultimately all of these goals can only be viably pursued within a multilateral framework. Hence, the United States has to strengthen rather than weaken its colleagueship in the present regional alliances and international organizations. Interestingly, greater and more cross-cutting ties would be a boon to peace in the Middle East, a lesson that is obviously making an impression on the United States as it seeks a more multilateral solution to the Palestinian question. The United States must act quickly and with resolution to consolidate its standing in regional alliances, as foreboding harbingers of potential disassociation have recently emerged. The Pew (2003) survey reported that a majority of Western European populations want more independence from the United States in diplomacy and security. In addition, U.S. allies have, for the first time, refused to reelect the United States to the UN Human Rights Commission (Nye 2002, 156). The deterioration of the United States' image within alliance networks and international organizations was quite evident with the overwhelming refusal of Bush's overtures, since September 2003, for help to rebuild and stabilize Iraq. Disconcertingly for the United States, this refusal for support has reflected not only disapproval, but also a strategic element of burden avoidance. Staying out of such controversial undertakings not only saves resources, but it also lowers security risks facing U.S. allies and partner nations. Allowing the United States to supply the lion's share of occupation forces in Iraq and Afghanistan makes the United States the target of vituperation. This trend is visible in North Korea as well, where NATO allies and other nations can shift risk away from themselves by leaving WMD talks in a regional context rather than having them become a prime focus of the Security Council (Heisbourg 2004, 11).

Since the unilateralism encouraged by Bush served to weaken multilateral venues for addressing the United States' most pressing problems, the United States has been increasingly forced to carry more of the burden without help from others (Guoliang 2004, 79; Gallarotti 2010). This has compounded the problem of overstretch and raised the costs of foreign policy all the more. A legacy of brash unilateralism has further enhanced the problem of overstretch because it has given allies legitimate grounds for avoiding burden sharing. Although alienation and vituperation explain much of the reluctance to share the burden, NATO allies certainly have used American impunity in starting the Afghanistan and Iraq campaigns without proper consent and consultation as justification for skirting logistical support. And even when the United States was able to procure partners in the Iraq war, such as Britain, the difficulty of sustaining the campaign without communal contributions caused political backlashes that undermined the limited support the United States enjoyed. The Blair case had reverberation effects throughout the United States' alliance partners by discouraging support for these and other such U.S. undertakings (Halper and Clarke 2004, 264–7). Furthermore, a Pew (2003) survey reported that faith in the UN system was very low in the world at large. Such an absence of confidence can only mean more dependence on the United States to provide international public goods heretofore doled out by international organizations. Certainly this fear has been vindicated in the context of a variety of issues, as nations appear to be targeting the United States as the champion that will deliver them from their problems: Liberians and Palestinians have sought U.S. intervention; Afghanistan wants more U.S. aid; and Indonesia and the Philippines seek more U.S. assistance in fighting terrorism. Herein lies one of the more debilitating manifestations of the vicious cycle of unilateralism. As diminishing U.S. support for multilateral forums undermines the forums' effectiveness in addressing global problems, the burden will fall increasingly on the unilateral power of the dominant nation in the world: in this case the United States. It is bad enough that a unilateral posture forces the United States increasingly into an independent role in solving its own problems, but it also opens the United States to the prospect of being increasingly pressured to address the problems of other nations.

As noted, one of the principal adverse effects of the vicious cycle of unilateralism is that unilateral solutions are often far inferior to multilateral solutions in dealing with a nation's international problems. This has certainly been the case across U.S. foreign policy goals: terrorism, WMD, regional peacekeeping, environmentalism, democratic state building, international law, and human rights. American primacy has generated a tendency for unilateral solutions that are not only inferior in attending to these goals, but also have often proved counterproductive. As has been suggested in the context of moral hazard, softer power solutions grounded in multilateralism present the most viable long-term opportunities for realizing such goals. Developments in the Middle East and Asia represent a lucid microcosm of the intersection of these three goals and the concomitant inferiority of unilateral solutions in attending to them. The unilateralist orientation in this case was heightened by Bush's neoconservative disdain for diplomacy with autocratic governments, especially those targeted within the "axis of evil" and states fingered as sponsors of terrorism. Yet this disdain of working multilaterally with Iran and Syria has severely hamstrung the possibilities of substantive solutions to the Palestinian problem. Both nations would have significant pull in negotiations with the most militant Palestinian factions, and peace agreements could very well be forged. These peace agreements would be a potential pillar to achieve all of the U.S. goals in the Middle East: discouraging the need for WMD, abating terrorism, and promoting liberal political and economic reforms. But the United States not only shunned Iran and Syria under Bush, it also continued to coerce and isolate them. Greater confrontation made cooperation with these states even more difficult, leaving the United States increasingly alone as a champion of democracy and political stability in the region (Kaplan 2008, 168–72).

Similarly, with respect to WMD and democracy in Asia, Bush initially chose to unilaterally confront Kim Jong-il, as Bush disdained diplomacy with North Korea and China. The China card has been especially important and fragile. Yet China is the most influential nation in Asia with respect to North Korea, so any viable multilateral solution regarding North Korea would have to feature China prominently. Once more, the neoconservative disposition against working with autocratic states hampered the only viable long-term solution to WMD and liberal transformation in Asia. As Bush spurned such diplomacy, Kim Jong-il became more politically entrenched and increasingly anxious to develop a deterrent against a U.S. invasion. However, it became clear to Bush that disdain for diplomacy had further alienated China and North Korea, which meant that the United States would have increasingly been forced to contemplate unilaterally coercive solutions, solutions that would continue to prove counterproductive (Kaplan 2008, 69–76).

With respect to peacekeeping and state building, the superiority of UN and other multilateral solutions over unilateral initiatives, such as in Iraq and Afghanistan, has been starkly demonstrated. Haiti and Kosovo provide interesting foils to Iraq and Afghanistan. The problems of unilateral engagement in the latter states have been duly chronicled earlier in this chapter. Conversely, collective engagement in the former territories manifested effects that attest to the utility of multilateral strategies. In both these territories, multilateral strategies promoted effective burden-sharing strategies with manifold effects in eliminating security threats and conditioning political forces to coalesce around expectations generated by the peacekeeping forces. Much of this derived from the greater legitimacy accorded multilateral peacekeeping operations and solutions. But in addition to the obvious advantages in terms of burden sharing and legitimacy, the multilateral solutions provided relatively low-cost exit strategies for the United States. Disengagement was enhanced by multilateral commitments for post-conflict stabilization. Moreover, the United States never became a principal target for retaliation, given that it avoided an imperialistic presence. And more generally, state building proceeded on perceptions of political balance in the emerging domestic regimes and institutions. However, in Afghanistan and Iraq, the United States has found itself cursed with a lack of all three outcomes: little burden sharing, even less legitimacy, and, finally, very high-cost exit strategies (Malone 2003; Thakur 2003; Stepanova 2003).

With respect to human rights and international law, the United States' principal goals have been adversely affected not only by its preemptive security posture, but also by its reticence about supporting the ICC. American support for the court would be a classic example of how moderation in attending to direct goals can create milieu effects that enhance those goals far more than a recalcitrant unilateral posture and glaringly attests to the inferiority of unilateral solutions. U.S. reticence on the court under Bush focused on the protection of American peacekeepers in international operations (i.e., ensure the protection of American constitutional rights even when abroad). Fears centered on erstwhile enemies of the United States using the ICC as a legal platform from which to attack Americans. Such might be the case if initiatives arose that targeted the actions of American peacekeepers as crimes under the jurisdiction of the Court (e.g., accidental firing on a civilian target that results in deaths). However, such fears of a politicized court are unfounded. Because the court is an ancillary mechanism to national courts in prosecuting international crimes, the United States would have first right to investigate and prosecute cases involving American peacekeepers. The argument that American peacekeepers should be completely unaccountable for their actions is indefensible. The only possible glitch in the first-right clause would be a case in which a nation harboring an American peacekeeper refused to extradite that suspect but chose to prosecute him/her itself. Even in such a case, the likelihood of foreign prosecution is remote, as extradition is a diplomatic question and the United States has firm agreements on extradition with virtually all other nations. Thus, the downside of supporting the court appears slim, but the upside is substantial for American interests, and this upside represents opportunities lost if the court is weakened by a lack of U.S. support. First, the court would allow the United States to step back from the role of world policeman that has generated such a negative image. Spreading the burden of prosecuting international criminals would help abate perceptions of American tyranny, which in turn would enhance the safety of Americans overseas and promote the desirability of American democracy and capitalism.[42] Second, prosecution of suspects would be enhanced, as erstwhile enemies of the United States would be more likely to extradite suspects to the ICC than to the United States or any of its allies. Finally, the charter of the ICC is heavily grounded in American law and constitutional rights. For all intents and purposes, it gives the appearance of having been written by American lawyers. Supporting the ICC gives the United States the opportunity to export the American system of jurisprudence to the world at large with regard to selected crimes. What better way to extend the protection of constitutional rights to Americans in the international system? Furthermore, by staying out of the court, the United States also risks the consequences of leaving international criminal law in the hands of others, that is, being

[42] After March 2005, the United States has pushed the Security Council to allow ICC engagement in prosecuting war crimes in Sudan. This is a clear manifestation of the usefulness of the court for U.S. foreign policy. After the debacle in Somalia, the court represents a means of relieving the United States of the risky roles of international policeman and judge in especially dangerous regional conflicts.

in a powerless position to prevent other nations from passing laws that conflict with American interests (Gallarotti and Preis 1999; Nolte 2003).

Multilateralism also appears superior to unilateralism in the issue of promoting environmentalism. The Bush stand on the Kyoto Protocol shows similar opportunities lost with respect to American business and the economy. Like the ICC, the United States used its participation in Kyoto to shape it significantly in its own interests (staggered cuts, emissions trading). Thus, a weakening of Kyoto because of American departure interrupted the exportation of American environmental policies to other countries. But in pulling out, the United States also left the fate of multilateral environmental control in the hands of others, clearly an inferior position from which to prevent undesirable international policies. In short, departure enervated American international environmental influence. The argument that adhering to the emission limits of Kyoto would burden businesses with extra costs and reduce economic growth fails to appreciate the opportunities Kyoto carried for the United States. First, greater environmentalism would promote the environmental industry, one in which the United States has both an absolute and a comparative advantage. Losses in international sales incurred by some industries burdened by environmental costs would be made up for in part by increased sales in other industries. Moreover, American firms are highly adaptable to changing environmental standards because of stricter and frequent changes in regulations at home, so general limits may give American companies an international competitive advantage if they can adapt to the limits faster than other companies. It therefore is not clear that the American economy will suffer a net decrease in growth as a result of stricter emissions standards. On the contrary, a stricter environmental milieu may carry opportunities for greater macro- and microeconomic growth (Gallarotti 1995a; Assuncao 2003).

Along with U.S. advantages in environmental technologies and production methods, it is clear that the call for greenhouse-gas curbs has become politically compelling in all developed nations. The United States is faced with political pressure to enact these curbs, even in the absence of an international treaty.[43] Interestingly, much of this pressure to consolidate some national initiative to curb greenhouse gases in the last years of the Bush presidency came from American industry itself, which feared more draconian measures by a new administration and hence pushed

[43] In fact, a number of U.S. states have proposed state laws that impose the Kyoto quotas on their residents.

to lock the nation into a system of more moderate cuts before future administrations propose more drastic standards. Bush, however, opted for a more decentralized system of cuts whereby nations would unilaterally select appropriate levels. The motivating force behind this plan was the hope that in conjunction with the United States' own unilateral cuts, other nations (first China and India in this iteration) would feel pressured to follow suit and thus generate a sort of additive regime for promoting a solution to global warming. Such a regime would in fact be far inferior to a multilateral regime given its decentralized character, which is inefficient and ineffective for dealing with the main problem of carbon emissions – the collective level of such emissions across nations. Appropriate collective levels can only be determined and managed within a multilateral regime, as iterated-additive diplomacy lacks the institutional capacity to effectively and efficiently set such levels. A multilateral regime also provides the advantages of an international market for emissions trading, a diplomatic forum to negotiate relief through quota realignments, as well as domestic political capital for American politicians to sell painful cuts to their constituents. Such a decentralized regime as championed by Bush would not produce results very different from the free-for-all system that would exist without a strong international agreement. Even worse, it would generate even greater problems. Introducing such a system based on unilateral and limited multilateral standards would introduce a type of moral hazard that would lock nations into what amounts to a bounded system of curbs; that is, its existence would dampen initiates for other international greenhouse regimes (McKinnon and Power 2008; Assuncao 2003).

In sum, the United States has been victimized by a vicious cycle of unilateralism under the Bush Doctrine. By forsaking important soft venues and sources of international influence available through multilateral initiatives, the United States has found itself in the unenvious position of having to take up a greater unilateral burden in a period when its preponderant international presence has already generated excessive burdens.

Failure in Decision Making

To a large extent, the failures of the Bush Doctrine reflected more fundamental failures in decision making. These failures manifested themselves with respect to the five prescriptions (for instituting Cosmopolitical power strategies) presented in chapter 1. Indeed, Bush and his leading advisors fell woefully short in the perspicacity necessary to effectively monitor, evaluate, and manage U.S. power.

With respect to the first prescription (continually questioning theories of power and continual power audits), the Bush administration proved surprisingly rigid in its evaluation of foreign policies. Theories of security were heavily grounded in an orientation founded on the utility of large conventional forces and nuclear deterrence. The U.S. administration held rigidly to these models, even though outcomes across the major goals of foreign policy reflected broad failures. The United States was so distracted by these models that they wrongly equated success in larger conventional confrontations (wars in Iraq and Afghanistan) with winning the wars against terrorism, WMD, and autocracy. The Bush administration continued to bank on its military primacy to fight the battle against terrorism. Yet the weapons and strategies proved ill equipped to confront such an amorphous threat. Indeed, the use of such weapons and strategies made the problem of terrorism worse. The administration also banked on its nuclear and conventional supremacy as wedges that would deliver liberal regime transformation and reduce the threat of WMD. This, too, proved to be an illusory, and ultimately a counterproductive, conviction.

With respect to the second and third prescriptions (assessing national strength in net rather than nominal terms, and being sensitive to the manifold consequences of power-seeking strategies), the Bush administration proved equally deficient. In essence, countervailing responses (adverse negative feedback) arose across a plethora of international sources and also served to deliver a crushing blow to American influence across the international system (more terrorist attacks, fewer cooperative allies, and adverse balancing effects by target nations). These feedback effects manifested themselves as complex and manifold consequences and produced net effects that neutralized the nominal influence of America's arsenal of hard power resources. Once more, the compelling perceptions of America's hard power primacy distracted the Bush administration from the fact that broad negative feedback effects were rendering the use of such hard power resources self defeating. Thus, perceptions of U.S. strength were largely illusory when net effects and complexity were factored in.

The Bush administration also failed on the fourth prescription by not addressing the disjuncture between actual foreign policy outcomes and American hard power. The Bush administration made few fundamental changes in its strategies to combat terrorism, WMD proliferation, and autocracy even in the face of outcomes suggesting that not only were these strategies failing, but that they were actually enhancing the threats in all three areas. The strategies continued to bank on U.S. military strength and coercive diplomatic weight in world politics, even though such resources continually proved insufficient to deliver the goods in terms of foreign policy outcomes. Belief systems among Bush and his leading advisors never deviated from a conviction that American hard power primacy would ultimately dictate outcomes somewhere down the road.

Finally, with respect to the last prescription, the Bush Doctrine was a model of rigidity rather than flexibility in the conduct of foreign policy. Coercive diplomacy and conventional force dominated the agenda for bringing about Bush's three sacred goals. This restricted use of American power was in large part driven by several factors. First, there was the doctrine's conviction that American hard power primacy was too great to ultimately fail in delivering on the three goals. This belief persisted even in the face of continual setbacks. But Bush also made commitments to a course so confrontational that it was difficult to disengage from or annul it. Starting with such a strategy made responses to foreign problems path dependent. Having started with tough and large-scale actions (threat and invasion), it was hard to retreat significantly from such brinkmanship because this strategy, for the administration, represented an opening move in a chicken game. It was, of course, feared that backing away and taking refuge in a more restrained set of diplomatic options would have compromised the resolve of the United States in the perceptions of opponents. Bush also made a domestic commitment to the American public to stay the course in a resolute war against the threats faced by the United States. It was feared that backing off from this promise would have compromised Bush's domestic political standing. Yet again, Bush's own perceptions of American hard power led him all too easily to promises that effectively boxed him into a rigid course of action against the threats to the United States. Ultimately, the United States' own conventional military primacy served to suffocate alternative military and non-military responses to terrorism, WMD, and nation building (i.e., muscle-boundedness). One of the most disempowering consequences of this rigid posture on the part of Bush was in neglecting and undermining important means of foreign policy tied up in soft power strategies. Integrating more of such strategies promised to enhance the ability of the administration to achieve its most treasured foreign policy goals.

In sum, the Bush legacy of disempowerment has indeed been compelling. Perhaps few foreign policies have been as controversial across

American history. Yet, concomitantly, few have been as important in generating lessons about the art of foreign policy. Certainly there are important lessons here for the Obama and future administrations. Heeding these lessons will be necessary for future administrations to deliver the United States from the disempowering legacy forged by Bush.

6

Case Study of Soft Empowerment

The Power of Modern American Culture

Soft power traditionally has been seen as manifesting itself largely through culture. In fact, American soft power has, to a large extent, derived from the compelling influence of America's alluring culture. Culture fits the more popular, but limited, vision of soft power. It is soft (does not modify behavior coercively); it is intangible; and it is pervasive and compelling in the world. The power of American culture is more extensive in its manifestations than the soft power analyzed in Chapter 4. These cases chronicled a somewhat more restricted manifestation of soft power in looking at the empowering effects of nations copying the economic policies of other nations. The manifestations of the soft power of culture are broader. They do have elements of emulation, but emulation goes far beyond just copying economic policies. It applies to emulation across issue areas (political, economic, legal, and social) and across actors (within both government and civil society). But the allure of culture and its capacity to enhance national influence are embedded in a much wider appeal than that which is represented by emulation alone. This appeal derives broadly from the endearment a soft power nation can generate, and this endearment manifests itself in pervasive and manifold ways. Also, as seen in the case studies in Chapter 4, the case of the soft empowerment of American culture attests to the workings of a Cosmopolitan process of power. Indeed, the compelling effects of American culture derive to a large extent from America's hard power, principally its economic power. This economic power generates many chariots through which culture itself is disseminated throughout the world. To the extent that these chariots are robust, the allure of American culture becomes that much more compelling. Also consistent with the Cosmopolitan vision of power, the soft power facilitated by the hard power of American primacy serves to enhance American hard power. As with the cases in Chapter 4, a distinct Cosmopolitan cycle of mutual reinforcement appears between hard and soft power in the context of American culture. The allure of American culture has opened up manifold opportunities for the United States to enhance its hard power (economically, militarily, and politically), and this hard power has served to make American culture all the more alluring. The power of American culture today is especially crucial to the influence of the United States, as it has served as an important counterweight to Bush's toxic foreign policy legacy, which has undermined much American soft power in his eight years as president.

As with the case studies of soft power in general, there has also been insufficient process tracing with respect to analyses of American culture, notwithstanding that American culture has generated sufficient attention among scholars who have studied soft power. Indeed, extant analyses have been restricted either in terms of the issue areas covered or the chronicling of the manifold manifestations of American cultural power. Nye's (2002, 2004a, 2004b) work features extensive coverage, but he focuses more on the sources of American cultural power than the processes through which this cultural power translates into enhanced influence. Similarly, Yasushi and McConnell (2008) feature some analysis of American cultural power, but like Nye's work, the analysis concentrates more on the sources than on the specific benefits. The analyses in Lennon (2003) concentrate principally on how cultural power can be used to combat terrorism. Fraser (2003) addresses some of the benefits of American cultural power for the United States but focuses on how American media and culture serve as vehicles for raising the appeal of the United States among foreign populations. In evaluating the theory of soft power and recommending avenues of future research into the concept, Lukes (2007, 97) offers several leading questions but never asks for a greater clarification and detailed analysis of how cultural power actually benefits a soft power nation. This chapter attempts to fill these gaps by analyzing the myriad processes through which American culture has empowered the United States.

As with the case studies in Chapter 4, the case of American culture at best is a weak test of the process of soft empowerment and the theory of Cosmopolitan power. It is a single case chronicling the effects of a pervasive culture. More such cases of cultural effects would have to be undertaken to produce a stronger test. Moreover, it would be necessary to look at the effects of cultures that are not very pervasive so as to limit problems of selecting on the dependent variable (King, Keohane, and Verba 1994, 129–49). However, the American case nonetheless features some redeeming qualities as a laboratory to evaluate soft empowerment and a Cosmopolitan vision of power. It may be the most salient case in history in terms of the international pervasiveness of a national culture. Indeed, the technological factors responsible for the dissemination of American culture are more advanced than at any other epoch in history. In no other epoch did a national culture have as powerful a set of chariots to carry it around the globe. This greater magnitude gives the analysis of cultural power the potential to be that much more illuminating (i.e., process tracing) about the mechanics of the process of soft empowerment. Moreover, because it may be history's most salient case of the soft empowerment of culture, it serves important falsification functions for assessing the value of soft power and of a Cosmopolitan vision of power. In this respect, it serves a crucial-case function as a most likely case (Eckstein 1975; Gerring 2004, 347; King, Keohane, and Verba 1994, 209–12).

The Endearing Allure of American Culture

Perhaps no other source of American soft power has been as compelling as American culture (Fraser 2003, 2008). The cultural power that emanates from America has been both glorified and criticized. Critics of the present exportation of American culture have branded it as "imperialistic" (Tomlinson 1991; Sardar and Davies 2002; Barnet and Cavanagh, 96; LeFeber 1999).[1] In this vision, it appears more as indoctrination than a result of indigenous preferences (Klein 1999; Sklair 1995). Yet non-critics and critics alike attest to the addictive power of American culture, the latter seeking to encapsulate or defend against the fallout from American cultural penetration (Sklair 1995; Mander and Goldsmith 1996; Klein 1999; Sardar and Davies 2002).[2] Irrespective of disagreements about

[1] Sardar and Davies (2002) and Huntington (1996) have produced explicit chronicles of the adverse reactions from the penetration of American culture, which have caused a "clash of civilizations" and led many to "hate Americans." Nye (2004b, 35–44) and Fraser (2003) also discuss anti-American sentiment among nations.

[2] Some scholars view the cultural transformation emanating from globalization as representing more of a synthesis of American and local culture than outright American cultural imperialism; they have used terms such as hybridization, glocalization, and syncretism (Pieterse 1995, Epitropoulos and Roudometof 1998, and Roudometof and Robertson 1998). But even these scholars attest to American culture as the principal model for transformation across cultures, notwithstanding the degree of synthesis with local values and practices.

the redeeming qualities of American culture, the signs of the addictive qualities of American culture are pervasive – a clear manifestation that in the context of the proliferation of Western culture in general, America has maintained a pronounced superiority in the competition over ideas (Fraser 2003). Regarding the influence of American culture, there is a consensus across scholarship that the United States clearly enjoys unrivaled cultural primacy in the modern world. This advantage has increased with the end of the Cold War, developments in global demographics (40 percent of the world population is aged twenty-one or younger), and the onslaught of the information age (Barnet and Cavanagh 1996). Sardar and Davies (2002, 117) have underscored the preponderant influence of American culture, noting that it is "in the process of replicating itself in the rest of the world." Even in an age when American soft power has been seriously compromised by its domestic and foreign policies (as demonstrated in Chapter 5), Nye (2004b) still identifies American culture as the predominant source of America's soft power.[3] In this context, America has emerged as the leading disseminator of global culture. Fraser (2003, 260) argues that despite some adverse reactions to America's cultural domination of the world through the media, pop lifestyle, and corporations, it still reigns as the foremost "model society" on the face of the Earth. As he notes, "more people [are] seeking to emigrate to the United States than are actively engaged in a Jihad against it."

Survey results on global attitudes have attested to the compelling qualities of American culture. The extensive Pew (2003) survey (of thousands of people across forty-four nations) affirms the positive perceptions accorded the "American lifestyle." Results show a positive perception of the United States, very favorable views of American media and entertainment, strong admiration of American technological capacity, and a preference for American products. Whereas the results on perceptions of American democracy and multinationals are mixed, large pluralities tend to show support for both. Moreover, these survey results show that people strongly embrace the major vehicle of American cultural dissemination – globalization. People strongly support free markets, travel, communication, interdependence, and the media. The support for democracy and capitalist values embodied in U.S. culture are reaffirmed by

[3] It is a testament to the resilience of American cultural soft power that even among the populations of Muslim nations, which have been most affected by Bush's toxic foreign policy and that have shown great displeasure with the president and his policies, surveys show that people still remain strongly favorable to many American values and institutions (Inglehart and Norris 2003 and Pew 2003).

the *Human Values and Beliefs* surveys (Inglehart, Bazanez, and Moreno 1998). These international surveys show strong support for political values such as political freedom, participation in government, open government, individual autonomy, and individual development. They also demonstrate similar support for economic principals such as the accumulation of wealth, business, and technological development. The soft power of American culture is enhanced all the more by the rise of popular culture as an important shaper of ideology and lifestyles across the globe. Barnet and Cavanagh (1996, 76) attribute American youth culture's social-psychological primacy to the fact that it "fills the vacuum left by the pervasive collapse of traditional family life, the atrophying of civil life, and the loss of faith in politics that appears to be a worldwide trend." Indeed, the United States has achieved cultural primacy in the global community, and this primacy has produced a compelling magnet for the world at large. As Sadar and Davis (2002, 65) observe, "Today, the globe is much more like an extension of American society, where-mostly-all too willing individuals and communities embrace American culture and values."

Gitlin (1998) cites four important factors that account for the competitive superiority American culture enjoys over other cultures. First, he underscores limited competition in the American historical tradition. This limited competition has allowed it to entrench itself strongly while cultural battles were raging overseas because of differing historical traditions. To quote Gitlin (1998, 77),

> For at least a century and a half, America's prime cultural tradition has been to entertain and thereby to cultivate popularity. It never had to fight to establish its legitimacy against an established high culture. Already a generation before the Civil War, it reigned supreme over its ecclesiastical rivals.

Second, he notes that American culture has the advantages of being "pre-tested" in a multicultural environment. American society is so heterogeneous that any cultural trends that succeed in the United States appear to have already passed an important litmus test and would seem well adapted to an international cultural marketplace that features a similar heterogeneity. Third, given the social diversity in the United States, American culture emerges as more of a "mélange" or hybrid system than other cultures. Thus, with so many possible points of appeal emanating from this diversity, it is bound to "out-compete" other less heterogeneous societies whose cultures generate fewer points of potential appeal (see also Pieterse 1995).

Finally, he argues that the very philosophic foundation of American culture is "fun," which gives it many advantages over cultures that are founded on more Austere or Solemn mindsets.[4]

The Chariots of American Culture

The chariots of American culture are generated by its global economic and political primacy (i.e., a Cosmopolitan interconnection between hard and soft power, each reinforcing the other). Gitlin (1998) speaks of these chariots as America's "supply-side advantage" in the competition among cultures. This primacy has served to vigorously disseminate American culture across the globe in the form of ideas, images, products, physical structures, organizations, and people. Such dissemination has resulted in various cultural backlashes, but it has nonetheless generated a great deal of attraction among foreign populations and governments alike (Sklair 1995; Mander and Goldsmith 1996; Huntington 1996; Sardar and Davies 2002). Whereas the chariots of American soft power in the context of culture represent hard power resources that contribute to America's economic and political primacy, the reception of the culture itself is very much a soft power process (i.e., perceptions that endear the culture to a global population).

First, economic primacy has delivered primacy over the means of communication. No other nation rivals the United States in its power to deliver information. The driving force behind America's cultural domination is the domination of communication. Ultimately, the competition for cultural supremacy becomes a competition over ideas (Blinken 2003; Kaufman 2003).[5] This competition, in turn, ultimately becomes a competition over the venues of communication. To quote Nye (2004b, 31),

> The ability to share information – and to be believed – becomes an important source of attraction and power.... The countries that are likely to be more attractive and gain soft power are those with multiple channels of communication that help to frame issues....

[4] Gitlin (1998, 78) notes that as early as the 1940s, American psychologists were talking about the emergence of a "fun" culture in America (Wolfenstein and Lieites 1950). See also Barnet and Cavanagh (1996).

[5] Ideas and culture overlap, of course, but are not synonymous. Some ideas (norms, ideologies, and beliefs) are not transmitted as vigorously through cultural penetration as others. For example, accepting popular fads in entertainment may not generate equal acceptance of a political or economic culture. Yet cultures do transmit general orientations that are pervasive, even if some of the elements make a slower and indirect impact. American culture itself exudes a general political, social, and economic orientation, which manifests itself in different forms and in different intensities through a variety of venues.

America, with its preponderant lead in information-transmission capacity, is indeed the great global communicator. It produces and exports far more movies, television programming, and radio programs than any other nation; it produces and transmits far more multimedia content and also digitized content because of its preponderant lead in information technologies; it produces and disseminates more advertisements than any other nation; it publishes and exports more books than any other nation; and its technological lead makes it the greatest source of distance learning (as most of the educational resources are produced in and disseminated from the United States). It may be a telling testament to the influence of this power over information that the capacity to attract global audiences is pervasive even among recipients who are not very familiar with the English language, from people mouthing words to American songs phonetically to foreign audiences watching American television programs that are neither dubbed nor subtitled. Beyond this, in a world where English is the lingua franca, the message hits home even harder. This message is marshaled on a technological capacity for information dissemination that is unmatched in history (De Grazia 2005; Cowen 2008; Fraser 2003, 2008; Nye 2004b; Gitlin 1999; Sklair 1995; Barnet and Cavanagh 1996).[6] This gives the United States far greater power than any other nation in the world with respect to its "access to other societies" (Haskel 1980).

In addition to primacy in information technology and media, the United States stands as an exporter of its culture through the multinational corporation (MNC). America is the largest foreign direct investor in the world, and American MNCs employ more foreign workers than the MNCs of any other nation. By 2005, the value of American non-bank multinational corporations (both parents and affiliates) superseded 3 trillion dollars, with a workforce of more than 30 million (International Labor Organization 2009; United States Census Bureau 2009). As a vehicle of American culture, the MNC manifests itself in various ways. Each MNC is more than just a workplace, but also a place of education about the American lifestyle and products. Employment geared toward the manufacture and sale of products produced by American multinationals must be founded on familiarity with the mother country. This takes place through educational initiatives ranging from mission statements for foreign executives and blue-collar workers that exude American

[6] DeGrazia (2005, 206) goes so far as to assert that early on the U.S. film industry was "self-consciously rivalrous about its role in shaping cultural trends."

values to direct education about American geography and lifestyles for people employed in outsourced phone banks.[7] Also, the integration of a foreign and American expatriate workforce encourages cross-cutting social linkages that bring foreign employees into a greater familiarity with American culture. This cultural imprinting is compounded by the fact that a disproportionate number of top jobs are held by Americans; thus, the cross-cutting effects are compounded by the admiration resulting from a hierarchical relationship (i.e., company superiors are accorded greater admiration as role models). Furthermore, the company re-creates the American experience in foreign locations in a number of ways. The peripheral industries that arise bring environments and services from the mother country that appeal to expatriate Americans, from restaurants to schools. And of course, the physical plant of the foreign subsidiary itself exudes many features of American life and common values. In these respects, with the direct investment of American capital, elements of American life are exported as well. Moreover, the endearment and allure generated by this exportation of American culture is compounded by the tendency of MNCs to invest in public goods that benefit both foreign workers and the communities where they reside. The value of MNCs in this regard was poignantly displayed during the period of divestment in South Africa. With this divestment, all of the public goods that MNCs in South Africa were providing were eliminated – schools, day care centers, education, subsidized housing for workers, and infrastructures that brought significant benefits both to community residents and workers (Vogel 2005; Gitlin 1999).

The cultural impact and penetration of MNCs is compounded by a third chariot: the penetration of foreign nations by American civil society. Just as the United States is the greatest source of foreign direct investment and large-scale exporter of workers overseas, it is also the most prolific exporter of people in the form of students, tourists, and nongovernmental organizations (NGOs) in the world. Of the more than sixty thousand NGOs functioning in more than three hundred countries, a preponderant number originated as American organizations. More than 30 million American tourists visited foreign nations in 2006, and more than 190,000 American students studied abroad in 2004. The transient ambassadors of

[7] The Microsoft mission statement stresses the value of the "... company, individual workers, customers, openness, passion for work, challenges, self-improvement, quality work, and personal excellence." This range of values encapsulates a fairly liberal-capitalist orientation of political economy, one that accords well with an American vision of labor, politics, and business (Microsoft Mission Statement 2009).

American culture (tourists and students) compound the penetration and impact made by the American expatriates (permanent ambassadors) who are employed in various capacities in foreign nations and the organizations that operate in those nations.[8] The tourists reinforce the admiration for images of prosperity and primacy, given that they are purchasing luxury goods and demonstrating extensive liquidity relative to the foreign hosts observing them. They also provide economic opportunities for foreign merchants and businesses that endear them all the more as supporters of local and national economies. Perhaps an even greater per-capita impact is generated by students studying abroad. These students generate far more intimate contacts with local populations, given their economic dependence and arrangements governing study abroad. They intermix with foreign youth and serve to influence perceptions among future leaders and captains of industry. Also, they often live with foreign families, bringing American ideas and practices into the intimacy of foreign homes. The NGOs compound this cultural impact in a permanent way by bringing both Americans and their values/ideas to foreign countries (Epitropoulos and Roudemetof 1998; Katsuji and Kaori 2008; International Trade Administration 2009a).

Fourth, as a magnetic entrepot, the United States serves as an important chariot of American culture. Blinken (2003, 282) underscores this magnetic appeal of the United States: "[W]hen people vote with their feet, the United States wins in a landslide." This chariot of American culture manifests itself via four main vehicles: students, tourists, immigrants, and foreign companies. The United States attracts more tourists than any other nations. In 1999, more than 49 million tourists visited the United States. No nation attracts more foreign students. In 2006, more than 560,000 foreign students were enrolled in U.S. institutions of higher education. No other nation attracts more immigrants. The United States attracts six times more immigrants than the second-leading destination nation, Germany. There are presently 14 million legal foreign workers in the United States. Another 20 million are estimated to be illegal immigrants. No other nation attracts more foreign direct investment. As of 2007, the United States had attracted 2.7 trillion dollars in foreign direct investment.

As with American penetration across foreign borders, this penetration of American borders serves similar functions in disseminating American

[8] Epitropoulos and Roudemetof (1998) underscore the influence of American tourism after World War II in transforming foreign cultures.

culture abroad. The foreign presence in the United States compounds the exportation promoted by the United States' cultural supply-side. Foreign visitors and residents export American culture back to their home nations either through communication or upon leaving to reclaim their foreign residency. Like Americans abroad, these individuals become ambassadors of American culture as well, bringing American images, values, and lifestyles into their domestic societies. These are even more powerful ambassadors of American culture, given that they generate far greater trust and legitimacy among their compatriots relative to Americans. The exportation also has a strong material element that enhances the allure of the culture: profits from businesses and remittances manifest themselves as symbols of the prosperity of the United States and thus generate admiration (International Trade Administration 2009b; Nye 2004b, 33, 34; Institute of International Education 2006; Krigman 2008; International Labor Organization 2009; United States Census Bureau 2009).

A fifth chariot is a subset of the power of American corporations, but its influence is especially compelling, so it is discussed separately. This chariot is driven by the power over images generated in the offices on Madison Avenue in New York City. The power of the advertising industry in the United States dwarfs the power of advertising in all other nations. The United States is by far the greatest promoter of products in the world and therefore has the most compelling influence not only over consumption patterns, but also in establishing the psychological foundations of consumption. Even in its origins in the early twentieth century, American advertising companies assumed global dominance and rode this wave of primacy to become one of the most powerful forces influencing global consumption preferences. In establishing these foundations, the American advertising industry has concomitantly sold American culture and lifestyles to foreign populations. Such psychological salesmanship is consistent with the interconnection between lifestyles and products. Advertisers must sell a lifestyle in order to sell a product. No corporate promotion strategy better exemplifies this than Nike. Great athletes, the quest for personal excellence, rugged individuality, the virtues of youth and beauty, materialism, the quest for wealth and success, the virtues of freedom, entitlement, and the need for instant gratification are all salient values and images geared toward producing a consumption psychology that, in turn, promotes consumption patterns. Once people are sold on images and values, they will naturally be attracted to the products designed to appeal to those values and images. In this case, the single-greatest market for Nike products is the American market itself, so the promotion of Nike products must be oriented heavily around American cultural values. And in instituting such a structure of values and images, the promotion itself ends up selling American culture to the world at large. The manifestations of the dissemination of culture through advertising have been pervasive and absolutely compelling in imprinting an appreciation of American culture on foreign populations, as various studies have demonstrated. Of course, the dissemination of culture through advertising is compounded and ultimately consummated by consumption of the products themselves, as these products are a constant reinforcement mechanism for the appeal of American culture (De Grazia 2005; Klein 1999; LeFeber 1999).

The American educational system represents a sixth chariot of American culture. American higher education enjoys primacy over all other nations in a variety of dimensions. It represents the most prodigious cradle of ideas in the world, and invariably, many of these ideas are tied to the values espoused in the source nation. As noted just above in this section, no country exports more students and academics, no country hosts more students and academics, and no country exports more books to the world than the United States. Furthermore, no nation produces more research across the academic disciplines. American universities and researchers dwarf all others in the amount of knowledge disseminated. This involves both the movement of ideas through published venues (most scholarship emanates from the United States) as well as through human contact (more conferences are held in the United States). Finally, more international conference attendees are American that any other nationality. Thus, the United States is the most prodigious exporter and importer of academic ideas.

Do academic ideas necessarily disseminate American values? In some cases, as with purely scientific findings, the answer might be no. However, because the vehicles for transmitting these ideas have a nationality, the recipients of the ideas will have to come into contact with American values, whether through reading English (discussed later in this section) or through the physical contacts generated by the United States' primacy (visit American universities, receive American colleagues).[9] In many cases, the ideas are directly connected to American values themselves. Many dominant modes of thinking and models espoused across disciplines do exude visions that are consistent with American ideas and

[9] In many cases, the admiration of America's intellectual achievements has driven a vast global movement of emulation in academic and educational institutions (Schott et al. 1998, 18).

values. Many models of governance exude republican and democratic orientations; economists largely embrace principles consistent with liberalism and free trade; sociologists work within frameworks that often underscore pluralism and diversity; and models of corporate management exude a veneration of the virtues of free enterprise and profitability. In effect, the dominant ideas in higher education, which are imprinted into the psychologies of people throughout the world, spring in large part from the dominant culture. This results in the formation of "epistemic communities" (i.e., groups of intellectual leaders across issue areas) that share common images and ideas about solving problems founded to some significant degree in American values.[10] In this respect, the vast body of international expertise that is drawn upon across domestic and global issue areas has inculcated strong elements of American culture (Altbach and Peterson 2008; Schott et al. 1998; Institute of International Education 2006).

The seventh chariot derives from political and military, as opposed to economic, hard power. This chariot is the international politico-military presence of the United States across the globe. This presence is prodigious. Gardner (2005, 127) has referred to the United States' current politico-military presence as a "third wave" of American imperialism. Johnson (2004, 2006) has also labeled it an "empire." The military presence has been indeed gargantuan, with more than seven hundred military bases in more than 130 nations and employing approximately 2.5 million people. This is complemented by a military force of approximately 1.5 million, with another 1.5 million in reserve. Furthermore, military operations have generated a need for complementary and ancillary functions and services that have expanded the American presence abroad. Private companies servicing military operations (Halliburton, DynCorp) and companies contracted to provide postwar reconstruction services (Bechtel, Perini) have considerably expanded the U.S. presence. This presence is further compounded by the fielding of more embassies and diplomatic personnel than any other nation.

The diplomatic corps and ancillary industries generate substantial and obvious elements of soft power. It is in their nature to engage foreign elites and local populations in ways that nurture an endearing image for the United States. Yet even the military presence has generated much more soft power than traditionally has been acknowledged. Military operations in foreign nations, like private corporations, engage in a variety

[10] On epistemic communities, see *International Organization* (1992).

of relations with local populations and elites that generate opportunities for those groups. Vigorous civil-military operations are a salient characteristic of military operations throughout the world. These relations are quite beneficial to local populations, as military operations provide extensive public goods in the localities in which they are carried out (e.g., jobs, joint military operations, education, social services, access to American goods and technology). To a large extent, these public goods derive from a pacification imperative. Military operations can be most effective when embraced by local communities. In this respect, even the United States' most celebrated hard power resource (military operations) generates some soft power for the United States as well (Hartman 2007; Johnson 2004, 2006; Piven 2004, 15–17; Department of Defense 2007).

Finally, the English language itself is the eighth and possibly the most potent chariot of American culture. English is the global lingua franca. It is taught as the principal second language in virtually every nation in grammar schools and above. Just as the American greenback is the dominant global currency, the English language is the dominant cultural currency. There is no better testament to the primacy of a nation than the degree to which its language and currency are used. Because the United States is a leader in so many fields of human endeavors, the knowledge of English is essential for ambitious people who seek access to the very best opportunities in their nations and abroad (e.g., top jobs, best products, finest schools, most popular forms of entertainment).

Any language is so inextricably tied to its national culture that it may be the most salient manifestation of the culture itself. Learning a language is synonymous with learning the national culture to which it is tied. Because learning a language is so culturally contextual, the standard language pedagogy unfolds in a series of exercises that feature prevalent national customs, values, images, and geography. The literal terminology is culturally oriented enough, but the idiomatic expressions that are commonly used are even more so. However, even the value of the language as a vehicle for disseminating the culture is modest compared with the value of the language as a tool to access the culture itself. All of the other chariots of American culture become that much more influential when foreign people acquire the language skills to ride these chariots toward a meaningful experience with the culture itself. This reflects a common interaction tendency among all of the chariots. Not only does each chariot serve to transmit American culture around the world, but each also has an impact on the other chariots in compounding their effectiveness.

Of course, no single chariot features the pervasive interaction effects of language in enhancing the influence of other chariots (Nye 2004b).

Empowerment through Culture: General Applications

In essence, the power of American culture serves to create a world in the United States' own image. At the most extreme level, there is direct emulation among both civil society and governmental policies. At other levels, societies and governments are favorably disposed to the United States and its interests. In effect, a global milieu is created that facilitates the interests of American civil society and the interests of the American state.[11] What does it mean in terms of national influence to create a world in one's own image? Much of this augmentation of influence occurs through compounding the hard power resources that have served as chariots for the spread of American culture, in this sense demonstrating a Cosmopolitan interaction process of power augmentation. This section considers more general aspects of American empowerment through the endearing allure of American culture on three dimensions: social, economic, and political.

Socially, Americans themselves and American organizations become more influential. The extensive social penetration facilitated by American cultural primacy makes the world far more accessible to both Americans and American organizations. This cultural primacy manifests itself socially in lower costs of interpenetration. In a world where the transaction costs of interpenetration are lower for Americans and American organizations, Americans and their organizations will become more influential players. Socially, the transaction costs for Americans are lower in an Americanized world. Irrespective of the degree to which Americans are actually embraced when they travel to foreign lands or by foreign visitors, functioning in an Americanized world drives down the transaction costs of the citizens of the dominant culture. Tourists and expatriates can function in fairly familiar conditions even when living outside the hard shell of the United States. Communication is easy, dollars are accepted or interchangeable everywhere, restaurants have familiar names, shopping can be done in the same stores one frequents in the United States, and the general environment is not entirely alien when American television

[11] Kurlantzick (2007) underscores how China has recently embraced the idea that its culture can serve as an effective means of enhancing its global political and economic interests. In the service of this idea, China has instituted an aggressive public diplomacy initiative to promote the dissemination of Chinese culture internationally.

programs and songs fill the airwaves. Accommodating visitors to the United States also renders lower transaction costs for Americans and foreign travelers for the same reasons. Foreigners already will be experiencing far greater proliferation of the American culture in their nations, which makes transitions easier for them and accommodation easier for host Americans. At the broadest social level, Americans will be the most visible people in the world (whether as travelers or hosts). The ideas and values they carry will, in turn, be more pervasive than those of any other people. This global penetration on the part of American society will generate a plethora of soft power elements for Americans: respect, admiration, esteem, and endearment. These elements will, in turn, create a greater disposition on the part of foreign populations to address the needs of Americans. At this broadest social level, the needs of Americans will achieve primacy over the needs of other people in global society. In this respect, Americans themselves will experience greater influence in the world at large (Barnet and Cavanagh 1996; Pieterse 1995).

The U.S. government has historically valued the importance of this social penetration for American influence in the world community in general and for foreign policy specifically. From the administration of Woodrow Wilson to the present, the U.S. government has continued to maintain close ties to the power centers that manage media for the purposes of promoting specific and broad foreign policy goals. Whether for the purpose of acquiring allies, winning wars, or competing against menacing ideologies, using technological chariots to foster a positive image of the United States, and thereby win the hearts and minds of key elites and populations, has long been a principal objective of American foreign policy. Consequently, American television, radio, and Hollywood have been historically valued as important wedges for U.S. power. In this respect, the U.S. government has been and still is strongly invested in winning a "media war" (Ross 2003; Kaufman 2003; Fraser 2003, 2008).

The soft empowerment process is similar with respect to organizations that originate in the United States. As noted, there are presently sixty thousand NGOs operating in three hundred countries and territories, and American-founded NGOs are far more numerous than NGOs originating in any other nation. A preponderance of these American-founded NGOs has an international mandate (INGOs). The expansion of American civil society has ridden the wave of the proliferation of INGOs, especially since the end of the Cold War. The global reach of these organizations has especially expanded in the past twenty-five years. Their impact has cut across every dimension of human relations – social, economic, and political. And behind this vanguard, American society has enjoyed especially numerous opportunities for soft empowerment. As with American citizens at a broader social level, organizational primacy is also facilitated by American cultural primacy. The organizations will be far more visible than the organizations founded in other nations. Their missions will likely strike more resonant chords among foreign populations, given the primacy of American values and images that pervade the world. Joining such organizations and keeping up with their activities will be that much easier given the lower transaction costs of dealing with language and accessing the organization itself (e.g., far more elaborate Web sites, more foreign liaisons, more foreign offices, superior membership outreach). As with American citizens at the broadest level of social interaction, American organizations will also enjoy a global community in which their needs and missions achieve primacy vis-à-vis the organizations founded in other nations. This primacy, in turn, will translate into far greater influence in the global community vis-à-vis foreign-born organizations.

There is no greater testament to the importance of American NGOs operating abroad for the greater influence of the United States than the fact that the U.S. government has historically funded, supported, and worked in conjunction with a plethora of such organizations vigorously throughout its recent history. Along with diplomats who increase the influence of the United States across nations, these NGOs have also come to spearhead important initiatives that supplement and complement both broad and specific foreign policy goals: from undermining the conditions conducive to terrorism, to alleviating poverty, to promoting democratic transition. Much of this support has come from the United States Agency for International Development (USAID), which declares in its mission statement a "... purpose [that centers around] furthering America's foreign policy interests in expanding democracy and free markets" and states that the organization "receives foreign policy guidance from the U.S. Secretary of State" (USAID 2009). NGOs have always functioned as a crucial vanguard for American foreign policy, whether supported by government funding or not. The government investment in NGOs is in large part an extension of broader public diplomacy initiatives designed to interface American culture with foreign cultures for the purpose of promoting U.S. interests abroad, but it also facilitates the implementation of specific initiatives consistent with U.S. foreign policy (Repeta 2008; Ross 2003; Crowell 2008; Lempert 1998; Katsuji and Kaori 2008).

Economically, cultural primacy presents a myriad of opportunities for enhancing the influence of American multinational corporations and, more generally, for enhancing the health and influence of the American economy. The power of culture is manifested directly in the form of perhaps the most potent source of non-price competition for American products in the global market. Economically, there is no greater promoter of American products and corporations than American culture itself. The dissemination of American culture through the many vehicles of the information age amounts to free advertising for American industry. Insofar as cultural values and products are inextricably linked, American culture appears to be the great promoter of consumerism oriented around American products. The dominance of the English language alone gives American multinationals a greater wedge into the international economy. In this respect, American culture serves as a potent source of product diversification that maintains the competitive position of American products in foreign markets. This is especially important in enhancing the demand for American products, as this "cultural diversification" often compensates for a loss of competitiveness in other dimensions of product quality and image. Thus, even with American products that may be deteriorating in quality and other non-price characteristics, the cultural appeal generated by American soft power has buoyed the demand for such products based on consumer esteem for image.[12]

An especially poignant testament to this culturally driven consumption has appeared in an area where the quality of products has suffered extensively during the past three decades: American sedans. Even though American sedans marketed outside the United States have been plagued with a number of poor qualities that have decreased their desirability on the part of foreign consumers, the American affiliation has bolstered a product diversification that has maintained demand based on cultural image. Whether they appeal to younger consumers looking to reify long-standing images of being "California cool" or older consumers aiming to experience fantasies of a cultural connection, American sedans have found some robust sources of marketing in the cultural connection (Fleder and Hosanagar 2007, 2008; Cowen 2008; Fox 1998; LeFeber 1999). Christopher Ellis, representative director and president of Chrysler Japan Company, Ltd., attests to this cultural product diversification among Japanese consumers: "Our buyers like the American lifestyle that our cars suggest. They want to drive something unique" (Betros 2009).

[12] This cultural diversification for American products today serves a similar function to the emulation of free trade for the British in the nineteenth century; both buoyed the demand for the products of these nations as the competitiveness of these products deteriorated on various dimensions.

LeFeber's (1999) chronicle of the rise of Nike as a global power, with far-reaching influence across global markets, stands as a testament to the economic soft empowerment through American culture as a source of product diversification. Like many other apparel MNCs, Nike's beginnings were inauspicious. Yet the powerful dynamic created by the team of Phil Knight (Nike's CEO) and Michael Jordan (Nike's principal global salesman) would go on to produce a global empire whose image was carried forth by perhaps the most recognized symbol in the world – the swoosh. In the most direct manifestations of the rise of Nike, ingenious marketing strategies combined to maximize global appeal and, carried forth on the chariot of Madison Avenue, vigorously injected the swoosh and the Nike mystique into every society, with an especially powerful impact among younger consumers. However, the underlying source of this global economic success story was American culture itself. As noted, the images on which marketing relied tapped into prevalent images of American culture (noted in the discussion of Madison Avenue as a vehicle of American culture) that were already pervasive in global society.[13] In this respect, the Michael Jordan connection was crucial. Jordan had already become the most famous athlete in the world and among one of the most recognizable faces in global society. Jordan himself became a beacon for an American lifestyle that transcended any single person and conveyed an image of superiority and excellence that could be captured through the products themselves. Thus, the products became symbols and enablers for foreign consumers, even if subliminally for many, who sought to indulge in an American dream. To a large extent, Knight and Jordan ended up selling a product that made Nike the dominant line in the global market for apparel. But selling this product was easy. Indeed, "swooshifying" the world was easy because Nike was selling an already highly desirable set of traits that the swoosh symbolized – American culture.

The Nike boom served as a testament to the compensatory effects that cultural product diversification can have for the American economy. As traditional product lines sagged in many countries, the sales of apparel and footwear picked up the slack, maintaining vibrant export markets

[13] Fox (1998) underscores the social context of global advertising; products are promoted in social situations that convey prevalent values, practices, and customs. America's cultural primacy has been so great that the dominant social settings of global advertising have indeed manifested American culture. So influential an advertising tool has this American context become that foreign companies even use such a social context to sell products to non-American consumers. Indeed, American culture has become a template for global advertising.

for American products. So strong was the appeal of Nike products that they generated a far more inelastic demand than do most luxuries. In fact, there were very odd consumption patterns in which people in less developed nations were spending significant amounts of their income to purchase Nike products.[14] The compensation dynamic underlying the culturally driven consumption was clear: American cultural primacy made a number of product lines extremely lucrative because such products were seen as the ultimate trendsetters, with American products occupying the cutting edge of style (Fleder and Hosanagar 2007, 2008; Cowen 2008; LeFeber 1999; Fox 1998).

This is an especially important wedge for maintaining American economic primacy in a postindustrial economy in which demand for products appears to be shifting from "needs" (which are being largely met by greater competition in traditional product lines) to "wants." In such luxury-driven markets, U.S cultural primacy will pay especially high dividends, as it represents a source of increasingly greater allure relative to "need" criteria – that is, a more competitive image can make up for shortfalls in product quality (Ruediger 2005). But beyond Nike and the selling of products, advertising in the area of an American social context further reinforces U.S. cultural primacy. To quote Fox (1998, 151): "Far from being innocuous, ads are a powerful political force that reinforce the cultural meanings that a majority would consider normal, such as the 'acceptable kinds' of freedom, individuality, relationships and gender roles." In this respect, there is a compound interaction between cultural primacy and the global marketing of products that serves to reinforce the cultural influence of the United States.

Furthermore, being the most desired place of residence and target for investment in the world generates many opportunities for enhancing the health and influence of the American economy. Although much of the attraction is generated by purely economic opportunities, there is an important cultural component. Immigrants will know about American values and more about the language relative to other countries simply because American culture is so globally pervasive. Aside from minimizing transaction costs of relocating, people and businesses also respond to the attractiveness of a culture they have grown to know better than any other aside from their own. In being the most prolific social magnet in

[14] A similar dynamic appeared in the American market, as poor inner-city youth were spending significant proportions of their disposable incomes on Nike footwear (LeFeber 1999).

the world, the United States benefits from the influx of large and diverse amounts of human capital that can bring many sources of strength to the American economy.[15] The economic benefits are distributed widely across the hierarchy defined by the development of human capital in labor markets. At the lower end, there is an endless supply of unskilled labor that can fill every niche in that segment of the American demand for labor. At the higher levels of human capital development, the tendency toward attracting middle-class immigrants and the "brain drain" fills important needs for specific expertise in the high-end market for labor (from language skills to scientific skills). Thus, with the extensive supply of human capital driven by America's magnetic geographic appeal, the American labor market should function at a far higher level of productivity vis-à-vis other nations that cannot attract the number and diversity of immigrants to fill every niche. Beyond the enhancement of economic influence created by the brain drain, the expertise in leading technologies with military applications will enhance the politico-military primacy of the United States as well. This supply of people makes the American economic machine achieve far greater results and become a more powerful global force (Borjas 2006; Alsalam and Smith 2005; Ottaviano and Peri 2005).[16]

In addition to filling labor niches, the influx fills important investment niches that also generate economic benefits. Foreign direct investment in the United States responds to similar points of attraction. The United States provides many purely economic reasons for the attraction of foreign capital, but the cultural attraction that compounds this economic attraction is also compelling, and for similar reasons (lower transaction costs and endearing perceptions of a culture). Investment decisions across nations have historically shown a keen sensitivity to proximity in "psychic space." Like people, foreign capital benefits the American economy. The greater abundance and diversity of products and services domestically

[15] Critics of such influx warn of the social, political, and economic price that the United States must pay. See, for example, Huntington (2004).

[16] Although there is less controversy regarding the benefits that immigration carries for employers, and thus American businesses themselves, there is extensive debate about the precise redistributional effects that U.S. immigration generates with respect to wealth between immigrant and domestic American labor. But even with regard to the impact on American domestic labor (which numerous studies suggest is adversely affected in terms of the initial effects of immigrant labor), Alsalam and Smith (2005, 29) cite secondary changes in labor markets that can mitigate some of the negative effects of the initial impact of immigration. On this debate, see Borjas (2006), Alsalam and Smith (2005), and Ottaviano and Peri (2005).

reduces the prices of such goods to domestic consumers, but it also reduces the costs of doing business on the part of domestic firms. Inputs, expertise, and essential services can be attained more cheaply because of the greater proximity. Also, greater opportunities for more efficient mergers can put American businesses in a stronger global position. Finally, ethnic investment (restaurants and other ethnic-capital businesses) provides diverse and low-cost options to American consumers, raising American real incomes, which in turn carries benefits for the sale of American products in the home market. Additionally, these businesses are also important consumers of American intermediary goods (Davidson 1980; Kogut and Singh 1988).

As an exporter of direct investment, America also benefits economically from cultural primacy. Establishing businesses overseas and interfacing with foreign subsidiaries renders lower transactions costs for American companies. Their operations are well-known because of the pervasive exposure to American business education, the language is familiar, and there are numerous overlapping points of identification. This, in turn, gives American businesses abroad a competitive advantage over domestic competitors in carrying out transborder operations, from enhancing intrafirm trade to avoiding state interference that might adversely affect transactions. A compelling manifestation of culturally driven receptivity for investment and business practices in foreign markets has come in the contexts of the super-corporation and standardization. Weak antitrust laws in the United States have encouraged mega-mergers, creating corporate giants (Disney-ANC and Time Warner-Turner Broadcasting). The success of super-chains (Walmart, Toys "R" Us, McDonald's) has established a mode of standardized international operation that can overwhelm local businesses. Together, these twin towers of American economic power have enjoyed significant opportunities in the international marketplace. Growth and success have become self-sustaining; the big and the rich have been getting bigger and richer. Each has fed on the American cultural frenzy and has also reinforced it by becoming economic ambassadors. American culture has been a dynamic source of strength for American business in a global marketplace (Klein 1999).

Politically, the cultural primacy of the United States has translated into a number of sources of empowerment in the global arena. One such important source has been international organizations and regimes. A common refrain in leftist scholarship on such institutions has been that they are manifestations of the "institutionalization of hegemony." Drawing on a Gramscian (1988) vision of governance that itself was inspired by the Marxist (1972) belief that the ideas of a dominant society are the ideas of the dominant classes, this line of argument portrays the existence and functioning of these important institutions as consistent with the prevailing balance of hard power in the international system. Indeed, for these scholars, such institutions function in the interests of the nations that are most powerful. This, however, is not done through coercion; rather, it is accomplished through the legitimation of their visions and interests in the form of institutions founded on the collective management of international relations.[17] Although leftists have identified this less coercive form of influence, they have not as carefully explored the deeper structure of its origins.[18] At a deeper level, regarding how the ideas of the dominant nations translate into the dominant ideas about international governance, we see the relevance of cultural primacy in shaping broad visions and models for solving international problems that are consistent with the visions and interests of the dominant cultures themselves. This raises the issue of the formation of epistemic communities (International Organization 1992). The idea of epistemic communities goes well beyond the most direct sources of influence in the form of dominant diplomats and leaders of these institutions being deferential to the interests of the dominant nations. Epistemic communities represent a deeper and more ingrained source of soft power that manifests itself in the very culture of governance and problem solving that permeates these institutions, from their directors to the rank and file of bureaucrats charged with even the most mundane responsibilities (Altbach and Peterson 2008).[19]

Because the United States presently enjoys such cultural primacy, the lion's share of the formation of soft power will favor the United States. The Bretton Woods institutions represent a poignant manifestation of the United States' epistemic influence. Aside from the very political origins of the WTO, the IMF, and the World Bank, in which the direct orchestration of institutional designs have given U.S. interests great prominence in such institutions (i.e., a wide array of norms and rules giving the United States

[17] The Neo-Marxist literature is extensive, but especially valuable and representative works can be found in Cox (1980, 1987), Gill (1993), Sklair (1995), and Murphy (1994).

[18] As noted in chapter 1, the soft power manifest in international organizations and regimes is not envisioned in as adversarial a context as it is in the leftist literature. Indeed, the treatment here posits far less conflict of interests across the hierarchy of nations governed by such arrangements.

[19] Altbach and Peterson (2008) underscore the power of American educational and academic primacy in forging shared cognitive experiences that create these epistemic communities oriented around American values and models for problem solving.

privileges and power over proceedings and outcomes), there is a deeper source of soft empowerment for the United States in these institutions that both derives from and is reinforced by its cultural power. All of the power elite in such institutions and all of the mid-level functionaries have had extensive exposure to American culture, ideas, and education. In this respect, they manifest the effects of cultural imprinting.

In terms of education, the connections have been both direct (learning in American graduate schools) and indirect (learning from people educated by people who were educated in American graduate schools). The constant physical exposure to the United States and Americans through travel and interactions among staff (made up predominantly of Americans) reinforces the cultural imprinting of education. In the case of the IMF, this institution carries on educational functions for both its own staff and foreign elites with whom staffers will eventually negotiate.[20] Because these foreign elites are in a global demographic most affected by American cultural imprinting (travel, associations, and education), the fundamental manifestations of soft power are further reinforced in terms of generating outcomes consistent with U.S. interests. Furthermore, the leaders and higher-level staffers have strong ties to business-elite circles that are strongly imprinted by American culture. Thus, there is reinforcement from other processes of elite socialization at the inner sanctum of decision making at these institutions.

The resulting institutional visions of these Bretton Woods institutions at the very core of decision making gravitate around belief systems and images that are most pervasive among American economists – trade liberalization, privatization, private investment, protection of property rights, limited government involvement in the economy, deregulation, the development of financial markets, free capital markets, the promotion of exports, economic development, investments based on market principles, political freedom and empowerment, and fiscal austerity. The organizational output that will be consistent with these visions will ultimately serve numerous important American foreign interests: creating markets for trade, creating greater opportunities for direct and indirect investment, creating macroeconomic conditions that assure profitability for American banks undertaking development lending (i.e., structural adjustment policies), protecting American patents and monopolies, building and consolidating capitalism in foreign states, establishing the preconditions for

[20] This is done through two institutions: the IMF Institute and the Internal Economics Training initiative.

democratic transition, creating economic dependence, and forging the foundations of geostrategic alliances. In this respect, cultural imprinting in the Bretton Woods institutions has produced significant political and economic influence for the United States in the global political economy (Stiglitz 1992; Bird 1996; Abdalla 1979).

With respect to the process of cultural imprinting, the formation of epistemic communities goes well beyond the Bretton Woods institutions and impacts a substantial cross-section of international organizations and regimes. This is to be expected, as the level of expertise required by leaders and staffers in these organizations brings these individuals into the demographic circle of greatest exposure to American culture and education. Moreover, the foreign elites with which they coordinate and negotiate are also very much in that demographic. Thus, there is consistency in organizational and problem-solving models across the spectrum of actors in the inner sanctums of decision making.

Aside from the Bretton Woods institutions, studies on epistemic communities in regimes and organizations have shown a pervasive impact of U.S. cultural primacy as a source of influence on experts who have been instrumental in framing solutions to important international problems. In these cases, the American component within the epistemic communities (both direct and indirect) has been of significant importance in driving decisions, and institutional outcomes have often reflected a consistency with important goals of American foreign policy. Such studies analyzed the General Agreement on Trade in Services (GATS) within the General Agreement of Tariffs and Trade (GATT), the regime governing nuclear arms control among the superpowers during the Cold War, the international management of whaling, the regulation of chlorofluorocarbons (CFCs), central bank regulation, and the international food aid regime (Drake and Nicolaidis 1992; Adler 1992; Peterson 1992; Haas 1992; Kapstein 1992; Hopkins 1992).

Nations have long used education and academia as means of foreign policy. One especially glaring manifestation was the structure of colonial systems of education, designed to stabilize colonial relations through cultural imprinting. The U.S. government has long appreciated the power over ideas deriving from America's educational and academic standing as an important tool of foreign policy, especially after World War II. The United States fought an educational and academic Cold War with the Soviet Union and communism by sponsoring a variety of programs that would expose both students and elites from communist nations to American ideas and values (from Fulbrights to educational exchange programs intended to inculcate American values in potential foreign leaders). Although the enemies of the state have changed over time, the tools have not. Government-funded programs to export American education and scholarship are still vigorously pursued in the context of U.S. foreign policy, whether to mend diplomatic relations or deradicalize prospective terrorists (Crowell 2008; Altbach and Peterson 2008).

To compound the soft empowerment of American culture through its impact on international governmental organizations and regimes, American influence is further enhanced through the cultural impact the United States has had on NGOs. NGOs are strongly influenced by the pervasive penetrating effects of American institutions, ideas, and people, just as international governmental organizations are. The elites, staffers, and principal clients of NGOs tend to be of a demographic that has either directly or indirectly had significant exposure to American ideas and education. This has encouraged the rise of numerous communities across a variety of issues that share some elements of consensual knowledge grounded in American values, ideas, and models for problem solving. International outcomes generated by the workings of these NGOs have shown strong consistencies with both broad and specific foreign policy goals. It is no surprise, then, that the U.S. government has traditionally funded such NGOs generously (Katsuji and Kaori 2008, 266).

There is no greater testament to the political value of the soft empowerment deriving from American culture than the U.S. government's vigorous promotion of public diplomacy around the world (Ross 2003; Blinken 2003; Kaufman 2003). The purpose of American public diplomacy is to interface American and foreign cultures so as to create "mutual understanding" and lasting relationships that keep foreign populations and elites favorable to U.S. interests and foreign policy objectives. Former Ambassador Christopher Ross (2003, 252) articulates a common goal of public diplomacy as "... winning hearts and minds, making friends and influencing enemies, building [a] policy context [and] protecting U.S. values." Public diplomacy aims low relative to conventional diplomacy. Whereas the later aims at direct influence through face-to-face negotiations with heads of state and other important decision makers, public diplomacy works at the roots of foreign relations by promoting cultural penetration among elites, specific groups, and the public at large. Whereas high diplomacy seeks to generate specific political outcomes, public diplomacy cultivates sentiments in foreign civil societies that create a psychological environment conducive to the emergence of such outcomes. American public diplomacy is manifest in a variety of ways. At a more direct governmental level, public diplomacy is principally carried out through the vehicle of the public affairs sections of foreign embassies. The initiatives include dissemination of information to individuals and groups, distributing important information to foreign media, sponsoring cultural exchange programs, sponsoring educational programs, and developing a variety of other venues of contact between Americans and foreign civil societies. The political benefits are potentially significant (Ross 2003).[21]

Studies of both elite and popular initiatives to promote political transformations in their societies attest to the importance of cultural imprinting in driving the agents of change. The values and ideas inculcated in these agents have proven instrumental in driving them to actions that have brought about political outcomes consistent with American foreign policy goals within their respective nations (Yurchak 2006; English 2000; Bergmann 1998; Lempert 1998; Fraser 2008). This process will be discussed in more detail in the next section below, and examples presented, with respect to its relevance to specific American foreign policy goals involved in democratic transition.

At the broadest level, U.S. influence has been so enhanced by such a pervasive culture that it has, to a large extent, shaped the world in its own image. As Sardar and Davis (2002, 65) succinctly note, "If the world is America, then it follows as a natural corollary that the interests of America should be the interests of the world."[22]

Empowerment through Culture: Specific Applications to America's Big Three Goals of Foreign Policy

While the power of American culture enhances the general influence of the United States in the global system, it can also facilitate important specific goals of American foreign policy. It can do this by enhancing the soft power strategies (discussed in Chapter 5) that are instrumental in helping to effectively deliver the big three goals of American foreign policy. These *cultural-value-added* processes are based on the need to gain broad support on the part of foreign populations and elites in the service of American foreign policy objectives.

For some scholars, the most potent weapon against the dangers that face the United States in the current world system (terrorism, autocratic

[21] NGOs are, of course, a principal vehicle for American public diplomacy.

[22] It is a testament to the cultural primacy of the United States that such an admission was made by authors whose book is principally about why the United States is despised in the global community.

regimes, and WMD) is not the U.S. military-industrial complex, but American cultural values themselves. The real battlefield of significance in these wars is not military, but the battlefield of ideas and values. American cultural penetration will be a powerful weapon on such a battlefield (Nye 2004b; Fraser 2003; Blinken 2003; Kaufman 2003; Gallarotti 2004). Cultural-value-added processes carry important points of leverage to deliver on each of the three major goals of foreign policy.

Political and Economic Transition

The challenge of promoting democracy and capitalism, as demonstrated, has been set back by Bush's hard power crusade. The toxic legacy of his policy will have to be reversed if future administrations wish to effectively pursue these goals. As noted in chapter 5, this will require softer strategies that are capable of creating public and elite endearment to American actions and policies. This will mean positive engagement through diplomacy, cooperation, economic partnerships, disaggregated political initiatives (local, regional, and national), and public diplomacy. These would essentially be strategies of "political pacification" designed to promote political and economic transformation as well as reduce the burden of such transformation. This would involve political and economic engagement for the purpose of state building, state rescue, and economic development. Stronger states and more vibrant economies would eliminate much of the breeding ground for authoritarian regimes. The means to promote regime transformation, suggested in chapter 5, consist of bilateral, multilateral, and public efforts to inject and create the political and economic resources to produce robust states and economies, which in turn would generate the foundations of democracy and capitalism.

However, these foundations can also emerge from a deeper and more fundamental level, one that involves the political and economic manifestations of broadly pervasive ideologies and shared values through cultural penetration. These elements involve the battle over ideas in the public space. It is in this context that cultural-value-added processes can be most effective in bolstering the solutions suggested in chapter 5, and together, these soft power facilitators of transformation will be far more effective.

The dominance of American culture promotes political and economic change both directly and indirectly. Thousands of foreign politicians and bureaucrats live and are educated in the United States or have been extensively exposed to American culture within their home nations. Their return to their home countries or inculcation at home is accompanied by an appreciation of American political values and institutions, along with the power to create policies that impact both their own people and the United States (Nye 2004b, 45). This process also takes place over a greater mass of politically enfranchised individuals, as larger groups of people are subject to the same experiences as elites. Nye (2004b, 48–51) attributes major democratic uprisings and transformations in recent history (e.g., Soviet Union, China, Iran, and Europe) to such cultural penetration. His most compelling claim regards the cultural underpinnings of the end of the Cold War, with American political and economic ideals shaping the course of regime transformation among the more progressive elements in Soviet politics. The classroom, radio, movies, and television have all been dynamic vehicles of American democratic values (Fraser 2003, 2008).

Transformations in Eastern Europe and the fall of the Iron Curtain were strongly influenced by American culture. From the time of Peter the Great in the eighteenth century, Russia has experience a long tradition of influence by Western culture and institutions. The fall of the Iron Curtain owed much to Western cultural penetration, with American culture as its vanguard. The penetration disseminated shared values and images that made both elites and the public more receptive to Western and American institutions. Ultimately, the fall of the Wall and political transformation in Eastern Europe reflected in great part a cultural transformation of Eastern European society. This transformation laid the foundations for salient political outcomes (Lempert 1998; Blinken 2003; Fraser 2008; Bergmann 1998).

From a broad public perspective, Yurchak's (2006) analysis of the transformation of the Soviet Union after World War II demonstrates how the ultimate fall of the Soviet state was the culmination of a number of internal shifts occurring "at the level of everyday life" (282). Many of these shifts were manifestations of American cultural penetration, which in effect "deterritorialized" Soviet culture.[23] Interestingly and paradoxically, it was Soviet ideology itself that fostered much of this transformative cultural penetration. This ideology openly embraced internationalism, cultural creativity, and innovation, but it failed to produce objective standards by which external cultural influences into the Soviet Union

[23] The famous Czech intellectual and political reformer Zdenek Mlynar succinctly captured the reformist public sentiment that emerged from exposure to America and the West: "... entire generations of young people became convinced that in fact the standard of living of Americans was incomparably higher than ours" (Gorbachev and Mlynar 2002, 36).

could be evaluated. Thus, Soviet citizens could embrace American cultural values and images without creating inconsistencies within their own ideological attachment to Soviet communism. In many cases, the Soviet state itself promoted this cultural penetration through making direct consumption possible (radio broadcasts on state media venues) and tolerating the use of a broad range of products and practices.

When looking at the elite level in the reform movement in Eastern European nations, it is clear that the reformers and their initiatives were manifestations of broader cultural transformation occurring behind the Iron Curtain (Yurchak 2006). Among the elite reformers was evident a cosmopolitan exposure to American and Western culture that sowed the seeds of their reformist orientations. Gorbachev himself recalls the influence of his exposure to Western ideas during his university years, one that would become manifest in his later historic reforms: "... [the university] opened up an entire world of ideas for us: the Vedas of India, Confucianism, Plato and Aristotle, Machiavelli and Rousseau. The history of human thought, a world we had not known, excited our minds.... For us Soviet Communists there was a lot of hope at that time that everything would change in the direction of greater openness and democracy" (Gorbachev and Mlynar 2002, 22, 27). Both Gorbachev and Mlynar's visions of socialism were heavily grounded in Western ideals. To quote Gorbachev again, "In discussing the fate of the socialist idea in the past, present, and future, [Mlynar] and I proceeded from a *value-based* vision of socialism, one to which Western European Social Democracy adheres" [italics in original] (Gorbachev and Mlynar 2002, 8).[24] English (2000, 3) affirms the impact of a new "identity" among Soviet elites as a fundamental source of political transformation. His analysis suggests that "a sine qua non of the cold war's sudden and peaceful end ... [was] the rise of a global, 'Westernizing' identity among a liberal policy-academic elite" in the Soviet Union. The emergence of this epistemic community among reformers was at the root of the great transformation that engulfed the region and ultimately brought down the communist state.

As cultural penetration of Eastern Europe increased after the fall of the Wall, the attachment to American values and institutions increased concomitantly. Socially, these nations moved to more cosmopolitan

[24] English (2000, 3) notes that "Gorbachev came under the influence of [Western] ideas and, together with his core group of political allies, embraced the new thinking *weltanschauung* and his new thinkers' ambitious agenda *before* his boldest steps of the later 1980s" [italics in original].

environments that reflected broad American values and practices. Legally, American principles of civil rights, due process, and criminal justice became more widespread. Economically, capitalist institutions proliferated. Politically, reforms pushed common American institutions such as separation of power and federalism. Surveys have continued to show strong support in Eastern Europe for American culture and institutions (Lempert 1998).

Some may scoff at the analogies between political transition during the Cold War and such prospects for transition in the current period, especially with so much of the Muslim world lined up ideologically against the United States. Yet it must be admitted that the ideological divide of the Cold War appeared compelling as well, and great transformations occurred there. Moreover, it is a testament to the allure of democracy and capitalism that surveys of Muslim nations tend to show that, despite Bush's toxic foreign policy legacy, Muslim populations remain favorable to American democratic political and economic institutions (Inglehart and Norris 2003; Pew 2003).

Epistemic community effects also manifest themselves with respect to America's influence over political and economic transition in the community of nations. As noted above in the previous section, much of the international superstructure that promotes development and state building is founded on models that exude the desirability of democratic governance and capitalism. Development agencies have vigorously promoted solutions that promote and thrive under democratic governance and capitalism – economic openness, social mobility, private property, governmental accountability, effective and efficient governance, industrialization, and cosmopolitanism. In strong measure, common models of development and state building that are pervasive in American academia and elite political spheres are strongly congruent with the international institutions that are charged with economic and political development. Moreover, the international superstructure proceeds from a vision of political rights and institutions that are strongly grounded in Western, and more predominantly American, laws and norms. There is no more telling testament to this epistemic effect with respect to this political superstructure than the specific rights contemplated in the Universal Declaration of Human Rights that was created and promoted by the UN General Assembly. This is an especially important document, because UN and UN-sanctioned initiatives that promote political development, human rights, and economic development are either founded on these rights or consistent with them. The Declaration is a striking recollection of the political and legal philosophy expounded in the principal documents of the founding of the American nation – the U.S. Constitution and the Declaration of Independence (Brown 2000; Stiglitz 2002; Bird 1996; Abdalla 1980).

Terrorism

The fight against terrorism under Bush largely failed because it attacked the symptoms rather than the causes. Fighting terrorism at the roots requires soft power. As noted in chapter 5, soft power solutions promise to be powerful weapons in fighting terrorism. The strategies mapped out there rely principally on the effectiveness of international cooperation and appropriate U.S. actions and policies to create a milieu that promotes sustainable security. From a military perspective, soft power can make hard power solutions that much more effective by creating networks of indigenous support that would help root out terrorists. At a more general level that encompasses social, economic, and political outcomes, soft power in the form of diplomacy and economic development can interdict fundamental causes of terrorism. Such initiatives can undermine the political, economic, and social conditions that are breeding grounds for terrorism in sensitive regions around the world. Most of these initiatives encompass state-to-state relations and public support initiatives created by appropriate actions and policies in promoting the foundations for sustainable security. Yet the cause against terrorism can be enhanced all the more by cultural-value-added processes.

As Desker and Ramakrishna (2003, 52) note, the war against terror is more of a "political and ideological war" than a military war. It is in this political and ideological war that cultural-value-added processes can be most effective. Such solutions to combat terrorism can manifest themselves in several ways that undermine the milieus that encourage anti-American radicalization. One occurs more directly through a social filter in the form of a cultural penetration that deradicalizes youth, whereas others work through a more indirect filter of political and economic transformation.

With respect to the power of cultural penetration through a social filter, the dissemination of values and images can serve as a potent wedge to abate the radicalization of youth. Muslim populations are largely penetrable by American culture. As Roy (2004) has noted, globalization is increasingly "deteritorializing" Islam. Muslim societies have preponderantly been pervaded by elements that have effectively Westernized their cultures, synthesizing religious beliefs with more modern and cosmopolitan cultural values and practices. This "re-Islamisation" of the Muslim world has served to deliver societies much closer to the American image. Re-Islamisation has, in fact, not been as difficult to consummate as some may believe. Demographic trends show that Muslim populations preponderantly embrace modern cosmopolitan values. Large majorities disapprove of terrorism, are opposed to fundamentalist Islamic governance, and are against Islamist organizations and movements. In fact, Islamist parties tend to do very poorly in general elections. Even among the more extreme Muslim elements, the Islamists themselves, demographic trends appear to favor American cultural penetrability on various dimensions. Most Islamist movements are not strictly "traditional" (e.g., Taliban), but of a more modern form. The leaders themselves are largely composed of a penetrated demographic – people who have been extensively exposed to Western culture and education, both directly and indirectly. Moreover, there is great diversity in values and practices among the rank-and-file followers, such that there is no pervasive counterweight that could repel cultural penetration. In fact, many such modern Islamist values and political platforms are consistent with those of Americans: anti-monarchical, pro-egalitarianism, pro-meritocracy, pro–human rights, pro–self-determination, pro–economic development, and generally antitraditional in many political, social, and religious respects (Kurzman 2008). It is no surprise, then, that surveys of Muslim nations tend to show that Muslim populations remain favorable to many American values and institutions (Inglehart and Norris 2003; Pew 2003).

Studies have attested to the power of American culture, especially American youth culture, in transforming mindsets in ways that have brought about general social psychologies antithetical to the consummation of anti-American radicalization. The values generally entrench cognitive orientations diametrically opposed to profiles normally equated with terrorist psychology: antipolitical, anticivic, antitraditional, materialistic, secular, cosmopolitan, modern, individualistic, ahistorical, and self-gratifying. In effect, this cognitive conditioning through cultural penetration cuts at the very core of values that inspire and perpetuate terrorism: political, civic-mindedness, religious, communitarian, traditional, historical, self-denial, and sacrifice (Bergamnn 1998; Lempert 1998; Barnet and Cavanagh 1996; Gitlin 1999; Epitropoulos and Roudometof 1998). Perhaps the best testament to the effectiveness of cultural penetration through this social filter is that Muslim nations with strong religious elements in their political systems feature cultural initiatives designed to abate such penetration. Yet notwithstanding this "cultural police" posture, youth culture in these nations is still pervaded by vigorous underground pockets of indulgence in Western culture and practices (Fraser 2008; Barnet and Cavanagh 1996).

The impact of this cultural penetration can also manifest itself in more indirect ways that undercut the perpetuation of social milieus favorable to terrorist activities. In this respect, such penetration can undermine social networks that support terrorist activities within the larger societies in which terrorists function. Cultural conditioning within the greater social milieus promotes values that make the public at large less invested in terrorist activities. Like the deradicalized youth, people will be less sympathetic to such activities, so they will be less likely to undertake the sacrifices necessary to harbor and support terrorist. Also, in spreading such values, cultural penetration gives the larger societies greater incentives to turn against such activities. Locals can be more easily bribed to turn in terrorists, and informers more easily recruited. Moreover, cultural penetration makes the public more invested in preventing such activities, because the lifestyles they find more favorable might be compromised by extensive terrorist activities. In this respect, people will be more influenced by threats of domestic police intervention or international economic sanctions that disrupt their lives.[25] History has overwhelmingly attested to the fact that insurgencies live or die based on the level of support they receive from local populations (Gallarotti 2010; Nagl 2002). In the words of Takeyh and Gvosdev (2003), terrorist networks especially thrive when they have "a home."

With respect to the other indirect filters through which cultural penetration functions, political and economic transformation can also create milieus unfavorable to the birth and sustenance of terrorist activities. In creating a milieu favorable to democracy and capitalism, cultural penetration concomitantly creates a toxic landscape for terrorism. Colin Powell best expressed this relationship: "[A] shortage of economic opportunities is a ticket to despair. Combined with rigid political systems, it is a dangerous brew."[26] This occurs through several processes. Capitalism leads to greater economic opportunities that undercut the deprivation and other natural logistical factors that generate incentives for terrorism (e.g., leisure time, isolation). Also, economic openness reinforces the very

[25] This suggests another Cosmopolitan interaction process between hard and soft power in the context of fighting terrorism: the soft power cultivated through cultural penetration makes hard power strategies against terrorism (sanctions) that much more effective.

[26] Quoted in Windsor (2003, 263).

cultural penetration that serves a deradicalizing function. Political openness created by democracy encourages greater economic openness, of course, but it serves other antiterrorist functions as well. Political openness, like economic openness, reinforces the very cultural penetration that serves a deradicalizing function. Political openness undermines the control of information, making it more difficult for states and terrorist groups to win people over with propaganda. Such openness also channels political activism and opposition into more moderate forms, rather than the extreme forms (which are a breeding ground for terrorism) created by more repressive regimes. In addition to economic development, political openness promotes human development, which undermines the deprivation and other logistical conditions conducive to terrorism. Finally, democratic governance tends to produce stronger (i.e., better-governed) states, which would be more effective at containing terrorist elements. It is no surprise that the U.S. government stepped up its support of democratization programs in the Middle East, such as the Millennium Challenge Account and the Middle East Partner initiative, after 9/11(Windsor 2003; Desker and Ramakrishna 2003; Radelet 2003).

Finally, epistemic effects that raise U.S. influence in dealing with the problem of international terrorism are amply visible in the vision of terrorism propounded in the major Security Council resolutions on the subject (SC 1189, 1269, 1368, 1373, 1377, 1998, 1999, and 2001). The language suggests strong international imprinting of American images of terrorism and American models for counterterrorist strategies. According to the language of these resolutions, all acts of terrorism are lumped together as international crimes and threats to humanity. Interestingly, there is no categorization of terrorist activities as political insurgencies or retributions, or any categorization of such activities as local or domestic crimes. This international criminalization of terrorism creates a pervasive expectation that all nations should align with the United States in stamping out terrorist activities. In fact, very strong language in the resolutions reifies that expectation. Thus, America's war becomes the world's war. Also, the international criminal aspect is raised by linking terrorism to a broad array of transnational crimes (e.g., drug trafficking, arms trafficking, and money laundering), making each terrorist activity that much more assailable. The language also designates the United States as a principal target – another manifestation of turning America's problem into the world's problem. This is further evident in language that poignantly declares terrorist activities violations of the UN Charter. Some of the language also suggests that in the face of a threat to national security, nations have the right to defend themselves unilaterally, giving nations great leeway in combating both actual and suspected terrorist activities. Finally, the language suggests that financial and logistical support of counterterrorism is an international responsibility, promoting financial burden sharing with the United States.

Weapons of Mass Destruction

As with political-economic transformation and terrorism, the fight against WMD can be promoted by a broad array of soft power strategies. It was demonstrated in chapter 5 how sustainable security against WMD also requires soft power solutions (Newhouse 2003). Regional security communities in which the United States has a strongly integrated role would have to be constructed. Again, as with terrorism, the strategies of prevention, indirect methods, disaggregation, limited-scale engagement, and a structure of endearing actions and foreign policies would be required for sustainable security against the threat of WMD. They would be implemented in fundamentally similar ways as in the war against terror. This, again, would rely on foreign receptivity to American involvement in national and local security initiatives, as well as on receptivity among allied and partner nations in building multilateral initiatives to support plans for sustainable security. As with political-economic transformation and terrorism, the soft power initiatives can be bolstered by the effects of cultural penetration. Therefore, these cultural-value-added processes also serve important functions in the war against the proliferation of WMD. Many of these functions derive from the impact that cultural penetration can have on enhancing political-economic transformations and limiting the spread of terrorism.

A number of cultural-value-added processes work through political and economic filters that promote economic and political transition. As demonstrated in the analysis in chapter 5, the threat of WMD has been intertwined with the politics of the regimes that have attempted to use such weapons to further their foreign policy goals. North Korea, Iran, and Pakistan have invested political capital in leveraging such weapons as an effective means of keeping potential enemies at bay, as well as to generate more robust geostrategic positions in their regions. The investments in these weapons have come more from autocrats than from civil societies. Surveys have shown that the priorities of civil societies are much more consistent with those of economic and political transition (Inglehart and Norris 2003; Pew 2003). In this respect, the United States has been far more worried about the possession of WMD by some regimes than by others. Given this set of overlapping outcomes and exigencies, it would appear that for American foreign policy, promoting democratic and economic transition would go far in abating such threats to American security. First, the United States could better forge direct ties with regimes that follow the capitalist-democratic route, to which dominant patterns in interstate relations attest (i.e., more extensive ties appear among similar regimes). The relations could be bolstered by greater military and economic aid, thus consolidating relations forged on the springers of political and economic similarities. Second, empowering civil society politically and economically would go far in reducing the quest for WMD. As just noted, surveys suggest that populations across such nations crave political and economic empowerment more than they support the acquisition of WMD. Such empowerment will feed into a less recalcitrant and expansionist foreign policy, as civil society will have a stake in maintaining both political and economic opportunities, which could be compromised by the quest for WMD. People become invested in discouraging such a quest in fear of losing connections with the West that could reinforce their political and economic gains (e.g., fear of sanctions and economic losses from divestment – another manifestation of Cosmopolitan interaction effects between soft and hard power). In this respect, the cultural processes that promote political and economic transition will filter through society in ways that conterminously discourage the quest for WMD. The battle over politics and the economy in strong measure is synonymous with the battle against proliferation. Much as the war against terror is an "ideological and political war," so too is the war against proliferation (Desker and Ramakrishna 2003).

The consummation of better relations forged from political and economic convergences would introduce a complex feedback system reinforcing the abatement of proliferation. Autocrats have gained much political leverage from poor relations with the United States in promoting the development of WMD. A great deal of the political fuel for galvanizing public and elite support from proliferation has been created by autocrats who have underscored the potential threat from military invasions by the United States or their allies (e.g., Israel). WMD have been touted as the only effective deterrent against such prospects. Poor relations with the United States have made this fuel all the more potent. Undermining the foundations of the rationale through better relations forged from political and economic convergence would, in turn, rob autocrats of such political leverage and make the quest for proliferation that much harder. Also, as noted, this would be reinforced by the economic and political stake that civil societies in these nations have in good relations with the United States and the West (Johnson 2004, 285; Kegley and Raymond 2007, 102; Jervis 2003a; Garner 2005, 12; "The Other Struggle" 2007, 16).

Yet the political and economic filter works also from the ground up in removing the popular support for the acquisition of WMD. As noted in the discussion of deradicalization among prospective terrorists, the cultural penetration in autocratic regimes reradicalizes politics in ways that depopulate the extreme elements that supply the foundations of support for menacing autocrats. As American cultural penetration moves politics toward the center, popular moods will be in greater conflict with policies that seek to buttress aggressive foreign policies supporting the acquisition of potent weapons. These moods will create large cross-sections of society that develop a stake in preventing such policy orientations for the same reasons that penetration creates popular cadres that support initiatives to uproot terrorist cells in their societies – because, as noted, political and economic gains may be threatened by just such policies. Yet this grassroots effect generates greater political effects that feed back to promote even more possibilities of regime change. Popular moods generated by penetration mean far greater support for moderate elites in politics, whose newfound popular support can translate into greater influence over domestic and foreign policies, all of which weaken the political support for recalcitrant autocrats swinging destructive weapons from their belts. And of course, with the ascent of more moderate elites into the inner sanctum of political power, there is a greater "demographic effect" (i.e., those especially exposed to American culture) that bolsters prospects for regime transformation and policies that discourage proliferation (Bergamnn 1998; Lempert 1998; Barnet and Cavanagh 1996; Gitlin 1999; Epitropoulos and Roudometof 1998).

As with both political-economic transition and terrorism, epistemic effects of the international war against WMD have also demonstrated strong cultural imprinting and thus have raised the influence of the United States in its quest to limit proliferation. Adler (192, 108) aptly notes, "...knowledge related to arms control cannot be separated from values." The NPT regime, in fact, is oriented around a set of goals and expectations that conform closely to American interests and psychologies about the proliferation of WMD. Expectations and goals about preventing the spread of nuclear technologies with military applications are more definitive and robust than goals and expectations about disarmament; hence, the regime disproportionately works in favor of nuclear weapons states (NWS). For non-nuclear weapons states (NNWS), the language of the treaty issues firmer expectations about nonproliferation, both from the demand side (NNWS are not to attempt to obtain nuclear military technology) (Article 2) and from the supply side (NWS are not to attempt to provide such technology to NNWS) (Article 1). Development of nuclear technology is specifically relegated to nonmilitary uses. Also, the International Atomic Energy Agency (IAEA) is charged with generating safeguards for limiting the ability of NNWS to develop nuclear military capabilities (Article 3). And whereas the nonproliferation initiatives more vigorously construct a set of rules to deny nuclear arms to NNWS, this is not the case with respect to NWS. In the set of rules and expectations regarding disarmament among NWS, the language is sufficiently vague so as not to impose the same constraints that the treaty imposes on NNWS. In this respect, Article VI of the NPT states, "Each of the Parties to the Treaty undertakes to pursue negotiations in good faith on effective measures relating to cessation of the nuclear arms race at an early date and to nuclear disarmament, and on a treaty on general and complete disarmament under strict and effective international control." This does not require NWS to conclude such a treaty, but only to negotiate in good faith.

Monitoring and implementation through the IAEA further compounds the epistemic effect of the NPT, as the conception of nuclear technology informing the operations of the IAEA very much reflects standards originating in the period in which the United States was the leader in developing and designing nuclear technology, both military and nonmilitary. Thus, scientific cognitions about the precise nature of nuclear technologies and their potential uses have been very much colored by American academia and science, given that American scientists established the cognitive precedents of nuclear technology.[27] Smith (1987) attests to the strength of these epistemic effects in establishing the cognitive foundations of the NPT regime, and these effects were magnified all the more by the fact that the principal institutionalization of the regime occurred during a period of decline in America's relative hard power.

Public Diplomacy

One of the keys to enhancing the cultural-value-added processes in delivering all of America's big three foreign policy goals will be a more vigorous

[27] According to Smith (1987, 277), America's cognitive lead in the issue of nuclear technology had a strong impact on the development of the NPT regime because, as he notes, "[the regime] was built... on convergent expectations prior to any well-developed pattern of interaction."

public diplomacy initiative on the part of future administrations. A number of scholars have attested to the importance of such an initiative in promoting American foreign policy objectives in these as well as other issues (Windsor 2003; Kaufman 2003; Ross 2003; Desker and Ramakrishna 2003; Blinken 2003).

Ross (2003) has underscored the effectiveness of public diplomacy as a major weapon against terrorism. This is clear in the United States' greater push to expand initiatives in public diplomacy against terrorism after 9/11. Public diplomacy continues to be a "high priority investment" for the U.S. government in this cause. As Ross (2003, 259) notes, we must "harness the power of U.S. culture" in undermining the conditions that breed terrorism and hatred of America. Ross (2003, 260) adds that there has always been a link between "perceptions of the United States and the country's national security." Windsor (2003) has emphasized the need for more extensive and efficient public diplomacy in order to promote political-economic transitions. In this respect, Windsor calls for greater government funding and more extensive involvement in initiatives that tap a variety of venues: journalists, official diplomatic contacts, civic groups, human rights organizations, and development agencies.

Blinken (2003) has marshaled a broad prescriptive plan for enhancing public diplomacy to fight terrorism, but his prescriptions would also enhance the quests to deliver regime transformation and abate the spread of WMD. In his view, the United States must reinvigorate its application of public diplomacy in a multistep initiative that calls for strengthening research on public opinion, developing a rapid response capability for public affairs problems, greater empowerment of American diplomats, increasing the number of diplomatic posts outside of capital cities, better utilization of foreign media, bolstering the Voice of America and creating new media and information outlets, developing and supporting outside partners, cultivating foreign opinion leaders, greater collaboration with the private sector, and greater utilization of public figures in disseminating information and values overseas.

Although the United States will need to step up public diplomacy for gaining all three major foreign policy goals, the application of soft power resources must be comprehensive and go beyond culture (Winsor 2003; Kaufman 2003; Blinken 2003). Winning the cultural war will pay far fewer dividends if the United States does not undertake actions and foreign policies that concomitantly endear the United States and its interests to foreign nations and their peoples. Cultural soft power will not be enough to deliver U.S. foreign policy goals. This was clear under the Bush Doctrine, so future administrations have a strong test case underscoring the need to be more comprehensive in producing soft power policies and actions (Sardar and Davis 2002; Kaufman 2003; Blinken 2003; Andoni 2003).

In sum, the means of soft power that America enjoys are numerous and varied. One specific manifestation of this soft power is the influence that can be derived from America's cultural penetration of the world. This cultural-value-added process of soft power can enhance the already robust and numerous means of soft power with which the United States is endowed. Much of this penetration is delivered on the shoulders of U.S. hard power resources. Yet the hard power resources not only deliver American cultural soft power, they are also enhanced by it. Cultural soft power delivers many sources of leverage for the United States at a general level of global influence. The primacy of culture promotes the primacy of American foreign interests abroad. But at a more specific level of the United States' big three foreign policy objectives (political and economic transition, WMD, and terrorism), the soft power of American culture generates many avenues for success. At both general and specific levels, cultural power interacts with hard power in a Cosmopolitan fashion. Indeed, each feeds on the other in ways that maximize the United States' global clout.

7

Conclusions

Cosmopolitan power offers an alternative to conceptions of power that have traditionally diverged along paradigmatic lines. Realists have embraced the centrality of hard power to the exclusion of soft power. Neoliberals and Constructivists have gone to great pains to reject such strong conceptualizations of world politics in pushing visions that gravitate around elements of soft power. The two conceptions of power are not only far more compatible than the paradigmatic battlefield suggests, but also are necessary components of any process of power management that purports to optimize national influence in world politics. Not only are the paradigms not antithetical with respect to building a theory of such a process, but they actually rely on one another to construct such a theory. Both hard and soft power are necessary elements in the power inventory of nations that seek to attain the greatest possible influence given their resources. The idea of Cosmopolitan power embraces such a vision of power and is founded on principles that suggest points of convergence among the three major paradigms of international relations. Such points of convergence can be developed to forge a new, and more integrated, paradigm of international politics: Cosmopolitik.

Toward a New Paradigm of International Relations: Some Thoughts on a Pre-Theory of Cosmopolitik

The Cosmopolitan theory of power suggests some strong foundations on which to develop a new paradigm in international politics – a paradigm of Cosmopolitan Politics, or Cosmopolitik. The Cosmopolitan theory of power is restricted to one issue area, but success in this issue area is inspiring because paradigmatic cleavages have appeared to be strongest in this particular issue. If some common ground could be forged in one of the most controversial and divisive issues among practitioners of the competing paradigms – that of power – then the prospects for theoretical interfacing on less contentious issues appears promising. The following thoughts suggest some pre-theoretical foundations that might serve to inspire a greater systematic logic that integrates Constructivism, Neoliberalism, and Realism into such a new paradigm.[1] A number of attempts have been made to synthesize elements of these paradigms, and the logic that follows recalls some of the points made in that literature in the context of the logic of Cosmopolitan power.[2]

The case studies of both the classical and modern realists attest to the compatibility of all three paradigms within a single consistent logic. Critiques of inconsistencies within the work of these great authors fail to appreciate broader views that each author possessed regarding human relations and world politics. The great works of the Realists analyzed in this book dispelled the common belief that great thinkers cannot be expected to produce a harmonious logic. They did indeed produce such a logic, which essentially and pervasively underscored the essential compatibility between cooperation and norms, on the one hand, and commonly venerated principles of Realism, on the other. These principles include the optimization of power, the interest in survival and quest for security, the importance of material capabilities, the centrality of states, and rational action.[3] These principles of Realism, as prescriptive categories, depend on both cooperation and normative behavior to be fully realized. This idea was vindicated extensively in the logic of the magnum opus of each Realist author considered in this book. For each author, these principles could best be achieved through a delicate balance among

[1] For at least two decades, scholars have embraced the idea of improving explanations of international relations through pluralistic perspectives and paradigmatic synthesis (Lapid 1989).

[2] On attempts at synthesis among the various paradigms, see Wendt (1999), Barkin (2003), Williams (2003), Sterling-Folker (2002), Johnston (2008), Onuf (2008), Hall (1997), Jervis (1970), Copeland (2000), Walt (1987), Fukuyama (2006), and Ikenberry and Kupchan (2004).

[3] Like all major paradigms, Realism is a battleground and in no way represents a consensual logic. The principles cited here are often underscored as being pervasive across various strands of Realism, so they are employed here. On variations across Realist thought, see Donnelly (2000) and Doyle (1990).

norms, cooperation, and material power resources (i.e., by joining hard and soft power).[4] This idea of an optimal synthesis in attending to the goals of states could form a fundamental mantra from which could be built a more general and systematic theory of international relations. This mantra exists within an integrated set of the three fundamental categories that formerly have been synonymous with each of the three paradigms: norms (Constructivism), cooperation (Neoliberalism), and power (Realism). Although such a logic is well beyond the intentions of this pre-theoretical exercise, a few thoughts can be issued regarding some building blocks for such logic, even if preliminary and scant.

The logic of Cosmopolitan power suggests that norms and cooperation, rather than being constraints to national power and thus incompatible with power itself, can function as instruments of national power.[5] Paradoxically, even in constraining nations, these phenomena can actually empower nations. In this sense, all of the paradigms can merge around the idea of power optimization through the indulgence in normative action and cooperation. From this conceptualization of power springs a broader set of theoretical tenets involving the nature of international relations. The resulting theory, once considered within the dynamic nature of world politics, becomes even more compelling as changes in the international system, highlighted in Chapter 1, make the need for such a more synthetic theory ever more acute. In the evolving nature of international politics, a broader theory constructed from a Cosmopolitan logic of power becomes increasingly relevant as a means of understanding international relations.

This evolving nature, in enhancing the value of soft power, fundamentally raises the value of cooperation and norms as important components of a nation's power lexicon.[6] In this respect, the apparently paradoxical idea of constraints being empowering attains greater vindication. Each of the major changes in international politics in the modern age cited in Chapter 1 raises the value of norms and cooperation in ways that

4 In comparing paradigms and assessing possibilities for interfacing, Barkin (2003) and Keohane and Nye (1989) stress the need to study the relationship between material power on one hand and cooperation and norms on the other.

5 Hall (1997b) validates this idea by demonstrating how moral authority can function as a source of power.

6 This broader theory of Cosmopolitik promises to be more dynamic than either Realism and Constructivism, whose critics have cited tendencies for some categories within these paradigms to be static (Barkin 2003). Sterling-Folker (2002) has underscored the possibilities for integrating Realism and Constructivism through such a more dynamic (i.e., evolutionary) approach to international politics.

attend to the fundamental principles of empowerment stressed by Realism. The evolution of military technology (both WMD and conventional weaponry) has delivered a world in which hard military power no longer holds a monopoly as an ultimate means of statecraft, because major wars are far too destructive to perpetrate and continue (Jervis 2002; Mueller 1988). Consequently, norms and cooperation gain greater utility as coercion and force become less useful as a means of foreign policy. So constraints gain utility as a means of attaining foreign policy objectives in the world system. The increasing usefulness of norms and cooperation relative to force is further enhanced by interdependence and globalization. As the fate of nations is increasingly intertwined, constraints become even more essential as a means of attaining foreign objectives, because the infliction of harm onto other nations in such a world amounts to self-punishment on various dimensions of state and non-state action. Indeed, cooperation and normative action are the best vehicles for attaining foreign objectives in an interconnected world.

Also, such constraints gain greater usefulness as means of foreign policy because of the rise of the guardian state and the spread of democracy. The guardian directive in politics has raised material well-being to the very highest pedestal in political platforms. This pushes nations to strive for cooperation and goodwill for the purposes of enhancing economic opportunities that lead to growth and development. This is compounded by a democratic ethic that underscores the rule of law and fair play as the foundations of politics, which are, to a large extent, exported to international relations. Finally, the growing importance of regimes and international organizations makes the constraints embodied in norms and cooperation essential to national well-being, as nations can obtain foreign objectives in these institutions only through cooperation and normative behavior. Yet as much as the changing world has raised the usefulness of cooperation and norms, it is always the case that such soft power resources must be complemented by hard power for the optimization of national influence. Material resources round out the optimal power portfolio for nations in the modern world system, which still contains sufficient elements of anarchy to make material power essential.

Another avenue for building a general theory from the components of all three paradigms is to explore how norms and cooperation contribute to the leading principles of Realism – the optimization of power, the interest in survival and quest for security, the importance of material capabilities, the centrality of states, and rational action. With respect to the optimization of power and material capabilities, this book has averred that such optimization can occur only through the integration of the power resources espoused by all three paradigms. With respect to the prescriptive principles involving survival and quest for security, it is clear that survival and security are best promoted by such a diversification among power resources, both constraints and material sources of power. This also derives trivially from the logic of Cosmopolitan power. If power is the principal means through which survival and security are effected, then surely optimal power will deliver optimal security.[7] Thus, an integrated vision of power best delivers survival and security. The centrality of states can be consistent with all three paradigms, and in fact, Neoliberals and Constructivists have not contested the primary role of states in shaping international politics (Wendt 1999; Barkin 2003; Keohane and Nye 1989). Yet neither have Realists claimed that states are the only important actors in world politics. Although international politics has been portrayed as state-centric by Realists, it is clear that other actors have been accorded influence in shaping international outcomes (Waltz 1959).

In constructing an integrated general theory of international politics, the central decision-making processes that drive action in international politics assume an important role. Historically, there has been disagreement about the incompatibility of normative processes espoused by Constructivists and rational processes espoused by Realists and Neoliberals (Barkin 2003). However, there are significant possibilities for interfacing the decision processes, especially in a changing international system that continues to make the utility functions of individual nations more interconnected (i.e., creates joint utility functions). With respect to the mechanics of human psychology, Realists and Neoliberals contend that actors are rational, whereas Constructivists propose that actors conceive of themselves as existing within well-defined social structures that affect their fates and therefore determine their individual objectives (Baldwin 1993; Mearsheimer 2001, 31; Wendt 1999, 1). Synthesizing the two delivers a decision-making process that could be referred to as social rationality. Although individual nations may be able to optimize their welfare, security, and/or power by independently pursuing their rational self-interest (i.e., the Adam Smith rule), it is often the case that these

[7] Williams (2003) demonstrates that Constructivist visions of security (i.e., specifically the work on securitization by the Copenhagen School) can interface effectively with Realist visions of security. On the Copenhagen School of security studies, see Guzzini and Jung (2004).

individual goals (and certainly the group's goals) can be compromised by individual nations acting in complete independence from each other. It was this realization that made the contributions of game theory so important to the social sciences. In many cases, the only way to attain desired individual (as well as group) outcomes in strategic cases (i.e., that carry both elements of cooperation and competition) is to frame one's utility in terms of both the individual and the group. Only by considering the goals of the group can individuals within that group best attend to their particularistic goals. The Prisoner's Dilemma, of course, stands as the classic example. The structure of strategic interaction leads to a Nash noncooperative equilibrium within which individuals attain their second-worst outcome by acting independently of each other. Both individuals and the group can do much better by conceptualizing the game in terms of collective utility and thus deliver superior payoffs to individuals and the entire group alike. In this respect, being socially rational is synonymous with individual rationality. We could construe such socially-grounded rational action as constituting complex rationality.

With regard to the work on human rationality, especially in economics, the synthesis of decision-making processes embraced by the three leading paradigms of international relations (thus espousing a vision of complex rationality) is neither unprecedented nor startling. The work of Neoliberalism, with its emphasis on institutions as means of solving market problems, emerges from the tradition of the economics of imperfect markets (the work on transactions costs, externalities, information, public goods, and bounded rationality) and game theory.[8] The work has been more than sufficiently recognized, having generated numerous Nobel prizes during the past four decades (eight in game theory alone). The mainstream scholarly legacy goes back to the nineteenth century at least and has manifested itself in the twentieth century in the work of a legendary cadre (Ronald Coase, Herbert Simon, George Akerlof, Joseph Stiglitz, Oliver Williamson, John von Neumann, Oskar Morgenstern, Kenneth Arrow, Reinhard Selten, John Nash, and John Harsanyi, among others). The voluminous body of work has sufficiently and definitively demonstrated the rationality of employing institutions to mediate strategic behavior and correct for other market imperfections so as to achieve higher levels of

[8] Even offensive Realists have embraced the idea of framing decisions based on interdependence with other actors. As Mearsheimer (2001, 37) proclaims, "[states] think carefully about... how other states will react to their moves." Even for Realists, there is ample incentive to cooperate in anarchy. Baldwin (1997) has argued that the quest for security need not be zero-sum; thus, possibilities for group or mutual security do exist.

utility, and it has shown that individual utility often can be realized only by optimizing the utility of the group.[9]

Constructivists do not deny that agents have interests and goals, and pursue such goals as best as they can with the resources they possess (Onuf 1998a, 60; Wendt 1999, 113). Onuf (1998a, 60) even calls such behavior "rational." In this respect, Constructivists, Neoliberals, and Realists all have the capacity to embrace a vision of rationality in which actors are pursuing well-specified objectives deriving from some structure of preferences.[10] The norms embraced by Constructivists have also been integrated into rational decision-making processes by social scientists for some time.[11] Norms and institutions have been analyzed as phenomena that can facilitate individual and collective utility in strategic situations (Brahms 1994; Taylor 1987; Ullman-Margalit 1977). Normative behavior has been envisioned as serving a plethora of functions (from signaling to constraints against defection) that facilitate the delivery of Pareto-superior outcomes for individuals and groups in strategic situations. In this respect, fundamental moral dictates embraced by Constructivists can be quite consistent with the rationality espoused by Realists and Neoliberals. The economics literature on the rationality of morality is extensive and compelling with respect to the possibilities for integrating Realist, Neoliberal, and Constructivist visions of rationality, thus producing a vision of complex rationality.[12]

In sum, the Cosmopolitan theory of power has suggested significant opportunities for a greater interfacing of the three leading paradigms in international relations – Realism, Constructivism, and Neoliberalism. If the three paradigms can carve out common ground on what historically has been considered the most divisive issue among these paradigms, hope

[9] Keohane's *After Hegemony* (1984) has become one of the most celebrated Neoliberal adaptations of the economics literature on imperfect markets.

[10] The main difference between the Realists and Neoliberals, on one hand, and the Constructivists, on the other, is how they conceptualize the formation of interests. For the former, interests derive from a more materialistic foundation based on objective incentives (exogenous). For the latter, interests are socially constructed and subjectively contingent (endogenous). See Wendt (1999, 114).

[11] This depiction of a Constructivist vision does not wish to suggest that Constructivists are only interested in norms. The contributors to this paradigm show a great deal of diversity in what they consider important processes and issues in international politics. I emphasize norms because such phenomena are especially useful points of paradigmatic interfacing. On the variety within the Constructivist vision of international politics, see Adler (2002).

[12] Much work has been done in this genre. For some illuminating contributions, see especially Stark (1995) and Phelps (1975).

for such an interfacing may appear bright. Hopefully the fate of theorizing in international relations is destined to follow the path of a more general intellectual evolution toward more interdisciplinary understandings of human action. In this respect, it will be neither fruitless nor dilettantish to follow a general trend that looks for answers at the crossroads of human knowledge.

Appendix

Formal Model of Cosmopolitan Power

Optimizing Power Through Diversification, a Model of Optimal Diversification among Hard and Soft Power Resources

Let us assume that nations wish to optimize influence through some investment in power resources. Assume that they can employ two kinds of resources: hard (HP) and soft (SP). These can be thought of as factors in the production of international influence and depicted as isoquants $I_1 \ldots I_4$ (see Figure 6). These influence curves represent all combinations of HP and SP for a given level of influence, so they are functions of HP and SP. The curves are convex over the factors of production, suggesting the standard structure of diminishing marginal productivity in factors of production. This is consistent with the depiction of standard returns to the application of power resources in the international relations literature on power, as it is posited that as we move toward the extremes (i.e., where nations are predominantly relying on one set of power resources), nations will have to substitute increasingly greater amounts of the prevalent resources for the lesser-used resources to maintain the same level of influence. This is depicted by a flattening of the curves in relation to the respective axes as we move away from the origin (Nye 2002, 162; Keohane and Nye 1989, 11). Movement along any influence curve represents the same level of influence at differing combinations of power resources, or the marginal rate of substitution among inputs $d\text{SP}/d\text{HP}$, alternatively the marginal rate of technical substitution. Higher levels of influence are attained as one moves out from the origin to higher influence curves. The full amount of resources that a nation may bring to bear on investing in influence can be depicted by a standard isocost line or

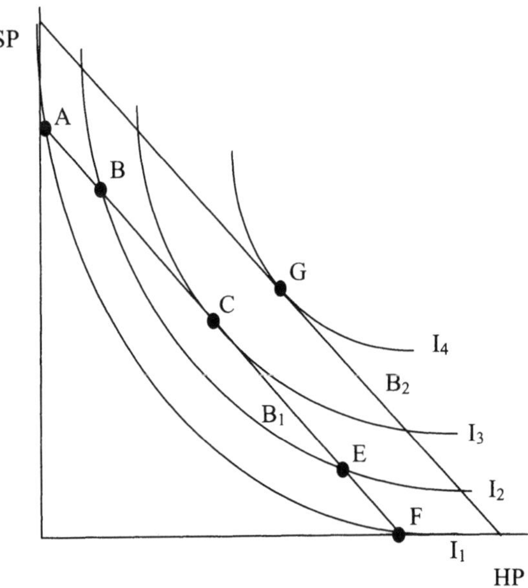

FIGURE 6. The Production of Influence I

budget constraint, defined as f(HP,SP) with standard slope – P_{HP}/P_{SP}.[1] It represents all combinations of hard and soft power that can be purchased by a nation given their prices P_{HP} and P_{SP}. The constraint B_2 in Figure 6 represents a larger budget than B_1 and therefore makes higher levels of influence attainable. Thus, output can be defined as

$$P_{HP}HP + P_{SP}SP \tag{1}$$

It will therefore be the goal of a nation to choose some mix of power inputs to attain an equilibrium at the highest possible isoquant or influence curve, given its budget, which is the point where the ratio of prices of the two power inputs should be equal to the marginal rate of substitution defined by the influence curve, so in general

$$P_{HP}/P_{SP} = MP_{HP}/MP_{SP} \tag{2}$$

[1] The standard assumption of a constant marginal rate of substitution in expenditures among inputs is generally reasonable and useful. However, as noted above, in the case of power, this may not always be the case. Investments in one kind of resource may enhance the other kind of power, as when the cultivation of goodwill helps to secure military bases, for example. It is useful, however, to view the decision to invest in power resources as a choice, especially given that so many investments in one kind of power are usually at the expense of gains in other kinds of resources. Certainly, the literature on power emphasizes this point.

which leads to general equilibrium condition

$$MP_S/P_S = MP_D/P_D = \cdots = MP_U/P_U \quad (3)$$

where S, D, and U are inputs. Thus, in this particular case, given budget constraint B_1, optimization at point C is attained at power output

$$MP_{HP}/P_{HP} = MP_{SP}/P_{SP} \quad (4)$$

Given standard isoquant curves, the benefits of diversification are fairly compelling. Let us look first at corner solutions at points A and F. Where there is complete specialization in either kind of resource, the levels of influence would be lower than at a diversified equilibrium like point C, as these points are on a lower influence curve (I_1 rather than I_3). The application to international relations is compelling. At the hard power extreme, a nation that completely disdains cooperation and uses coercive unilateral means to extract compliance to its wishes will likely generate the image of a pariah, which in turn will generate much hostility in the community of nations. Nations will resist it to the greatest possible extent, which means that all of its gains will have to be directly extracted against the wishes of other nations. Moreover, nations will want to exclude it from any multilateral arrangement designed to generate benefits for its members. Thus, any movement on the budget line B_1 from point C to point F would constitute hard disempowerment, in that higher levels of influence have been foregone because of increasing reliance on hard power (i.e., the nation has in fact weakened itself). Choosing to stay at point F would constitute the most extreme form of hard disempowerment in terms of opportunities for greater influence that are being foregone; thus, opportunity costs are very high.

Conversely, nations at the soft power extreme will be paper tigers. Although such saintly states are generally respected and venerated, they have limited unilateral means with which to attain their goals in world politics. They will not even be able to defend themselves. This would be considered a case of soft disempowerment – weakening oneself from pursuing strategies that are excessively reliant on soft power. Graphically, soft disempowerment would be represented by movement on the budget line B_1 from point C to point A.

Some diversification from extreme corner solutions makes higher levels of influence attainable (e.g., at I_2). At point B, the saintly state has adapted some hard power resources in its foreign policy, and although it is still well respected, it now has some muscle that it can use to attain some goals that were heretofore impossible, especially with respect to hostile nations (i.e., its enemies can no longer act with impunity). Similarly, in contemplating a movement from point F to point E, the state that was formerly at a hard power corner solution will benefit from the acquisition of some soft power; other nations will be more amenable to its interests and goals, thereby increasing its influence (i.e., enjoy soft empowerment). Yet in this case, the nation has retained sufficient muscle to compel other nations if it has to. Optimal influence given budget B_1 would be attainable at point C on curve I_3, which in Figure 6 suggests a roughly equal distribution of hard and soft power resources.[2]

Optimal equilibrium is dependent on the structure of the budget line and influence curves. With respect to the budget line, a greater endowment of resources would naturally make higher levels of influence attainable. A nation with budget constraint B_2 could attain higher levels of influence (optimal equilibrium at point G) than a nation with a constraint of B_1. At point G, a nation has significantly more of both kinds of resources and can attain far greater influence than a nation limited to point C. Of course, as in the case of a B_1 constraint, a nation may squander influence because it fails to diversify its resources in the most productive way (e.g., attain equilibrium on I_3 – where it intersects with B_2).

2 Perfectly equitable diversification need not be an optimal equilibrium; much depends on the shape of the budget constraint and influence curves, as will become clear. Moreover, an interior solution (i.e., one that promotes diversification rather than specialization) follows from the assumptions that isocost and isoquant functions conform to some standard structures – that is, the assumption about production technologies contemplates a structure for the budget line that is not so skewed as to encourage corners solutions, and the assumption about nations facing diminishing marginal utility with standard convexity structures over differing inputs also works in favor of an interior solution. These assumptions do not seem unreasonable, as nations derive utility from both hard and soft power in the world system, and both kinds of power resources are necessary for a robust arsenal of power resources. Therefore, we should see conventional marginal utility effects as nations move too far to one extreme at the expense of the other power resource. Moreover, there does not appear to be any unusual or significantly skewed relative technological capabilities in the production of power resources that would excessively advantage the creation of one power resource over another. Nor does there appear to be significantly skewed relative technological capabilities that would excessively advantage the productivity of one set of power resources over another. Consequently, the assumed production technologies and utility functions proposed here appear reasonable, and therefore interior solutions also appear to be strongly encouraged. But even with the standard assumptions, corner solutions are still possible if relative prices are strongly skewed and influence curves are either very steep or very flat in relation to the budget line functions (see the discussion regarding Figure 7 later). In sum, there is no guarantee of a diversified portfolio of power resources, but under assumptions that appear reasonable with respect to the quest for influence in international relations, it appears that such an outcome will be strongly encouraged.

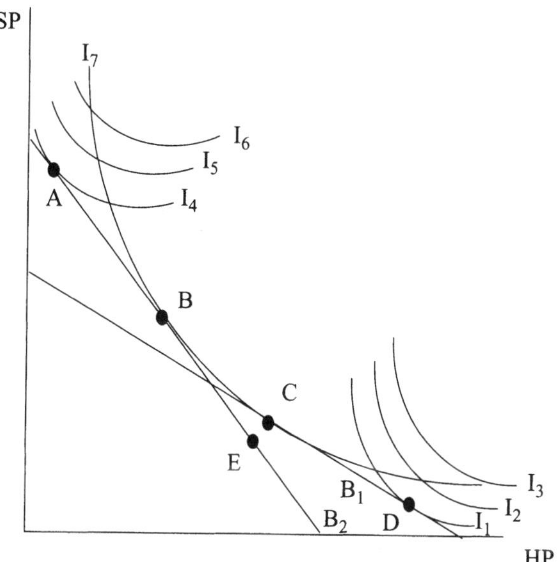

FIGURE 7. The Production of Influence II

Optimality may also shift as a result of a change in the relative prices of the resources. Let us assume that for some reason, soft power resources become cheaper relative to hard power resources. This would be represented by a clockwise rotation of the budget line, B_1 to B_2 in Figure 7. What was an optimal equilibrium at point C is no longer attainable given the new relative prices. Maintaining the same ratio of resources would lead to lower levels of influence at point E (i.e., a lower influence curve). The new optimal equilibrium would be at point B.[3] The logic is fairly straightforward; as one kind of resource has become relatively cheaper, a nation will tend to substitute it for the more expensive resource given a fixed budget.

The structure of influence is essentially a reflection of the marginal rate of substitution between resources, which in turn represents relative productivity among the resources. In Figure 7, two kinds of structures

[3] Just like factors of production, power resources – even the most intangible ones – are attainable at a price. In this example, soft power resources have become more affordable relative to hard power resources. For example, keeping a nation militarily strong may become terribly expensive, while possibilities for international diplomacy may become more abundant as a result of the proliferation of international organizations. Although influence remained the same in this example (moved along I_7), such need not be the case, as the income effects of a relative price change may well make higher influence curves attainable.

are depicted in influence curves $I_1 \ldots I_6$. $I_1 \ldots I_3$ represent a structure of marginal substitution that favors hard power resources. The steeper curves depict a situation in which progressively larger amounts of soft power resources have to compensate for the loss of any given level of hard power resources. This suggests the greater productivity of hard power relative to soft power resources as the incremental addition of very few hard power resources can compensate for the loss of far more soft power resources. Conversely, influence curves $I_4 \ldots I_6$ suggest far greater relative productivity in soft power resources. The flatter curves suggest that a few soft power resources can do the work of far more hard power resources. The differing equilibria generated by the differing productivity structures are predictable. Where hard power resources are far more productive, you would expect a composition heavily weighted in their favor (at point D). The converse will be true when soft power resources are more productive (point A).[4]

Interestingly, if one differentiates perceptions from reality, it is possible to deduce quite a complex set of functions: both budget and influence. For example, nations may perceive endowment levels below actual levels and continue to attain suboptimal levels of influence. Conversely, nations that perceive inflated endowments may be consistently frustrated by attaining only modest influence. Also, nations will desire differing baskets of resources depending on how they view international politics. Nations that believe hard power resources to be relatively more expensive may favor soft power in their foreign relations. Similarly, nations will be more favorable to soft power resources if such resources are considered relatively more productive as well. Conversely, nations will opt for hard over soft power if the latter is perceived relatively more costly and/or less productive. Realists, for example, would feature a perception of influence that is depicted by influence curves $I_1 \ldots I_3$ in Figure 7. Consequently a Realist basket will be predominantly composed of hard power resources (at point D), as Realists believe such resources to be more valuable in attaining essential goals in international politics. Constructivists and Neoliberals will feature perceptions more consistent with $I_4 \ldots I_6$, with an equilibrium somewhat more favorable to soft power resources relative to Realists (at point A). In sum, nations will favor one set of

4 Such steep or flat influence curves could create corner solutions if they are excessive enough. However, assumptions about normal structure of productivity among hard and soft power resources appear to discourage excessively skewed influence functions that would create corner solutions.

resources to the extent that they perceive those resources to be relatively more productive and/or relatively less costly. But unless such perceptions are in the extreme, it is clear that some diversification will yield greater influence over a homogeneous basket of power resources.

Endogenizing Risk

Let us now factor risk into national preferences. We compute an investment function defined by diversification among investments that differ in risk and returns. In this case, returns to hard and soft power would differ in magnitude, not be strongly-positively correlated, and the variability in returns among the activation of the sources of power (i.e., risk) would differ. With respect to the correlation among the returns, there is no reason to suspect that returns from soft and hard power will vary identically in the same direction. The reason for this is that the source of compulsion is different. There is no reason to think that a positive image will generate precisely similar outcomes, with respect to encouraging nations to comply to your wishes, to those that might be engendered by force, threats, or bribery. It is, however, reasonable to posit that returns from the activation of hard power resources have the potential of generating higher returns than those of soft power resources in the short run. Such a property derives from the nature of the power resources. Hard power resources are far more stark and menacing in nature, thus creating greater urgency to comply. A threat of military force or economic sanctions can encourage a higher level of compliance as well as timelier compliance than, for example, some diplomatic plea from a nation that traditionally shuns the use of force. Noncompliance or limited compliance will, in the short run, be devastating in the first instance, but not in the second instance. Therefore, there would appear to be a bias in favor of more moderated short run compliance to soft power activation (i.e., lower returns in the short run).

It is also in the nature of hard power to create greater variability in returns than would soft power.[5] Again, threat of force or economic sanctions can, if sufficiently menacing, generate some excessive amount of compliance from the threatened nation (i.e., very high returns in terms of influence). However, such reliance on force or economic warfare will also generate great animosity, which may in fact lead to some forms of

[5] Traditional measures of risk are calculated in terms of variability, most commonly the standard deviation of returns.

retaliation instead of compliance. Moreover, the more widespread and extreme the initial strong-armed tactics, the greater the potential adverse reactions to those tactics (e.g., the target nations may retaliate to a greater extent and others may join in the retaliation). Even in the case of hard power activation that does not have such martial properties, there is the potential for greater variability in the reaction of target nations. In the case of economic agreements that promote trade or investment or even foreign aid initiatives, for example, the returns to such carrots can be very high (e.g., open markets, secure alliances, maintain strategic strongholds), but reactions can also be extremely adversarial, thus seriously compromising influence over target nations (e.g., anti-imperialist sentiments that lead to poor diplomatic relations with the donor nation, or even terrorism). Conversely, returns to soft power activation will likely be less variable (i.e., more consistent) in the short run. A positive image and diplomatic virtue will neither create the extreme urgency conducive to excessive and timely compliance nor generate adverse reactions characterized by excessive animosity. Target nations that care about their own image will likely comply to some extent (thus rendering positive influence for the sender nation), but such compliance will likely be limited by the target nations' own particularistic goals. In sum, in the short run, the ideas of hard power exhibiting higher returns with greater variability (i.e., risk), soft power featuring lower returns and lower risk, with the returns from each not being strongly-positively correlated all appear plausible.[6]

[6] In the long run, however, things may change. Continued use of strong-armed tactics may so alienate other nations that they become increasingly adversarial, producing an international system whose outcomes are far less favorable for the aggressor nation. Also, as noted in chapter 1, where commands lack specificity or monitoring limitations exist, excessive hard power strategies may find their higher returns diminished somewhat by x-inefficiencies. So too, returns from sustained use of soft power strategies may increase returns over the long run , especially in the case of emulation. So longer term effects may alter the structure of returns in the long run in a manner that diminishes the disparity in returns, and in some cases may even promote higher net-returns to soft power strategies (i.e., hard disempowerment).

Long run risk structures, however, will not be transformed to the same extent since sustained hard power would not be expected to create a risk structure that converges toward a soft risk structure. In fact, there may be more of a divergence in the long run, hence compounding the short run disparity. But excessive reliance on soft power may generate other kinds of threat in an anarchic world (i.e., vulnerability to invasions or coercion), so here you might have an increasing risk associated with excessive reliance on soft power. This suggests an incentive to diversify sufficiently toward hard power to the extent that such menacing threats would be deterred. Once a nation has established such a minimum safety net, then it is not unreasonable to assume that nations value the achievement of their foreign policy goals without excessive swings in the nature

TABLE 2. *Risk and return of hard and soft power assets*

	Return	Risk
Asset S	2%	4%
Asset H	4%	10%

Under such conditions we can clearly see the benefits of diversification.[7] Let us model such a situation with hard and soft power resources being represented as assets or investment instruments (see Table 2). Asset S (soft power resource) represents an asset that has a relatively modest return as well as a modest level of risk (2 percent and 4 percent, respectively). Asset H (hard power resource) generates a higher return subject to greater risk (4 percent and 10 percent, respectively). Also, the returns are not strongly-positively correlated (in these estimates assumed to be .1). The risk/return profiles of these assets are therefore consistent with a profile representing hard and soft power, with hard power exhibiting both a higher risk and return than does soft power.

Let us use only these two assets in constructing a portfolio. Such a portfolio can vary continuously between one composed entirely of asset S (in which case portfolio risk and return will be precisely that of asset S – point A in Figure 8) to one that is composed entirely of asset H (which would feature a portfolio risk/return equal to that of H – point E). A risk/return frontier can be mapped out between these two points by varying the composition of the portfolio between these two

of the outcomes (i.e., want to avoid a roller coaster of variability in such outcomes). Furthermore, while emulation and x-efficiencies deriving from soft power may generate higher returns, they will more likely be consistent, which would render more limited variation in returns. Moreover, both in the long and the short runs, there is no reason to think that returns to the activation of both soft and hard power would be strongly-positively correlated. Hence, irrespective of long run effects with respect to returns, as long as the risk structures of the two assets are not as strongly affected in the long run, the investment model does a good job capturing both the short and long run mechanics of the advantages of diversification (as does the production model articulated in the previous section).

7 According to modern portfolio theory, when you have assets whose returns are not strongly-positively correlated, you can generate a joint (i.e., portfolio) risk-return combination that is superior to any of the risk-return combinations of the individual assets. This advantage of diversification manifests itself in the reduction of portfolio risk as you move from a correlation among the returns of the assets from +1 (perfect positive correlation) to -1 (perfect negative correlation) for any given portfolio composition.

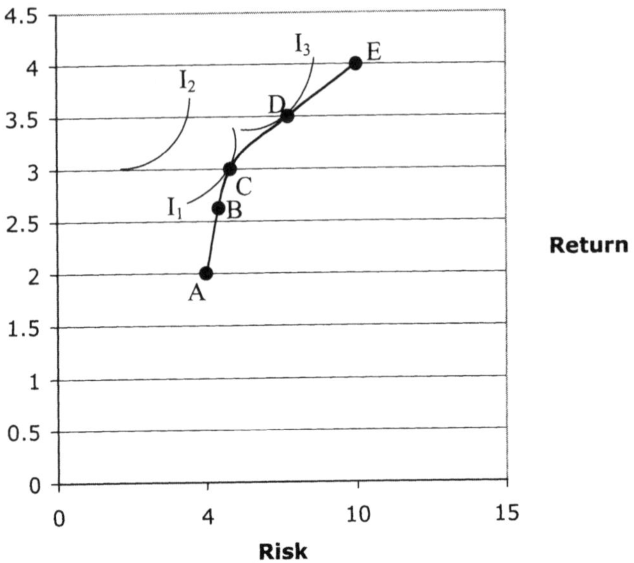

FIGURE 8. Influence and Risk

extremes. Referring back to the production model above in the previous section, this frontier is a mapping of all possible equilibrium points on production budget line B_i such that $dB_i = dI_j$ given differing factor composition preferences that now endogenize risk. In this respect, simple points of production on the production possibility frontier have been converted into risk-adjusted returns (a function of the best possible risk/return combinations). Function AE in Figure 8 represents just such a mapping. Included are indifference curves over returns (I_1, I_2) that also endogenize risk. They progress directly northwest, which suggests conventional investment preferences that favor higher returns with lower risk. A somewhat more risk-neutral investor might exhibit preference structure I_3, which suggests greater tolerance of risk for a higher return. The portfolio return (PR) is computed as follows:

$$\text{PR} = W_S R_S + W_H R_H \tag{5}$$

where W represents the respective weight of each asset in the portfolio (varying between 0 and 100 percent), and R represents the return of the respective asset. The level of portfolio risk is computed by equation 6, where P(K) is the total portfolio risk, W represents the respective weights of the assets in the portfolio, K is the respective level of risk for each individual asset, and C_{SH} is a measure of the correlation between the returns of the respective assets (assumed to be .1).

$$P(K) = \sqrt{W_S^2 K_S^2 + W_H^2 K_H^2 + 2 W_S W_H C_{SH} K_S K_H} \qquad (6)$$

Inspecting the risk/return possibilities presented by diversification in Figure 8, we can see that over some range departing from a portfolio exclusively composed of soft power, from point A to point C, diversifying can actually create a win/win situation in that a higher return can be achieved with only a slight increase in the level of risk. But from the other extreme (point E), a portfolio composed exclusively of hard power, significant risk can be averted merely by sacrificing a modest increment of returns. So sacrificing 1 percent in returns can reduce risk by 4.19 percent (from point E to point C). In relative terms, such a diversification would cut risk by approximately half at the cost of sacrificing only a quarter of the returns. Hence, disproportionate risk can be eliminated through diversification away from a high risk option (point E). Two equilibria are modeled here; equilibrium at point C represents that of an investor with conventional risk preferences, while equilibrium at D represents an investor that is less risk averse. Point B would represent a possible equilibrium point for a nation that is more risk averse. Optimization is achieved at

$$dI = dRR \qquad (7)$$

where I represents a function of investor preferences and RR is the risk/return frontier. With respect to the mapping of this investment equilibrium over a production equilibrium (modeled above in the previous section), a final general equilibrium is defined by fulfillment of conditions in equations 3 and 7, or

$$MP_S/P_S = MP_D/P_D = \cdots = MP_U/P_U \text{ at } dI = dRR \qquad (8)$$

Operationalizing Strategies for Optimization

Finding the optimal mix of soft and hard power resources will be challenging for decision makers. Doing so will require great perspicacity on their part. These decision makers will have to follow several important guidelines in both monitoring and evaluating power. These guidelines are presented in the form of prescriptions delineated in Chapter 1.

References

Abdalla, Ismail. 1980. "The Inadequacy and Loss of Legitimacy of the International Monetary Fund." *Development* 22: 46–65.

Adler, Emanuel. 1992. "The Emergence of Cooperation: National Epistemic Communities and the International Evolution of the Idea of Nuclear Arms Control." *International Organization* 46 (Winter): 101–46.

Adler, Emanuel. 2002. "Constructivism and International Relations." In *Handbook of International Relations*. Edited by Walter Carlsnaes, Thomas Risse, and Beth A. Simmons, 177–91. London: Sage.

Allawi, Ali A. 2007. *The Occupation of Iraq: Winning the War, Losing the Peace*. New Haven: Yale University Press.

Alsalam, Nabeel A., and Ralph E. Smith. 2005. *The Role of Immigrants in the U.S. Labor Market*. U.S. Congress. Washington, D.C.: Congressional Budget Office, November.

Altbach, Philip G., and Patti McGill Peterson. 2008. "Higher Education as a Projection of America's Soft Power." In *Soft Power Superpowers: Cultural National Assets of Japan and the United States*. Edited by Watanabe Yasushi and David L. McConnell, 37–53. Armonk, N.Y.: M.E. Sharpe.

Alterman, Jon B. 2004. "Not in My Back Yard: Iraq's Neighbors' Interests." In *Reshaping Rogue States*. Edited by Alexander T. J. Lennon and Camille Eiss, 357–71. Cambridge: MIT Press.

Altig, David, and Ed Nosal. 2002. "'Dollarization:' What's in It (or Not) for the Issuing Country?" Federal Reserve Bank of Cleveland, http://imf.org/external/np/leg/sem/2002/comfl/eng/na.pdf.

Andoni, Lamis. 2003. "Deeds Speak Louder Than Words." In *The Battle for Hearts and Minds: Using Soft Power to Undermine Terrorist Networks*. Edited by Alexander T. J. Lennon, 262–81. Cambridge: MIT Press.

Ansari, Ali M. 2004. "Continuous Regime Change from Within." In *Reshaping Rogue States*. Edited by Alexander T. J. Lennon and Camille Eiss, 265–282. Cambridge: MIT Press.

Arreguin-Toft, Ivan. 2005. *How the Weak Win Wars: A Theory of Asymmetric Conflict*. Cambridge: Cambridge University Press.

Assuncao, Lucas. 2003. "Turning its Back to the World? The United States and Climate Change Policy." In *Unilateralism and U.S. Foreign Policy*. Edited by David M. Malone and Yuen Foong Khong, 297–317. Boulder: Lynne Rienner.

Axelrod, Robert. 1984. *The Evolution of Cooperation*. New York: Basic Books.

Axelrod, Robert, and Robert O. Keohane. 1985. "Achieving Cooperation under Anarchy: Strategies and Institutions." *World Politics* 38 (October): 226–54.

Bachrach, Peter, and Morton S. Baratz. 1962. "Two Faces of Power." *American Political Science Review* 56 (December): 947–52.

Bachrach, Peter, and Morton S. Baratz. 1963. "Decisions and Nondecisions: An Analytical Framework." *American Political Science Review* 57 (September): 632–42.

Bagehot, Walter. [1873] 1921. *Lombard Street: A Description of the Money Market*. New York: E.P. Dutton.

Bairoch, Paul. 1989. "European Trade Policy, 1815–1914." In *Cambridge Economic History of Europe*, vol. 8. Edited by Peter Mathias and Sidney Pollard, 1–160. Cambridge: Cambridge University Press.

Baldwin, David A. 1989. *The Paradoxes of Power*. New York: Basil Blackwell.

Baldwin, David A., ed. 1993. *Neorealism and Neoliberalism: The Contemporary Debate*. New York: Columbia University Press.

Baldwin, David A. 1997. "The Concept of Security." *Review of International Studies* 23 (January): 5–26.

Baldwin, David A. 2002. "Power and International Relations." In *Handbook of International Relations*, 177–91. Edited by Walter Carlsnaes, Thomas Risse, and Beth Simmons. London: Sage.

Barkin, J. Samuel. 2003. "Realist Constructivism." *International Studies Review* 5:325–42.

Barnet, Richard, and John Cavanagh. 1996. "The Homogenization of Global Culture." In *The Case Against the Global Economy and for a Turn Toward the Local*. Edited by Jerry Mander and Edward Goldsmith, 71–77. San Francisco: Sierra Club.

Barnett, Michael, and Raymond Duvall. 2005. "Power in International Politics." *International Organization* 59 (Winter): 39–75.

Barnett, Roger W. 2003. *Asymmetrical Warfare: Today's Challenges to U.S. Military Power*. Washington, D.C.: Brassey's.

Barro, Robert J. 1995. "Inflation and Economic Growth." *NBER Working Papers*, 5326. Cambridge, Mass.: National Bureau of Economic Research.

Barry, Brian. 1972. "Warrender and His Critics." In *Hobbes and Rousseau: A Collection of Critical Essays*. Edited by Maurice Cranston and Richard S. Peters, 37–65. Garden City, N.Y.: Anchor.

Bartlett, C. J. 1993. *Defence and Diplomacy: Britain and the Great Powers 1815–1914*. Manchester, U.K.: Manchester University Press.

Beck, Ulrich. 2005. *Power in the Global Age: A New Global Political Economy*. Malden, Mass.: Polity Press.

Bedford, David, and Thom Workman. 2001. "The Tragic Reading of the Thucydidean Tragedy." *Review of International Studies* 27 (January): 51–67.

Beitz, Charles R. 1979. *Political Theory and International Relations*. Princeton: Princeton University Press.

Berenskoetter, Felix. 2007. "Thinking about Power." In *Power in World Politics*. Edited by Felix Berenskoetter and M. J. Williams, 1–22. London: Routledge.

Bergmann, Peter. 1998. "The Specter of Americanisierung, 1840–1990." In *American Culture in Europe: Interdisciplinary Perspectives*. Edited by Mike-Frank G. Epitropoulos and Vitor Roudomentof, 67–90. Wesport: Praeger.

Bergsten, C. Fred. 1994. *Dilemmas of the Dollar*. Armonk, N.Y.: M.E. Sharp.

Berridge, G. R. 2001. "Machiavelli: Human Nature, Good Faith, and Diplomacy." *Review of International Studies* 27 (October): 539–56.

Betros, Chris. 2009. "Chrysler Makes its Mark in Japan." *Japan Today*, http://www.japantoday.com/category/executive-impact/view/chrysler-nakes-its-mark-in-japan, April 23.

Betts, Richard K. 2002. "The Soft Underbelly of American Primacy: Tactical Advantages of Terror." *Political Science Quarterly* 117:19–36.

Bird, Graham. 1987. *International Financial Policy and Economic Development*. London: Routledge.

Bird, Graham. 1996. "The International Monetary Fund and Developing Countries: A Review of the Evidence and Policy Options." *International Organization* 50 (Summer): 477–511.

Blinken, Anthony J. 2003. "Winning the War of Ideas." In *The Battle for Hearts and Minds: Using Soft Power to Undermine Terrorist Networks*. Edited by Alexander T. J. Lennon, 282–98. Cambridge: MIT Press.

Bock, Gisela, Quentin Skinner, and Maurizio Viroli, eds. 1990. *Machiavelli and Republicanism*. Cambridge: Cambridge University Press.

Booth, Ken. 1991. "Security in Anarchy: Utopian Realism in Theory and Practice." *International Affairs* 67 (July): 527–45.

Bordo, Michael D., and Hugh Rockoff. 1996. "The Gold Standard as a 'Good-housekeeping Seal of Approval.'" *Journal of Economic History* 56 (June): 389–428.

Borjas, George J. 2006. "The Impact of Immigration on the Labor Market." Paper prepared for the Conference on Labor and Capital Flows in Europe Following Enlargement. Organized by the International Monetary Fund, the Joint Vienna Institute, and the National Bank of Poland, January.

Boserup, Anders, and Andrew Mack. 1975. *War without Weapons: Non-Violence in National Defense*. New York: Schocken Books.

Brahms, Steven J. 1994. *Theory of Moves*. Cambridge: Cambridge University Press.

Brass, Paul. 2000. "Foucault Steals Political Science." *Annual Review of Political Science* 3:305–30.

Brooks, Stephen G., and William C. Wohlforth. 2008. *World Out of Balance: International Relations and the Challenge of International Primacy*. Princeton: Princeton University Press.

Brown, Seyom. 2000. *Human Rights in World Politics*. New York: Longman.

Brzezinski, Zbigniew. 2007. *Second Chance: Three Presidents and the Crisis of American Superpower*. New York: Perseus.

Bull, Hedley. 1977. *The Anarchical Society: A Study of Order in World Politics*. New York: Columbia University Press.

Bull, Hedley. 1981. "Hobbes and the International Anarchy." *Social Research* 41 (Winter): 717–38.

Butters, H. C. 1985. *Governors and Government in Early Sixteenth-Century Florence 1502–1519*. Oxford: Clarendon.

Calleo, David. 2003. "Power, Wealth and Wisdom." *The National Interest* 72 (Summer): 5–15.

Carr, Edward Hallett. 1964. *The Twenty Years' Crisis 1919–1939*. New York: Harper.

Carr, Edward Hallett. 2000. "An Autobiography." In *E. H. Carr: A Critical Approach*. Edited by Michael Cox, xiii-xxii. Houndmills, U.K.: Palgrave.

Cartwright, David. 2000. *A Historical Commentary on Thucydides*. Ann Arbor: University of Michigan Press.

Cerny, Philip G. Forthcoming. "Reconfiguring Power in a Globalizing World." In *Handbook of Power*. Edited by Stuart Clegg and Mark Haugaard. London: Sage.

Clarke, Kevin A., and David M. Primo. 2007. "Modernizing Political Science: A Model-Based Approach." *Perspectives on Politics* 5 (December): 741–53.

Cohen, Benjamin J. 2003. "Monetary Union: The Political Dimension." In *The Dollarization Debate*. Edited by Dominick Salvatore, James W. Dean, and Thomas D. Willett, 221–37. Oxford: Oxford University Press.

Connell, William J. 2005. "Introduction." In *The Prince*, by Niccolo Machiavelli, 1-34. Boston: Bedford/St. Martin's.

Connor, W. Robert. 1984. *Thucydides*. Princeton: Princeton University Press.

Copeland, Dale C. 2000. "The Constructivist Challenge to Structural Realism." *International Security* 25 (Autumn): 187–212.

Cornford, Francis M. 1907. *Thucydides Mythistoricus*. London: Edward Arnold.

Cox, Michael. 1999. "Will the Real E. H. Carr Please Stand Up?" *International Affairs* 75 (July): 643–53.

Cox, Michael, ed. 2000. *E. H. Carr: A Critical Approach*. Houndmills, U.K.: Palgrave.

Cox, Michael. 2001a. "A Guide to the Secondary Literature on E. H. Carr." In *The Twenty Years' Crisis 1919–1939*, by Edward Hallett Carr. Edited by Michael Cox, lxiv–lxxi. Houndmills, U.K.: Palgrave.

Cox, Michael. 2001b. "Introduction." In *The Twenty Years' Crisis 1919–1939*, by Edward Hallett Carr. Edited by Michael Cox, ix–lviii. Houndmills, U.K.: Palgrave.

Cox, Michael. 2007a. "Hans J. Morgenthau, Realism, and the Rise and Fall of the Cold War." In *Realism Reconsidered*. Edited by Michael Williams, 166–94. Oxford: Oxford University Press.

Cox, Michael. 2007b. "Is the United States in Decline – Again?" *International Affairs* 83: 643–53.

Cox, Robert W. 1980. "The Crisis of World Order and the Problem of International Organization in the 1980s." *International Journal* 35 (Spring): 370–95.

Cox, Robert W. 1987. *Production, Power, and World Order: Social Forces in the Making of History*. New York: Columbia University Press.

Crane, Gregory. 1998. *Thucydides and the Ancient Simplicity: The Limits of Political Realism*. Berkeley: University of California Press.

Crenshaw, Martha. 2003. "Coercive Diplomacy and the Response to Terrorism." In *The United States and Coercive Diplomacy*. Edited by Robert J. Art and Patrick M. Cronin, 305–58. Washington, D.C.: U.S. Institute of Peace Press.

Crowell, William G. 2008. "Official Soft Power in Practice: U.S. Diplomacy in Japan." In *Soft Power Superpowers: Cultural National Assets of Japan and the United States*. Edited by Watanabe Yasushi and David L. McConnell, 207–23. Armonk, N.Y.: M.E. Sharpe.

Curley, Edwin. [1651] 1994. "Introduction." In *The Leviathan*, by Thomas Hobbes, viii-xlvii. Indianapolis: Hacket.

Dahl, Robert A. 1957. "The Concept of Power." *Behavioral Science* 2: 201–15.

Dahl, Robert A. 1965. *Modern Political Analysis*. Englewood Cliffs, N.J.: Prentice-Hall.

Dahl, Robert A. 1974. *Who Governs? Democracy and Power in an American City*. New Haven: Yale University Press.

Davidson, William H. 1980. "The Location of Foreign Direct Investment Activity: Country Characteristics and Experience Effects." *Journal of International Business Studies* 11 (Autumn): 9–22.

De Alvarez, Leo Paul S. 1999. *The Machiavellian Enterprise*. Dekalb: Northern Illinois University Press.

"Defending and Advancing Freedom: A Symposium." 2005. *Commentary* (November).

De Grazia, Sebastion. 1989. *Machiavelli in Hell*. Princeton: Princeton University Press.

De Grazia, Victoria. 2005. *Irresistible Empire: America's Advance through Twentieth-Century Europe*. Cambridge: Harvard University Press.

Department of Defense. 2007. "Active Duty Military Personnel by Rank/Grade." August 31, http://siadapp.dmdc.osd.mil/personnel/MILITARY/rg0708.pdf.

Desker, Barry, and Kumar Ramakrishna. 2003. "Forging an Indirect Strategy in Southeast Asia." In *The Battle for Hearts and Minds: Using Soft Power to Undermine Terrorist Networks*. Edited by Alexander T. J. Lennon, 45–64. Cambridge: MIT Press.

Deudney, David. 2007. *Bounding Power: Republican Security Theory from the Polis to the Global Village*. Princeton: Princeton University Press.

Deutsch, Karl W. 1966. *The Nerves of Government*. New York: Free Press.

de Wijk, Rob. 2003. "The Limits of Military Power." In *The Battle for Hearts and Minds: Using Soft Power to Undermine Terrorist Networks*. Edited by Alexander T. J. Lennon, 3–28. Cambridge: MIT Press.

Digeser, Peter. 1992. "The Fourth Face of Power." *Journal of Politics* 54 (November): 977–1007.

Donnelly, Jack. 2000. *Realism and International Relations*. Cambridge: Cambridge University Press.

Doyle, Michael W. 1990. "Thucydidean Realism." *Review of International Studies* 16 (July): 223–37.

Doyle, Michael W. 1997. *Ways of War and Peace*. New York: Norton.

Drake, William J., and Kalypso Nicolaides. 1992. "Ideas, Interests, and Institutionalization: 'Trade in Services' and the Uruguay Round." *International Organization* 46 (Winter): 37–100.

Dunne, Tim. 2000. "Theories as Weapons: E. H. Carr and International Relations." In *E. H. Carr: A Critical Approach*. Edited by Michael Cox, 217–33. Houndmills, U.K.: Palgrave.

Eckstein, Harry. 1975. "Case Study and Theory in Political Science." In Handbook of Political Science, vol. 7, *Political Science: Scope and Theory*. Edited by Fred Greenstein and Nelson Polsby, 79–133. Reading, Mass.: Addison-Wesley.

Ellis, Jason D. 2004. "The Best Defense: Counterproliferation and U.S. National Security." In *Reshaping Rogue States*. Edited by Alexander T. J. Lennon, and Camille Eiss, 50–72. Cambridge: MIT Press.

Elrod, Richard. 1976. "The Concert of Europe: A Fresh Look at an International System." *World Politics* 28 (January): 149–74.

English, Robert D. 2000. *Russia and the Idea of the West: Gorbachev, Intellectuals, and the End of the Cold War*. New York: Columbia University Press.

Epitropoulos, Mike-Frank G., and Victor Roudometof. 1998. "Youth Culture and Lifestyle in Modern Greece." In *American Culture in Europe: Interdisciplinary Perspectives*. Edited by Mike-Frank G. Epitropoulos and Vitor Roudomentof, 119–44. Westport, Conn.: Praeger.

Etheridge, Eric. 2009. "How 'Soft Power' got 'Smart.' New York Times, January 14, http://opinionator.blogs.nytimes.com/2009/01/14/how-soft-power-got-smart/.

Evans, Graham. 1975. "E. H. Carr and International Relations." *British Journal of International Studies* 1: 77–97.

Ewans, Martin. 2005. *Conflict in Afghanistan: Studies in Asymmetric Warfare*. London: Routledge.

Falk, Richard. 1997. "The Critical Realist Tradition and the Demystification of Interstate Power: E. H. Carr, Hedley Bull and Robert W. Cox." In *Innovation and Transformation in International Studies*. Edited by Stephen Gill and James H. Mittelman, 39–55. Cambridge: Cambridge University Press.

Femia, Joseph V. 2004. *Machiavelli Revisited*. Cardiff, U.K.: University of Wales Press.

Ferguson, Niall. 2003. "Power." *Foreign Policy* (January/February): 18–27.

Fetter, Frank. 1965. *Development of British Monetary Orthodoxy 1797–1875*. Cambridge: Harvard University Press.

Fielden, Kenneth. 1969. "The Rise and Fall of Free Trade." In *Britain Preeminent: Studies of British World Influence in the Nineteenth Century*. Edited by C. J. Bartlett, 76–100. London: Macmillan.

Finlayson, Jock A., and Mark W. Zacher. 1981. "The GATT and the Regulation of Trade Barriers." *International Organization* 35 (Autumn): 561–602.

Finley, M. I. 1985. "Appendix." In *History of the Peloponnesian War*, by Thucydides, 607-20. Translated by Rex Warner. New York: Penguin.

Fischer, Markus. 2000. *Well-Ordered License: On the Unity of Machiavelli's Thought*. Lanham, Md.: Lexington.

Fleder, Daniel, and Kartik Hosanagar. 2007. "Recommender Systems and Their Impact on Sales Diversity." Proceedings of the 8th ACM Conference on Electronic Commerce, 192–9.

Fleder, Daniel, and Kartik Hosanagar. 2008. "Blockbuster Culture's Next Rise or Fall: The Impact of Recommender Systems on Sales Diversity." Networks, Electronic Commerce, and Telecommunications Institute, Working Paper #07–10, April, 1–45.

Forde, Steven. 1992. "Varieties of Realism: Thucydides and Machiavelli." *The Journal of Politics* 54 (May): 372–93.

Forde, Steven. 2000. "Power and Morality in Thucydides." In *Thucydides' Theory of International Relations*. Edited by Lowell S. Gustafson, 151–73. Baton Rouge: Louisiana State University Press.

Foucault, Michel. 2000. *Power*. Translated by Robert Hurley et al. New York: The New York Press.

Fox, Steve. 1998. "African-American Images in German Advertising, 1987–1992: The Uses of Imagined Diversity." In *American Culture in Europe: Interdisciplinary Perspectives*. Edited by Mike-Frank G. Epitropoulos and Vitor Roudomentof, 145–62. Wesport, Conn.: Praeger.

Frankel, Jeffrey, and Andrew Rose. 2002. "An Estimate of the Effects of Common Currencies on Trade and Income." *Quarterly Journal of Economics* 117: 2.

Fraser, Matthew. 2003. *Weapons of Mass Distraction: Soft Power and American Empire*. New York: St. Martin's Press.

Fraser, Matthew. 2008. "American Pop Culture as Soft Power: Movies and Broadcasting." In *Soft Power Superpowers: Cultural National Assets of Japan and the United States*. Edited by Watanabe Yasushi and David L. McConnell, 172–87. Armonk, N.Y.: M.E. Sharpe.

Frieden, Jeffry. 2003. "The Political Economy of Dollarization: Domestic and International Factors." In *Dollarization*. Edited by Eduardo Levy Yeyati and Federico Sturzenegger, 305–33. Cambridge: MIT Press.

Fukuyama, Francis. 2006. *America at the Crossroads*. New Haven: Yale University Press.

Gallarotti, Giulio. M. 1985. "Toward a Business-Cycle Model of Tariffs." *International Organization* 39 (Winter): 155–87.

Gallarotti, Giulio M. 1993. "The Scramble for Gold: Monetary Regime Transformation in the 1870s." In *Monetary Regimes in Transition*. Edited by Michael Bordo and Forrest Capie, 15–67. Cambridge: Cambridge University Press.

Gallarotti, Giulio M. 1995a. "It Pays to be Green: The Managerial Incentive Structure and Environmentally Sound Strategies." *Columbia Journal of World Business* 30 (Winter): 38–57.

Gallarotti, Giulio M. 1995b. *The Anatomy of an International Monetary Regime: The Classical Gold Standard, 1880–1914*. New York: Oxford University Press.

Gallarotti, Giulio M., and Arik Y. Preis. 1999. "Politics, International Justice, and the United States: Toward a Permanent International Criminal Court." *UCLA Journal of International Law and Foreign Affairs* 4: 1–54.

Gallarotti, Giulio M. 2000. "The Advent of the Prosperous Society: The Rise of the Guardian State and Structural Change in the World Economy." *Review of International Political Economy* 7 (Spring): 1–52.

Gallarotti, Giulio M. 2004. "Nice Guys Finish First: American Unilateralism and Power Illusion." In *Independence in an Age of Empires: Multilateralism and Unilateralism in the Post 9/11 World*. Edited by Graham F. Walker, 225–36. Halifax, Nova Scotia: Center for Foreign Policy Studies, Dalhousie University.

Gallarotti, Giulio M. 2005. "Hegemons of a Lesser God: The Bank of France and Monetary Leadership under the Classical Gold Standard." *Review of International Political Economy* 12 (October): 624–46.

Gallarotti, Giulio M. 2008. "More Revisions in Realism: Hobbesian Anarchy, the Tale of the Fool and International Relations Theory." *International Studies* 45: 167–92.

Gallarotti, Giulio. M. 2010. *The Power Curse: Influence and Illusion in World Politics*. Boulder: Lynne Rienner Publishers, Inc.

Ganshof, Francois L. 1996. *Feudalism.* Translated by Philip Grierson. Toronto: University of Toronto Press.

Gardner, Hall. 2005. *American Global Strategy and the War on Terrorism*. Aldershot, U.K.: Ashgate.

Garst, Danicl. 1989. "Thucydides and Neorealism." *International Studies Quarterly* 33 (March): 3–27.

George, Alexander L., and Andrew Bennett. 2005. *Case Studies and Theory Development in the Social Sciences*. Cambridge: MIT Press.

George, Alexander L., and Timothy J. McKeown. 1985. "Case Studies and Theories of Organizational Decision Making." *Advances in Information Processing and Organization* 2: 21–58.

Gerring, John. 2004. "What is a Case Study and What Is It Good For?" *American Political Science Review* 98 (May): 341–54.

Gill, Stephen, ed. 1993. *Gramsci, Historical Materialism and International Relations*. Cambridge: Cambridge University Press.

Gilpin, Robert. 1975. *U.S. Power and the Multinational Corporation: The Political Economy of Foreign Direct Investment*. New York: Basic Books.

Gilpin, Robert. 1981. *War and Change in World Politics*. New York: Cambridge University Press.

Gilpin, Robert. 1986. "The Richness of the Tradition of Political Realism." In *Neorealism and Its Critics*. Edited by Robert. Keohane, 301–21. New York: Columbia University.

Gitlin, Todd. 1998. "The Adorable Monsters of American Culture: Mickey Mouse, Bruce Willis, and the Unification of the World." Paper based on a lecture ("Liberty and Vulgarity: The Appeals of American Culture"), given on September 18, 1998 at a conference on "America Beyond its Borders" at the University of Marne-la-Vallée, Marne-la-Vallée, France, http://www.paradigme.com/sources/SOURCES-PDF/Pages%20de%20Sources06-2-1.pdf.

Goldstein, Judith, and Robert O. Keohane. 1993. Ideas and Foreign Policy: An Analytic Framework." In *Ideas and Foreign Policy: Beliefs, Institutions, and Political Change*. Edited by Judith Goldstein and Robert O. Keohane, 3-30. Ithaca: Cornell University Press.

Goodnight, G. Thomas. 1996. "Hans J. Morgenthau in Defense of the National Interest: On Rhetoric, Realism and the Public Sphere." In *Post Realism: The Rhetorical Turn in International Relations*. Edited by Francis A. Beer and Robert Hariman, 143–65. East Lansing: Michigan State University Press.

Gorbachev, Mikhail, and Zdenek Mlynar. 2002. *Conversations with Gorbachev*. Translated by George Shriver. New York: Columbia University Press.

Gramsci, Antonio. 1988. *Prison Letters*. London: Zwan.

Guarini, Elena Fasano. 1990. "Machiavelli and the Crisis of the Italian Republics." In *Machiavelli and Republicanism*. Edited by Gisela Bock, Quentin Skinner, and Maurizio Viroli, 17–40. Cambridge: Cambridge University Press.

Guoliang, Gu. 2004. "Redefine Cooperative Security Not Preemption." In *Reshaping Rogue States*. Edited by Alexander T. J. Lennon and Camille Eiss, 73–85. Cambridge: MIT Press.

Guzzini, Stefano. 1993. "Structural Power: The Limits of Neorealist Power Analysis." *International Organization* 47 (Summer): 443–78.

Guzzini, Stefano, and Dietrich Jung, eds. 2004. *Contemporary Security Analysis and Copenhagen Peace Research*. London: Routledge.

Haas, Peter M. 1992. "Banning Chlorofluorocarbons: Epistemic Community Efforts to Protect Stratospheric Ozone." *International Organization* 46 (Winter): 187–224.

Hall, Peter M. 1997a. "Meta-Power, Social Organization, and the Shaping of Social Action." *Symbolic Interaction* 20: 397–418.

Hall, Rodney Bruce. 1997b. "Moral Authority as a Power Resource." *International Organization* 51 (Autumn): 591–622.

Harper, Stephen and Jonathan Clarke. 2004. *America Alone: Neoconservatives and the Global Order*. New York: Cambridge Universtiy Press.

Hanson, Donald W. 1984. "Thomas Hobbes's 'Highway to Peace.'" *International Organization* 38 (Spring): 329–54.

Hartman, Thomas R. 2007. "A Realist Approach to Soft Power Production." Paper presented at the annual meeting of the American Political Science Association, Chicago, Ill., September 1.

Haskel, Barbara G. 1980. "Access to Society: A Neglected Dimension of Power." *International Organization* 34 (Winter): 89–120.

Haslam, Jonathan. 1999. *The Vices of Integrity: E. H. Carr, 1892–1982*. London: Verso.

Haslam, Jonathan. 2000. "E. H. Carr's Search for Meaning." In *E. H. Carr: A Critical Approach*. Edited by Michael Cox, 21–35. Houndmills, U.K.: Palgrave.

Hay, Denys, and John Law. 1989. *Italy in the Age of the Renaissance 1380–1530*. London: Longman.

Heisbourg, Francois. 2004. "A Work in Progress: The Bush Doctrine and Its Consequences." In *Reshaping Rogue States*. Edited by Alexander T. J. Lennon and Camille Eiss, 3–18. Cambridge: MIT Press.

Herz, John. 1957. "Rise and Demise of the Territorial State." *World Politics* 9 (April): 473–93.

Hobbes, Thomas. [1651] 1994. *The Leviathan*. Edited by Edwin Curley. Indiannapolis: Hacket.

Hoffmann, Stanley. 1981. *Duties Beyond Borders*. Syracuse: Syracuse University Press.

Hopkins, Raymond F. 1992. "Reform in the International Food Aid Regime: The Role of Consensual Knowledge." *International Organization* 46 (Winter): 225–64.

Howe, Paul. 1994. "The Utopian Realism of E. H. Carr." *Review of International Studies* 20: 277–97.

Huntington, Samuel P. 1971. *Political Order in Changing Societies*. New Haven: Yale University Press.

Huntington, Samuel P. 1996. *The Clash of Civilizations and the Remaking of World Order*. New York: Simon & Schuster.

Huntington, Samuel P. 2004. *Who Are We? The Challenge to America's Identity*. New York: Simon & Schuster.

Ignatieff, Michael. 2003. "Canada in the Age of Terror-Multilateralism Meets a Moment of Truth." *Options Politiques* (February): 14–18.

Ikenberry, G. John. 2001. "Getting Hegemony Right." *The National Interest* 63 (Spring): 17–24.

Ikenberry, G. John, and Charles A. Kupchan. 2004. "Liberal Realism: The Foundations of a Democratic Foreign Policy." *The National Interest* 77 (Fall): 38–49.

Inglehart, Ronald, Miquel Basanez, and Alejandro Moreno. 1998. *Human Values and Beliefs: A Cross-Cultural Handbook*. Ann Arbor: University of Michigan Press.

Inglehart, Ronald, and Pippa Norris. 2003. "The True Clash of Civilizations." *Foreign Policy* (March/April): 62–70.

Institute of International Education. 2006. "New Enrollment of Foreign Students in the U.S. Climbs in 2005/06," http://www.iie.org/Content/NavigationMenu/Pressroom/PressReleases/New_Enrollment_of_Foreign_Students_in_the_U_S__Climbs_in_2005_06.htm.

International Labor Organization. 2009, http://actrav.itcilo.org/actrav-english/telearn/global/ilo/multinat/multinat.htm.

International Organization. 1992. *Special Issue on Knowledge, Power and International Policy Coordination*. Edited by Peter M. Haas. Winter, 46.

International Trade Administration. 2009a. Office of Travel and Tourism Industries, http://tinet.ita.doc.gov/cat/f-2006-101-002.html.

International Trade Administration. 2009b. Office of Travel and Tourism Industries, http://tinet.ita.doc.gov/view/f-1999-203-001/index.html.

Isaac, Jeffrey C. 1987. *Power and Marxist Theory: A Realist View*. Ithaca: Cornell University Press.

James, Scott C., and David A. Lake. 1989. "The Second Face of Hegemony: Britain's Repeal of the Corn Laws and the American Walker Tariff of 1846." *International Organization* 43 (Winter): 1–29.

Jefferson, Thomas. 1774. "Summary Review of the Rights of British America." In *The Works of Thomas Jefferson*, http://oll.libertyfund.org.

Jervis, Robert. 1970. *The Logic of Images in International Relations*. Princeton: Princeton University Press.

Jervis, Robert. 1976. *Perception and Misperception in International Politics*. Princeton: Princeton University Press.

Jervis, Robert. 1978. "Cooperation under the Security Dilemma." *World Politics* 30 (January): 167–214.

Jervis, Robert. 1988. "The Political Effects of Nuclear Weapons: A Comment." *International Security* 13 (Autumn): 80–90.

Jervis, Robert. 1993. "International Primacy: Is the Game Worth the Candle?" *International Security* 17 (Spring): 52–67.

Jervis, Robert. 1997. *System Effects: Complexity in Political and Social Life*. Princeton: Princeton University Press.

Jervis, Robert. 2002. "Theories of War in an Era of Leading-Peace Power." *American Political Science Review* 96 (March): 1–14.

Jervis, Robert. 2003a. "The Compulsive Empire." *Foreign Policy* (July/August): 82–87.

Jervis, Robert. 2003b. "Understanding the Bush Doctrine." *Political Science Quarterly* 118 (Fall): 365–88.

Jervis, Robert. 2005. "Why the Bush Doctrine Cannot Be Sustained." *Political Science Quarterly* 120 (Fall): 351–77.

Johnson, Chalmers. 2004. *The Sorrows of Empire: Militarism, Secrecy and the End of the Republic.* New York: Metropolitan.

Johnson, Chalmers. 2006. *Nemesis: The Last Days of the American Republic.* New York: Metropolitan.

Johnson, Laurie M. 1993. *Thucydides, Hobbes, and the Interpretation of Realism.* Dekalb: Northern Illinois Press.

Johnson Bagby, Laurie M. 1996. "Thucydidean Realism: Between Athens and Melos." In *Roots of Realism.* Edited by Benjamin Frankel, 169–93. London: Frank Cass.

Johnson, Whittle. 1967. "E. H. Carr's Theory of International Relations: A Critique." *Journal of Politics* 29 (November): 861–84.

Johnston, Alastair Iain. 2008. *Social States: China in International Institutions, 1980–2000.* Princeton: Princeton University Press.

Jones, Charles. 1997. "Carr, Mannheim, and a Post-positivist Science of International Relations." *Political Studies* 45: 232–46.

Jones, Charles. 1998. *E. H. Carr and International Relations: A Duty to Lie.* Cambridge: Cambridge University Press.

Kagan, Donald. 1991. *Pericles of Athens and the Birth of Democracy.* New York: Free Press.

Kagan, Donald. 2003a. *The Peloponnesian War.* New York: Viking.

Kagan, Robert. 2003b. *Of Paradise and Power: America and Europe in the New World Order.* New York: Alfred A. Knopf.

Kaplan, Fred. 2008. *Daydream Believers: How a Few Grand Ideas Wrecked American Power.* Hoboken: John Wiley & Sons.

Kapstein, Ethan Barnaby. 1992. "Between Power and Purpose: Central Bankers and the Politics of Regulatory Convergence." *International Organization* 46 (Winter): 265–88.

Katsuji, Imata, and Kuroda Kaori. 2008. "Soft Power of NGOs: Growing Influence beyond National Boundaries." In *Soft Power Superpowers: Cultural National Assets of Japan and the United States.* Edited by Watanabe Yasushi and David L. McConnell, 262–77. Armonk, N.Y.: M.E. Sharpe.

Kaufman, Edward. 2003. "A Broadcast Strategy to Win Media Wars." In *The Battle for Hearts and Minds: Using Soft Power to Undermine Terrorist Networks.* Edited by Alexander T. J. Lennon, 299–313. Cambridge: MIT Press.

Kavka, Gregory S. 1986. *Hobbesian Moral and Political Philosophy.* Princeton: Princeton University Press.

Kegley, Charles W. Jr., and Gregory A. Raymond. 2007. *After Iraq: The Imperiled American Imperium.* New York: Oxford University Press.

Kennedy, Paul. 1987. *The Rise and Fall of the Great Powers*. New York: Random House.

Kennedy, Robert F. 1969. *Thirteen Days: A Memoir of the Cuban Missile Crisis*. New York: Norton.

Kenwood, A. G., and A. L. Lougheed. 1999. *The Growth of the International Economy 1820–2000*. London: Routledge.

Keohane, Robert O., and Joseph S. Nye Jr. 1989. *Power and Interdependence*. Glenview, Ill.: Scott, Foresman and Co.

Keohane, Robert O. 1984. *After Hegemony: Cooperation and Discord in the World Political Economy*. Princeton: Princeton University Press.

Keynes, John Maynard. [1913] 1971. Indian Currency and Finance in *The Collected Writings of John Maynard Keynes*, vol 1. London: Macmillan.

Keynes, John Maynard. [1919] 1988. *Economic Consequences of the Peace*. New York: Penguin.

Kindleberger, Charles P. 1975. "The Rise of Free Trade in Western Europe." *Journal of Economic History* 35 (March): 20–55.

Kindleberger, Charles P. 1984. *A Financial History of Western Europe*. London: George Allen & Unwin.

Kindleberger, Charles. 1986. *The World in Depression 1929–1939*. Berkeley: University of California Press.

King, Gary, Robert O. Keohane, and Sidney Verba. 1994. *Designing Social Inquiry: Scientific Inference in Qualitative Research*. Princeton: Princeton University Press.

Klein, Naomi. 1999. *No Logo*. New York: Picador.

Kogut, Bruce, and Harbir Singh. 1988. "The Effect of National Culture on the Choice of Entry Mode." *Journal of International Business Studies* 19 (Autumn): 411–32.

Koskenniemi, Martti. 2001. *The Gentle Civilizer of Nations: The Rise and Fall of International Law 1870–1960*. Cambridge: Cambridge University Press.

Krasner, Stephen D. 1976. "State Power and the Structure of International Trade." *World Politics* 28 (April): 317–47.

Krasner, Stephen D., ed., 1983. *International Regimes*. Ithaca: Cornell University Press.

Krigman, Eliza. 2008. "Number of Illegal Immigrants in U.S. Closer to 20 Million," http://ohmygov.com/bloges/general_news/archive/2008/04.10/number-of-illegal-immigrants-in-u-s-may-be-closer-to-20-million.aspx, April 10.

Krisch, Nico. 2003. "Weak as Constraint, Strong as Tool: The Place of International Law in U.S. Foreign Policy." In *Unilateralism and U.S. Foreign Policy*. Edited by David M. Malone and Yuen Foong Khong, 41–70. Boulder: Lynne Rienner.

Kristol, Irving. 1995. *Neoconservatism: The Autobiography of an Idea*. New York: Free Press.

Kubalkova, Vendulka. 1998. "'The Twenty Years' Catharsis: E. H. Carr and IR." In *International Relations in a Constructed World*. Edited by Vendulka Kubalova, Nicholas Onuf, and Paul Kowert, 25–57. Armonk, N.Y.: M.E. Sharpe.

Kupchan, Clifford. 2004. "Real Democratik." *The National Interest* 77 (Fall): 26–37.

Kurlantzick, Joshua. 2007. *Charm Offensive: How China's Soft Power is Transforming the World*. New Haven: Yale University Press.

Kurzman, Charles. 2008. "Bin Laden and Other Thoroughly Modern Muslims." In *The Globalization Reader*. Edited by Frank J. Lechner and John Boli, 353–7. Malden, Mass.: Blackwell.

Lambakis, Steven, James Kiras, and Kristen Kolet. 2002. "*Understanding 'Asymmetric' Threats to the United States*." Fairfax: National Institute for Public Policy.

Lankov, Sergei. 2007. "How to Topple Kim Jong Il." *Foreign Policy* (March/April): 70–74.

Lapid, Yosef. 1989. "The Third Debate: On the Prospects of International Theory in a Post-Positivist Era." *International Studies Quarterly* 33: 235–54.

Lasswell, Harold D., and Abraham Kaplan. 1950. *Power and Society: A Framework for Political Inquiry*. New Haven: Yale University Press.

Lebow, Richard Ned. 2001. "Thucydides the Constructivist." *American Political Science Review* 95 (September): 547–50.

Lebow, Richard Ned. 2003. *The Tragic Vision of Politics: Ethics, Interests and Orders*. Cambridge: Cambridge University Press.

Lebow, Richard Ned. 2008. *A Cultural Theory of International Relations*. Cambridge: Cambridge University Press.

Lebow, Richard Ned, and Robert Kelly. 2001. "Thucydides and Hegemony: Athens and the United States." *Review of International Studies* 27 (October): 593–609.

LeFeber, Walter. 1999. *Michael Jordan and the New Global Capitalism*. New York: Norton.

Leibenstein, Harvey. 1966. "Allocative vs. X-Efficiency." *American Economic Review* 56 (June): 392–415.

Lempert, David. 1998. "The Colonization of the Russian Political and Legal System." In *American Culture in Europe: Interdisciplinary Perspectives*. Edited by Mike-Frank G. Epitropoulos and Vitor Roudomentof, 91–118. Wesport, Conn.: Praeger.

Lennon, Alexander T. J., ed. 2003. *The Battle for Hearts and Minds: Using Soft Power to Undermine Terrorist Networks*. Cambridge: MIT Press.

Lennon, Alexander T. J., and Camille Eiss, eds. 2004. *Reshaping Rogue States*. Cambridge: MIT Press.

Lindert, Peter. 1969. *Key Currencies and Gold 1900–1913* in *Princeton Studies in International Finance, No. 24*. Princeton: Princeton University Press.

Lindsay, Alexander D. 1962. *The Modern Democratic State*. New York: Oxford University Press.

Linklater, Andrew. 1997. "The Transformation of Political Community: E. H. Carr, Critical Theory and International Relations." *Review of International Studies* 23: 321–38.

Linklater, Andrew. 2000. "E. H. Carr, Nationalism and the Future of the Sovereign State." In *E. H. Carr: A Critical Approach*. Edited by Michael Cox, 234–57. Houndmills, U.K.: Palgrave.

Lloyd, S. A. 1992. *Ideals as Interests in Hobbes Leviathan: The Power of Mind over Matter*. Cambridge: Cambridge University Press.

Lobell, Steven E. 2008. "Second Face of Security Strategies: Anglo-German and Anglo-Japanese Trade Concessions during the 1930s." *Security Studies* 17: 438–67.

Lukes, Steven. 1974. *Power: A Radical View*. London: Macmillan.

Lukes, Steven. 2007. "Power and the Battle for Hearts and Minds: On the Bluntness of Soft Power." In *Power in World Politics*. Edited by Felix Berenskoetter and M. J. Williams, 83–97. London: Routledge.

Lukes, Timothy J. 2001. "Lionizing Machiavelli." *American Political Science Review* 95 (September): 561–75.

Lynch, Cecilia. 1994. "E. H. Carr, International Relations and the Social Origins of International Legal Norms." *Millennium: Journal of International Relations* 23: 589–619.

Machiavelli, Niccolo. 2005. *The Prince*. Translated by William J. Connell. Boston: Bedford/St. Martin's.

Machiavelli, Niccolo. 1996. *Discourses on Livy*. Translated by Harvey C. Mansfield Jr. and Nathan Tarcov. Chicago: University of Chicago Press.

Mack, Andrew. 1975. "Why Big Nations Lose Small Wars: The Politics of Asymmetric Conflict." *World Politics* 27 (January): 175–200.

Malcolm, Noel. 2002. *Aspects of Hobbes*. Oxford: Oxford University Press.

Maliniak, Daniel, Amy Oakes, Susan Peterson, and Michael Tierney. 2007. *The View from the Ivory Tower: TRIP Survey of International Relations Faculty in the United States and Canada*. Williamsburg: College of William and Mary.

Malone, David M. 2003. "A Decade of U.S. Unilateralism." In *Unilateralism and U.S. Foreign Policy*. Edited by David M. Malone and Yuen Foong Khong, 19–38. Boulder: Lynne Rienner.

Malone, David M., and Yuen Foong Khong, eds. 2003. *Unilateralism and U.S. Foreign Policy*. Boulder: Lynne Rienner.

Mander, Jerry, and Edward Goldsmith, eds. 1996. *The Case Against the Global Economy and for a Turn toward the Local*. San Francisco: Sierra Club.

Mansfield, Harvey C. Jr. 1979. *Machiavelli's New Modes and Orders: A Study of the 'Discourses on Livy.'* Ithaca: Cornell University Press.

Mansfield, Harvey C. Jr. 1996. *Machiavelli's Virtue*. Chicago: University of Chicago Press.

Maoz, Zeev. 1989. "Power, Capabilities, and Paradoxical Conflict Outcomes." *World Politics* 41 (January): 239–66.

Marx, Karl. 1972. "The German Ideology." In *The Marx-Engels Reader*. Edited by Robert W. Tucker, 110–64. New York: W.W. Norton.

McCloskey, Donald N. 1980. "Magnanimous Albion: Free Trade and the British National Income, 1841–81." *Explorations in Economic History* 17 (July): 303–20.

McKinnon, John D. 2008. "Bush's Vision of NATO Takes Root." *Wall Street Journal*, 3 April, A7.

McKinnon, John D., and Stephen Power. 2008. "Bush to Call for Greenhouse-Gas Curbs." *Wall Street Journal*, 16 April, A1, A16.

McNeil, William H. 1982. *The Pursuit of Power: Technology, Armed Force, and Society since A.D. 1000*. Chicago: University of Chicago Press.

Meade, Walter Russell. 2004. "America's Sticky Power." *Foreign Policy* (March/April): 46–53.

Mearsheimer, John. J. 2001. *The Tragedy of Great Power Politics*. New York: Norton.

Microsoft Mission Statement. 2009, http://www.samples-help.org.uk/mission-statements/microsoft-mission-statement.htm.

Milner, Helen V. 1988. *Resisting Protectionism: Global Industries and the Politics of International Trade*. Princeton: Princeton University Press.

Milner, Helen V. 1991. "The Assumption of Anarchy in International Relations: A Critique." *Review of International Studies* 17: 67–85.

Monten, Jonathan. 2007. "Primacy and Grand Strategic Beliefs in US Unilateralism." *Global Governance* 13 (January–March): 119–39.

Morgenthau, Hans J. 1951. *In Defense of the National Interest: A Critical Examination of American Foreign Policy*. New York: Knopf.

Morgenthau, Hans J. 1967. *Scientific Man vs. Power Politics*. Chicago: University of Chicago Press.

Morgenthau, Hans J. 1969. *A New Foreign Policy for the United States*. New York: Praeger.

Morgenthau, Hans J. 1978. *Politics Among Nations: The Struggle for Power and Peace*. New York: Knopf.

Mueller, Dennis C. 1997. *Perspectives on Public Choice: A Handbook*. Cambridge: Cambridge University Press.

Mueller, Dennis C. 2003. *Public Choice III*. Cambridge: Cambridge University Press.

Mueller, John. 1988. "The Irrelevance of Nuclear Weapons: Stability in the Postwar World." *International Security* 13 (Autumn): 55–79.

Mueller, John. 2004. *The Remnants of War*. Ithaca: Cornell University Press.

Murphy, Craig N. 1994. *International Organization and Industrial Change: Global Governance since 1850*. New York: Oxford University Press.

Murray, A.J.H. 1996. "The Moral Politics of Hans Morgenthau." *The Review of Politics* 58: 81–107.

Nagl, John A. 2002. *Counterinsurgency Lessons from Malaya and Vietnam: Learning to Eat Soup With a Knife*. Westport, Conn.: Praeger.

Newhouse, John. 2003. "The Threats America Faces." *World Policy Journal* 19 (Summer): 21–37.

Niebuhr, Reinhold. 1932. *Moral Man and Immoral Society*. London: Scribner.

Niou, Emerson M. S., and Peter C. Ordeshook. 1994. "'Less Filling, Tastes Great': The Realist-Neoliberal Debate." *World Politics* 46 (January): 209–34.

Nolte, Georg. "The United States and the International Criminal Court." In *Unilateralism and U.S. Foreign Policy*. Edited by David M. Malone and Yuen Foong Khong, 71–94. Boulder: Lynne Rienner.

Nossel, Suzanne. 2004. "Smart Power." *Foreign Affairs* (March–April): 131–43.

Nye, Joseph S. Jr. 1990a. *Bound to Lead: The Changing Nature of American Power*. New York: Basic Books.

Nye, Joseph S., Jr. 1990b. "Soft Power." *Foreign Policy* 80 (Fall): 53–71.

Nye, Joseph S. Jr. 2002. *The Paradoxes of American Power: Why the World's Only Superpower Can't Go It Alone*. New York: Oxford University Press.

Nye, Joseph S. Jr. 2003. "The Velvet Hegemon: How Soft Power Can Help Defeat Terrorism." *Foreign Policy* (May/June): 74–75.

Nye, Joseph S. Jr. 2004a. *Power in the Global Information Age: From Realism to Globalization*. London: Routledge.

Nye, Joseph S. Jr. 2004b. *Soft Power: The Means to Success in World Politics*. New York: Public Affairs.

Onuf, Nicholas G. 1989. *World of Our Making: Rules and Rule in Social Theory and International Relations*. Columbia: University of South Carolina Press.

Onuf, Nicholas G. 1998a. "Constructivism: A User's Manual." In *International Relations in a Constructed World*. Edited by Vendulka Kubalova, Nicholas Onuf, and Paul Kowert, 58–78. Armonk, N.Y.: M.E. Sharpe.

Onuf, Nicholas G. 1998b. "Everyday Ethics in International Relations." *Millennium: Journal of International Studies* 27: 669–93.

Onuf, Nicholas G. 2008. "Structure? What Structure?" Paper presented at a conference at Aberystwyth University, U.K., September 15–17.

Orwin, Clifford. 1994. *The Humanity of Thucydides*. Princeton: Princeton University Press.

Osgood, Robert E., and Robert W. Tucker. 1967. *Force, Order and Justice*. Baltimore: Johns Hopkins University Press.

Ottaviano, Gianmarco I. P., and Giovanni Peri. 2005. "Rethinking the Gains from Immigration: Theory and Evidence from the U.S." Center for Economic Policy Research Discussion Paper No. 5226, September.

Pellicani, Luciano. 1976. *Gramsci: An Alternative Communism*. Stanford: Hoover Institute.

Peterson, M. J. 1992. "Whalers, Cetologists, Environmentalists, and the International Management of Whaling." *International Organization* 46 (Winter): 187–224.

Pew Research Center. 2003. "Views of a Changing World 2003," http://people-press.org/reports/display.php3?ReportID=185.

Phelps, Edmund, ed. 1975. *Altruism, Morality, and Economic Theory*. New York: Russell Sage.

Pieterse, Jan Nederveen. 1995. "Globalization as Hybridization." In *The Globalization Reader*. Edited by Frank J. Lechner and John Boli, 99–105. Malden, Mass.: Blackwell.

Piven, Francis Fox. 2004. *The War at Home*. New York: New Press.

Plamenatz, John. 1977. "In Search of Machiavellian 'Virtu.'" In *The Prince*. Edited by Robert M. Adams, 217–26. New York: Norton.

Pocock, J. G. A. 1975. *The Machiavellian Moment: Florentine Political Thought and the Atlantic Republican Tradition*. Princeton: Princeton University Press.

Poggi, Gianfranco. 1978. *The Development of the Modern State*. Stanford: Stanford University Press.

Polanyi, Karl. 1957. *The Great Transformation*. Boston: Beacon Press.

Polsby, Nelson W. 1980. *Community Power and Political Thought: A Further Look at Problems of Evidence and Inference.* New Haven: Yale University Press.

Preble, Christopher A. 2009. *The Power Problem: How American Military Dominance Makes Us Less Safe, Less Prosperous, and Less Free.* Ithaca: Cornell University Press.

Radelet, Steve. 2003. "Will the Millennium Challenge Account Be Different?" In *The Battle for Hearts and Minds: Using Soft Power to Undermine Terrorist Networks.* Edited by Alexander T. J. Lennon, 342–61. Cambridge: MIT Press.

Rahe, Paul A. 1996. "Thucydides' Critique of Realpolitik." In *Roots of Realism.* Edited by Benjamin Frankel, 105–41. London: Frank Cass.

Reiter, Dan, and Alan C. Stam. 2002. *Democracies at War.* Princeton: Princeton University Press.

Repeta, Lawrence. 2008. "Mr. Madison in the Twenty-first Century: Global Diffusion of the People's 'Right to Know.'" In *Soft Power Superpowers: Cultural National Assets of Japan and the United States.* Edited by Watanabe Yasushi and David L. McConnell, 245–61. Armonk, N.Y.: M.E. Sharpe.

Report of the Center for Strategic and International Studies Commission on Smart Power. 2007. Washington, D.C.: Center for Strategic and International Studies.

Rice, Condoleezza. 2000. "Promoting the National Interest." *Foreign Affairs* 79 (January/February): 45–62.

Rich, Paul. 2000. "E. H. Carr and the Moral Quest for Revolution in International Relations." In *E. H. Carr: A Critical Approach.* Edited by Michael Cox, 198–216. Houndmills, U.K.: Palgrave.

Romilly, Jacqueline de. 1963. *Thucydides and Athenian Imperialism.* New York: Barnes and Noble.

Rosecrance, Richard. 1999. *The Rise of the Virtual State: Wealth and Power in the Coming Century.* New York: Basic.

Ross, Christopher. 2003. "Public Diplomacy Comes of Age." In *The Battle for Hearts and Minds: Using Soft Power to Undermine Terrorist Networks.* Edited by Alexander T. J. Lennon, 251–61. Cambridge: MIT Press.

Rotberg, Robert I. 2003. "The New Nature of Nation-State Failure." In *Reshaping Rogue States.* Edited by Alexander T. J. Lennon and Camille Eiss, 79–93. Cambridge: MIT Press.

Roy, Olivier. 2004. *Globalized Islam: The Search for a New Unmah.* New York: Columbia University Press.

Rubin, Barry. 2004. "Lessons from Iran." In *Reshaping Rogue States.* Edited by Alexander T. J. Lennon and Camille Eiss, 141–53. Cambridge: MIT Press.

Rudowski, Victor A. 1992. *The Prince: A Historical Critique.* New York: Twain.

Ruediger John. 2005. "Globalized Culture, Consumption and Identity." Translated by Gunilla Zedigh. Baden, http://artrelated.net/ruediger_john/globalized-culture.html.

Ruggie, John Gerard. 1983. "International Regimes, Transactions, and Change: Embedded Liberalism in the Postwar Economic Order." In *International Regimes.* Edited by Stephen D. Krasner, 195–232. Ithaca: Cornell University Press.

Russell, Greg. 1990. *Hans J. Morgenthau and the Ethics of American Statecraft.* Baton Rouge: Louisiana State University Press.

Russett, Bruce, and John R. Oneal. 2001. *Triangulating Peace: Democracy, Interdependence, and International Organization.* New York: Norton.

Salvatore, Dominick, James W. Dean, and Thomas D. Willett, eds., 2003. *The Dollarization Debate.* Oxford: Oxford University Press.

Sardar, Ziauddin, and Merryl Wyn Davies. 2002. *Why Do People Hate America?* New York: Disinformation.

Sasso, Gennaro. 1977. "The Origins of Evil." In *The Prince.* Edited by Robert M. Adams, 206–16. New York: Norton.

Saul, S. B. 1960. *Studies in British Overseas Trade 187–1914.* Liverpool: Liverpool University Press.

Schmidt, Brian C. 2007. "Realist Conceptions of Power." In *Power in World Politics.* Edited by Felix Berenskoetter and M. J. Williams, 43–63. London: Routledge.

Schott, Thomas, Jun Kanamitsu, and James F. Luther. 1998. "The U.S. Center of World Science and Emulating Centers: Japan and Western Europe." In *American Culture in Europe: Interdisciplinary Perspectives.* Edited by Mike-Frank G. Epitropoulos and Vitor Roudomentof, 15–38. Wesport, Conn.: Praeger.

Shambaugh, David. 2004. "China and the Korean Peninsula: Playing for the Long Term." In *Reshaping Rogue States.* Edited by Alexander T. J. Lennon, and Camille Eiss, 171–86. Cambridge: MIT Press.

Skinner, Quentin. 1981. *Machiavelli.* In *Great Political Thinkers.* Oxford: Oxford University Press.

Skinner, Quentin. 1990. "Machiavelli's 'Discorsi' and the Pre-humanist Origins of Republican Ideas." In *Machiavelli and Republicanism.* Edited by Gisela Bock, Quentin Skinner, and Maurizio Viroli, 121–42. Cambridge: Cambridge University Press.

Skinner, Quentin. 1996. *Reason and Rhetoric in the Philosophy of Hobbes.* Cambridge: Cambridge University Press.

Sklair, Leslie. 1995. *Sociology of the Global System.* Baltimore: John Hopkins University Press.

Smith Adam. [1759] 2002. *The Theory of Moral Sentiments.* Edited by Knud Haakonssen. Cambridge: Cambridge University Press.

Smith, Michael. 1986. *Realist Thought from Weber to Kissinger.* Baton Rouge: Louisiana State University Press.

Smith, Roger K. 1987. "Explaining the Non-Proliferation Regime: Anomalies for Contemporary International Relations Theory." *International Organization* 41 (Spring): 253–81.

Smith, Tony. 2007. *A Pact with the Devil.* New York: Routledge.

Snyder, Jack. 1991. *The Myth of Empires: Domestic Politics and International Ambition.* Ithaca: Cornell University Press.

Sommerville, Johann P. 1992. *Thomas Hobbes: Political Ideas in Historical Context.* New York: St. Martin's Press.

Speer II, James P. 1968. "Hans Morgenthau and the World State." *World Politics* 20 (January): 207–27.

Souza, Philip de. 2002. *The Peloponnesian War 431* B.C.*–404* B.C. New York: Routledge.

Stark, Oded. 1995. *Altruism and Beyond.* Cambridge: Cambridge University Press.

Sterling-Folker, Jennifer. 2000. "Competing Paradigms or Birds of a Feather? Constructivism and Neoliberal Institutionalism Compared." *International Studies Quarterly* 44 (March): 97–119.

Sterling-Folker, Jennifer. 2002. "Realism and the Constructivist Challenge." *International Studies Review* 4: 73–100.

Stiglitz, Joseph E. 2002. *Globalization and Its Discontents.* New York: Norton.

Takeyh, Ray, and Nikolas Gvosdev. 2003. "Do Terrorist Networks Need a Home?" In *The Battle for Hearts and Minds: Using Soft Power to Undermine Terrorist Networks.* Edited by Alexander T. J. Lennon, 94–107. Cambridge: MIT Press.

Taylor, Michael. 1987. *The Possibility of Cooperation.* Cambridge: Cambridge University Press.

Temes, Peter S. 2003. *The Just War: An American Reflection on the Morality of War in Our Time.* Chicago: Ivan R. Dee.

"Terrorism Index." 2007. *Foreign Policy* (September/October): 60–67.

Thakur, Ramesh. 2003. "UN Peacekeeping Operations and U.S. Unilateralism and Multilateralism." In *Unilateralism and U.S. Foreign Policy.* Edited by David M. Malone and Yuen Foong Khong, 153–80. Boulder: Lynne Rienner.

"The Other Struggle in the Gulf." 2007. *Economist* (September 8): 16.

"The World's Most Dangerous Place." 2008. *Economist* (January 5): 7.

Thomas, Jim. 2008. "Sustainable Security: Developing a Security Strategy for the Long Haul." Center for a New American Security, 3–19, http://www.cnas.org/en/cms/?1924, April.

Thucydides. 1985. *History of the Peloponnesian War.* Translated by Rex Warner. New York: Penguin.

Tomlinson, John. 1991. *Cultural Imperialism: A Critical Introduction.* London: Pinter.

Ullman-Margalit, Edna. 1977. *The Emergence of Norms.* Oxford: Clarendon Press.

United States Census Bureau. 2009, http://www.census.gov/compendia/statab/cats/business_enterprise/multinational_companies.html.

United States Military Index. 2008. *Foreign Policy* (March/April): 71–77, http://www.cnas.org.

USAID. 2009. "About USAID," http://www.usaid.gov/about_usaid/, May 4.

Van Evera, Stephen. 1999. *The Causes of War: Power and the Roots of Conflict.* Ithaca: Cornell University Press.

Vincent, John. 1981. "The Hobbesian Tradition in Twentieth Century International Thought." *Millennium: Journal of International Studies* 10 (June): 91–101.

Viroli, Maurizio. 1990. "Machiavelli and the Republican Idea of Politics." In *Machiavelli and Republicanism.* Edited by Gisela Bock, Quentin Skinner, and Maurizio Viroli, 143–72. Cambridge: Cambridge University Press.

Viroli, Maurizio. 1998a. *Machiavelli.* Oxford: Oxford University Press.

Viroli, Maurizio. 1998b. *Nicolo's Smile: A Biography of Machiavelli*. New York: Farrar, Straus and Giroux.

Vogel, David. 2005. *The Market for Virtue: The Potential and Limits of Corporate Social Responsibility*. Washington, D.C.: Brookings Institution.

von Hippel, Karin. 2003. "Democracy by Force: A Renewed Commitment to Nation Building." In *Reshaping Rogue States*. Edited by Alexander T. J. Lennon and Camille Eiss, 108–29. Cambridge: MIT Press.

Walt, Stephen M. 1987. *The Origins of Alliances*. Ithaca: Cornell University Press.

Walt, Stephen M. 1999. "Musclebound: The Limits of U.S. Power." *Bulletin of the Atomic Scientists* 55 (March/April): 1–5, http://www.thebulletin.org/article.php?art_ofn=ma99walt.

Waltz, Kenneth. 1959. *Man, the State, and War*. New York: Columbia University Press.

Waltz, Kenneth. 1979. *Theory of International Politics*. Reading, Pa.: Addison Wesley.

Walzer, Michael. 1977. *Just and Unjust Wars*. New York: Basic.

Warrender, Howard. 1957. *The Political Philosophy of Hobbes: His Theory of Obligation*. Oxford: Clarendon.

Weber, Max. 1978. *Economy and Society*. Berkeley: University of California Press.

Welch, David A. 2003. "Why International Relations Theorists Should Stop Reading Thucydides." *Review of International Studies* 29 (July): 301–19.

Wendt, Alexander. 1992. "Anarchy Is What States Make of It: The Social Construction of Power Politics." *International Organization* 46 (Spring): 391–425.

Wendt, Alexander. 1999. *Social Theory of International Politics*. Cambridge: Cambridge University Press.

White, James Boyd. 1984. *When Words Lose Their Meaning: Constitutions and Reconstructions of Language, Character and Community*. Chicago: University of Chicago Press.

White House. 2002a. *National Security Strategy of the United States (NSS)*. Washington, D.C., September.

White House. 2002b. *National Strategy to Combat Weapons of Mass Destruction*. Washington, D.C., December.

White House. 2006. *National Security Strategy of the United States (NSS)*. Washington, D.C., September.

Whitfield, J. H. 1977. "Machiavelli's Use of 'Ordini.'" In *The Prince*. Edited by Robert M. Adams, 194–205. New York: Norton.

Williams, Mary Frances. 1998. *Ethics in Thucydides: The Ancient Simplicity*. Lanham, Md: University Press of America.

Williams, Michael C. 1996. "Hobbes and International Relations: A Reconsideration." *International Organization* 50 (Spring): 213–36.

Williams, Michael C. 2003. "Words, Images, Enemies: Securitization and International Politics." *International Studies Quarterly* 47: 511–31.

Williams, Michael C. 2005. *The Realist Tradition and the Limits of International Relations*. Cambridge: Cambridge University Press.

Wilson, Peter. 2000. "Carr and his Early Critics: Responses to the Twenty Years' Crisis, 1939–46." In *E. H. Carr: A Critical Approach*. Edited by Michael Cox, 165–97. Houndmills, U.K.: Palgrave.

Wilson, Peter. 2001. "Radicalism for a Conservative Purpose: The Peculiar Realism of E. H. Carr." *Millennium: Journal of International Relations* 30: 123–36.

Windsor, Jennifer. 2003. Promoting Democratization Can Combat Terrorism." In *The Battle for Hearts and Minds: Using Soft Power to Undermine Terrorist Networks*. Edited by Alexander T. J. Lennon, 362–80. Cambridge: MIT Press.

Wirtz, James J., and James A. Russell. 2003. "U.S. Policy on Preventive War and Preemption." *The Nonproliferation Review*, 10 (Spring): 113–123.

Wolfenstein, Martha, and Nathan Leites. 1950. *Movies: A Psychological Study*. Glencoe, Ill.: Free Press.

Woodruff, Paul. 1993. *Thucydides on Justice, Power, and Human Nature*. Indianapolis: Hackett.

Wright, Robin. 2008. "Since 2001, a Dramatic Increase in Suicide Bombings." *Washington Post*, April 18, A18.

Yarmolinsky, Adam, and Gregory D. Foster. 1983. *Paradoxes of Power: The Military Establishment in the Eighties*. Bloomington: Indiana University Press.

Yasushi, Watanabe, and David L. McConnell, eds. 2008. *Soft Power Superpowers: Cultural National Assets of Japan and the United States*. Armonk, N.Y.: M.E. Sharpe.

Yurchak, Alexi. 2006. *Everything Was Forever Until It Was No More: The Last Soviet Generation*. Princeton: Princeton University Press.

Index

Made in the USA
Middletown, DE
28 June 2017